Furry Fandom Conventions,
1989–2015

Furry Fandom Conventions, 1989–2015

Fred Patten

Furword by Kathleen C. Gerbasi

McFarland & Company, Inc., Publishers
Jefferson, North Carolina

LIBRARY OF CONGRESS CATALOGUING-IN-PUBLICATION DATA

Names: Patten, Fred, 1940– author.
Title: Furry fandom conventions, 1989–2015 / Fred Patten ;
furword by Kathleen C. Gerbasi.
Description: Jefferson, North Carolina : McFarland & Company, Inc.,
Publishers, 2017 | Includes index.
Identifiers: LCCN 2016050917 | ISBN 9781476663814
(softcover : acid free paper) ∞
Subjects: LCSH: Human-animal relationships—Social aspects. |
Anthropomorphism in art. | Anthropomorphism in literature. | Fantasy. |
Costume—Social aspects. | Subculture.
Classification: LCC QL85 .P38 2017 | DDC 591.5—dc23
LC record available at https://lccn.loc.gov/2016050917

BRITISH LIBRARY CATALOGUING DATA ARE AVAILABLE

**ISBN (print) 978-1-4766-6381-4
ISBN(ebook) 978-1-4766-2688-8**

© 2017 Fred Patten. All rights reserved

*No part of this book may be reproduced or transmitted in any form
or by any means, electronic or mechanical, including photocopying
or recording, or by any information storage and retrieval system,
without permission in writing from the publisher.*

Front cover illustration by Yamavu, 2014

Printed in the United States of America

*McFarland & Company, Inc., Publishers
Box 611, Jefferson, North Carolina 28640
www.mcfarlandpub.com*

To Steve Gallacci
without whom there would be no furry fandom
as we know it today

and to

Mark Merlino and Rod O'Riley
organizers of the first furry fandom convention

Acknowledgments

This book would not have been possible without the help of many people and groups within furry fandom who have provided the information herein. My apologies to any whom I may have inadvertently left out.

I would like to especially thank Higgs Raccoon for running down much of this information, and for corresponding with many present and past convention members for me. He has effectively served as the assistant editor of this book via e-mail. (He's not even in North America.)

Zack Friedrich (a.k.a. skippyfox) has also been very helpful in not only answering questions about his own convention, but in getting information about others for me. FuzzWolf of FurPlanet Productions passed many questions to the Furry Convention Leadership Roundtable (http://flcr.info/) for the representatives of many conventions to answer. Taffka Unicorn (that should be in Cyrillic) has answered all my questions about RusFURence and furry fandom in Russia in general. Blue_Panther has done the same for furry fandom in Switzerland. There are too many fans to list who are veterans of one convention, and have taken this opportunity to get it documented in detail through the years.

Thanks to all of the conventions that have sent me their logo or mascot, or one of their website banners or posters or conbook covers or T-shirts, or a similar illustration for publication in this book.

The WikiFur website has been a goldmine of historical information about discontinued conventions, and conventions that have not bothered to keep any records.

Unfortunately, some convention committees have an attitude of "we're here to have fun, not to engage in bureaucracy." They have no interest in keeping records or in documenting their own pasts.

Furry Fandom Conventions was conceived of with the intent that it be published in 2015 for the 25th anniversary of the first furry convention, which was held in 1989. Of course, it took longer to find a publisher for the book than was expected. I would like to thank McFarland & Company, Inc., Publishers, for bringing my book to reality.

Enjoy, and if you haven't attended a furry fan convention yet, may this book inspire you to do so.

Contents

Acknowledgments

vi

Furword by Kathleen C. Gerbasi

1

Preface

3

Introduction

5

The Conventions

13

**Between pages 124 and 125 are 8 color plates
containing 23 photographs**

Appendix: Furry Convention Attendance Milestones

221

Index

223

Furword
by Kathleen C. Gerbasi

Who knew?! Really, seriously I ask, who could have known there were so many furry cons nearly everywhere in the world. Well the answer is Mr. Fred Patten, noted author and historian of science fiction and the furry fandom. Fred knew and now you can too! Fred has researched and produced this amazing book, *Furry Fandom Conventions*. It is an exhaustive compendium of what appears to be virtually all known furry conventions on the planet. In case you wonder, it is possible to attend a furry convention on every continent except Africa and Antarctica as of the printing of the book. Yes indeed, anthropomorphic fans are global and some travel very serious lengths to attend furry conventions.

As a furry researcher, of course I know that furries have a world-wide presence and that there were many more conventions than those of which I had personal knowledge. But this book not only catalogues dates and locations of furry cons all over the globe, but also reports many key interesting and important facts about them, such as number of attendees, guests of honor, special activities, charity recipients and much, much more.

In fact the book is jam packed with fascinating tidbits of furry history, including what I imagine are some pretty obscure facts. My personal favorite is that at FurFright 2007 apparently a random attendee, fursuiter JD Puppy, was selected as a guest-of-honor. I can only imagine how thrilled any furry would be to be selected as guest-of-honor for a con! That could be a grand tradition that other cons might adopt. I also learned that Robert C. King is credited as the first to coin the word "fursuit."

The book is a must read for scholars of popular culture, history of culture, sociology, ethnography, and anthropology who wish to understand the development and spread of the furry fandom. I think it would also be absolutely fascinating to see all of the cons in the book displayed in GIS format on a giant map of the world with years added as a variable, but that could just be the quantitative scientist in me.

This book is also an invaluable resource for anyone just plain interested in following the rise of the furry convention from very humble beginnings at ConFurence 0 (1989) in California with 65 attendees to Anthrocon 2015 with 6,389 attendees and over 1,400 participants in the fursuit parade.

I think the book is also an invaluable resource for anyone planning a fan based convention. It details all furry cons, not only the ones that have flourished and grown over the years but also the short–lived, unsuccessful cons. It is clear from reading the con descriptions which

Furword by Kathleen C. Gerbasi

factors contribute to con successes and failures. Additionally, con planners and organizers can glean ideas for new activities which they might want to add to their convention.

In summary, I was very pleasantly surprised how much I learned from *Furry Fandom Conventions* and I think it is an amazing and invaluable resource for scholars, furries and furry scholars alike.

Kathleen C. Gerbasi is a social psychologist, anthrozoologist, and professor of psychology at Niagara County Community College of the State University of New York. She is the first behavioral scientist, along with her co-authors, to publish a peer-reviewed, scientifically-based study of furries: "Furries from A to Z (Anthropomorphism to Zoomorphism)" (2008) in the journal Society and Animals.

Preface

I have been an enthusiast of one form or another of science fiction and fantasy for my whole life. I was born in Los Angeles, California, on December 11, 1940. I discovered science fiction when I was nine years old, when my father brought Robert A. Heinlein's newly published *Sixth Column* from the L.A. Public Library. Public libraries did not accept paperbacks during the 1950s when many original paperback science fiction novels, anthologies, and collections were published, so I started a personal "library for books that other libraries won't have" during my adolescence. I attended UCLA from 1959 to 1963, graduating with a B.S. in history in 1962 and a M.L.S. in library science in 1963; my M.L.S. thesis was on the books of science fiction author Andre Norton.

In 1960, while a student at UCLA, I attended my first meeting of the weekly (Thursday evenings) Los Angeles Science Fantasy Society (established 1934), and I have been a participant in science fiction and related fandom activities ever since. I published my first mimeographed fanzine, *Foofaraw*, in 1961, and had my first book review published in 1962. I was employed as a librarian from 1963 to 1990, mainly as a cataloguer in Hughes Aircraft Company's Company Technical Document Center from 1969 until I was laid off in 1990. From 1991 to 2002, I was the first employee of Streamline Pictures, specializing in the licensing and dubbing of Japanese anime for American theatrical, television, and home video sales.

During that time I was an active hobbyist in many science fiction and fantasy fandoms. I became active in comic-book fandom as well and wrote ¡*Supermen South!* about Mexican comic-book superheroes, for the comics fanzine *Alter-Ego* in 1965. During 1972–1975 I was the co-owner (with Richard Kyle) of Graphic Story Bookshop in Long Beach, California, an early science fiction/comics specialty bookshop and the first in America to import foreign comics including Japanese manga. It was through this shop I discovered Japanese manga and anime. I co-founded (with Mark Merlino) the Cartoon/Fantasy Organization (C/FO) in May 1977, the first anime fan club in the U.S. and Canada. (I and other early anime fans claim credit for introducing the Japanese fan word "cosplay" to America, which today has almost completely replaced "costuming" and "masquerading" even outside of fandom.) I have been on many science fiction convention organizing committees, including several times as chairman. In 2006 I received a special Life Achievement Award from the World Science Fiction Convention, "in recognition of a lifetime of service to the fandom."

From 2002 to 2005, I was a freelance writer specializing in Japanese anime. I had monthly columns for three anime and comics specialty magazines, *Animation World Network*, *Comics*

Buyer's Guide, and *Newtype USA*. I had a major stroke in March 2005, and since then I have been paralyzed, living in a convalescent hospital bed in Southern California, where I communicate with the outside world through a MacBook Pro computer.

I have become more and more involved in furry fandom since 1980. During the 1980 World Science Fiction Convention in Boston, I participated in the first events that led to the evolution of furry fandom—the meeting with Steve Gallacci at that convention's Art Show, and the informal gatherings around him at other science fiction and comics conventions to discuss funny animals. I was a founding member of *Rowrbrazzle*, the quarterly furry Amateur Press Association, in 1984, publishing a pioneering furry fanzine, *Lettres de Coquefredouille*, for it. I became *Rowrbrazzle*'s official editor from 1989 until my stroke in 2005. I was at the first furry convention in January 1989, and was an attendee of practically every furry convention on the west coast of America and several "back east" until my stroke. I co-founded the annual Ursa Major Award for the best anthropomorphic work in (currently) eleven categories, and I am still on its organizational Anthropomorphic Literature and Arts Association (ALAA, http://www.ursamajorawards.org/). I was elected to the Australian Fandom Conventions' global Furry Hall of Fame in 2011, and I am a current member of the Furry Writers' Guild (FWG; http://furrywritersguild.com/).

Besides writing two books about animation (*Watching Anime, Reading Manga: 25 Years of Essays and Reviews* [Stone Bridge Press, September 2004] and *Funny Animals and More: From Anime to Zoomorphics* [Theme Park Press, March 2014]), I have specialized in editing ten anthologies of furry short fiction, including the first anthology of furry fiction, *Best in Show: 15 Years of Outstanding Furry Fiction* (Sofawolf Press, July 2003). The latest is *Gods with Fur; And Feathers, Scales, …* (FurPlanet Productions, June 2016). I have been a furry literary book reviewer since January 1990, at first for paper magazines like *Yarf!: The Magazine of Applied Anthropomorphics* (69 issues, 1990–2003), and later for several online magazines, currently for *Flayrah* and *Dogpatch Press*. I also review non-furry books for the online *AmoXcalli*, and write a weekly animation column for *Cartoon Research*. I have written numerous articles on furry history including "An Illustrated History of Furry Fandom, 1966–1996" and "Funny Animals in World War II Propaganda."

When I had my stroke in 2005, my collection was donated to the University of California, Riverside, forming the Fred Patten Special Collection on Science Fiction and Animation, a part of the UCR Library's Eaton Collection of Science Fiction & Fantasy. My holdings of furry literature, fanzines, and ephemera have given the UCR Library the most extensive collection of furry material in the world.

Introduction

The first furry convention was ConFurence 0, held in Costa Mesa, California, on January 21–22, 1989. That makes 2015 the 26th anniversary of furry fandom's conventions. And, boy, have they grown! The unnoticed furry fans of 1989 would be dumbfounded by today's Anthrocon, welcomed by Pittsburgh for putting an average of $5.5 million dollars into the local economy each year, and asked by Guinness World Records to provide an accurate count of fursuiters, the fans who dress up in full-body anthropomorphic-animal costumes. Annual furry conventions today have spread to Australia, Brazil, Canada, China, the Czech Republic, Italy, Japan, Malaysia, Poland, Russia, Singapore, Switzerland, Ukraine, and points between, with no signs of stopping.

First, though, a distinction between furmeets and furry conventions. Essentially, a furmeet is a big informal furry party of only one day or weekend without memberships or admissions, while a furry convention has a convention committee, paid memberships and badges, a hotel or similar public venue, lasts two or more days, has guests of honor, a theme, a charity, a souvenir book and T-shirt, may be incorporated, etc., and is almost always continued annually. Some furmeets are more than house parties, are held annually, have some fursuits, and use the convention name, such as SylCon, an invitational New Year's Day house party for 20 to 30 fans at a farm/resort at the Lutter am Barenberge in the Harz Mountains of Germany, from 1996 to 2008; or Zillercon, a skiing and snowboarding event held each January since 2001 at a lodge or other skiing location in the Austrian or Swiss Alps; or the Cologne FurDance, a fursuit rave (with its own website) held semi-yearly since 2008 in Köln/Cologne, Germany; or the annual Furry Cruise from a South Florida port around the Caribbean since 2005, described as like a regular cruise ship vacation with fursuits. But if this list were to include every big or regular furry gathering since 1989, it would grow to unmanageable size! Please excuse any arbitrary exclusions of "so-called conventions" that are really not. Some annual furmeets have grown to become conventions, and at that point they are included here.

Another major distinction is that furmeets are usually limited to local furs. Even when a furmeet is open, such as a picnic or barbecue or São Paulo's bowling Furboliche, it is expected that only members of the local furry community or rare known visitors from other furry communities will attend. A convention is usually open to and encourages out-of-town furs, often from around the world, and the general public, usually with a website. It is expected that a sizeable minority to a majority of convention attendees will be strangers. One of the purposes of furry conventions is to proselytize: to attract new fans, to encourage the attendance of furs from other communities, and to form friendships.

Introduction

For those interested, you are invited to see Jeff Jonas' history of early East Coast furry fandom, which includes many of the furry parties that preceded the first East Coast furry conventions: http://meep.us/furry/. Also Huscoon's video history map of the growth of furry conventions in North America might be of interest: pic.twitter.com/tZKbMSdKAl.

This list does not include established science fiction conventions with large furry tracks, such as Chicago's DucKon or New York's I-CON. It should also be pointed out that the number of fursuits in a parade is seldom the same as the number of fursuits at a given convention. Some fursuiters do not bother to participate in the parade. Also, some attendees may have more than one fursuit, which they wear on different days or loan to other fans to wear. The number of fursuits in the parade is usually the only statistic that most conventions make. Further, some veteran furry fans may have more than one fursona. Popular artist Tamara Jeanette is known as both Meezer and RedCoatCat, and sometimes is a Guest of Honor under one name or the other, or both. Finally, I have used the slang word "conbook" throughout to refer to those convention publications called by a variety of names: convention book, program book, souvenir book, memory book, and so on.

During the month before *Furry Fandom Conventions* was delivered to the publisher, there was considerable Internet and e-mail discussion throughout furry fandom about the destructive conduct at RainFurrest 2015 in Seattle that resulted in one of the largest and best-established annual conventions having its hotel contract canceled, and its planned 2016 convention indefinitely postponed. Is there anything that convention organizers can do at a 2,700+-attendee convention to prevent a minority's irresponsible behavior from causing serious hotel damage before it happens? For one thing, try to prevent it rather than taking the attitude that since it's not an officially programmed activity, the convention isn't responsible for it. Most conventions have printed Rules of Conduct. Dronon, a veteran furry fan from Winnipeg, has commented on the Flayrah furry discussion group, "Rules only go so far—the key is atmosphere. Expectation. I've argued that furry cons are a kind of 'reality bubble' we create to let out our furry side. Within that space, there's less willingness to acknowledge the norms of behavior that we want to escape from. For a good chunk of the fandom, that's part of the fandom's appeal. [...] I saw something similar at Midwest FurFest years ago—don't know if it's still done—the police would show up on Saturday night and just casually walk around briefly. They loved the dance, they took photos, and the fursuiters formed a conga line around them."

There are a few more last-minute, breaking-news events that I would like to mention: (1) the awarding of top honors (the 2016 Spirit of Slamdance winner) to the 81-minute independent documentary *Fursonas*, directed by Dominic Rodriguez and produced by Olivia Vaughn, released on January 25, 2016, at the 22nd annual Slamdance Film Festival, January 22–28, 2016 in Park City, Utah, focusing on emerging filmmakers and low-budget independent films. *Fursonas*, about "The fascinating phenomenon of 'furries,' or people who don anthropomorphic full-body costumes for role-playing purposes," as a review in *Variety* (February 3, 2016) put it, was begun in 2012 as a Pittsburgh college film class project. In 2013 it was awarded a $10,000 development grant from The Sprout Fund, "enabling Pittsburgh's community of filmmakers, videographers, and multimedia artists to showcase their approach to community innovation and receive support for their work." *Fursonas* was chosen to open the 2016 Slamdance Film Festival. It has since been picked up by the distributor Gravitas Ventures for worldwide release; (2) the announcement in February 2016 of Furrnion, the first full-scale furry convention in Spain, to be held in Madrid in January 2017 with programming in both English and Spanish. www.furrnion.org. (3) the high-profile release of the Disney Studios' animated fantasy feature *Zootopia*, about a world of intelligent animals in which humans do not exist, in early March 2016. (The exact date has differed between various countries from February 10 to late March 2016, but was generally on the weekend of March 3 and 4.) Furry fans around the world used e-mail and social media such as Facebook and Twitter to organize theater parties of dozens to hundreds to attend the local premiere together, sometimes dressed in fursuits where the theater managements allowed it. In Stockholm, where the Swedish release of *Zootopia* coincided with the NordicFuzzCon 2016 convention, the committee rented an entire 250-seat theater, a 15-minute walk from the convention hotel, and organized a communal walk to the theater and an exclusive screening in English with Swedish subtitles. The special event was coordinated in advance through the NordicFuzzCon 2016 website, which included a professional-quality cartoon painting indistinguishable from Disney's own publicity art, by Silverfox5213, a Malaysian furry artist. Many of the organized theater parties included amateur illustrated banners. One party in a 145-seat theater was upgraded to a 225-seat theater, and still developed a waiting list. Planned *Zootopia* theater parties, many including an informal furmeet before or after, were also reported throughout the U.S. and in Brazil, Canada, México, the Philippines, Russia, and Singapore.

Today furmeets and furry conventions have spread throughout North America, Europe, and Australasia. A one-day "Morph Parade" in Bangkok, Thailand, announced as a "Kemono Only Event" (for fursuiters only), on November 7, 2015, between 10:00 a.m. and 3:00 p.m., drew approximately 400 participants. A second parade is scheduled for October 29, 2016. Such furmeets are also becoming more common in Latin America. An intriguing article on fursuiters in Lima, Peru, in Lima's *El Comercio* on May 19, 2015, "Furry Fandom: la Comunidad de los Muñecos de Peluche en Lima," says that "En Latinoamérica, Chile es un pais privilegiado para el 'furry fandom'" ["In Latin America, Chile is a privileged country for 'furry fandom'"]. That's news to most furs. Brazil has two gatherings; the Abando campout with ties to Canada's Camp Feral!, and the one-day Furboliche bowling furmeet. Furboliche most recently had 248 fans on October 31, 2015, including 61 in fursuits, from across Brazil in a São Paulo bowling palace. But there's nada in Chile.

Recent laws in France banning any masked head coverings in public places have made French fursuit gatherings technically illegal, but they are recognized as harmless social gatherings, usually under 100, and the laws are not enforced against them—although they are usually well-policed.

If furmeets and furry fandom conventions are still considered colorfully oddball by the general public, there are so many around the world that they are no longer misidentified as gatherings of animal-masked terrorists, or of sexual deviants who hold orgies in their fursuits in hotel hallways. There is probably a furry convention in your city. If there isn't yet, don't be surprised when one is started.

Timeline

Furry Fandom Conventions is primarily about furry fandom's conventions, arranged in alphabetical order. Unfortunately, this gives a poor chronological view of how the fandom has developed.

Furry fans themselves have debated as to when it started. Some have argued in favor of its beginning with the popularity of newspaper comic strips and animated cartoons in the 1910s and 1920s, with such funny animals as Old Doc Yak (goat), Felix the Cat, Oswald the Lucky Rabbit, and Mickey Mouse. Krazy Kat in the newspaper comic strip by George Herriman became so prestigious that there was a 1922 ballet, *Krazy Kat: A Jazz Pantomime*, by John Alden Carpenter, later adapted into a symphonic piece. In Britain, there were similar fandoms for Rupert Bear and for the trio of Pip (dog), Squeak (penguin), and Wilfred (baby rabbit). A Wilfredian League of Gugnuncs fan club grew so large with thousands of members that it held annual meetings for several years in the Royal Albert Hall. Its 1920s and 1930s membership badges are valuable collectibles today. Three British military medals awarded to servicemen who had served throughout World War I were popularly known as the Pip (1914 or 1914–15 Star), Squeak (British War Medal), and Wilfred (British Victory Medal) medals. There were Mickey Mouse Clubs throughout the U.S. and Canada in the 1930s.

But these fandoms, especially the organized clubs, were all commercial enterprises. The Mickey Mouse Clubs were organized by the Walt Disney Company as a copyrighted spinoff primarily to increase the theatrical cartoons' popularity, and secondarily to sell children's merchandise. They were little different from the Superman clubs, the Captain Marvel clubs, the Little Orphan Annie clubs, the Lone Ranger clubs, and similar children's clubs with songs, secret handshakes, and knickknacks such as decoder rings, whistles, lapel pins, and clothing patches that were sold to their members. They were at best fandoms for individual funny animal characters and their supporting friends, not for the genre.

Furry fandom has evolved from science fiction fandom, which began in the 1930s, and comics fandom, which developed in the 1960s. It is generally assumed to have gotten its start at the annual World Science Fiction Convention in Boston, Massachusetts, in 1980, when Steve Gallacci, a young U.S. Air Force technical illustrator, entered a painting of a cat-woman in flight gear standing next to a highly detailed fighter aircraft in the convention's art show. The disparity of the funny animal and the realistic aircraft drew attention. Gallacci explained that the painting was from an idea he was developing for a science fiction comic book about bioengineered animal-peoples so far in the future that they had forgotten their origins. He had file folders full of sketches for his story that he showed. Several of the fans who gathered around him found through discussions that many of their favorite stories were those featuring intelligent animal characters, such as the novels *Animal Farm* and *Watership Down* in science fiction, Disney's animated *Robin Hood* in movies and *Kimba the White Lion* in television, and *Donald Duck* and *Pogo Possum* in comic books and strips. As Gallacci got out of the Air Force and began attending science fiction and comics conventions along the West Coast in the early 1980s, the crowd of fans around him grew. Many were amateur cartoonists, and they traded sketches of their own anthropomorphic characters.

Some of these fans were members of a fanzine club, *Vootie*, "the fanzine of the Funny Animal Liberation Front," published bimonthly from April 1976. It was a closed cartoonists' club, but when it was discontinued in 1983, one of its members, Mark Schirmeister, started a similar club, *Rowrbrazzle*, as its replacement, beginning in February 1984. Two key differences were that *Rowrbrazzle* allowed text articles such as reviews and critiques about funny animals as well as cartoons, enabling funny animal fans who were not cartoonists to join; and accepted discussions of the early activities of funny animal fandom, proving in print that a separate furry fandom (not yet named) existed by that point.

During the early 1980s the first furry fans got together during science fiction fandom and comics fandom conventions, notably the annual Westercons and San Diego Comic-Cons. Furry fans began holding distinct parties at the 1985 Westercon in Sacramento, California, organized by Mark Merlino and Rod O'Riley of Southern California, and "official" furry room parties with flyers posted throughout the hotels, the first at the Westercon 39 science fiction convention in San Diego in July 1986. It was these flyers announcing a "Furry Party" at science fiction and comics conventions during the late 1980s that led to the popular name of "furry fandom." In 1987 Mark Merlino attempted to publicize the annual BayCon in San Jose as the science fiction convention at which furry fans should gather. (Merlino also attended the 1987 Worldcon in Brighton, England, and held a furry room party there. Many first-generation British furry fans attributed this party with introducing them to the concept of furry fandom.) The 1987 and 1988 BayCons did have large attendances of furry fans, but hostility from several of the BayCon's non-furry science fiction fan attendees who objected to "having their convention co-opted by non-s-f fans" made a strong furry presence unfeasible. At the 1988 BayCon, Kris Kreutzman's Furry Party flyers were graffitied into "Skunkfuckers Party" flyers, and the graffitiers then used the "Skunkfuckers" posters to try unsuccessfully to get the furry fans expelled from the convention. (Anime fans were also made to feel unwelcome at early BayCons.) There were also informal furry parties on the east coast during the late '80s. Merlino & Co. concluded that furry fans needed their own convention.

When the ConFurences began in 1989, most furry fans used their real names or nicknames, and dressed in street clothes except for specific masquerades. The fandom and conventions were centered around furry art and literature. Common activities were trading drawings in sketchbooks, asking a fan artist to sketch on your registration badge (usually done for free), and looking for furry fanzines and books like *Jonathan Livingston Seagull, Watership Down, Tailchaser's Song,* or the latest furry-oriented science fiction and fantasy paperbacks in the Dealers' Den. (There were no furry specialty publishers until the early 2000s.)

On February 1–2, 1992, English fan Ian Curtis held the "First British Furry Micro-Con" at his home in the village of Yateley, in Surrey, Southern England. The occasion was the visit to England of a half-dozen American furry fans who had attended the 1992 International Comics Festival in Angoulême, France, in January. Curtis invited furry fans throughout Britain (only about a dozen); six came. The dozen American and British furry fans spent the weekend partying at Curtis' home. More importantly, Curtis enjoyed himself so much that in April 1994 he began a series of quarterly open weekend "Housecons," starting with Housecon 3 to include his February 1992 party and a June 1993 party held by Jan Paxton at his home in South Wales. Curtis' Housecons become a tradition for the next several years, drawing approximately 15 attendees each, including some furry fans from Germany. These and a series of annual UK Fur CONs, little more than parties organized through FurryMUCK, kept the concept of furry conventions alive in Britain, and helped lead to the EuroFurences and later conventions in Central Europe.

Around 1992 or 1993, the makeup of the ConFurence evolved. Fursuits became more prominent. The influx of new attendees brought an increasing number who did not have any familiarity with science fiction or comics fandom, who had learned about furry fandom and the ConFurences over the Internet. The newcomers included many who were used to adopting personas for role-playing games, and preferred to be known by furry personas (fursonas) that were flamboyantly pseudonyms, like Aerofox and Neo PanTyger. Many refused to let their real names become known.

The earliest continuous annual furry fandom convention, not counting the now-discontinued ConFurence, was EuroFurence. It was started in 1995 by two German fans at the countryside farmhouse of one's parents. Nineteen fans attended. From there EuroFurence has grown, moving into the largest hotel in Berlin with over 2,000 attendees. EuroFurence has met in the Czech Republic, the Netherlands, and Sweden, but it has moved about within Germany since 2004. Other continuous European furry conventions began in Russia in 1999, France in 2003 (unfortunately, it did not last), the Czech Republic and Poland in 2005, Switzerland, Ukraine, and England in 2008 (and Scotland in 2011), Denmark and Finland in 2011, Italy in 2012, and Sweden in 2013. Outside Europe, there have been furry conventions in Australia since 2006, New Zealand since 2007, Brazil and Japan since 2008, the Philippines since 2014, and China (both the mainland and Taiwan), Malaysia, and Singapore since 2015 (with Thai Tails, Thailand's first furry convention scheduled for January 2016).

In North America, the ConFurence in Southern California was alone from 1989 to 1995. During the early 1990s furry fans got several east coast science fiction conventions to add furry programming to their events. The first separate eastern furry convention was Furtasticon in Philadelphia in 1995. Others quickly followed: Albany Anthrocon (which moved to Philadelphia, then to Pittsburgh) and Memphis in 1997, Ontario and Seattle in 1998, Orlando and San Jose in 1999, Chicago in 2000, Atlanta in 2004, Denver in 2007, and a flood of others. They have not all prospered, but most of them have grown from annual conventions of a few hundred attendees to 1,000 or 2,000 or more.

By 1997, the wearing of fursuits and the use of fursona names only was becoming common; the importance of Fursuit Parades and "headless lounges" where a fursuiter could remove his or her animal head and relax, grew. Convention paper or cardboard membership badges around 2000 commonly included the names of the convention and the member in tiny type, with most of the badge blank to allow for an individualized cartoon or a commissioned painting. By this time many furry artists specialized in taking commissions for membership badges all convention long, often with elaborate cartoon color portraits of the member's fursona. By the 2010s, membership badges had evolved to laminated plastic ones printed with full-color cartoon paintings, often by an artist guest-of-honor, with the attendee's name on a transparent overlay strip at the bottom. Many members add a second badge with a full-color individualized cartoon portrait of the member's animal fursona.

It should be mentioned that from the early 1990s through the early 2000s, especially through the three years of the CritterConDiegos, a major furry fan activity was attending the Comic-Con International in San Diego, California, to hang out around the tables of Radio Comix, Terrie Smith, Jim Groat, Steve Gallacci and Lance Ikegawa, and other furry specialty exhibitors. Cartoonist Mitchell Beiro was "discovered" at a San Diego Comic-Con around 1990 and invited to join furry fandom. This lasted until the mid–2000s when, one by one, these exhibitors could no longer afford Comic-Con's rising table prices and disappeared, and individual furry fans at the Comic-Cons no longer had natural gathering spots.

Beyond the conventions, furry fandom developed several fanzines or amateur magazines during the 1990s and early 2000s such as *Anthrolations, Fantastic Furry Stories, FurryPhile, FurVersion, Morphic Tales, Mythagoras, PawPrints Fanzine, South Fur Lands* (in Australia), *Yarf! The Journal of Applied Anthropomorphics,* and *Zoomorphica*. These were usually edited and published by an individual fan or small club, were photo-offset, contained editorials, articles, stories and illustrations, and were available by mail order and on sale at furry conventions. They disappeared during the 2000s when rising postage prices made them unprofitable. They and the Internet enabled furry fans to stay in contact between conventions. Furry specialty book publishers such as FurPlanet Productions, Rabbit Valley Books, and Sofawolf Press appeared during the 2000s. Two annual furry literary awards began: the Ursa Major Award, voted upon by international furry fans and administered by the Anthropomorphic Literature and Arts Association (ALAA) since 2001, and the Cóyotl Award, administered and voted upon by members of the Furry Writers' Guild (FWG) since 2012. Several furry artists have been able to support themselves largely by taking commissions for paintings and book jacket art, and by selling limited-edition art prints. One artist sold a painting for $10,000 at a 2004 furry convention art show auction. Full-body fursuits have become so elaborate and so desirable that several specialty makers have become commercial manufacturers under such names as Blue Fox Fursuits and Clockwork Creature Studio, charging up to several thousand dollars for a custom-made fursuit.

This timeline shows how the culture of furry conventions and furry fandom has grown and evolved; from the ConFurences in Southern California in 1989 to the ConFURence Easts in 1994, to European conventions with EuroFurence in Germany in 1995, back to Albany AnthroCon in 1997, to Canada's outdoor Camp Feral! in Ontario in 1998, to Further Confusion in Northern California in 1999, and to the explosion in furry conventioneering during the 2000s throughout North America and Europe, including its spread to Australia, Japan, and Latin America.

The Conventions

Abando

Abando was created in 2008, after discussion on the Furry Brasil forum and a visit by Ekevoo to Canada's Camp Feral!, as an outdoor camping event on WToboe's farm near São Paulo, Brazil during Brazil's Carnival season. It was started in emulation of Canada's Camp Feral! It moved to Intervales State Park (Parque Estadual Intervales), also near São Paulo, when it outgrew WToboe's farm. There are no charities or Fursuit Parades. It is for age 18+ only. Attendees receive a conbook, a T-shirt, and sometimes a reusable cup to cut down on the waste of cups. The T-shirts (a different one each year) are all by Jrrhack except in 2011 when it was by Reyes Wolf. Abando and Camp Feral! are often cross-promoted as sister camps. An Abando animated teaser on the Camp Feral! website reads: "Too much snow? Want to warm up? Come and enjoy the tropical summer At Brazil's most traditional camping con!"

Name & Date	Theme	Location	Attendance
Abando 2008 February 2–5, 2008	none	Sitio Maio, São Roque	15
Abando 2009 February 21–24, 2009	none	Sitio Maio, São Roque	22
Abando 2010 February 13–16, 2010	Hawaii: Aloha, Abando!	Sitio Maio, São Roque	37
Abando 2011 March 5–8, 2011	UFO Hunters	Sitio Maio, São Roque	55
Abando 2012 February 18–21, 2012	Mayas; The Sons of the Sun	Intervales state park, Ribeirão Grande	50
Abando 2013 February 9–12, 2013	Furries of the Sea!	Intervales state park, Ribeirão Grande	55
Abando 2014 March 1–4, 2014	Japan: The Daimyō Lands	Intervales state park, Ribeirão Grande	73
Abando 2015 February 6–9, 2015	The Mafia of Arts	Intervales state park, Ribeirão Grande	68

Events

Abando 2008: The first Abando was organized after Ekevoo from Brazil attended Canada's weeklong outdoor Camp Feral! in 2007. The staff were six fans led by Reyres Wolf. The staff prepared three meals a day. Activities were similar to Camp Feral!'s: workshops, board games, movie nights, and sports including foam-bat battles, Frisbee tossing, lake swimming, a nighttime campfire, and water-balloon rugby.

Guests of Honor: Tiamat (furry artist)
Chairmen or Organizers: Reyres Wolf (chairman), staff Ångström, Ekevoo, Isra, JrrHack, WToboe

Abando 2009: It was mostly the same.
Guests of Honor: Yanazaki (furry artist)
Chairmen or Organizers: Reyres Wolf (chairman); staff Aniki Geelong, Ekevoo, Jrrhack, Tanuki Gokuhi, WToboe; collaborators Koush, Shadow

Abando 2010: Again the same, with the addition of a theme. This was the last year that Reyres Wolf led the staff.
Guests of Honor: Carykaiba (furry artist)
Chairmen or Organizers: Reyres Wolf (chairman); staff Aniki Geelong, Ekevoo, Jrrhack, Koush, Tanuki Gokuhi, WToboe; collaborators Shadow, Silverbolt

Abando 2011: The same. It was noted that the comfortable capacity of Toboe's farm had become far exceeded.
Guests of Honor: Fificat (furry artist; cancelled at last minute)
Chairmen or Organizers: Aniki Geelong (chairman); staff Ekivoo, Jrrhack, Silverbolt, Tanuki Gokuhi, WToboe; collaborators Josepp, Koga Silverdragon, Flam

Abando 2012: The annual outing moved to the larger Intervales State Park in Ribeirão Grande, a nature reserve with cascades, caverns with guided tours, and much wildlife. The new site included housing, a lodge, a restaurant, a pool, and a sports field, but there was no camping or cell phone service. Meals were provided through the park management.
Guests of Honor: (none)
Chairmen or Organizers: Aniki Geelong (chairman); staff Ekivoo, Jrrhack, Koush, Silverbolt, Tanuki Gokuhi, WToboe; collaborator Loba Teimosa

Abando 2013: The same as in Abando 2012. Potoroo, the chairman of Canada's Camp Feral!, spent the week following Abando 2013 as the house guest of São Paulo's furry community.
Guests of Honor: Lucas Raymond (Potoroo)
Chairmen or Organizers: Aniki Geelong (chairman); staff Casshan, Ekevoo, Henrik, Jrrhack, Koush, Loba Teimosa, Silverbolt, Tanuki Gokuhi, WToboe; collaborator White Raccoon

Abando 2014: The same as in Abando 2012.
Guests of Honor: (none)

Abando logo. Art by Tanuki Gokuhi. Used with permission.

Chairmen or Organizers: Aniki Geelong (chairman); staff Casshan, Ekevoo, Jrrhack, Koush, Loba Teimosa, Silverbolt, Tanuki Gokuhi, WToboe, Tui, White Raccoon

Abando 2015: Abando was booked online in 37 minutes. An official mascot was chosen: Obi ("green" in Tupi-Guarani), an anthropomorphized local teiú lizard (large enough to eat mice). It was announced that Abando had reached the park's capacity, and would move next year to a school camp with room for 140 attendees. (But it announced in early 2016 that Abando was being discontinued after that year's camp because it was growing larger than its staff could handle.)

Guests of Honor: (none)

Chairmen or Organizers: Aniki Geelong (chairman); staff Casshan, Ekevoo, Jrrhack, Koush, Loba Teimosa, Silverbolt, Tanuki Gokuhi, WToboe, Tui, White Raccoon

All Fur Fun

AFF was meant to replace the discontinued Conifur Northwest in Seattle. The CN committee donated its materials such as Art Show hangings to AFF just before the convention. The Ridpath was a charmingly colorful hotel, about a hundred years old, with rococo statuary all around the lobby and a big old-fashioned fireplace. Unfortunately, it had a large non-furry regular clientele and was never very furry-friendly. A move to a convention center did not offset committee dissatisfaction with a lack of incorporation. AFF was also faced with another replacement of Conifur Northwest created the same year; the better-organized RainFurrest in Seattle. Although there was never any animosity between the two conventions, the Northwest furry community just did not consider AFF necessary.

Name & Date	Theme	Location	Attendance	Parade
All Fur Fun 2007 March 30–April 1, 2007	none	Ridpath Hotel, Spokane, WA	110	25 (estimated)
All Fur Fun 2008 April 18–20, 2008	Pajama Party	Ridpath Hotel, Spokane, WA	165	?
All Fur Fun 2009 May 15–17, 2009	Ancient Greece	Mirabeau Park Hotel & Convention Center, Spokane Valley, WA	197 (estimated)	50

Events

All Fur Fun 2007: Events included a Dealers' Den, an Art Show and Auction, a Fursuit Parade, numerous fursuiting and crafting workshops, a writing workshop led by furry author Phil Geusz, a dance, and an ice cream social. There was a T-shirt with the AFF logo on the front and the full-color convention book cover by Shadow Wolf on the back.

Guests of Honor: Katie Hofgard (Shadow Wolf) (furry artist)

Chairmen or Organizers: Sean Ravencraft (Moorcat)

All Fur Fun 2008: A theme was added. 2, the Ranting Gryphon did a rant. There was an Ice Cream Social. The animal group Wolf People brought a tame wolf for a nature demonstration. Complaints were that there were no Con Suite or hotel air conditioning, the hotel elevators broke down on the first day of the convention and were never fixed, and the hotel had no restaurant but did have a "swanky night club" filled with non-fan drunks every night, some of whom molested the fursuiters. The police came on one night. The T-shirt and conbook cover were by Foxy Fennec.

Guests of Honor: Juliana Fennec (Foxy Fennec) (furry artist)

Chairmen or Organizers: Sean Ravencraft (Moorcat)

All Fur Fun 2009: Scheduled events included two dances, Giant Fursuit origami planning, a Masquerade, a Fursuit Olympics, workshops on making fursuits and ears 'n' tails, a military furs brunch and a panel, and "Whose Fur" hosted by Mursa. Art Show sales were about $1,400. The 2008 Ursa Major Awards were presented at AFF 2009. The T-shirt and conbook cover were both collaborations by FlintHoof and Wicked Sarah.

Guests of Honor: Dan Canaan (FlintHoof, furry artist), Special G-o-H Sarah Krueger (Wicked Sarah, furry artist/sculptor)

Chairmen or Organizers: Sean Ravencraft (Moorcat)

This was the final AFF. AFF 2010 was cancelled due to the lack of incorporation and committee resignations. By 2011, it was generally agreed that AFF was dead.

Antheria

Antheria 2010 was organized under the auspices of Anthro International Entertainment, to "continually bring a remarkable event of impeccable professionalism and integrity to the southern California area." It was generally considered as unnecessary, being too close to the already-established CaliFur. It was plagued with cancellations and rearrangements, and disappeared after two years.

Name & Date	Theme	Location	Attendance
Antheria 2010 October 1–3, 2010	Anthropolis	Best Western Sunrise Hotel, Redondo Beach, CA	~400
Antheria 2011 September 30–October 2, 2011	Egyptian Underworld	Marina Hotel, Redondo Beach, CA	?

Events

Antheria 2010: Antheria 2010 was organized under the auspices of Anthro International Entertainment, to "continually bring a remarkable event of impeccable professionalism and integrity to the southern California area." The theme was actually only described vaguely as "an ancient Roman theme," but it was unofficially called "Anthropolis." The convention was originally scheduled for the Westin Los Angeles Airport Hotel, but was changed less than a week before the convention due to the last-minute cancellation of the contract by the Westin. The new hotel was across the street from the beach, and a five-minute walk from the Redondo Beach pier and amusement arcade. Fursuiters mingled with tourists there and posed for photos. There were performances by Bucktown Tiger and J Tigerclaw, 2, the Ranting Gryphon, and Uncle Kage; and numerous dances. On one night the main ballroom was occupied by a bridal shower, and some fursuiters were invited to attend for photographs. The mascot was Lionitus, created by Agent Elrond. The 32-page conbook had a color front and back cover by Agent Elrond, and an 11-page gallery of Roman-themed anthro animal art. Agent Elrond was appointed the Mayor of Antheria 2010 for her hard work for the convention; a position intended to become elective in future years.

Guests of Honor: Stan Sakai, Special G-o-H Matthew Ebel, Mark Merlino

Chairmen or Organizers: Matthew Wayne Davis (2, the Ranting Gryphon), Jibba Foxcoon

Antheria 2011: The 28-page souvenir book had a cover by Mike Kazaleh.

Guests of Honor: Mike Kazaleh (cartoonist, animator)

Chairmen or Organizers: Daniel Branton

Antheria 2012 was expected but was never announced.

Anthro New England

Anthro New England (ANE) is a furry convention in Cambridge, Massachusetts. It is incorporated as Anthro New England, Inc.

Anthro New England 2015 poster. Art by Kittitara. Used with permission.

Name & Date	Theme	Location	Attendance	Parade
Anthro New England 2015 February 27–March 1, 2015	The American Revolution: Boston Strong	Hotel Regency Cambridge, Cambridge, MA	757	165

Events

Anthro New England 2015: Most of the program consisted of the traditional opening and closing ceremonies, fursuit games and dances, panels, and raves. There was a Cambridge Police K-9 presentation. The conbook cover was by Fivel. Valhund did the T-shirt.

Guests of Honor: Valhund, Fivel (furry artists)
Charity: MA Vest-a-Dog ($10,000)
Chairmen or Organizers: Nexus Folf, Logn, KotaHusky

Anthrocon

The Anthrocon, the third American furry convention, originated as the Albany Anthrocon in 1997 when it was created in Albany, New York. It dropped the Albany when it moved out of that city as too small.

Name & Date	Theme	Location	Attendance	Parade
Albany AnthroCon 1997 July 3–6, 1997	An East Coast Furry Con	Omni Albany Hotel, Albany, NY	500 (estimated)	no record
Albany AnthroCon 1998 July 3–5, 1998	Here Be Dragons	Omni Albany Hotel, Albany, NY	600	no record
Anthrocon '99 July 1–4, 1999	The Furry Revolution	Valley Forge Hilton, King of Prussia, PA	804	no record
Anthrocon 2000 June 29–July 2, 2000	Furries of Myth and Legend	Valley Forge Hilton, King of Prussia, PA	1,128	no record
Anthrocon 2001 July 27–29, 2001	Furries in Flight	Adam's Mark Hotel, Philadelphia, PA	1,457	no record
Anthrocon 2002 July 12–14, 2002	Invention	Adam's Mark Hotel, Philadelphia, PA	1,648	no record
Anthrocon 2003 July 17–21, 2003	Creatures of the Night	Adam's Mark Hotel, Philadelphia, PA	1,949	no record
Anthrocon 2004 July 6–11, 2004	Summer Games	Adam's Mark Hotel, Philadelphia, PA	2,404	no record
Anthrocon 2005 July 7–10, 2005	Heroes	Wyndham Franklin Plaza Hotel, Philadelphia, PA	2,370	140
Anthrocon 2006 June 15–18, 2006	Making History	Westin Hotel [&] David L. Lawrence Convention Center, Pittsburgh, PA	2,489	191
Anthrocon 2007 July 5–8, 2007	Looking to the Future	Westin Hotel [&] David L. Lawrence Convention Center, Pittsburgh, PA	2,849	353
Anthrocon 2008 June 26–29, 2008	It's a Jungle Out There!	Westin Hotel [&] David L. Lawrence Convention Center, Pittsburgh, PA	3,390	453
Anthrocon 2009 July 2–5, 2009	OMG Aliens!	Westin Hotel [&] David L. Lawrence Convention Center, Pittsburgh, PA	3,776	640
Anthrocon 2010 June 24–27, 2010	Modern Stone-Age Furries	Westin Hotel [&] David L. Lawrence Convention Center, Pittsburgh, PA	4,238	713

Name & Date	Theme	Location	Attendance	Parade
Anthrocon 2011 June 23–26, 2011	Anthropomorphic Institute of Magic	Westin Hotel [&] David L. Lawrence Convention Center, Pittsburgh, PA	4,400	854
Anthrocon 2012 June 14–17, 2012	A Midsummer Night's Dream	Westin Hotel [&] David L. Lawrence Convention Center, Pittsburgh, PA	5,179	1,044
Anthrocon 2013 July 4–7, 2013	The Fast and the Furrious	Westin Hotel [&] David L. Lawrence Convention Center, Pittsburgh, PA	5,577	1,300
Anthrocon 2014 July 3–6, 2014	Secret Societies	Westin Hotel [&] David L. Lawrence Convention Center, Pittsburgh, PA	5,861	1,326
Anthrocon 2015	Viking Invasion!	Westin Hotel [&] David L. Lawrence Convention Center, Pittsburgh, PA	6,389	1,460

Events

Albany AnthroCon 1997: Albany AnthroCon was the idea of Roger Wilbur. It became the first furry annual convention to stake out a major public holiday. It was almost cancelled because, unknown to the convention, the contact at the convention's first hotel, the Desmond Albany Hotel, had resigned and left the state without making the arrangements for the convention; and by the time this was discovered in June, it was too late to book the hotel. Only last-minute hard work by Brent Edwards (Chip Unicorn) got the Omni as a replacement. Despite the short-notice change in hotels, the convention had a large attendance. The mascots were Max Cat and Sophia Ferret. There was regular convention programming with moderated panels and workshops on writing and drawing. In addition to the dealers' room and the Art Show, there was an Internet Room run by Tigerwolf. Events included a Plush Gathering, Steve Plunkett's Puppet Show, a charity auction, a Masquerade, a Club Fur dance, and a closing Pizza Party. Randy Fox (Yappy Fox) started AnthroCon's annual Fursuit Parades, with what may have been the earliest official Fursuit Parade. Dr. Samuel "Uncle Kage" Conway told his stories on the pool deck. The city's 4th of July fireworks in the nearby Empire State Plaza were a major attraction. After the convention, Gary Akins produced a "highlights" video of it.

Albany AnthroCon held the first furry fandom awards ceremony, for an award voted on by the public [since the 1996 ConFurence presentation of the Golden Sydney Award, for the promotion of furry fandom, was committee-chosen], for the Moreau Awards for furry fandom's favorite creators. All convention members who preregistered before February 1 were sent nomination forms, and the nominees were voted upon at the convention. At the Moreau presentations, about 20 attendees voted.

Best Furry Artist: Vicky Wyman
Best Furry Comic Artist: Terrie Smith
Best Furry "Alternative" Artist: Peter Stoller (for his "Jack Salem" Fursuit)
Best Furry Writer: Watts Martin (for "A Gift of Fire, A Gift of Blood")
Best Furry Publisher: Silverfox Publications
Best Furry Work: Yarf!
Best Furry Computer-Related Work: Eric W. Schwartz (of animation fame)
Best Furry Virtual Environment: Furrymuck
Best of Breed: Theodore Geisel (Dr. Seuss)

Guests of Honor: Daphne Lage (furry artist), Watts Martin (furry author), David L. Pulver (game designer).

Charity: Therapy Dogs, Inc. ($2,200).
Chairmen or Organizers: Roger Wilbur (Aloyen Youngblood)

Albany AnthroCon 1998: The activities of the first AnthroCon were repeated and expanded upon. There were around 75 events scheduled, including special interest group meetings; panels on such subjects as anthropomorphic-animal advertising mascots and "Cleaning Up Our Past"; a puppet show by Steve Plunkett and a Story Hour by Uncle Kage; and a Saturday-night performance by Purple Nurple Live! The previous year's Moreau Awards were not repeated; the committee considered them a failure since only about twenty members out of 500 had bothered to attend and vote. The 44-page Program Book had a cover by Jim Groat. The second AnthroCon had over forty staff members; Roger Wilbur was the official Chairman (CEO), but most of the convention was co-ordinated by Jonah E. Safar as Organizational Director. The T-shirt was by Jim Groat. There was general agreement that a larger hotel was needed for next year.

Guests of Honor: Jeffrey A. Carver (s-f author), Jim Groat (furry cartoonist); Fandom G-o-H: Dr. Samuel Conway
Charity: Whiskers, a cat rescue group ($3,092)
Chairmen or Organizers: Roger Wilbur (Aloyen Youngblood)

Anthrocon '99: Anthrocon (lower-case "c") became the new name for Albany AnthroCon, because it was no longer in Albany. It moved to the Valley Forge Hilton in the Philadelphia suburb of King of Prussia, Pennsylvania, under the new leadership of Dr. Samuel C. Conway (Kagemushi or Uncle Kage). The convention had outgrown Albany altogether, so it was turned over to Uncle Kage with the Albany committee's best wishes. Memberships were 845 and actual attendance was 804. Convention-long features included an Art Show, an Artists Alley, a Dealers' Room, and a board and computer gaming room. (The Art Show and Dealers' Room had separate Adult sections.) Events were categorized as workshops, seminars, artist demos, hands-on demos, round table discussions, panels, and Special Interest Groups. Special events included a charity auction, a masquerade, and dances. The 76-page conbook had a color wraparound cover by Vicky Wyman. The T-shirt was by Sara Palmer (Caribou).

Guests of Honor: S. Andrew Swann (s-f author), Vicky Wyman (furry artist).
Charity: Great Valley Nature Center ($3,600).
Chairmen or Organizers: Dr. Samuel C. Conway (Uncle Kage)

Anthrocon 2000: In 2000, Anthrocon became the second furry convention to top 1,000 attendees. Chairman Dr. Samuel "Uncle Kage" Conway was prominent throughout Anthrocon 2000 as the master of ceremonies in a "mad scientist" white lab smock. The attendance of 1,128 made AC the new "largest furry convention ever." The AC 2000 Program Book was 72 pages with a color wrap-around cover by Caribou. Panelists included many notable furry artists and writers. Fursuits seemed everywhere. The T-shirt was by Jason Holmgren (Rafferty). The hotel was clearly becoming too small for the growing Anthrocon.

Guests of Honor: Paul Kidd (furry author), Sara Palmer (Caribou; furry artist)
Charity: Great Valley Nature Center ($6,534)
Chairmen or Organizers: Dr. Samuel C. Conway (Uncle Kage)

Anthrocon 2001: Attendance jumped sharply. This was the first Anthrocon in Philadelphia (barely; it was just inside the city line). The most talked-about feature of Anthrocon 2001 was the Adam's Mark's four elevators and three escalators to the third floor that kept breaking down. Attendees re-dubbed the convention to "Staircon" and the theme to "Furries in Flight(s of Stairs)," a comment on having to walk up and down the stalled escalators, and the hotel's stairs to get to their rooms. Furry standup comedian 2, the Ranting Gryphon, in his first Antrocon appearance, made the elevators a main feature of his rant, and several last-minute Art Show entries featured the stairs. Most of the grousing was good-natured, since the Adam's Mark was the longtime home of s-f fandom's Philcon convention, and the furry fans knew about the notorious stairs. The closing of the Art Show bidding was marked by an advancing wall of giant pencils. At future Philadelphia Anthrocons, the giant pencils were used by the Dorsai Irregulars to get badge check volunteers. After the Anthrocon moved to Pittsburgh, the owners of the giant pencils (who live in Connecticut) transferred to FurFright there. Fans went out of their way to show friendship to the DeCarlos. The recently-fired, veteran Archie Comics artist had been adopted as A Cause by all of comics fandom. DeCarlo had named *Josie and the Pussycats* after his wife decades earlier, and when he asked for a share in the comic's profits, Archie Comics had fired him. At eighty, he was too old to get a new job, and Archie Comics' lawyers had prevented him from drawing his most popular creations, Josie and Sabrina, the Teen-Age Witch, for his fans. DeCarlo seemed bemused by the attention that he was getting from furry fandom since he had never drawn furry characters—the fans dubbed him a furry artist for creating Josie's cat-costume—but he reveled in it. (Anthrocon 2001 was one of his last fan conventions. He died in December.) The "automated" convention registration broke down on the first day, creating a vast logjam of fans waiting to get their badges. It was estimated that the wait was three hours for people at the rear of the line, making some fans miss first-day panels. The Art Show was large but notably lacking in original paintings. Attendees included furry fans from all around the world. Anthrocon 2001 got a long, favorable writeup in the *Wayne Suburban* newspaper, "Invasion of the Furries" by Rob Staeger. Bill Holbrook did a color wraparound cover featuring his *Kevin & Kell* characters for the 76-page Program Book. The charity was a nearby service that provided horses for physically handicapped children. The T-shirt had a front by Herbie Hamill (Herbie Bearclaw) and a back by Sara Palmer (Caribou).

Guests of Honor: Bill Holbrook (newspaper/Internet cartoonist), Dan DeCarlo (comic book artist) and his wife, Josie

Charity: Reins of Life ($7,237)

Chairmen or Organizers: Dr. Samuel C. Conway (Uncle Kage)

Anthrocon 2002: Membership badges were upgraded from "old-fashioned" cards in clear holders to illustrated laminated plastic. Several fans lamented the disappearance of individual mostly-blank badges that could be personalized by an artist. (Many fans have since worn both that year's laminated badge and a personalized illustrated badge, some choosing a permanent elaborate mini-painting by a popular fan artist, and others coming with a blank card each year for a new drawing.) There were the usual Funday Pawpet Show, Uncle Kage's Story Hour, Masquerade, Comedy Club improve show, and Fursuit Parade and photo session. One of the Masquerade skits was "The History of Ferret Aviation." Chairman Uncle Kage personally led a reporter from the *Philadelphia Inquirer* around in the hope of getting a favorable story. The charity auction included Uncle Kage promising and getting a Mohawk haircut. The T-shirt was done as a contest, won by Grimal.

Guests of Honor: Heather Bruton (fantasy artist), and s-f author Lisanne Norman (s-f author). There were two "special guests," Dan DeCarlo's widow Josie, and furry artist Herbie Bearclaw.

Charity: Canine Partners for Life ($13,280)

Chairmen or Organizers: Dr. Samuel C. Conway (Uncle Kage)

Anthrocon 2003: There was the usual abundance of panels, workshops, and furry RPGing. Bill Holbrook was a popular panelist on the WebComics panel. There were a Funday PawPet Show and a VCL mixer. There was dancing on Friday night to DJs Dragonboy's and Genki's records, and on Saturday night to a live performance by the Fear Liston 4-piece rock band. There were a Video Room, an Internet Room, and lots of fursuits. Attendees enjoyed complaining about the hotel's erratic elevators, but the Supersponsors' Lounge was complimented for lots of good food. The 76-page conbook had a wraparound color cover by Guy Gilchrist. The T-shirt was by Mark Rogers. Convention security was provided by the Dorsai Irregulars.

Guests of Honor: Guy Gilchrist (newspaper/comic-book cartoonist), Mark E. Rogers (*Samurai Cat* creator)
Charity: Support Our Shelters ($8,348)
Chairmen or Organizers: Dr. Samuel C. Conway (Uncle Kage)

Anthrocon 2004: This was the first furry convention to top 2,000 attendees. This was the final Anthrocon to meet at the Adam's Mark Hotel, which had the largest convention space in Philadelphia, before it was demolished. The notorious elevators were, if not fixed, at least improved. The AC Board of Directors first discussed moving to Pittsburgh for its larger convention facilities. The two guests-of-honor were asked to each present an Art Show "Guest of Honor's Choice Award." There were the usual Fursuit Parade and Uncle Kage's Story Hour. Anthrocon, Inc., announced a 2004 revenue of $106,131.99 and expenditures of $110,331.06. The T-shirt had a front by Michel Gagné and a back by Stan Sakai; they both collaborated on the 76-page wraparound color conbook cover.
Guests of Honor: Michel Gagné (animator/illustrator), Stan Sakai (cartoonist)
Charity: Forgotten Felines & Fidos ($7,200)
Chairmen or Organizers: Dr. Samuel C. Conway (Uncle Kage)

Anthrocon 2005: Anthrocon moved due to the planned demolition of the Adam's Mark Hotel. This was the only year that attendance declined. The new hotel had slight space arrangement problems that required a smaller Art Show and Dealer's Rooms, and moved the Internet Lounge to the second floor lobby. Despite the problems, the new hotel was considered only a temporary problem because the committee promised to move to better quarters next year. The 2004 Ursa Major Awards presentations were at Anthrocon 2005. This was the first year that statistics for the number of fursuits in the Fursuit Parade were kept. There was a huge unplanned furpile in the upper level of the lobby, when it was found to have a fantastic view and most of the fursuiters rushed there with their cameras. An empty bottle in the Art Show had a note saying that the bottle's genie had gone to see Uncle Kage's Story Hour; Kage bought it for $25. Anthrocon, Inc., reported $125,169.78 in income and $112,542.73 in expenses. Peter Laird did the 76-page conbook wraparound color cover. There were two T-shirts, by Peter Laird and by Tim Albee.
Guests of Honor: Peter Laird (*TMNT* co-creator), Timothy Albee (*Kaze, Ghost Warrior* creator)
Charity: Greater Philadelphia Search & Rescue ($6,470)
Chairmen or Organizers: Dr. Samuel C. Conway (Uncle Kage)

Anthrocon 2006: Anthrocon moved from Philadelphia to Pittsburgh. The "last brick" from the demolished Adam's Mark Hotel was auctioned off for $200. 2, the Ranting Gryphon gave a rant. There was considerable friction between many dealers, who were used to setting up their tables at their own convenience and bring in their own food for meals, and the convention center which was a Union signatory and required the tables to be set up by Union personnel, and required the dealers to buy their food from the overpriced convention eateries. Some of the late-night parties were hassled by hotel management. The 72-page wraparound color conbook cover and the T-shirt were by Scott Shaw! The convention was covered by five local TV stations or newspapers. Frozen Oasis hosted a room party, but it was controversially shut down after fifty minutes by Dorsai Irregulars security due to complaints from other rooms of too much noise. Two years after Anthrocon 2006, it was recorded in the 2008 Guinness Book of Records as the "largest furry fan club."
Guests of Honor: Scott Shaw! (animator/comic-book artist), Diane Duane (s-f author), Tom Smith (filker)
Charity: The Western Pennsylvania National Wild Animal Orphanage ($5,845)
Chairmen or Organizers: Dr. Samuel C. Conway (Uncle Kage)

Anthrocon 2007: The convention started unofficially the previous weekend when fans began arriving in hotels and gathering for partying and fursuit-wearing. By Tuesday the Westin lobby was filled. All attendees received a "furvey survey" from the Niagara County Community College. A claim was made to Guinness World Records for "Most Mascots in a parade" that the Guinness World Records organization let Anthrocon know was being verified. The Westin Hotel sold out its room block and the Omni William Penn Hotel was used as Anthrocon's overflow hotel. Besides the $6,608 that was raised for Animal Friends, an additional $1,000 was donated from Time Warner in October for a Time Warner Community Service Grant. Around $32,000 was spent in the Artists Alley, which sold out. Anthrocon, Inc., reported $186,002.90 in revenue and $157,490.40 in expenses. Numerous attendees commented on how friendly Rob Paulsen was. The 72-page wraparound color conbook cover and the T-shirt were by Carolyn Kelly featuring *Pogo* characters. Frozen Oasis hosted a three-room suite dance party and rave. Three protestors against the "Furfags" stood across the street from the convention center in the rain. Rather than counter-protesting, Uncle Kage provided umbrellas for them.

Anthrocon received favorable Pittsburgh newspaper, radio and TV publicity. The Chicago Cubs and the Milwaukee Brewers baseball teams were booked into the same hotels as Anthrocon for games against the Pittsburgh Pirates; the Cubs moved to a different hotel before the convention to get away from the "wacky animal people," according to the Cubs' manager in the Chicago press. The Brewers stayed at the Westin, without any complaints during Anthrocon; however, several ballplayers complained after the convention about the "creepy" Fursuiters. The Brewers lost several games, giving rise to jokes about "the Curse of the Furries." There was the first mention in convention reports of how friendly the local restaurants were. Several of them visually appreciated the furry fans' trade. One, Fernando's Café, was especially noted. "Found on the block neighboring the Westin, Fernando's was renowned for having embraced the furry gathering with above and beyond support. For the weekend they would change the name of the restaurant to "Furnando's" (embroidered upon shirts), drew blue paw marks on the sidewalk, and offered attendees special discounts. The owner also showed great courage on an infamous day during Anthrocon 2007 [...]" "On Friday, at Fernando's Café, AllFur Radio was having a live show. During said show, [a non-fur] showed up and started being extremely rude and harassing the furs because they were getting discounted food. Fernando [DeCarvalho] chased the person off the establishment, and told them not to harass the furs. This person decided to pick up a brick and smash it over Fernando's head." Fernando was briefly hospitalized with a fractured skull.

Guests of Honor: Rob Paulsen (voice actor), Mark Evanier (TV animation/comic-book writer), Carolyn Kelly (Walt Kelly's daughter/current Pogo cartoonist)

Charity: Animal Friends ($6,608)

Chairmen or Organizers: Dr. Samuel C. Conway (Uncle Kage)

Anthrocon 2008: AC 2008 became the first furry convention to top 3,000 attendees. Veteran Disney animator/writer Floyd Norman did not feel worthy to be "honored," so he was made the "Guest of O.K." Furry specialty publisher Sofawolf Press and others released new books and other products at the convention. Local classic rock radio station WDVE 102.5 tried to film an unauthorized Anthrocon video report but was shut down by Security. Floyd Norman did both the 72-page Program Book wraparound color cover and the T-shirt. Anthrocon, Inc., reported $215,694.29 in revenue and $201,455.62 in expenses. Anthrocon 2008 shared the Westin with the New York Yankees, in Pittsburgh to play against the Pittsburgh Pirates. The Yankees' security staff demanded that all of the furries clear out of the lobby when the Yankees came through, ostensibly because the Yankees, as "America's Team," were considered a target for terrorism and the security folks did not like having people there with their faces covered. Anthrocon complied the first time by tricking the attendees into running upstairs by sending someone out to spread the rumor that "Uncle Kage is drunk and telling stories that the board of directors doesn't want him to" in an upstairs ballroom. After that, the Dorsai Irregulars provided extra assistance to keep any Yankees "safe" when crossing the lobby.

"Guest-of-O.K.": Disney Legend Floyd Norman
Charity: Pittsburgh Parrot Rescue ($11,900)
Chairmen or Organizers: Dr. Samuel C. Conway (Uncle Kage)

Anthrocon 2009: The growing attendance forced some functions such as registration and the Dealers' Den to move to larger quarters in Hall B of the Convention Center, twice as large as Hall C used from 2006 to 2008. The secondary and tertiary overflow hotels changed, due to the popular Omni William Penn being already booked for 2009. A "First Fursuiter of 2009" award was won by fursuiter Hallow Fox. The charity donation included the proceeds of both the charity auction and raffle, and a Sunday benefit comedy show by 2, the Ranting Gryphon and Uncle Kage. The three Guests-of-Honor collaborated on the wraparound color cover of the 48-page conbook. The T-shirt was by Ben Balistreri. Anthrocon, Inc., reported $196,409 in revenue and $213,639 in expenses.

Guests of Honor: Joe Harris (creator of Underdog and the Trix Rabbit), Bob Boyle (creator of *Wow! Wow! Wubbzy!*), Ben Balistreri (design supervisor of *Foster's Home for Imaginary Friends*)
Charity: The Animal Rescue League's Wildlife Rehabilitation Center ($8,992.69)
Chairmen or Organizers: Dr. Samuel C. Conway (Uncle Kage)

Anthrocon 2010: AC 2010 became the first furry convention with over 4,000 attendees. The Program Guide listed 164 separate events, divided into Guests of Honor presentations, Convention (opening & closing ceremonies, charity auction, etc.), Art, Family, Social & Fandom, Fursuit, Gaming, Performance, Puppet, Science & Technology, Videogaming, and Writing. There was a minor pre-convention controversy when Anthrocon banned two-time previous attendee David Ross from returning, for known to openly carry a gun, despite Ross' protests that it was legal where he had worn it and that he had never tried to bring one into Anthrocon. An attendee clowning dangerously on the convention center's roof the day before AC 2010 got the roof closed to AC attendees by convention center security, except for the scheduled Rooftop Drum Jam and Dance, limited to 35 attendees. (The guards also made an exception for an attendee who wanted to propose marriage on the roof at sunset, and his girlfriend.) Anthrocon, Inc., reported $373,926 in revenue and $376,346 in expenses. This included $125,304 in revenue and $125,966 in expenses for the Art Show and Artists' Alley. The 44-page conbook had a wraparound color cover by James Gurney, who did the T-shirt. There was mention in a con report of an Anthrocon flag flying over the convention center.

Guests of Honor: James Gurney (s-f artist), Jim Martin (director of *Sesame Street*)
Charity: Fayette Friends of Animals ($12,849)
Chairmen or Organizers: Dr. Samuel C. Conway (Uncle Kage)

Anthrocon 2011: Anthrocon tied with the ConFurences for longevity—15 of them. Attendees came from 39 countries. The 4,400 attendees reportedly booked all the hotel rooms in Downtown Pittsburgh. Uncle Kage was quoted in the *Pittsburgh Post-Gazette* as saying that "he believed the event would have pulled in even more attendees if the city had followed through on a languishing initiative to build more hotels Downtown. […] When Downtown hotels became fully booked in mid–May, Anthrocon registration dropped off dramatically, Mr. Conway said. Many furry fans are already bunking four to a room—the Westin's limit. Mr. Conway said that he doubts the event will grow further unless more rooms are made available near the center." The article also said that the attendees would "spend an estimated $5.3 million at Downtown businesses." (After the convention the actual amount was reported as $5.7 million.)

Notable events included an Anthropoly quiz panel, a "My Little Pony" panel, a Fursuit Friendly Dance, Uncle Kage's Story Hour, and the Masquerade. G-o-H Peter Beagle was usually accompanied by his close friend and agent, Connor Cochran. Several fans visited Pittsburgh's Space Center in their fursuits. An extensive social psychology survey, first conducted online during February by Dr. Courtney Plante (Nuka), then a graduate student at the University of Waterloo [Ontario] and Dr.

Kathy Gerbasi of Niagara County Community College of the State University of New York as part of their "Anthropomorphic Research Project," was followed up at Anthrocon 2011; the results were posted online. (Nuka attended several furry conventions from 2010 on as a psychology speaker and fursuiter as a neon-furred blue kitty wearing a lab coat.)

Anthrocon, Inc., reported $392,805.02 in revenue and $405,563.74 in expenses. This included $123,526.67 in revenue from the Art Show and Artists' Alley. The 60-page conbook had a wraparound color cover by Andy Runton, who did the T-shirt.

Guests of Honor: Andy Runton (cartoonist), Peter S. Beagle (s-f author)
Charity: ToonSeum: Pittsburgh Museum of Cartoon Art ($11,522)
Chairmen or Organizers: Dr. Samuel C. Conway (Uncle Kage)

Anthrocon 2012: AC 2012 was originally scheduled for June 21–24, but in August 2011 it announced its move back to June 14–17 at the request of the municipal government to make a "very rare opportunity to host an event that they have been wanting to host for many years." The event, officially a secret, was rumored from the start to be the National Hockey League Entry Draft; this was confirmed in October. In return, AC 2012 was awarded an additional hundred hotel rooms within walking distance of the Convention Center. During April-May 2012, Anthrocon was widely "appreciated" in local news for helping to keep Fernando's Café open. As reported in the *Huffington Post* in May, the café (which had been an Anthrocon favorite since 2006 for its Anthrocon decorations, "Fernando's" T-shirts, animal-themed menu, and discounts to furry fans) had announced that it would have to close on April 27 due to the recession. Anthrocon's CEO Dr. Conway started a fund-raising campaign and on April 21, an Anthrocon committee presented café-owner Fernando DeCarvalho with $21,000; not enough to save the restaurant, but enough to keep it open through that June's convention.

Anthrocon, Inc., reported $472,019.59 in revenue and $448,383.48 in expenses. This included $124,781.27 in revenue from the Art Show and Artists' Alley. The 56-page conbook had a tete-a-beche color cover; half by Dev Madan, half by Mike Kazaleh. Dev Madan drew the T-shirt.

Guests of Honor: Dev Madan (Sly Cooper art director), Mike Kazaleh (cartoonist/animator)
Charity: Hello Bully ($20,656)
Chairmen or Organizers: Dr. Samuel C. Conway (Uncle Kage)

Anthrocon 2013: AC 2013 contracted room space with seven of Pittsburgh's ten Downtown hotels. It received favorable pre-convention newspaper and TV news coverage, noting that Anthrocon was one of the ten largest conventions in Pittsburgh and was expected to add over $6 million to the local economy. A post-convention article was headlined "Largest parade of people in fur suits: Pittsburgh breaks Guinness world record." Seviche's restaurant offered free "Nibbles and Bits" menu items to people who posed for a photograph with fursuiters and posted it to Facebook or Twitter. Fernando's Café, which had remained open during AC 2012 and had been sold afterward but had remained a café, was temporarily renamed the Furryland Café with Fernando as returning manager for the weekend. City management requested that Anthrocon produce a T-shirt that could be sold throughout the city during the convention. The "Anthrocon .... Rocking Pittsburgh, PA Since 2006" multicolor-on-black shirt by German furry artist Tani Da Real, only on sale outside the convention, was an instant sell-out at gift shops throughout Pittsburgh, many going to people who bought multiple shirts for sale on eBay. The 2012 Ursa Major Awards were presented at an awards ceremony. The 52-page conbook had a front cover by Larry Dixon. The T-shirt was by Tom Minton and Jasper. Anthrocon, Inc., reported $534,112 in revenue, and assets of $149,139.

Guests of Honor: Larry Dixon, Mercedes Lackey (s-f authors), Tom Minton (animator), Sardyuon (Japanese furry artist/fursuiter/juggler/acrobat)
Charity: Equine Angels Rescue ($31,000)
Chairmen or Organizers: Dr. Samuel C. Conway (Uncle Kage)

Anthrocon 2014: There were attendees from 25 countries and every U.S. state except North Dakota. The Schedule and Pocket Program was 76 pages with 153 events including "AC 2014 Charity Poker Tournament," "Advanced Fursuit Safety," "Disneyana and the Furry World," "Feline Friendly Furry Fiasco," "Ferret Photo Meet," "Furocity Radio Live," "Puppet Improv Workshop," and "You Can Be a Pawpet, Too!" As usual when AC meets during the July 4th holiday, the roof of the Convention Center was open on July 4th night to convention goers for one of the best views of fireworks in the city. The 40-page conbook had a wraparound color cover by AlectorFencer. The T-shirt was by Cupro Hastes. Anthrocon, Inc., reported income of $581,784, and assets after expenses of $170,839.

The mayor of Pittsburgh proclaimed July 5th to be Anthrocon Day. Numerous videos were posted to YouTube; some of recorded AC events like the Fursuit Parade, and some of performed music videos featuring fursuited fans. (Two outstanding examples by Kiba Wolf are https://www.youtube.com/watch?v=ckbNWlglrHg and https://www.youtube.com/watch?v=TBOxGwjMj18&feature=iv&src_vid=ckbNWlglrHg&annotation_id=annotation_4272641227.) The ToonSeum (AC 2011's charity) presented AC 2014 with its Gertie Award "For Exhibiting Great Character." The Carnegie Library of Pittsburgh participated with its mascot, an anthropomorphized giant library card.

Guests of Honor: Lee Tockar, Jim Cummings (voice actors)
Charity: The National Aviary ($32,372.79)
Chairmen or Organizers: Dr. Samuel C. Conway (Uncle Kage)

Anthrocon 2015: Two 9:00–2:00 a.m. shuttles were provided to five hotels. The Fursuit Parade for the first time included an outdoor route, marching around the hotel and back into it rather than going through it or the Convention Center. It was widely covered by the news media, which reported hundreds up to 5,000 non-attendees gathered to watch it. The media also reported that Anthrocon added an estimated $5.7 million to Pittsburgh's economy. The *Pittsburgh Post-Gazette* said that "Furries Seem to 'Nest' in Pittsburgh Year-Round" (July 8), reporting a monthly meeting of about two dozen furries at Fernando's Café, bowling and ice-skating meets, online forums like www.pa-furry.org, and other year-round activities, some in fursuits. The full-color conbook was 40 pages, and there was a separate 40-page Convention & Dining Guide with a congratulatory letter from the mayor of Pittsburgh, both with a cover by Cupro Hastes, who also did the T-shirt. A separate 76-page pocket Program Guide listed 188 events.

Guests of Honor: Kimlinh Tran (voice artist), Ted Giannoulas/San Diego Chicken (sports mascot)
Charity: Western Pennsylvania Humane Society ($35,910)
Chairmen or Organizers: Dr. Samuel C. Conway (Uncle Kage)

Anthrofest

Anthrofest, a.k.a. the International Anthropomorphics Festival or Festival Internationale de l'Anthropomorphisme, was an English-French bilingual furry convention in Montréal, Quebec. It was created in 2006 partly to replace the cancelled C-ACE in Ottawa; partly as a smaller alternative to larger furry conventions; and partly as a more informal convention emphasizing entertainment and a Mardi Gras atmosphere. It could not get a hotel booking for 2008, and faded away.

Name & Date	Location	Attendance	Parade
Anthrofest 2006 August 11–13, 2006	Doubletree Plaza Hotel, Montréal, Quebec	100	13
Anthrofest 2007 July 27–29, 2007	Doubletree Plaza Hotel, Montréal, Quebec	111	20

Events

Anthrofest 2006: Noble Wolf replaced Comic Creator of Recognition Graveyard Greg, who withdrew.
> *Guests of Honor:* Artist of Recognition FirestormSix, Fursuiter of Recognition Noble Wolf
> *Chairmen or Organizers:* Cnipur

Anthrofest 2007: Many events were fursuit-oriented. Anthrofest 2007 got a writeup the day before the convention by the *Montreal Gazette*; "Finally comfortable in their own fur."
> *Guests of Honor:* Artist of Recognition Palladinthug, Costumer of Recognition Furbo
> *Chairmen or Organizers:* Cnipur

AnthrOhio *see* Morphicon

Arizona Fur Con

Arizona Fur Con is a furry convention for the whole state, located in Phoenix. It is registered as Arizona Fur Convention LLC.

Name & Date	Theme	Location	Attendance	Parade
Arizona Fur Con 2013 October 11–13, 2013	Cowboy Campfire	Embassy Suites Phoenix-Scottsdale, Phoenix, AZ	533	114
Arizona Fur Con 2014 October 31–November 2, 2014	Undead Ghost Town	Pointe Hilton Squaw Peak Resort, Phoenix, AZ	537	117
Arizona Fur Con 2015 October 16–18, 2015	Furry Tales	Scottsdale Resort at McCormick Ranch, Scottsdale, AZ	725	121

Events

Arizona Fur Con 2013: The program included a dance contest, gaming, fursuiting, a masquerade, panels and workshops. A themed café presented a *My Little Pony* "Pinkie Pie Café Party." The conbook cover was by Myenia, and the T-shirt was by Jethro Kassis (Jethro).
> *Guests of Honor:* FurPlanet Productions (furry publisher; its staff), Special Guests Krista Campbell (Broadway costumer), Dimitri Davis (screenwriting consultant), Rukis (furry artist/author), Myenia (furry artist), Laura Garabedian (furry artist), Wicker (fursuit maker)
> *Chairmen or Organizers:* Danielle Kemper (Trick)

Arizona Fur Con 2014: Arizona Fur Convention LLC joined with Monkey Paw Entertainment, the organizer of several anime conventions, for greater backing and funding. A charity was added. The Gypsi Pirates were two swimming performers in mermaid costumes, Mermaid Lilith and Mermaid Lucia. They were scheduled to give a Friday performance in the hotel swimming pool, but they were ordered out by hotel security after the first moments because of the hotel's "no costumes in the pool" policy. Instead, they gave a "how to make a mermaid tail" demonstration/workshop. The conbook cover was by Celina Pike (Frost.Bite), and the T-shirt was by Laura Knapp (Immaterial).
> *Guests of Honor:* Rebecca Sharpe (fursuiter), Frost.Bite (furry artist), Gypsi Pirates (two mermaid performers), Matthew Wayne Davis (2, the Ranting Gryphon, furry standup comedian), Amadhia (professional musician), Uncle Kage (furry performer, chairman of Anthrocon)
> *Charity:* Cat A Do Cat Co-op ($1,300+)
> *Chairmen or Organizers:* Danielle Kemper (Trick), Greg Fennell

Arizona Fur Con 2015: AFC 2015 moved to a new hotel. Buck Hopper gave a voice acting workshop. The Gypsi Pirate mermaids returned and had full use of the pool. AFC 2015 added an experimental meal plan, with its hotel's cooperation, of a buffet lunch with a different menu each day, for the first 60 members to sign up for it; heavily subsidized by the convention. The conbook cover was by Laura Knapp (Immaterial), and the T-shirt was by Jethro Kassis (Jethro).

Guests of Honor: Uncle Kage (furry performer, chairman of Anthrocon), Telephone (fursuit maker), Danjiisthmus (furry artist), Albinotopaz (fursuiter), Matthew Wayne Davis (2, the Ranting Gryphon, furry standup comedian)

Charity: Cat A Do Cat Co-op ($5,525)

Chairmen or Organizers: Danielle Kemper (Trick), Greg Fennell, Tony Pineda

BerliCon

BerliCon is a small relaxicon for the Berlin furry community in a nature setting.

Name & Date	Theme	Location	Attendance
BerliCon 1 April 24, 2004	?	Gemeindehaus der Philipp Melanchthon Gemeinde, Berlin	23
BerliCon 2 April 30, 2005	?	Gemeindehaus der Philipp Melanchthon Gemeinde, Berlin	30
BerliCon 3 April 22, 2006	?	Gemeindehaus der Philipp Melanchthon Gemeinde, Berlin	34
BerliCon 4 June 15–17, 2007	?	Köpenicker Kanusport Club, Berlin	35
BerliCon 5 July 19–22, 2008	?	Zeltlagerplatz e.V. campground/hostel, Berlin	57
BerliCon 6 June 18–21, 2009	?	Zeltlagerplatz e.V. campground/hostel, Berlin	71
BerliCon 7 June 17–20, 2010	?	Zeltlagerplatz e.V. campground/hostel, Berlin	71
BerliCon 8 June 16–19, 2011	?	Abenteuerzentrum Grunewald e.V., Berlin	89
BerliCon 9 June 21–24, 2012	Nach uns die Sintflut	Abenteuerzentrum Grunewald e.V., Berlin	?
BerliCon 10 June 20–23, 2013	Auf die Jugend!	Abenteuerzentrum Grunewald e.V., Berlin	?
BerliCon 11 June 12–15, 2014	Damals wie Heute	Abenteuerzentrum Grunewald e.V., Berlin	?
BerliCon 12 June 18–21, 2015	Schlag 12	Abenteuerzentrum Grunewald e.V., Berlin	?

Events

BerliCon 1: There had been numerous furry house parties around Berlin; this one-day convention was an attempt to get everyone together at once. Memberships were €7. The Philipp Melanchthon Municipal House was a rented neighborhood hall with a main room, several smaller rooms including a basement set up with games such as table tennis, indoor football, and billiards, and a large grassy yard where a barbecue grill was set up. The program was informal socializing and game-playing

during the daytime, a barbecue dinner, and an evening watching a DVD movie on a projection screen. Attendees were welcome to take leftover food home. This first BerliCon has slowly grown.
Chairmen or Organizers: Kai-Uwe Wilke (Riffuchs), Phelan

BerliCon 2: The attendance of 30 presumably did not include the organizers because a progress report announced that the hall's limit was 30 attendees and 50 people. Memberships were €10, meals included. The activities were the same as the previous year. The program included staying over the night and breakfast the next morning. Waffles were emphasized.
Chairmen or Organizers: "The BerliCon Orga"

BerliCon 3: The progress report explained that the BerliCon date was chosen to be before the MMCs in early May and hopefully earlier than Walpurgis celebrations on May 1. It was intended to be a relaxicon compared to the MMCs and the EFs. There were a grill lunch and evening BBQ and movie night. A group photo was scheduled "depending on weather conditions." The BerliCon ended at 3:00 a.m. Sunday morning, but attendees got a Sunday morning breakfast before leaving.
Chairmen or Organizers: Arnold, CleanerWolf, Phelan, Kai-Uwe Wilke (Riffuchs)

BerliCon 4: The Köpenicker Kanusport Club is a canoeing club on the River Spree, offering "accommodation for all: comfortable sleeping rooms, quiet rooms and a campground. Located directly on the River Spree, and a large forest just outside the door, they can hardly be desired." The convention was organized as a relaxicon similar to the Camp Ferals!, beginning with a Friday 6:00 p.m. hot dinner followed by a movie night; a Saturday morning Dance Dance Revolution, an afternoon Fursuit Walk and evening Furdance and BBQ, "NovaFox's history lesson" and a group photo; and a Sunday "warm happening." An alternate event on Friday and Saturday nights was a "The Werewolves of Mirkwood" card game. There was a hot breakfast on Saturday and Sunday mornings. The T-shirt was by Isuna.
Chairmen or Organizers: Kai-Uwe Wilke (Riffuchs), Phelan, Marcus Dudziak (Hoyt), Jens-René Wiedemann (MafunDi)

BerliCon 5: The venue was in the Tegler Forest just outside northwest Berlin. Members roomed in the House Hostel. Aside from outdoor campground events, the convention took place in a large central tent. There were a Friday night barbeque with salad and soft drinks provided by the convention, and dances every evening. On Saturday a Pirate Radio broadcast by MafunDi was streamed into the Internet. The T-shirt was by Sethaa (front) and Silke Nischan (Isuna; back).
Chairmen or Organizers: Kai-Uwe Wilke (Riffuchs), Phelan, Marcus Dudziak (Hoyt), Jens-René Wiedemann (MafunDi)

BerliCon 6: There was an Art Show throughout the convention and a morning brunch/buffet each day. Events included a Thursday movie night; a Friday Fursuit Walk, BBQ dinner, and night scavenger hunt; a Saturday group photo and Fursuit photo, nighttime scavenger hunt, and pirate radio activities; and a Sunday feedback session. The T-shirt was by OliverFox (front) and Sethaa (back).
Chairmen or Organizers: Kai-Uwe Wilke (Riffuchs), Phelan

BerliCon 7: There was a breakfast/brunch/buffet every day, except on Thursday that started in the evening. Events included a Thursday evening film night and campfire; a Friday Fursuit activity, evening BBQ (with beer), nighttime scavenger hunt, and stories around the campfire; a Saturday group photo and fursuit activity including a fursuit photo, an evening awards ceremony for the winners of the scavenger hunt, Pirate Radio Fur "with delicious meals," and campfire activities; and Sunday feedback session. The T-shirt was by EosFoxx (front) and Sethaa (back).
Chairmen or Organizers: Kai-Uwe Wilke (Riffuchs), Phelan

BerliCon 8: The Grundwalheim Adventure Center is a three-acre wooded estate with leisure activities for youth groups and schools, including rope climbing and nature activities.
Chairmen or Organizers:

BerliCon 9: The translation of the theme, After Us the Deluge, was a reference to the Mayan calendar showing the world ending in 2012. The T-shirt was by Michaela Frech (Pan Hesekiel Shiroi).
Chairmen or Organizers:

BerliCon 10: The translation of the theme is About Youth!
Chairmen or Organizers:

BerliCon 11: The translation of the theme is Then and Now.
Chairmen or Organizers:

BerliCon 12: The translation of the theme is Strike 12. The schedule was: Thursday, noon open. Evening supper, karaoke, campfire. Friday, morning brunch. Afternoon, high ropes climbing for non-fursuiters and fursuiters. Evening, barbecue, fuchsjagd, campfire. Saturday, morning brunch. Afternoon, fursuit group photo, fursuitwalk through 2.5 km forest route, high ropes climbing, fursuit games (fursuiterspiele). Evening, victory celebrations, fox hunting, group photo, pirate fur radio, campfire, cocktail. Sunday, morning breakfast. Noon, closing session, leaving. The T-shirt was by OliverFox/Severus Blackpaw and EosFoxx. The illustrated plastic membership badges were by Riffuchs.
Chairmen or Organizers: "The ConOrga."

On December 21, 2015, BerliCon announced (translated), "A very sad day for us as Orga: there are no further plans for further BerliCon. We hereby wish to thank all our guests [for] the past twelve years—you were great!"

Biggest Little Fur Con

BLFC is a take on Reno, NV's motto, "The Biggest Little City in the World." It is organized by Reno Area Anthropomorphic Arts and Recreations (RAAAR), a.k.a. BLFCorp, with Brometheus Bear as fictional Chairman. It was preceded by PawFur 2012, a one-day trial convention on May 13, 2012, on the Arcade level of the Grand Sierra Resort, Nevada Foyer in Reno, NV; hosted by Reno's anime community that was already putting on an annual anime convention. PawFur was a success, but the anime group decided that two annual conventions was too much. PawFur was turned over to Reno's furry community, which organized as RAAAR to continue it. It became BLFC when it was established "for real."

Name & Date	*Theme*	*Location*	*Attendance*	*Parade*
Biggest Little Fur Con 2013 May 3–5, 2013	Roaring Twenties	Grand Sierra Resort, Nevada Foyer, Reno, NV	704	186
Biggest Little Fur Con 2014 March 28–30, 2014	80s Pop Culture	Grand Sierra Resort, Nevada Foyer, Reno, NV	1,442	485
Biggest Little Fur Con 2015 May 14–17, 2015	Utopia	Grand Sierra Resort, Nevada Foyer, Reno, NV	2,443	707

Events

Biggest Little Fur Con 2013: PawFur 2012 made Reno's furry community aware of how perfect the Grand Sierra Resort was for a furry convention, so it was eager to keep one going. The hotel had many fursuit-friendly activities including bowling, go-karting, and mini-golf, plus games like laser-tag and a discount movie theater. BLFC activities, all within one 44,000 square foot space, included an art show and dealers' den, a photo area, panels, dances including a fursuit dance competition (won by Apollo Husky), electronic and tabletop gaming, and a live podcast by Fur Media honoring furs in the military.

Guests of Honor: Spelunker Sal & Dreamous (furry artist-writer wife & husband), Wolfpup TK (fursuiter)
Charity: Nevada Humane Society ($3,000)
Chairmen or Organizers: Tyco

Biggest Little Fur Con 2014: A new annual program event was started; the Fursuit Bachelor Auction, at which fursuited "bachelors" were auctioned (one hour) as dance partners (one hour). Auction proceeds were added to the charity donation.
Guests of Honor: Linsey Huish (Sidian, furry artist, fursuiter), Kijani (fursuiter)
Charity: Safe Haven Rescue Zoo ($16,650)
Chairmen or Organizers: Tyco

Biggest Little Fur Con 2015: The Utopia theme was developed as a furry totalitarian dystopia, overthrown at the closing ceremonies with the motto "Brometheus has fallen; the revolution has begun!" YCH (Your Character Here) personalized art badges were sold for charity. The G-o-Hs were technically furry companies, represented by their staffs.
Guests of Honor: Rabbit Valley (furry publisher; Sean Rabbitt, Andrew Rabbitt, Brian Mogged), Mongoose Ink (furry writing/art business; Mitch de la Guardia)
Charity: Safe Haven Rescue Zoo ($34,000)
Chairmen or Organizers: Tyco

Biggest Little Fur Con logo. Art by BLFC staff. Used with permission.

C-ACE

C-ACE stood for Canadian Anthro and Cartooning Expo, initially. (The meaning of the acronym changed.) Programming emphasized furry creativity in art, costuming, music, and writing. All material was required to be a "clean" G or PG-13. A Sketch Pad Lounge was popular. "Some of the activities and features we have planned include an artshow, art shoppe (our combination artists' alley and dealer room), three rooms for panels or workshops (including a nearly 700 sq. ft. feature workshop), a con suite, video programming, a "Sketch Pad" (an artists' lounge where you can relax, draw, or chat with friends), a small gaming room, contests and art jams, and social events every evening." C-ACE was run by an Ontario-Registered Not for Profit Corporation.

Name & Date	*Location*	*Attendance*
C-ACE 2002 August 16–18, 2002	Courtyard Ottawa Downtown Hotel, Ottawa, Ontario	110
C-ACE 2003 May 30–June 1, 2003	Chimo Hotel, Ottawa, Ontario	160 (estimated)
C-ACE 2004 June 4–6, 2004	Chimo Hotel, Ottawa, Ontario	178
C-ACE 2005 June 3–5, 2005	Best Western Victoria Park Suites Hotel, Ottawa, Ontario	224
C-ACE 2006 June 23–25, 2006	Best Western Victoria Park Suites Hotel, Ottawa, Ontario	177

Name & Date	Location	Attendance
C-ACE 2007 June 8–10, 2007	Best Western Victoria Park Suites Hotel, Ottawa, Ontario	127

Events

C-ACE 2002: The convention hotel was located in one of the liveliest sections of Ottawa, with plenty of attractions nearby. Niall MacConaill conducted a Chocolate Social, giving attendees dozens of flavors of gourmet chocolates. A 2002 T-shirt was designed by Anya Schwartz.

Guests of Honor: Comic Artist Guest-of-Honour, Shawntae Howard; Instructor Guest-of-Honour, Scott Ruggels; two Newcomer Guests-of-Honour, furry cartoonists Amy Pronovost and Anya Schwartz

Chairmen or Organizers: Jeff Novotny (Orleans)

C-ACE 2003: Both the Dealers Room and the Art Show sold out. Niall MacConaill repeated his Chocolate Social by popular demand. The 2003 T-shirt was by Chris Goodwin.

Guests of Honor: Writer Guest-of-Honour Ted MacKinnon, Artist G-o-H Chris Goodwin, Newcomer G-o-Hs Jennifer Brook (Nalina), Amy Fennell (Lyosha) (artists)

Chairmen or Organizers: Orleans, Niall MacConaill

C-ACE 2004: The programming included life-drawing for artists, a writing contests, and MacConaill's popular Friday night Chocolate Social. The 3rd C-ACE was the venue of the 3rd annual Ursa Major Awards presentation. The T-shirt design was by Spunky.

Guests of Honor: Heather Bruton (fantasy artist), Jen Seng (Spunky) (newspaper cartoonist)

Chairmen or Organizers: Niall MacConaill, Chris Pilgrim (Feli)

C-ACE 2005: The convention was called the Canadian Arts and Cartooning Expo in pre-convention publicity and just C-ACE (unexplained) at the convention and in its publications. The program featured the usual, including the ever-popular Chocolate Social. Cara Mitten did the T-shirt.

Guests of Honor: Jo Walton (s-f author), Cara Mitten (Spacehyena, artist)

Chairmen or Organizers: Niall MacConaill

C-ACE 2006: The convention again called itself C-ACE without saying what the letters stood for. C$550 was donated to charity. The T-shirt was by Melita Curphy (Missmonster Mel), featuring one of her Fu dogs.

Guests of Honor: Julie E. Czerneda (s-f author), Mark Oakley (comic-book artist), Melita Curphy (animator)

Charity: ? (C$550)

Chairmen or Organizers: David Gordon

C-ACE 2007: Due to the steady decline in attendance, this was the final C-ACE.

Guests of Honor: Fiona Patton (Canadian fantasy author), Andrew Pidcock (Loopy Wolf) (artist/fursuiter)

Chairmen or Organizers: Niall MacConaill

Cal-Furr

Name & Date	Location	Attendance
Cal-Furr August 11–13, 2006	Best Western Hospitality Inn, Calgary, Alberta	30 (estimated)

Events

Cal-Furr: This convention was basically a party held in the evenings in the Willow Room at the Con-Version 22 s-f convention. The 30 furry attendees included seven fursuits. Announced events such as a dance, fursuiting events, and a dealer's den were either never held or were invisible within the larger s-f convention. It was organized as the Calgary Furry Convention over the Canadian Furs Livejournal community. There was some controversy over the Cal-Furr name, which some fans felt was too suggestive of a California convention. ConWild and Sci-Fur Con were suggested as alternates. It was academic, since Cal-Furr was never repeated.

Chairmen or Organizers: Lindsey Bladon (Silver Huskywolf)

CaliFur

CaliFur was created in 2004 in Orange County, California, as a replacement for the ConFurence, arbitrarily cancelled the year before despite protests. It is organized by the unincorporated FENEC Adventures ("Furries Enjoying the Natural Environments of California"), and is usually held in late May or early June. No records are kept on Fursuit Parades or charity donation totals, so those are unknown unless they were announced in news at the time.

Date	Theme	Location	Attendance	Parade
Califur 0 May 28–30, 2004	—	Atrium Hotel, Irvine	328	—
CaliFur 1 May 20–22, 2005	Welcome to the Islands	Holiday Inn Bristol Plaza, Costa Mesa	383	—
CaliFur 2 May 5–7, 2006	Furry Pirates	Holiday Inn Bristol Plaza, Costa Mesa	434	22
CaliFur 3 May 4–6, 2007	Our Favorite Furry Villains	Holiday Inn Bristol Plaza, Costa Mesa	496	25
CaliFur 4 May 16–18, 2008	Something Steampunk This Way Comes	Hyatt Regency, Irvine	587	64
CaliFur 5 June 5–7, 2009	On Safari	Irvine Marriott, Irvine	720	87
CaliFur 6 June 4–6, 2010	Fabulous Furry Funnies	Irvine Marriott, Irvine	851	no records kept
CaliFur 7 June 3–5, 2011	Post Apocalyptic	Irvine Marriott, Irvine	919	no records kept
CaliFur 8 June 1–3, 2012	The Roaring Twenties	Irvine Marriott, Irvine	949	199
CaliFur IX May 31–June 2, 2013	Furtual Reality	Irvine Marriott, Irvine	1,178	180 (estimated)
CaliFur X May 30–June 1, 2014	Hollywood Past and Present	Irvine Marriott, Irvine	1,206	140
CaliFur.11 June 5–7, 2015	Anime Kemono!	Irvine Marriott, Irvine	1,317	no records kept

Events

CaliFur 0 (2004): The first CaliFur was called CaliFur 0 because the ConFurences, which it replaced, started with ConFurence 0. The program was heavy on media entertainment and on participatory events in fursuits such as dancing around the hotel pool and photo sessions. There

CaliFur 0 conbook. Art by Foxfire. Used with permission.

was a Fursuit Parade, but no charity. Sub-level 03 performed a rave with flashing laser lights in a dry-ice fog. Clint Warlick sold a self-published collection of his popular "Jack Lynch" stories from *Yarf!* Parties went on all night; the hotel management showed up around 2:00 a.m. to politely ask the fans to be quieter so the non-fans in the hotel could sleep. The 20-page conbook had a color cover by Foxfire. Brian Wear did two T-shirts; one male and one female.

Guests of Honor: Foxfire (furry artist), Matthew Wayne Davis (2, the Ranting Gryphon). There were also four "special guests": Jefferson Swycaffer (s-f/furry author), Sub-level 03 (musical group), John Cawley (TopFox) (animation writer), and his wife Rachel Cawley (Cataroo) (furry artist)

Chairmen or Organizers: Robert K. Johnson Jr. (AlohaWolf), Zsa'nene Stevens (Zee or Tiger Eyes)

CaliFur 1 (2005): The return to the hotel that had hosted the first two ConFurences was played up. 2, the Ranting Gryphon served as Toastmaster. A charity was added. Brian Wear did the conbook cover, and Leo Magna did two T-shirts; one male and one female. Trapa of Seattle organized a CaliFur Train to assist Vancouver and Seattle fans to attend. Trapa set up the Convention Master registration system.

Guests of Honor: Brian Wear (artist), Ken Fletcher (s-f/furry cartoonist), Toastmaster Matthew Wayne Davis (2, the Ranting Gryphon)

Charity: The Moonridge Zoo, Big Bear, CA

Chairmen or Organizers: Robert K. Johnson Jr. (AlohaWolf), Zsa'nene Stevens (Zee or Tiger Eyes), Tank Winters (Trapa)

CaliFur 2 (2006): The CF staff all wore (or were supposed to) pirate costumes. In addition to the usual Art Show and Dealers' Room, a 17-foot electric giraffe was set up. An Ice Cream Social was on Friday. A Friday panel on "Furries and Boats" discussed furry pirates in galleons, the River in *Wind in the Willows*, and the swamp skiffs in *Pogo*. Saturday's programming included 2, the Ranting Gryphon, a Pet Auction, a Treasure Hunt, a Fursuit Parade and Presentation, and the evening Cabaret Fur Le Dance. The Saturday evening banquet was serenaded by appropriately drunken pirates. Sunday included the Art Auction and Talk-Back. The 28-page conbook had a wraparound color cover by Mitch de la Guardia, who did two T-shirts; a black-&-white one for sale to attendees, and a full-color one for Sponsors. Trapa again organized a CaliFur Train for Vancouver and Seattle attendees.

Guests of Honor: Lisanne Norman (s-f author), Mitch de la Guardia (furry artist)

Charity: Reptile and Amphibian Rescue Network (RARN)

Chairmen or Organizers: Zsa'nene Stevens (Zee or Tiger Eyes), Tank Winters (Trapa)

CaliFur 3 (2007): Featured events included an Ice Cream Social, a Celtic-style concert by Marc Gunn, the 2006 Ursa Major Awards presentation, and a Fursuit Dance on Friday; a Saturday Morning Cartoon Breakfast, a Fursuit Show & Tell, a Pet Auction, a "Mission Furpossible" variation of the Treasure Hunt (find and disarm a bomb before it explodes), the Fursuit Parade, the evening Cabaret Fur Le Dance and Saturday Night Dance on Saturday; and an Improv Workshop & Show and the Art Auction on Sunday. Fred Patten attended his first convention since his stroke, in a wheelchair, and a collection was taken for his medical expenses. Balaa did the conbook cover, and Shannon Stuart did the full-color T-shirt. Trapa organized a CaliFur Train for the last time. (He became the Co-Chairman of the new RainFurrest that August.) The hotel was generally considered too small for further growth.

Guests of Honor: Balaa, Roz Gibson (furry artists), Marc Gunn (singer)

Charity: Reptile and Amphibian Rescue Network (RARN)

Chairmen or Organizers: Zsa'nene Stevens (Zee or Tiger Eyes), Tank Winters (Trapa)

CaliFur 4 (2008): Events were keyed to the Steampunk theme, especially the costume design workshops. There was a Fursuit Parade. The Mustelid Fan Meet-Up was visited by a group trying to legalize ferrets as pets in California. The Disney theme park's Animation Academy set up a recruiting table in the Artist Alley. The 32-page conbook had a wraparound color cover by Kitsumi, who did the full-color T-shirt. CaliFur 4 was most memorable for the trouble it had with the hotel because of a Japanese wedding party there (dubbed "the drunken wedding of doom") at the same time. The hotel "officiously" put up signs and drapes to separate the CaliFur, but many CaliFur attendees felt that the hotel was more attentive to the wedding party "because the Japanese wedding party paid more money than the entire Califur hotel bill, for 1/10th the space." The convention committee promised to move to a new hotel next year. (The hotel actually had two other events; the Japanese wedding party, and a drunken high school [graduation?] party. Most CaliFur attendees conflated these into blaming a drunken Japanese wedding in their con reports. The hotel claimed to have put up the black curtain to protect the CaliFur from the high schoolers, who were seriously drunken and out of control. Some CaliFur staffers themselves approved of the photographing of parts of the convention without the attendees' permissions, which some attendees objected to.)

Guests of Honor: Kitsumi (fantasy artist), Keovi (fursuiter). Special G-o-H: Roy D. Pounds, II (Steamfox)

Charity: The Exotic Feline Breeding Compound, Apple Valley, CA

Chairmen or Organizers: Zsa'nene Stevens (Zee or Tiger Eyes), Tank Winters (Trapa)

CaliFur 5 (2009): The new hotel was very popular compared to the Hyatt Regency Hotel. CaliFur 5 also celebrated twenty years of Furry conventions. There was a poster. Bonnie Callahan gave several "how-to" art presentations. Fossil did the conbook cover, but he could not attend from Huntsville, Alabama. There were two T-shirts; one in color by Kitsumi, and one in black-&-white by Keovi. The Irvine Marriott staff were particularly friendly; some even bought ears and tails.

Guests of Honor: Bonnie Callahan (fantasy artist), Special G-o-H Matthew Wayne Davis (2, the Ranting Gryphon), Artist G-o-H Fossil the Undead Anthrosaur Artist

Charity: The Exotic Feline Breeding Compound, Apple Valley, CA

Chairmen or Organizers: Zsa'nene Stevens (Zee or Tiger Eyes), Daniel Branton (Rainhopper Roo)

CaliFur 6 (2010): The theme was furry comic strips. Miss Mab was the artist of the Internet strip *Dan and Mab's Furry Adventures*. Fossil was again unable to attend. Events included the Art Show, a Pet Auction, Rock 'n' Roll Toons (comedy acts and music), a Furry Night Live (FNL) performance, and the Cabaret Fur le Dance. Los Angeles rock radio station KROQ came to CaliFur for the first time. The 40-page conbook had a wraparound color cover by Amber Williams. The T-shirts were by (color) Kyteria of Anevern for Patrons, and (black-&-white) by Fossil for sponsors and regular attendees.

Guests of Honor: Comic Strip G-o-H Amber M. Williams (Miss Mab), Artist G-o-H Kytheria of Anevern, Fursuit G-o-H Lucky Coyote of Don't Hug Cacti Studios (fursuit makers), Special G-o-H Fossil the Undead Anthrosaur Artist

Charity: The Exotic Feline Breeding Compound, Apple Valley, CA

Chairmen or Organizers: Zsa'nene Stevens (Zee or Tiger Eyes), Sean Verezhensky (Hellfyre)

CaliFur 7 (2011): The theme was Post Apocalyptic. Radio station KROQ shared the convention space with CaliFur again. The 40-page program book had a wraparound cover by Matrices. The T-shirt and badges were by Mitti.

Guests of Honor: Mandi Tremblay (Touch My Badger; furry artist), Sara Howard (Matrices; furry artist, fursuiter), Special G-o-H Alflor Aalto (furry author)

Charity: The Cat House on the Kings

Chairmen or Organizers: Zsa'nene Stevens

CaliFur 8 (2012): The theme was The Roaring Twenties, with the tagline "Flappers and Gangsters, Movers and Shakers!" There were the usual ice cream social, and adult-only Fur Le Dance cabaret. The 2011 Ursa Major Awards were announced at an awards presentation. All events were on the hotel's main floor, except for the 2nd floor Con Suite. Registration badges were attractive but had the wearer's name on the back, making the attendees anonymous. The traditional furry convention program/souvenir book was replaced by a 20-page booklet that had little besides the program schedule, with a wraparound cover by Mochi. Fursuits containing "squeakers" were banned in the Dealers' Den. There were complaints of a lack of organization or information, with only the main events such as dances well publicized; and of little scheduled on Friday but late afternoon/evening registration, or on Sunday but teardown/closing ceremonies. An "Animation in the Early 20th Century" panel had featured veteran animator and longtime animation union president Tom Sito, but it was unannounced; and CaliFur attendees said after the convention that they'd've gone if they'd known that he was to be a speaker. The Saturday night dance began more than two hours late.

Guests of Honor: Mochi (furry artist, fursuiter)
Charity: World Wildlife Fund (WWF)
Chairmen or Organizers: Zsa'nene Stevens

CaliFur IX (2013): The Party Floor was cancelled. The Fursuit Parade was generally criticized as "a disaster." It was so hot in the outdoors gathering area around the hotel's pool that the 2:30 Parade was allowed to start a half-hour early, with the result that fursuiters arriving on time found that they had missed it. There were many new programming events, including an After Dark set of tracks for attendees 18 and over. Officially unconnected with CF IX, the AvantGarden art gallery, five miles away in nearby Santa Ana, CA, presented a "The Art of Furry Fandom" exhibit of 11 paintings and photographs by Steve Martin, Sherwood, Brown Wolf, and Changa Lion, curated by Rod O'Riley, from June 1–29, overlapping CF IX.

Guests of Honor: Maxwell Alexander Drake (s-f author), NecroDrone (furry artist)
Charity: California Wolf Center
Chairmen or Organizers: Zsa'nene Stevens

CaliFur X (2014): A "My First Furry Convention" panel was held for neofurs, and "Furry Gladiators" for fursuiters. Major events included: Friday, a screening of *Animalympics* with voice actor Michael Fremer (Henry Hummel, René Fromage & Kit Mambo, Bolt Jenkins, other major characters) present; Saturday, the 30th anniversary of Rowrbrazzle and the 20th anniversary of *The Lion King* fandom, both with panels, and the 2013 Ursa Major Awards were presented, for the third time; Sunday, a Q&A on fursuiting with g-o-h Beastcub, and a panel on Disney's 1994–1997 TV animation *Gargoyles* and the 20 years of its fandom, moderated by co-creator Greg Weisman. CaliFur's first Fursuit Dance Competition was held, with winners Okami (1st place), Telephone (2nd place), and Flinch (3rd place). The 20-page program book (cover by Megan Giles) again had little more than the program schedule.

Guests of Honor: Megan Giles (Dustmeat, artist), Beastcub (fursuiter), Special G-o-H: Greg Weisman (co-creator of Disney's *Gargoyles*)
Charity: Alpha K-9
Chairmen or Organizers: Zsa'nene Stevens

CaliFur.11 (2015): The day before CaliFur 2015, Thursday, June 4, was designated Furry Day at nearby Disneyland. Furs who wished to tour the park together were urged to meet at the main gates at 10:30 a.m., wearing green shirts and animal ears & tails, if possible. CaliFur.11 was organized with the help of its "brother convention," Kemocon 8 in Tokyo, in planning for the theme of Anime Kemono! The three-day video program was heavily devoted to Japanese animated theatrical features and TV series featuring anthropomorphic animals. Pepper Coyote played a rock concert. There was no program book, but the 26-page Program Guide had a black-&-white cover by Zhivago!, who also did the membership badge. The T-shirt was by Amadhia Albee. It was announced that CaliFur would move to a larger hotel next year. (CaliFur 2016 has been announced for the Fairplex Sheraton Hotel and Convention Center in Pomona, California.)

Guests of Honor: Amadhia Albee (creator of *Kaze: Ghost Warrior*), Rusty Shakleford (Zhivago Daemon, artist)
Charity: Animal Rescue Kansai (ARK) ($2,048)
Chairmen or Organizers: Zsa'nene Stevens, Justin Chan (VidWulf Silentstrider Spiritweaver)

CaliFur Diego

CaliFur Diego was an attempted successor to the ConFurence's CritterConDiegos; a furry mini-convention within San Diego, CA's Comic-Con International. It failed, largely because the Comic-Con itself was evolving to attract more of the general public and less furry fans. It was noted that the established furry exhibitors were disappearing one by one as the Comic-Con kept raising its table prices.

Name & Date	Location	Attendance
CaliFur Diego 2006 July 22, 2006	Main Ballroom, The Horton Grand Hotel, San Diego, CA	65 (estimated)
CaliFur Diego 2007 July 27–28, 2007	The Horton Grand Hotel, San Diego, CA	150 (estimated)
CaliFur Diego 2008 Not held		
CaliFur Diego 2009 July 24–25, 2009	The Hilton Bayfront Hotel, San Diego, CA	150 (estimated)

Events

Califur Diego 2006: The mini-convention (frankly a fur-meet) ran from 8:00 p.m. until midnight. The attendance was a sharp drop from the CritterConDiegos. Speculation at the event was that being held at the same time as the Comic-Con's Masquerade seriously cut into attendance.
Chairmen or Organizers: Rod O'Riley

CaliFur Diego 2007: It was held from 8:00 p.m. each evening, in two smaller rooms instead of one large room as the previous year.
Chairmen or Organizers: Rod O'Riley
Due to financial reasons, there was no CaliFur Diego 2008.

CaliFur Diego 2009: CaliFur Diego 2009 was in a suite rather than a ballroom. This was the final public CaliFur Diego. Since the organizers needed an attendance of about 200 to break even, the last two CaliFur Diegos were not financially successful. Around this time a lot of younger furry fans stopped going to the Comic-Con, if they had ever gone in the first place.

No CaliFur Diego was announced for 2010 and 2011. In 2012 it was revealed that it had devolved into an invitational private room party.
Chairmen or Organizers: Rod O'Riley

Camp Feral!

Camp Feral!, in the wilds of Ontario, was the first Canadian furry "convention" and the first furry event that was an outdoor campout in the wilderness (actually at a lodge in a provincial park). It has since spawned imitations from Brazil's Abando to Spain's short-lived Ibercamp.

Name & Date	Theme	Location	Attendance
Camp Feral! August 21–23, 1998	none	Camp Arowhon, Algonquin Provincial Park, Ontario	54 (estimated)
Feral! '99 August 14–18, 1999	none	Kinark Outdoor Centre, Haliburton Heights, Ontario	75 (estimated)

Name & Date	Theme	Location	Attendance
Camp Feral! 2000 August 16–20, 2000	none	Kinark Outdoor Centre, Haliburton Heights, Ontario	80 (estimated)
Feral! 2001 August 22–26, 2001	none	Kinark Outdoor Centre, Haliburton Heights, Ontario	90 (estimated)
Feral! 2002 August 21–25, 2002	none	Kinark Outdoor Centre, Haliburton Heights, Ontario	87
Feral! 2003 August 20–24, 2003	none	Kinark Outdoor Centre, Haliburton Heights, Ontario	70 (estimated)
Feral! 2004 August 25–29, 2004	none	Camp Arowhon, Algonquin Provincial Park, Ontario	85 (estimated)
Feral! 2005 August 27–31, 2005	Join the Tribe	Camp Arowhon, Algonquin Provincial Park, Ontario	103
Feral! 2006 September 2–6, 2006	none	Camp Arowhon, Algonquin Provincial Park, Ontario	132
Camp Feral! X August 27–31, 2007	none	Camp Arowhon, Algonquin Provincial Park, Ontario	80 (estimated)
Feral! 2008 August 24–28, 2008	none	Camp Arowhon, Algonquin Provincial Park, Ontario	92 (estimated)
Camp Feral! XII August 29–September 2, 2009	Wish You Were Here…	Camp Arowhon, Algonquin Provincial Park, Ontario	92 (estimated)
Feral! 2010 September 1–5, 2010	Feral! The 13th	Camp Arowhon, Algonquin Provincial Park, Ontario	94
Feral! 2011 August 31–September 4, 2011	It Came from Camp Feral!	Camp Arowhon, Algonquin Provincial Park, Ontario	111
Feral 2012 August 24–28, 2012	The Future Is Now!	Camp Arowhon, Algonquin Provincial Park, Ontario	123
Feral! 2013 August 22–26, 2013	Canadaiana	Camp Arowhon, Algonquin Provincial Park, Ontario	135
Feral! 2014 August 21–25, 2014	Algonquinos	Camp Arowhon, Algonquin Provincial Park, Ontario	147
Feral! 2015	Feral! The 13th Part 2: Jason vs. Shreddermoose	Camp Arowhon, Algonquin Provincial Park, Ontario	163

Events

Camp Feral!: The first Camp Feral! was organized by Ken Suzuki (P. Pardus), Terry Wessner, Dan Markey (Silfur), Benjamin Eren Robinson (Simba), and Colin Bolton (Wilykat), all of Toronto-area furry fandom, after having been inspired by Albany Anthrocon 1997; but they conceived of Camp Feral! as a furry convention with a difference. It was the first Canadian furry convention, and the first furry outdoor camp. Feral! 1998 met at Camp Arowhon in Algonquin Provincial Park in rural Ontario, a traditional Summer camp for children about three hours' drive from Toronto. It consisted of six residential cabins and a main cabin for communal dining, on the shore of a large lake. Memberships were C$125, with C$25 extra for a chartered school bus from downtown Toronto for those who did not have their own transportation or did not care to drive to the campsite. To cash checks and to qualify for insurance, FeralCom incorporated under the name of the Toronto Role-playing and Anthropomorphic Animal Costuming Society. TRAACS was listed as "a sponsor" of Camp Feral! Attendance was limited to 150, but only about 50 besides the committee attended the experimental first camp. Activities included 1½-hour workshops on art, writing, and fursuit-making (one of the rooms in the main cabin was turned into a headless Fursuit Lounge) by popular writers, artists, and fursuit-makers, evening campfire sing-alongs, and two evening dances in the main cabin, a high-school dance and a DJ dance. Daytime activities included the Camp's regular activities: swimming, kayaking, canoeing, sailing, and windsurfing; guided nature hikes, a wolf howl ("An Algonquin staff ecologist will make a spectacular and informative presentation on wolves as a sort of briefing session […] Patience and quietude is required to help communicate with the wolves of Algonquin and seemingly become one of the pack […]"), and a wide variety of team sports such as softball, volleyball, basketball, and soccer; archery, climbing, and outdoor camping instruction. There were afternoon games of Capture the Flag and the furry-friendly Predator & Prey. The event included the furry convention staples of a 20-page "Survival Guide" souvenir book and a T-shirt by Melissa Drake (MelSkunk) featuring Feral!'s cartoon mascot by Simba, an anthropomorphized lynx named Farley. Feral! 1998 was more than popular. Everyone complained that it ended too soon. Future Camp Feral!s have been five-day events.

Chairmen or Organizers: Ken Suzuki (P. Pardus)

Feral! '99: The convention committee for the second Camp Feral! met at Terry Wessner's Toronto apartment for months beforehand to plan a smooth gathering. The first Feral! had lost considerable money due to the C$125 being not nearly enough to offset expenses (Wessner covered the loss until future Ferals over several years could reimburse him), so 1999 memberships were doubled to C$250. Despite this, attendance increased to about 75 "campers." Camp Arowhon was not available, so Feral! '99 was held at the similar Kinark Outdoor Centre in the Haliburton Heights region of southeastern Ontario. The Kinark Centre was larger and more modernized than Camp Arowhon, but in general fans preferred the "rustic charm" of Arowhon. Also, Kinark's lake, dubbed Lake Nestea because of the leaf particles from nearby trees giving it a tealike hue, also gave the water a slimy feel. Activities were similar to the first year's. More animal-themed games were devised. Wessner went about the camp as a genial master-of-ceremonies. Campers in Kinark's fifteen animal-named cabins were encouraged to write and rehearse a group skit, for a contest of all the cabin's skits on the next-to-last day. Nexxus of FurNation set up an Art Show and sales service. The nighttime dances in the woods included a laser light show. The Survival Guide grew to 38 pages including a foldout map of the Centre. The T-shirt was by Wookiee/Nakira.

Chairmen or Organizers: Ken Suzuki (P. Pardus)

Camp Feral! 2000: Camp Feral! 2000 was also known as Feral! 2K. Some of the FeralCom shuffled positions but the committee was basically the same. Activities were also basically the same. A Feral! General [Art] Store was set up for a few hours on Friday evening, for campers to display and sell their artwork, PG and Adult. The most popular games were the Predator & Prey and the cabin skits. The Survival Guide had a color cover. The 2000 T-shirt was by Richard Bartrop and Wookiee/Nakira.

Chairmen or Organizers: Ken Suzuki (P. Pardus)

Feral! 2001: Feral! 2001 was the first Camp Feral! to feature a Guest of Honor. The FeralCom shuffled its positions again. The campers included one who drove to Toronto from Texas, and one each from Australia and Finland. Activities were about the same. Uncle Kage's Story Hour was added to the program, and Uncle Kage participated vigorously in many events. George F. Nemeier, Jr. (Tigerwolf) supplied two-way radios to keep exploring groups in contact with the base camp. The popular nighttime Furry Rave dance was repeated. There was a smash-the-piñata contest. The Survival Guide was 48 pages. Rebecca Ann Frey (BushyCat) did the 2001 T-shirt.

Guests of Honor: Dr. Samuel C. Conway (Uncle Kage)

Chairmen or Organizers: Ken Suzuki (P. Pardus)

Feral! 2002: The cost increased to C$295, plus C$30 extra for the chartered bus. Uncle Kage performed his Story Hour around the campfire. A Poetry Corner was led by Wotan. Saturday night's Feral! Woodland Rave featured DJs SnowWolf, Genki, Slay3r, and Chris Pardus. The Drum Circle had ritual TeleTubby sacrifices. The T-shirt, drawn by *Associated Student Bodies* artist Chris McKinley and colored by Hiker, was inspired by the Predator vs. Prey game. This was the first Feral! T-shirt to sell out at the con itself, requiring a re-order. Ginger's gay wolf-dog Falstaff was featured prominently in Feral! 2002's publications and publicity. Ken Suzuki, the head of the organizational team, took the title of "Head Honcho."

Guests of Honor: Ginger (furry artist)
Chairmen or Organizers: Ken Suzuki (P. Pardus)

Feral! 2003: This was the final Camp Feral! at the Kinark Outdoor Centre. In addition to the usual activities, a Poetry track was added to the programming because individual poetry readings at previous Camp Ferals had been so popular, including campers reading their own poetry in a "beatnik" coffee-house atmosphere. Two new games were a "Furvivor" scavenger hunt, and a "bead hunting" to collect the most wooden beads, one of which was given out for each workshop or other activity the camper attended. The FeralCom underwent an almost complete change, due to Terry Wessner moving away from Toronto. The 30-page Survival Guide contained many advertisements from Conifur Northwest, Anthrocon, and Further Confusion, showing the widespread support that Camp Feral! was gaining throughout furry fandom. The 2003 T-shirt was by Paf!

Guests of Honor: John Barrett (Roxicat), Krahnos ("the magi-dragon") (Canadian furry cartoonists)
Chairmen or Organizers: Dan Desveaux (Branwyn)

Feral! 2004: The game with wooden beads was repeated, as were all the previous events. The cabin whose campers had the most total beads won a prize, and the individual with the most beads won a free registration to Feral! 2005. The T-shirt was designed by Ginger.

Guests of Honor: Steve Domanski (Iyu) and Andrew French (Aethan), the writers of the *Circles* comic book published by Rabbit Valley)
Chairmen or Organizers: Verec, Lucas Raymond (Potoroo)

Feral! 2005: The program was more structured, centered around aboriginal motifs. There was an official flag, and the aboriginal theme was emphasized on that year's website. Campers were divided into four "clans" which were given different challenges. In addition to the usual activities was a four-hour canoe trip with cookout lunch through Algonquin Park's lakes and rivers. The guests-of-honor and Uncle Kage all participated vigorously. Chairman Potoroo said in his convention report that the cover by Anklebones and The Wormwood for that year's Survival Guide was "THE BEST CONBOOK COVER IN HISTORY." Anklebones and The Wormwood also designed the T-shirt around a "tribal" theme; the back of the shirt showed the 2005 official flag.

Guests of Honor: Anklebones and The Wormwood ("artists in residence"), Sean and Andrew Rabbitt (Rabbit Valley Comics), BanWynn Oakshadow (a.k.a. Uncle Oakie) (furry writer)
Chairmen or Organizers: Lucas Raymond (Potoroo)

Feral! 2006: Co-chairmen Potoroo and Patchouli apologetically announced that rising costs forced them to raise memberships to C$300, plus C$45 for the chartered bus from Toronto. The two guests-of-honor threw themselves into the usual activities, and performed as a comedy duo. A light rain throughout most of the camp had a greater percentage of the campers than usual participating in indoor activities, while the hardier campers did not let it keep them from the outdoor activities. Feral! 2006 had four mascots: Geist (Earth), Misha (Fire), Aelos (Wind), and Kabalo (Water). Each was the "patron" of one of the four "clans" that campers were divided among. The Clan Challenges were won by, in descending order, Wind, Water, Earth, and Fire. Camp Feral!'s "artists in residence,"

Camp Feral! 42

Anklebones and The Wormwood, designed a T-shirt for each mascot and painted a full-color cover for the Survival Guide that was auctioned off for C$450. BanWynn, one of the previous year's guests-of-honor, was a guest speaker. One of Feral! 2006's activities was to make plushies of the mascots. The four mascots were intended to be Camp Feral!'s permanent mascots in the future, but a dispute arose during the event between the FeralCom and the two artists over who owned their copyright. The result was that a different 2007 mascot was designed early, with the copyright clearly in the Camp's name.

Guests of Honor: Matthew Wayne Davis (2, the Ranting Gryphon), Dr. Samuel C. Conway (Uncle Kage)

Chairmen or Organizers: Lucas Raymond (Potoroo), Patchouli

Camp Feral! X: The new permanent camp mascots were the wolf Pawnee (or Pawnie, created by Ferris), with co-mascots Weeko, a female porcupine (created by Patchouli) and Ruger, a male deer (created by Gideon Hoss). Registration was now C$325 for regular campers, C$375 for Sponsors, and C$495 for patrons, plus the C$45 bus fee. The drop in attendance was popularly blamed upon the U.S. financial crisis. The programming, focused upon Camp Feral!'s tenth anniversary, centered around the four clans, but participation became voluntary rather than mandatory, freeing campers to choose other activities if they wished. A Feral Scavenger Hunt was added to the programming. Fifteen cabins took part in the final night's Cabin Skits, with the cabin of the three guests of honor, the "Snog Lodge," being voted the best skit. New furry publisher Bad Dog Books slated the first volume of its FANG anthology, the "little black book of furry [gay] fiction," for release to coincide with Feral! 2007. Two campers from Brazil enjoyed themselves so much that they founded Abando, Brazil's first furry camp, the next year. The Feral! Survival Guide featured a retrospective by Terry Wessner titled "It's Like Herding Cats, Only Moreso," a foreword by Camp Feral!'s founder, P. Pardus, and a gallery of art, maps, and "factoids" from the nine previous conbooks. The T-shirt was by Ferris.

Guests of Honor: Chuck Davies (Ferris), Gideon Hoss (of Club Stripes), Malcolm Earle (Max Black Rabbit) (Canadian furry artists)

Chairmen or Organizers: Lucas Raymond (Potoroo), Patchouli

Feral! 2008: Feral! 2008 had the usual events, but a major change was that attendance became limited to those 19 years old (drinking age) or older, for insurance purposes. This resulted in at least one veteran attendee dropping out because he could no longer bring his children. Several veteran staff members resigned to enjoy Camp Feral! as regular campers. The T-shirt was by Patches.

Guests of Honor: Chuck Davies (Ferris), Patches (Ontario artists)

Chairmen or Organizers: Lucas Raymond (Potoroo)

Camp Feral! XII: The Camp Feral! website was redesigned in January. Campers were encouraged to join early, to "become campers for the whole year," to contact each other through the website, and to learn of other events such as a pre–Feral! barbeque. Events included an opening night campfire tribal Drum Circle and sing-along, a Poetry Corner, an open mic Musicians' Circle, a Mixtape Dance, the traditional Summer Camp games, sports, and workshops. The 32-page conbook featured a color cover by Patches and an exclusive story by Kyell Gold. The T-shirt was by Zakkun. Camp Feral!'s three mascots (Pawnee the wolf, Weeko the porcupine, and Ruger the deer) were featured on both the conbook cover and the T-shirt.

Guests of Honor: Flain Falcon (host of furry podcasts Clawcast and Anthropod), Kyell Gold (furry author)

Chairmen or Organizers: Lucas Raymond (Potoroo)

Feral! 2010: The thirteenth annual Camp Feral! was themed around the *Friday the 13th* horror movies. Graphic designer Arius was added to the FeralCom to carry out the Feral! the 13th theme.

The basic advertisement was a mock movie poster showing mascot Pawnee the wolf with a machete and hockey mask, captioned "A summer camp … by a lake … miles from the nearest town. Plan for a bloody good time." Other posters were variants on this. The FeralCom began using YouTube to heavily promote the camp, with videos of past camps, video blogs (vlogs), and a series of webisodes featuring each annual theme, starring a pantomimed Pawnee. 2010s featured a fursuited Pawnee (with a hockey mask designed for his muzzle) coming to live with the Feral! staff during the several months' leadup to the camp. During the Camp, a "Jasonized" Pawnee Fursuiter prowled the camp "killing" campers who never knew where he would strike next. (Unfortunately, the "menace" was not entirely fictional. An unknown stomach flu struck several campers, one so badly that he was taken to a hospital as a precaution. The campers were reminded to wash their hands before and during meals, which apparently was enough to take care of that problem.) The 36-page conbook featured a color cover by Blotch showing the hocky-masked Pawnee sneaking up behind a horrified raccoon, and an exclusive story, "The Challenge," by Kyell Gold. The T-shirt was by Edgardo Sanchez, a Toronto nonfurry graphic designer.

Guests of Honor: Colson Grainger (musician), Ivybeth (artist)

Chairmen or Organizers: Lucas Raymond (Potoroo), Growler

Feral! 2011: The theme of "It Came from Camp Feral!" was a celebration of B sci-fi horror movies. In its videos beginning the previous November, Pawnee tried to protect Camp Feral! from the corrupting green ooze being spread by "Evil Nayo." Potoroo speculated that Camp Feral! had become the most video-heavy convention in furry fandom. Registrations were now C$350 for regular campers, C$400 for Sponsors, and C$495 for Patrons, plus C$45 for the round-trip bus from the Yorkdale Mall. The Musicians' Circle expanded to a drum kit, amps, and a PA system for open mic performing. The annual Friends of Feral award was begun, presented to those who had become frequent workers for the annual event over the years, and recorded on a permanent bronze plaque; the first recipients were Deuce and Miami. The Survival Guide cover was by Black Teagan, while Arius did the T-shirt.

Guests of Honor: Black Teagan (Teagan Gavet, artist), Rikoshi Kisaragi (Kevin Frane, author)

Chairmen or Organizers: Lucas Raymond (Potoroo)

Feral! 2012: The fifteenth Camp Feral! was called the Quintennial. Its theme was a retro-future space camp. A series of Futurecamp! videos showed the Feral! Committee preparing for Feral! 2012 in an alternate retro-future world, with Pawnee battling "Evil Simbaya" to prevent his takeover of the Camp a hundred years in the future, and restore the correct timeline. The Feral! bus stop in Toronto was moved from Yorkdale Mall due to renovations, to The Den (Potoroo's house; the furry commune where five Feral! staffers live). Artist/graphic designer Arius, who was responsible for Camp Feral!'s graphic design, was a special guest, announced as "in absentia" but he was able at the last minute to attend. Due to Camp Arowhon's reconstruction schedule, the old Rec Hall was replaced by a new Rustic Lodge for hockey, near TeePee Heights, during the midst of the Camp; used by Camp Feral! for dancing and cabin skits. The final events held in The Rec Hall were the 2012 Furry Improv and a screening of *The Hunger Games*. The Friends of Feral award went to Hiker and Loopy. The Survival Guide cover was by GT Skunkrat, and the T-shirt by Arius.

Guests of Honor: Gez Tank Skunkrat, a.k.a. Grimal (cartoonist), Arius (artist)

Chairmen or Organizers: Lucas Raymond (Potoroo)

Feral! 2013: The 16th Camp Feral! set a new attendance record with 135 campers. Its theme, Canadiana, celebrated Canadian culture: the Maple Leaf, etc. It was the final gathering to eat in the old Main Lodge, the focal point of Camp Algonquin since its foundation in 1934.

Guests of Honor: Anyare, Gishkeshenh, Patto (artists)

Chairmen or Organizers: Lucas Raymond (Potoroo)

Feral! 2014: Attendance rose again to 147 campers, only three short of the 150 limit set in 1998. The Feral! Committee's video series portrayed "Algonquinos" as a fantasy land being battled over by four houses based on High Fantasy themes, with Pawnee as a mystical woodland figure trying to bring peace.

Guests of Honor: Kihu (artist), Tempe O'Kun (author)
Chairmen or Organizers: Lucas Raymond (Potoroo)

Feral! 2015:

Guests of Honor: Edge (artist/musician), Eevachu (artist)
Chairmen or Organizers: Lucas Raymond (Potoroo)

Campfire Tails

Campfire Tails (CFT) is an outdoor camping event for Oregon furs. "Camp under the stars and explore the woods with furs from all over the west coast … and beyond!" It is "based on attendee-driven events called Happenings." A Happening is "an event of artistic significance" suggested or planned by one or more attendees, such as art exhibits, craft workshops, or musical performances throughout the camp, approved by the Chair. Attendance is limited to 18 or older. The cartoon mascot by NullEnigma is a happy fennec with its tail on fire.

Name & Date	Theme	Location	Attendance
Campfire Tails 2010 August 5–9, 2010	Down the Rabbit Hole	Ogden Group Camp, Deschutes National Forest, La Pine, OR	72
Campfire Tails 2011 August 4–8, 2011	Choose Your Own Adventure	Ogden Group Camp, Deschutes National Forest, La Pine, OR	94
Campfire Tails 2012 August 2–6, 2012	Keep Furry Weird!	Ogden Group Camp, Deschutes National Forest, La Pine, OR	135
Campfire Tails 2013 August 1–5, 2013	Outpost 27	Ogden Group Camp, Deschutes National Forest, La Pine, OR	113
Campfire Tails 2014 July 31–August 4, 2014	Caulk the Wagon and Float It	Ogden Group Camp, Deschutes National Forest, La Pine, OR	130
Campfire Tails 2015 July 30–August 3, 2015	Space Camp	Ogden Group Camp, Deschutes National Forest, La Pine, OR	143

Events

Campfire Tails 2010: Events the first year were themed around *Alice's Adventures in Wonderland*.
Chairmen or Organizers: C.S. Mounier

Campfire Tails 2011: The adventures were set in a parody of a picturesque 1979 resort summer camp.
Chairmen or Organizers: C.S. Mounier

Campfire Tails 2012: The theme was to bring out everyone's inner eccentric self. Hyperbole was encouraged.
Chairmen or Organizers: C.S. Mounier

Campfire Tails 2013: The theme was a post-apocalyptic camp and interactive environments.
Chairmen or Organizers: Devin

Campfire Tails 2014: "Caulk the wagon and float it" is an old Oregon Trail reference. There were a covered wagon piñata called "Hang the Wagon and Bash It," a costume contest, an improvisational skit, a western bottlecap casino, some craft and art events, and others. More events to fit the theme were discussed, such as a "shitty wagon race" in which teams would build cardboard wagons and attempt to race them across the river, but not carried out. As usual, a good number of events occurred that fell outside of the theme. The sponsor and patron gifts included wooden laser engraved coins showing the CT logo.

Chairmen or Organizers: Devin

Campfire Tails 2015: Themed items and happenings in 2015 consisted of a freeze-dried icecream social and patches gifted to patrons and sponsors, a bottle rocket workshop, a participatory burning art display (a camper brought a large wooden spaceship that attendees could draw on or decorate with thoughts and wishes they wanted to send off; at the end of the event the display was burned and a moment of silence held. It was a spectacular experience). Another display, The Infurnational Space Station, was built as a blacklight art display, art jam geodesic dome and dancefloor. Stargazing, a bunch of ham radio operators came out and set up a number of repeaters so they could communicate with the ISS, and there were lots of costumes and other improvised displays that took place..

Chairmen or Organizers: C.S. Mounier

CampFur

CampFur or Campfur is an annual Canadian 19+ outdoor tent or trailer furry campout in the mountains alongside the Coquihalla River near Hope, British Columbia; primarily for the BC Furries community. It is organized by Gizmo as a private event, with advance invitations required for approval. The CampFur website shows cartoon furry logos and photographs of all previous CampFurs. Large dogs are frequently present. Although the venue is not fursuit-friendly, there have been a few fursuiters. The theme is mostly reflected in the website furry art, not any campout activities.

Name & Date	*Theme*		*Attendance*
CampFur 2011 June 24–26, 2011	none		50
CampFur 2012 June 22–24, 2012	none		
CampFur 2013 June 20–23, 2013	Time to Get Leh'd		55
CampFur 2014 June 19–22, 2014	Furrst Blood		55
CampFur '15 June 25–28, 2015	SurviFur	—	76

Events

CampFur 2011: Typical camping out in the British Columbia wilderness. The main food was deep fried turkey and poutine.

CampFur 2012: Typical camping out activities again. The main feature was a whole pig roast over the campfire.

CampFur 2013: The theme was Hawaiian based.

CampFur 2014: The theme was based on the Stallone/Rambo movie *First Blood*.

CampFur '15: The theme was based on the *Survivor* TV program. Its motto was "Outfox—Outlast."

Central Midwest Furmeet

CMF (not to be confused with the Central Plains Fur Meet) was an outdoor camping activity for furs in the Kansas City area who were unable to attend larger gatherings. It emphasized small group activities like gathering around campfires and musical performing, and games like Capture the Flag.

Name & Date	Theme	Location	Attendance
Central Midwest Furmeet 2010 September 11–12, 2010	—	Camp Bloomington West, Clinton Lake, KS	22
Central Midwest Furmeet 2011 September 9–11, 2011	Fort Knight	Camp Bloomington West, Clinton Lake, KS	33
Central Midwest Furmeet 2012 September 14–16, 2012	Rock and Roll	Capital City KOA, Topeka, KS	?

Events

Central Midwest Furmeet 2010: Clinton Lake is near Lawrence, Kansas. CFM 2010 was announced by Rieko on Fur Affinity in May 2010. Even though Rieko had to withdraw, Steel the Wolf still organized it. Activities included Capture the Flag, kickball, foursquare, campfires, and meals.
Chairmen or Organizers: Steel the Wolf, Riyeko

Central Midwest Furmeet 2011: In addition to repeating the previous, a theme and charity were added, with a charity art raffle of donated artwork. An official video was made.
Charity: Pet Connection ($237)
Chairmen or Organizers: Steel the Wolf

Central Midwest Furmeet 2012: KOA stands for Kampgrounds Of America, a loose national confederation of private campsites. The Capital City KOA site was primarily for Recreational Vehicles, with facilities for non–RV campers including "large open tent sites, and three types of rental units. Our Cabin sleeps 4 and our bunkhouse sleeps 6. Both units have a refrigerator, outside cooking area, picnic table, and cable TV. Our Deluxe Cabin sleeps 4, has all the amenities of our other cabins plus, a full bath, mini kitchen, outside grill and campfire ring, (an excellent choice for the non-roughing it types)." The CMF 2012 website said: "The Captiol [sic] City KOA hosts a variety of ammenaties [sic] including fishing and swimming ponds, a hiking trail, a group event room, a large patio, a game room, indoor bathrooms and shower facilities, laundry facilities, wireless internet, and a large group fire ring along the shore of the largest pond." Attendees were urged to bring "a chair, some snacks, games, and a fursuit if you wish to costume." Attendees had to sign a "Partisipation" Agreement Form, or to get a parent's or legal guardian's signature if a minor.
Charity: Helping Hands Humane Society (of Topeka) ($230 [estimated])
Chairmen or Organizers: Steel the Wolf

On April 22, 2013, Steel the Wolf posted on Fur Affinity that he would not be able to organize CFM 4 for personal reasons. Although he offered to turn it over to someone else, and several others asked what the job entailed, there were no volunteers.

Central Plains Fur Con

Central Plains Fur Con grew out of the Central Plains Fur Meet, an outdoor furry convention begun in 2010 for Wichita, Kansas-area furs. It was organized in 2013 by Merkindesr and Dale Fox in downtown Wichita for those who preferred an indoor, hotel-type venue.

Name & Date	Theme	Location	Attendance
Central Plains Fur Con 2013 October 3–6, 2013	The Wizard of Pawz	Drury Plaza Hotel Broadview	97
Central Plains Fur Con 2014 November 6–10, 2014	Furry Fantasy	Drury Plaza Hotel Broadview	?
Central Plains Fur Con 2015 November 5–8, 2015	Food!	Drury Plaza Hotel Broadview	83

Events

Central Plains Fur Con 2013: CPFM 2013's theme was based on the 1939 Wizard of Oz movie. Rukis did the conbook cover. The T-shirt was by Svey.
   Guests of Honor: Rukis (furry artist/author)
   Chairmen or Organizers: Merkindesr (fursuiter, fursuit maker), Dale Fox (fursuiter)

Central Plains Fur Con 2014: CPFM 2014's theme was based on the Final Fantasy video game and TV animation. Laura Garabedian did the conbook cover. The T-shirt was by IdleValley.
   Guests of Honor: Laura Garabedian (furry artist)
   Chairmen or Organizers: Merkindesr (fursuiter, fursuit maker), Dale Fox (fursuiter)

Central Plains Fur Con 2015: The Food! theme was based on g-o-h Vantid's interest in organic gardening and cooking. Vantid did the conbook cover. The T-shirt was again by IdleValley.
   Guests of Honor: Amber Hill (Vantid; furry artist)
   Chairmen or Organizers: Merkindesr (fursuiter, fursuit maker), Dale Fox (fursuiter)

Central Plains Fur Meet

Central Plains Fur Meet is an outdoor furry convention like Oklacon intended for Wichita, Kansas-area furs. It started as an informal furmeet but since has added a guest of honor, programmed events, and badges.

Name & Date	Location	Attendance
Central Plains Fur Meet 2010 May 29–30, 2010	Cheney Lake Campground, Cheney, KS	22
Central Plains Fur Meet 2011 June 25–26, 2011	Lake Afton Campground, Wichita, KS	24
Central Plains Fur Meet 2012 May 18–20, 2013	Lake Afton Campground, Wichita, KS	36
Central Plains Fur Meet 2013 May 16–19, 2014	Lake Afton Campground, Wichita, KS	?
Central Plains Fur Meet 2014 May 22–25, 2014	Lake Afton Campground, Wichita, KS	?
Central Plains Fur Meet 2015 May ?, 2015	Lake Afton Campground, Wichita, KS	?

Events

Central Plains Fur Meet 2010: Events included swimming, art panels, a movie night, dances, and wood burning.
   Chairmen or Organizers: Merkindesr (fursuiter, fursuit maker), Dale Fox (fursuiter)

Central Plains Fur Meet 2011:
Guests of Honor: Luthien Nightwolf (furry artist)
Chairmen or Organizers: Merkindesr (fursuiter, fursuit maker), Dale Fox (fursuiter)

Central Plains Fur Meet 2012: Merkindesr and Dale Fox rented an air-conditioned pavilion for dances and a raffle.
Guests of Honor: Wolfaya (furry artist/fursuit maker)
Chairmen or Organizers: Merkindesr (fursuiter, fursuit maker), Dale Fox (fursuiter)

Central Plains Fur Meet 2013: Zahzu designed membership badges. Merkindesr and Dale Fox organized the Central Plains Fur Con in downtown Wichita for those who preferred an indoor event.
Guests of Honor: Zahzu (furry artist)
Chairmen or Organizers: Merkindesr (fursuiter, fursuit maker), Dale Fox (fursuiter)

Central Plains Fur Meet 2014:
Guests of Honor: Blitz Victor Foxtrot, Steven Powell (Idle Valley, furry artist)
Chairmen or Organizers: Merkindesr (fursuiter, fursuit maker), Dale Fox (fursuiter)

Central Plains Fur Meet 2015: CPFM 2015 was reduced by staff cutbacks to a small local gathering at an empty campground; no enclosed shelter, no free prepped food on a daily basis, no sound and DJ equipment for dances, and no movie night on a nine foot screen.
Guests of Honor: none
Chairmen or Organizers: Dale Fox (fursuiter)

ČeSFuR

ČeSFuR (pronounced "Chesfur") is a furry convention for the Czech Republic. The name is a play on the abbreviation for the united Czech and Slovak republics from 1990 to 1993: ČSFR (Česká a Slovenská Federativni Republika = Czech and Slovak Federative Republic). It is known for having an attendance from throughout Europe. ČeSFuRs before 2012 did not have an official theme though they may have had an unofficial one.

Name & Date	*Theme*	*Location*	*Attendance*	*Parade*
ČeSFuR 1 March 25–28, 2005	none	The Turistická ubytovna Pohoda, Březová nad Svitavou	33	
ČeSFuR 2 April 28–May 1, 2006	none	The Turistická ubytovna Pohoda, Březová nad Svitavou	44	
ČeSFuR 3 April 6–9, 2007	none	Bartošova pec, near Turnov	55	
ČeSFuR 4 March 21–24, 2008	none	Sluneční zátoka (Sun Bay) campground, Ledeč nad Sázavou	74	
ČeSFuR 5 July 15–18, 2009	none	The Hláska Hotel, Zlenice	74	
ČeSFuR 6 June 30–July 3, 2010	none	The Hláska Hotel, Zlenice	112	
ČeSFuR 7 July 14–17, 2011	none	Hotel Vltava, near Prague	86	
ČeSFuR 8 July 5–8, 2012	Apocalypse	Hotel Luna, Kouty (in the Bohemian-Moravian highlands)	107	

ČeSFuR X conbook. Art by Qzurr. Used with permission.

Name & Date	Theme	Location	Attendance Parade
ČeSFuR 9 June 27–30, 2013	Hippies	Hotel Luna, Kouty (in the Bohemian-Moravian highlands)	152
ČeSFuR 10 June 25–29, 2014	Treasure Island	Hotel Luna, Kouty (in the Bohemian-Moravian highlands)	180
ČeSFuR 11 June 24–28, 2015	Ancient Egypt	Hotel Skalský-Dvůr, Bystřice nad Pernštejnem	202

Events

ČeSFuR 1: The location was a tourist hostel in a small town in Eastern Bohemia. The 33 attendees were mostly from the Czech Republic and Slovakia, with a few from Austria, Germany, Great Britain, and the U.S. The convention was the usual mix of lectures, special interest groups, fursuit workshops, a Truth or Dare game, a furdance, a campfire, a charity auction, etc. There was a hiking trip to the nearby Punkva Caves, a popular cave system in the Moravian Karst featuring an underground river. The 4-page program book, this year and following, was in both Czech and English. The program book cover used the same T-shirt design by Olven.

Charity: The Zoological Garden of Brno city (5,000 Kč, 4,500 raised by the auction)
Chairmen or Organizers: Xkůň and staff

ČeSFuR 2: The unofficial theme was originally "Beneath Gods' Paws" but was changed to "Of Ancient Myths and Legends" before the convention. The attendance was specified as 32 from the Czech Republic and Slovakia, five from Poland, four from Russia, two from Germany, and one from Ukraine.

The activities were similar to the previous year's, with the addition of a barbeque, a dramatic performance around the theme, and a feast around the theme. Unfortunately, bad weather cut short or cancelled many of the outdoor events. The T-shirt was by Nera Akkari and Scheriff, with the latter's art featured on the 8-page conbook cover as well.

Charity: Regália, a horse shelter (8,000 Kč)
Chairmen or Organizers: Xkůň and staff

ČeSFuR 3: Bartošova pec was a guest hostel. Programmed events included the previous, plus an Artist Ambush, a game show, and a tearoom. The hiking trip was to the ruins of Frýdštejn Castle. The T-shirt design contest was won by Hossie and Tygřík, whose art was featured on the front and back of the T-shirt, respectively. Janys made the cover for the 20-page conbook, which became the usual size for the following years.

Charity: The Handicapped Wildlife Station in Libštát, of the Czech Union for Nature Conservation (20,000 Kč [$1,109])
Chairmen or Organizers: Michal Valášek (Altair), Mbili, Mysh, Xkůň

ČeSFuR 4: Events included the previous, plus an Art Show, a photo contest, a DDR tournament, a Fursuit Show, a band concert by The Puppits, and games inspired by TV game shows. The T-shirt was by Akela Taka and Janys; the former also designed the cover of the program book. This was the last ČeSFuR to take place in the spring. Because of particularly cold weather and related discomfort experienced by con-goers in 2008, a decision was made after that year's con to move the event to summer months, and permanently switch to hotel accommodation.

Charity: An animal rescue station in Pavlov, of the Nature Conservation Agency of the Czech Republic (about 12,000 Kč ($665)
Chairmen or Organizers: Altair, Ihaha, Mbili, Mysh, Peso, RustyFox and Xkůň, as "the Orgateam"

ČeSFuR 5: ČeSFuR 5 moved to the village of Zlenice, closer to Prague. In addition to the usual events, ČeSFuR 5 featured a bullwhip show and karaoke. The T-shirt design contest was won by Akela Taka and her design was used on the conbook cover as well.

Charity: An animal rescue station in Pavlov, of the Nature Conservation Agency of the Czech Republic (about 11,500 Kč)
Chairmen or Organizers: Altair, Ihaha, Mbili, Mysh, Peso, Vlk00, and Xkůň, as "the Orgateam"

ČeSFuR 6: The sharp increase in attendance was partly due to 22 more foreign furs, plus 16 more Czech attendees. More than a third of the attendees came from Poland, Germany, Russia, UK, Austria, and Hungary. In addition to most previous events, there were sushi tasting and a fursuit photoshoot. The T-shirt design contest was won by Olven. The conbook cover featured art from Sumie-dh.

Charity: An animal rescue station in Pavlov, of the Nature Conservation Agency of the Czech Republic (about 15,000 Kč [about $750])
Chairmen or Organizers: Altair, Ihaha, Mbili, Peso, TabbieFox, Vlk00, and Xkůň, as "the Orgateam"

ČeSFuR 7: The seventh year moved to a hotel closer to Prague and introduced a Guest of Honor for the first time. In addition to the usual events, a fursuit parade took place, with more than 20 fursuiters taking part. Activities included an Artists Ambush. Korrok won the T-shirt contest. The contribution from Sharley placed second and was used on the conbook cover.

Guests of Honor: Korrok (artist)
Charity: The handicapped wildlife station Praha-Jinonice (10,000 Kč).
Chairmen or Organizers: Ihaha, Mbili, TabbieFox, Tamu, Vlk00, and Xkůň, as "the Orgateam"

ČeSFuR 8: ČeSFuR moved to a new hotel in the Bohemian-Moravian highlands, with an indoor swimming pool and a nearby pond. 107 furs from 14 different countries have attended. The outdoor events included fireworks for the first time, which would become a regular attraction in the following years. The theme of the con was Apocalypse, alluding to year 2012 in which it took place. Olven won the T-shirt design contest, and the conbook cover was done by Mearú.

Guests of Honor: Mearú Dreamsong (artist)

Charity: An animal rescue station in Pavlov, of the Nature Conservation Agency of the Czech Republic (11,000 Kč)

Chairmen or Organizers: Greyfur, Ihaha, Raika, Tamu, Vlk00, and Xkůň, as "the Orgateam"

ČeSFuR 9: The attendance of 152 included fans from 18 different countries. Events included an auction, a campfire, a DDR, a furdance, a fursuit show, and a hiking trip. Sharley won the T-shirt design contest, and the conbook cover featured artwork from Wolfy-Nail.

Guests of Honor: Wolfy-Nail (artist)

Charity: Czech Society for Ornithology (14,000 Kč)

Chairmen or Organizers: Greyfur, Ihaha, Petboy, Raika, Tamu, Vlk00, Xkůň, as "the Orgateam"

ČeSFuR X: ČeSFuR was reported to be the biggest convention in the Czech Republic. Beginning with the tenth year, the con was extended by one additional day. This marked the third and last year in Hotel Luna, which was fully booked out by the convention's 180 attendees from 16 different countries. The extra day allowed for two nights with a campfire and three nights of furry dancing. Events again included a barbecue, a charity auction, a DDR setup, fireworks, and a fursuit show. A Fursuit Dance Contest was introduced. The theme was Treasure Island, and a Jolly Roger flag was hoisted over the consite for the duration of the con, to be auctioned off in the final charity auction. Memburu won the T-shirt design contest, conbook cover was done by Qzurr.

Guests of Honor: Qzurr (artist)

Charity: Raptor Protection of Slovakia (16,000 Kč)

Chairmen or Organizers: Xkůň, Vlk00, Raika, Tamu, Ihaha, as "the Orgateam"

ČeSFuR 11: ČeSFuR moved to the Hotel Skalský-dvůr, near Nové Město na Moravě and Lisek village in the midst of the Bohemian-Moravian highlands. It booked to capacity early, and late registrants were assigned to guest house beds. All lunches and dinners were included in the lodging price, and the ČeSFuR program included international tea brewing and drinking. There was a nightly campfire with cooking sausages and drinking beer. There was a short fursuit walk through the hotel and down to the local lake. There were several attendees from other European furry conventions such as Gdakon and RusFURence. A popular nearby tourist site was the 16th-century Pernštejn Castle. The T-shirt contest, from June 7 to 14, was won by Azshara kletete whose art was featured on the front; second place to Bluari whose art was featured on the ČeSFuR mugs. All five submissions were published in the conbook. An Egyptian mascot was Abayomi, a jackal, for the theme of Ancient Egypt. The charity was a public society for the preservation of the rainforest of Indonesia by buying part of the rainforest. The conbook cover was by Alassa.

Guests of Honor: EZwolf (filmmaker, fursuiter, photographer)

Charity: Prales detem (Wildwood for children) (12,000 Kč)

Chairmen or Organizers: Ihaha, Raika, Tamu, Vlk00, and Xkůň, as "the Orgateam"

China National Furry Party

This first furry convention in mainland China was originally planned as a separate event in an underground shopping center, but due to problems, it was finally held in conjunction with an anime convention. It is not yet known whether this will become an annual event. The name 神州萌兽祭 is translated as China National Furry Party, although since this sounds more like a political party, the translation may be liberalized as something like "China Critter Festival." The literal translation is "Cute Furry Festival of the Divine Land."

Name & Date　　*Location Attendance*

神州萌兽祭
July 18–19, 2015　　Nan Fung International Convention & Exhibition Center, Guangzhou　200+

Events

神州萌兽祭: The 2015 China National Furry Party was held in conjunction with an anime convention. Attendance is estimated at over 200 because all 200 commemorative tickets to the furry convention were taken. There were 12 fursuiters, although not all took part in the fursuit demonstration. Events included a fursuit show, a "lecture" about furry fandom, sales of furry related items, an art show and live painting. There was a 32-page conbook and a poster by BIABIA. BIABIA and 鲁肯 (Lu Ken) designed the commemorative ticket.

Chairmen or Organizers: 左一壹 (Zuo Yiyi) and 宅狮 (Zhai Shi, roughly "Indoorsy Lion")

CH-on

CH stands for Confoederatio Helvetica, the Helvetic Confederation; the official name of Switzerland. (It's Latin, from the days when the Roman legions first annexed the Alpine valleys.) CH-on was the first furry convention in Switzerland, organized on the Internet over "Furry.ch—das Schweizer Furryportal." It is a relaxicon in a rustic holiday house, emphasizing the Swiss Alps, little programming, and lots of meals. It is typified by the logo for CH-on 5 showing two anthropomorphized mountain goats eating cheese fondue.

Name & Date	Location	Attendance
CH-on June 12–15, 2008	A private residence, Morschach	40 (estimated)
CH-on 2 June 11–14, 2009	Gysenstein holiday house, near Bern	50 (estimated)
CH-on 3 June 3–6, 2010	Haus Marchgraben, Achseten, Adelboden	46
CH-on 4 June 23–26, 2011	Haus Marchgraben, Achseten, Adelboden	42
CH-on 5 June 7–10, 2012	Haus Marchgraben, Achseten, Adelboden	38

Events

CH-on: The first Swiss furry convention was held in a private residence/logging house belonging to a national hiking association in Morschach, near Lake Lucerne. The capacity of 40 furs was filled. It was organized by the Swissfurs.ch online association, headed by furry artist Blue_Panther. The program was themed for artists and fursuiters, with several workshops. There was a video and game room. A paper chase was held on the last day. The catered meals featured distinctively Swiss foods, especially cheese fondue in the evenings. The T-shirt was by Akeyla.

Chairmen or Organizers: Blue_Panther, naut, Pfluftel, Luxen, Patrix

Opposite: China National Furry Party poster. Art by BIABIA. Used with permission.

CH-on 2: CH-on 2 was in a larger holiday house with a capacity of 50. Membership was 170 CHF or €100. It featured a Fursuit day and an Artists' day, with workshops, a photoshoot, and a late night torch hike. The T-shirt was by Magus Lupus.

Chairmen or Organizers: Blue_Panther, naut, Doggy, Pfluftel, Patrix

CH-on 3: Adelboden is a popular resort village in the Bernese Alps. A shuttle bus was available from the Adelboden station to Achseten. The Achseten holiday house had a capacity of 70 with far more function space, so there was more than enough dorm and function room. Registration was 170/135/70 CHF, depending upon whether the member stayed at the holiday house for three, two, or one day(s). The Art and Fursuit days were dropped for a permanent music and game room, an Artists' Room, and several fursuit events such as a Photosuit and a Fursuit walk. The T-shirt was by Alpha_Ki.

Chairmen or Organizers: Blue_Panther, naut, Doggy, Pfluftel, Patrix

CH-on 4: CH-on 4 was held in the same holiday house as CH-on 3. Moving to the larger holiday home the previous year proved satisfactory, as the weather didn't allow for a lot of outdoor activities. The program was changed on short notice and involved a lot of card games, Music room and Video games, the Artists Room and an Art Roundtable, Fursuit Workshop, Whiskey Tasting and Cookie Backing. A shuttle service from the station was available for pre-registered attendees. The registration fee was CHF 170/135/70 for those staying three days, two days, or a single day. The T-shirt was by Blue_Panther.

Chairmen or Organizers: Blue_Panther, naut, Luxen, and Patrix as "Die Orga"

CH-on 5: The program remained the same as the previous years, but better weather allowed for more outdoor activities. Individual hiking groups formed and there also was a short excursion for fursuiting photo opportunities. On site provided once again a Music room, a Room for Card and Video games, the Artists Room for the Art Roundtable and Whiskey Tasting and Cookie Backing. Though there was a Room for Fursuiting needs, there was no specific workshop dedicated for Fursuiting this year. CH-on 5 boasted the help of a chef in the kitchen to provide even better and more "suffisticated" culinary fantasies all the day long. A shuttle service from the station was available for pre-registered attendees. The registration fee was CHF 170/135/70 for those staying three days, two days, or a single day. The T-shirt was by Kajito.

Chairmen or Organizers: Blue_Panther, naut, Luxen, and Patrix as "Die Orga"

CH-on was discontinued after 2012. CH-on 6 would have conflicted with ConFuzzled in the U.K. The organizers switched to the annual Golden Leaves Con and less organized furmeets instead.

CH-on T-shirt. Art by Akeyla. Used with permission.

Condition

Condition was one of several conventions created to replace C-ACE as a furry convention for Ontario. It was unique in being themed around a story created for the convention. A team of writers created the story, which was started in publicity before the convention began, recapped in a skit at the opening ceremonies, carried forward through events at the convention, and ended in a final skit at the closing ceremonies. The story's theme was the theme of the convention. The Board of Directors (CajunFox, Frostscar, and Cola) ran Condition; the Chairman position was ceremonial only, for public relations. The highest level of registration (sponsor) became the Story Arc Sponsor, and was written into the story. Two of the program events were an interactive spy game that determined major changes in the story, and an assassin game with Nerf guns and improvised imaginary weapons. Regular Condition features included the assassin games, the pool party, the booze in the sponsor lounge, and home cooked food instead of catered.

Name & Date	Theme	Location	Attendance	Parade
Condition: Zero Hour—Dropping the Bomb August 6–8, 2010		Four Points by Sheraton, London, Ontario	233	32
Condition: Red July 22–24, 2011		Four Points by Sheraton, London, Ontario	251	47
Condition: Blue July 27–29, 2012		Four Points by Sheraton, London, Ontario	?	?
Condition: Wasteland August 2–4, 2013		Four Points by Sheraton, London, Ontario	?	?
Condition vs. the Monsters August 1–3, 2014		Four Points by Sheraton, London, Ontario	?	?

Events

Condition: Zero Hour—Dropping the Bomb
Guests of Honor: Lucas Raymond (Potoroo, chairman of Camp Feral!), John Barrett (Roxikat, furry artist), Kamber Lane (fursuiter)
Charity: Salthaven Wildlife Rehabilitation and Education Centre (C$2,192)
Chairmen or Organizers: Frostscar

Condition: Red: The theme was "The People's Furry Con," a furry U.S.S.R.; and its war with Western furrydom. CajunFox, the chairman, was the Glorious Leader of the People's Furry Con. An anime track was added to the program.
Guests of Honor: Sophie Cabra (fursuit maker), Strype and Cooper Perian (furry artist couple)
Charity: Salthaven Wildlife Rehabilitation and Education Centre (C$10,586)
Chairmen or Organizers: CajunFox Windrunner

Condition: Blue: The theme was continued from last year, but segueing into the Jazz Era. "…carries on our story but is focused on the era of Jazz, the 1920s, 30s and 40s. The war is over! Hopefully, there won't be any mobsters."
Guests of Honor: Amber Williams, Mary E. Minch (Mary Mouse, furry cartoonist)
Charity: Salthaven Wildlife Rehabilitation and Education Centre (C$10,085)
Chairmen or Organizers: Brian Foster (Cola)

Condition: Wasteland: Caltroplay replaced Rikoshi (furry author), the original announced G-o-H, who was unable to attend.
Guests of Honor: Eevachu, Caltroplay (furry artists)

Charity: Salthaven Wildlife Rehabilitation and Education Centre
Chairmen or Organizers: CajunFox WindRunner

Condition vs. the Monsters: Fursuit maker Wolfbird was announced as a G-o-H but did not attend. It was announced before the convention that this would be its grand finale. Condition was planned to replace C-ACE, and for a four-year story arc. During that time, other Canadian furry conventions became established, and the story arc was finished. It was decided to have a fifth and final Condition to wrap everything up and give it a grand sendoff.

Guests of Honor: Sigil, Dixie von Fur (furry artists)
Charity: Salthaven Wildlife Rehabilitation and Education Centre
Chairmen or Organizers: Tyler

ConFurence

The ConFurence was the first furry convention. It was created in 1989 by Mark Merlino & Rod O'Riley, in Southern California's Orange County about thirty miles south of Los Angeles. Merlino & O'Riley had been attending s-f conventions and the San Diego Comic-Con throughout the 1980s, and they modeled the ConFurences upon these; but without what they felt was the unnecessary bureaucracy such as incorporating as a not-for-profit corporation or keeping statistics. Most of the basic formats and traditions of furry conventions were established by the ConFurences.

Name & Date	*Theme*	*Location*	*Attendance*
ConFurence 0 January 21–22, 1989	none	Holiday Inn Bristol Plaza, Costa Mesa	65
ConFurence 1 January 26–28, 1990	none	Holiday Inn Bristol Plaza, Costa Mesa	130 (estimated)
ConFurence 2 January 25–27, 1991	none	Holiday Inn Anaheim Resort, Anaheim	200 (estimated)
ConFurence 3 January 24–26, 1992	Our Furry World	Holiday Inn Anaheim Resort, Anaheim	400 (estimated)
ConFurence 4 January 22–24, 1993	In Search of Ancient Furries	Red Lion Costa Mesa, Costa Mesa	500 (estimated)
ConFurence 5 January 21–23, 1994	Furries In Space	Airporter Garden Hotel, Irvine	650 (estimated)
ConFurence 6 January 13–15, 1995	Magic and Morphs	Airporter Garden Hotel, Irvine	700 (estimated)
ConFurence 7 January 12–14, 1996	Furries in Force	Atrium Marquis Hotel, Irvine	900 (estimated)
ConFurence 8 January 16–19, 1997	Music & Mirth Reptiles	Buena Park Hotel and Convention Center, Buena Park	999
ConFurence 9 January 15–18, 1998	Furries in Love Furries Down Under	Buena Park Hotel and Convention Center, Buena Park	1,250 (estimated)
ConFurence 10 April 1–4, 1999	Looking Back at 10 Furry Years Year of the Rabbit	Town and Country Resort and Convention Center, San Diego	850
ConFurence 11 April 6–9, 2000	Furries in Asia	Irvine Hilton Hotel, Irvine	703
ConFurence 12 April 19–22, 2001	At the Movies	Hilton Burbank Airport & Convention Center, Burbank	640

Name & Date	Theme	Location	Attendance
ConFurence 2002 April 26–28, 2002	Furry Noir	Hilton Burbank Airport & Convention Center, Burbank	580
ConFurence 2003 April 25–27, 2003	The Furry West	Hilton Burbank Airport & Convention Center, Burbank	470

Events

ConFurence 0: For the first half-dozen or so years, the annual ConFurences had no competition. The attendance of ConFurence 0, so called because it was considered a dry run for the first "real" furry fan convention the next year, is debated. There were 90 signed-up members, but the attendance was only about 65. Furry fans from throughout North America and one from Australia, Steve Kerry, came. Memberships were $10. The first hotel asked, the Red Lion Costa Mesa, considered the expected attendance of 100 to be too small for it to bother with. The Holiday Inn Bristol Plaza, across the street, accepted the convention. The location of Costa Mesa, California, was conveniently next to the Orange County/John Wayne Airport, and was considered close enough to Disneyland for a trip there to be an attraction for the convention. The late January date was largely because those were otherwise dead weekends for hotel convention business.

ConFurence 0, formally the International Anthropomorphic Convention (the formal term was never popularly used), had two rooms of programming and a small dealers' room. The attendees included just about all of the big names in furry fandom. The Art Show brought in over $1,100, with the highest-selling painting, by Susan Van Camp, going for $450. The convention was too small and informal to have program moderators or speakers. Most attendees dressed normally, but there was a group meeting for "Furry Costuming," and one of the program events featured Robert Hill in costume as furry fan cartoonist Jerry Collins' "Hilda the Bambioid," a sexy deer-woman wearing bondage gear. This was before the word "fursuit" was coined. A filk contest was won by Tanith Teer for "Eyes of the Wolf." There was a screening of Mark Merlino's edited winter/summer TV special "movie" print of *Animalympics*. The 16-page Program Book cover was by Steve Martin. A ConFurence T-shirt featured a Ken Sample drawing of the convention's mascot, Mark Merlino's anthropomorphic fisher character Sydney Fisher. ConFurence 0 was the first furry convention at which many attendees complained of getting "the con crud" there—colds, the flu, or whatever. (The term, from s-f fandom, predates furry conventions.) This has been going on until today.

Chairmen or Organizers: Mark Merlino (Sylys), Rod O'Riley (as co-directors)

ConFurence 1:

ConFurence 0 was considered a big success, so a three-day ConFurence 1, the "first real furry convention," was organized. The attendance was an estimated 130 out of a membership of 145. Memberships were doubled to $20 for the three days. ConFurence 1 was the first to have Guests-of-Honor; all furry artists/cartoonists. Awards were presented, to Kay Shapero for "Furry" as Best Filk Award; to Ken Sample for "Winter Charge" for Art Show Best of Show; and to John Cawley as "Zorro the fox" for Best Costume. Significantly, the ConFurence was still imitating the s-f conventions at this time by holding a traditional Costume or Masquerade event instead of convention-long fursuiting. ConFurence 1 was the first to formalize the leaderless program events as "Special Interest Groups" where those interested in a topic were expected to get together and discuss it among themselves, rather than as a panel event with a programmed moderator and scheduled panelists. There was a Spaghetti Dinner. Phil Morrissey did a wraparound cover for the 24-page program book. The T-shirt was by Ken Sample, featuring Sydney Fisher again. Unofficially, ConFurence 1 saw the debut of the first issue of *Yarf!, the Journal of Applied Anthropomorphics*, which was to become the most prestigious and longest-running furry fanzine, lasting for 69 issues to September 2003.

Guests of Honor: Jim Groat, Monika Livingston, Martin Wagner
Chairmen or Organizers: Mark Merlino (Sylys), Rod O'Riley

ConFurence 2: The Holiday Inn Bristol Plaza's convention facilities were barely large enough for ConFurence 1. To have room to grow, ConFurence 2 in 1991 moved to the slightly larger Holiday Inn Anaheim Resort. ConFurence 2 had the first furry convention Ice Cream Social. There was a convention-long Video Room with its own schedule. Fred Patten organized a 33-artist art jam. Michael Payne won the Filk Contest with "Hope By Her Smile," inspired by Ken Sample's T-shirt for ConFurence 0. The Art Show auction brought in over $3,000. ConFurence 2 was the first furry convention to have attendees/speakers from outside furry fandom; Carl Gafford and Len Wein of Disney Comics. The 28-page "ConFurence Collection" had a wraparound cover by Jim Groat. The CF2 T-shirt was by Steve Martin.

Guests of Honor: Steve Gallacci, *Omaha, the Cat Dancer* creators Reed Waller and Kate Worley, Vicky Wyman.

Chairmen or Organizers: Mark Merlino (Sylys), Rod O'Riley

ConFurence 3: The tradition of having an official theme began. The first Cabaret Fur le Dance (not called that until the next year) was held, featuring Omaha Sternberg as Omaha, the Cat Dancer. Proceeds were donated to the medical expenses of Reed Waller, Omaha's creator. The Filk Contest was won by Christina Hanson for "Master of the Seventh Blade." The 32-page conbook had a wraparound cover by Steve Martin. There were three T-shirts, by Lia Graf (Tygger), Steve Martin, and Jack Cavanaugh.

Around 1992 or 1993, the makeup of the ConFurence evolved. Fursuits became more prominent. Also, the influx of new attendees brought an increasing number who did not have any familiarity with s-f fandom or comics fandom, but who had learned about furry fandom and the ConFurences over the Internet. The newcomers included many who were used to adopting personas for role-playing games, and preferred to be known by furry personas that were flamboyantly pseudonyms, like Aerofox and Neo PanTyger. Many refused to let their real names become known.

Guests of Honor: Dave Garcia, Chuck Melville, Taral Wayne (furry artists); "Special Media Guests": Jymn Magon and Mark Zaslove of Disney Afternoon TV's *TaleSpin*.

Charity: Reed Waller's medical expenses.

Chairmen or Organizers: Mark Merlino (Sylys), Rod O'Riley

ConFurence 4: The new hotel was the same one that had rejected ConFurence 0 as too small. The convention was dedicated to the memory of popular cartoonist Deal Whitley, the first notable furry fan to die (of sickle-cell anemia), on August 30, 1992. There was a Furry Rave dance in addition to the Cabaret Fur le Dance. Proceeds from the latter were donated to a Deal Whitley Fund at DuCret School of the Arts. A Pizza Feast replaced the Spaghetti Dinner. The Filk Contest was won by Bruce Lane with "Flying Purple Parking Meter." The Sci-Fi Channel covered the convention. Two oil paintings by Steve Gallacci sold for over $1,000. Reportedly the term "fursuit" began at or just after ConFurence 4, coined by Robert C. King for a Fursuit Mailing List. The 44-page conbook had a wraparound cover penciled by Terrie Smith and inked by Lia Graf, with backgrounds by Mitchell Beiro. The CF4 T-shirt was by Terrie Smith. This was the first "self-sustaining" ConFurence, paid for entirely by admission fees rather than partially by private donations.

ConFurence 4 in 1993 was the first furry convention to have serious trouble with its hotel. The Red Lion Inn was too large, with too many "mundanes" in the hotel. The ConFurence shared the hotel with a conservatively-dressed Amway convention. (I personally rode down on the elevator on one occasion from my room on an upper floor to the main convention floor. The elevator stopped a couple of floors lower and a large fursuiter [a wolf, as I recall] got on. A couple of floors lower and the elevator stopped for a group of Japanese businessmen. I will never forget the expression on their faces when they saw the fursuiter. They did not get on the elevator—but I would not be surprised if the hotel management heard from them.) The most serious conflict came when a hotel maid found Scott Malcolmson's costume in his room, "Veteran of the Psychotic Wars," which looked like a burlesque terrorist (with a unicorn head) with a cartoon bomb. She reported it to hotel security, which called the fire department and police to report a real bomb. The police sent a bomb squad, who, when they saw the obvious prop bomb, cited the hotel for making a prank call. (Malcolmson said that the Costa Mesa police bomb squad requested the prop for training purposes.) The security manager, who had expressed open hostility to the convention, was fired, but this did not endear the ConFurence to hotel management. From then on, any fan that left the hotel was required to show his or her room key as proof of being a registered guest to be readmitted. The ConFurence did not use the Red Lion Inn again, by mutual consent.

Guests of Honor: Mercedes Lackey (s-f author), Larry Dixon (s-f artist), Ken Fletcher (Furry artist).

Charity: Reed Waller's medical expenses.

Chairmen or Organizers: Mark Merlino (Sylys), Rod O'Riley

ConFurence 5: For the first time, the ConFurence seemed to have a "perfect" hotel. It was one conveniently of the hotels directly across from the Orange County/John Wayne Airport. It was the only convention in the hotel, and the majority of rooms were occupied by fans. The hotel staff were very friendly; some even wore ConFurence T-shirts. Attendees were enthusiastic about the hotel. In addition to the souvenir Program Book, attendees received a 12-page "Anime Gets Furry!" guide to furry Japanese anime and manga, illustrated by Michele Light and Terrie Smith. Programming included a writing workshop led by A. C. Crispin, and a "NitroCoon" Radio Show by Avi Melman. The Filk Contest was won by Dr. Samuel Conway with "I'm Going to ConFurence 5." The *Rowbrazzle* apa held a 10th Anniversary celebration with a special fanzine prepared during the convention for sale to the attendees on the last day. The CF5 T-shirt and 52-page wraparound Program Book cover were by Mitch Beiro.

Guests of Honor: Alicia Austin, Michael Capobianco, A. C. Crispin, Phil Foglio, Terrie Smith (a mixture of s-f and furry notables).

Charity: The Deal Whitley scholarship fund.

Chairmen or Organizers: Mark Merlino (Sylys), Rod O'Riley

ConFurence 6: The staff list grew to almost four dozen names, still led by co-Directors Mark Merlino and Rod O'Riley. Programming featured the two writers from the Disney *Gargoyles* TV program, Michael Reaves and Brynne Chandler-Reaves. The Video Room was split into two, one showing anime and the other showing programming based on the con theme; each having its own multipage guide. The Pearl Possum, a juice bar, was present. The Art Show auction was a disaster that ran for hours overtime, "trapping" bidders in it, due to the committee seriously underestimating the number of bidders and the length of time that many would bid on a painting. The Filk Contest was won by Michael Payne with "Gently Falling Rain." The attendees loved the Airporter Garden Hotel, which was filled to capacity, but reluctantly agreed that there was no room for further growth so the ConFurence would have to move to a larger hotel. The CF6 T-shirt and 56-page Program Book wraparound cover were by Daphne Lage.

Guests of Honor: Alan Dean Foster (s-f author), Ellisa Mitchell (s-f artist), Ed Zolna (furry specialty bookseller).

Charity: The Deal Whitley scholarship fund.

Chairmen or Organizers: Mark Merlino (Sylys), Rod O'Riley

ConFurence 7: By 1996, the first Furry conventions on the East Coast had started, and one in Europe. The Atrium Marquis Hotel was just the renamed Airporter Garden Hotel, next to the Orange

County Airport. The fans filled the hotel and overflowed into the Radisson Plaza Hotel next door. Notable attendees included Disney TV writer and creator of *TaleSpin* Jymn Magon, who was presented with the ConFurence's first (and only) Golden Sydney Award, for promotion of furry fandom (committee-awarded). The award consisted of a statuette of Sydney Fisher, the anthropomorphized fisher mascot of the ConFurences, by sculptor Ruben Avila. "Joining our mascot Sydney Fisher (the first female 007) this year is Atrium Marquis, the European ferret and his gerbil major-domo, Radisson." The Filk Contest was won by Seanan McGuire for "Tears Like Rain." The 60-page Program Book had a wraparound cover by Roz Gibson, and an article, "Looking Back: 10 Years of Furry Parties" by Rod O'Riley that was one of the first bits of furry historiography. The CF7 T-shirt was by Eric Schwartz, depicting Sydney Fisher as a *femme fatale*.

CF7 in 1996 is credited with starting the Fursuit Parades. The ConFurence had traditionally scheduled its costuming (mostly fursuiting) events during the afternoon, rather than in the evening like most s-f convention masquerades. By ConFurence 6, there were complaints from several dealers that they could not leave their tables in the Dealers' Dens to attend the costuming events. At CF7, the costumers were asked to parade in their costumes through the Dealers' Den before taking them off. This is popularly believed to have been the beginning of the furry convention Fursuit Parades.

There had been some criticism earlier about the overly public display of eroticism, and a perception that the con committee's publicity was aimed overly strongly at the gay community. By 1996 isolated criticism grew into public complaints, but the convention committee denied them and no evidence was ever produced. (It was not until 2015 that this was definitely disproven.)

Guests of Honor: Frank Kelly Freas and Laura Freas (s-f/fantasy artists), Michael Higgs, Eric W. Schwartz (furry artists), S. Andrew Swann (s-f author).

Charity: The Deal Whitley scholarship fund.

Chairmen or Organizers: Mark Merlino (Sylys), Rod O'Riley

ConFurence 8: The 1997 ConFurence moved to the larger Buena Park Hotel and Convention Center in Buena Park, California, next to Knott's Berry Farm, a major tourist attraction. It was nine stories tall, with a glass-walled penthouse, the City Lights ballroom, on the top floor; the Art Show was set up there. ConFurence 8 was the first to feature dual-themes. Some attendees claimed that, despite the official attendance total of 999, CF 8 had more than a thousand attendees. Most programming was of the usual Special Interest Groups. Friday evening featured the Ice Cream Social and a big Filk Concert. Saturday night had a poolside Fur Dance. Timothy Fay, from Minneapolis, had gotten his local TV channel, KARE, to send a news crew to cover the convention. The coverage noted the convention's adult nature but was generally positive. There were a half-dozen European fans wearing EuroFurence 2 T-shirts like a uniform. Karri Aronen came from Turku, Finland, which many fans considered a dare to Warner Bros.'s lawyers since they had threatened a lawsuit for his drawing pornographic cartoons with the *Tiny Toon Adventures* cast. There were more dance events than usual, including a Fur Dance in fursuits and a Purple Nurple Live! band. The Filk Contest tied with "Loot" by Lee Gold and "Cotillion" by Michael Payne. A guest briefly announced before the convention was Steven R. Boyett, author of furry favorite novel *The Architect of Sleep*, who cancelled when he realized this was a furry rather than a s-f convention. (The furry-hating Boyett said, "I'm more likely to make the world happy by engineering a furry-specific virus with a 99.99% mortality rate.") The 60-page Souvenir Book had a wraparound cover by Brian Harp. The minimalist T-shirt, by Michelle Light, was by far the most popular that the ConFurence ever produced. It was reprinted twice, and still sold out every time over the next couple of years.

ConFurence 8 took place in excellent weather after a week of rain. That and the larger size of the hotel were the best things about it, claimed most attendees. The hotel, dating from the 1920s, was in considerable disrepair. There was erratic hot water, often forcing fans to take ice-cold showers. The funky Ving card "cheese-grater" room keys often did not work. They were also unpopular for catching in pockets; many fans followed director Mark Merlino's lead in wearing his key around his neck with a lanyard. The two shaky elevators constantly seemed like they would break down at any minute. Signs in the elevators reading "Limit: 8 persons" had been graffitied to "8 fans or 16 mundanes," or limits for foxes, lions, Smurfs, and others. (A common sarcastic jibe among the members was about the obvious overweight nature of many fans.) The registration desk denied that it had received the reservations of many attendees from out of town. Fans revived the "Hotel from Hell" informal slogan of ConFURence East in 1995 as really deserved this time. On the last day of the convention, Mark Merlino was presented with a large petition demanding that the ConFurence move to a better and larger hotel. There were rumors that g-o-h Robert Sawyer was heard to remark that he did not consider the intelligent dinosaurs of his Quintaglio trilogy to be "furry," and that he had only accepted his g-o-h-ship to escape to Southern California from a Canadian winter.

After the convention, criticism increased sharply of "inappropriate public behavior," such as a young adolescent wearing only a strategically-placed Dixie cup gyrating lewdly in the lobby. There was a big argument over the Internet over whether someone had smeared one of the hotel elevators with semen. At the Con-Dor 5 s-f convention in San Diego on February 21–23, a post-mortem on ConFurence 8 led by Jeff Ferris had agreed that, aside from the problems, the Buena Park Hotel was too small for the ConFurence; which had been pointed out in the petition given to Merlino. Merlino got into an unruly shouting match when he announced in his presentation the next day that there was no reason for complaint because the Buena Park Hotel management had promised that there would be no problems next year, and besides a contract had already been signed. Merlino was accused to his face of being a liar. The complaints grew into a major criticism of the ConFurence's management, on such sites as alt.fan.furry for months.

Guests of Honor: Peter Beagle (fantasy author), Dr. Jane Robinson (dinosaur expert; filksinger), Robert J. Sawyer (s-f author).

Charity: The Deal Whitley scholarship fund.

Chairmen or Organizers: Mark Merlino (Sylys), Rod O'Riley

ConFurence 9: The 1998 ConFurence was the first furry convention to indisputably top a thousand attendees. (This was also the ConFurence's high point.) By this time the CF committee and staff had grown to over fifty fans, still led by Mark Merlino and Rod O'Riley. ConFurence 9 was generally considered to be very enjoyable, despite any previous complaints. There was a History of Furry Fandom program with Fred Patten, one of the earliest furry fans; Mark Merlino, who co-created the first furry convention; Drew Maxwell, one of the creators of FurryMuck and the furry presence on the Internet; Sven Tegethoff, who had just taken over running the EuroFurences; and others, that was videotaped and has since been posted on YouTube. The ConFurence 9 Souvenir Book was 56 pages and included stories and art from 41 people, with a wraparound cover by Margaret Carspecken. There was news coverage by three foreign TV crews, from Brazil, Britain (ITV), and France. The Filk Song Contest was won by Kay Shapero with "Hollow Hills." The biggest problem was caused by the State Board of Equalization's insistence that dealers had to go to the SBE office in Santa Ana to get their permits instead of getting them at the hotel. The SBE office was nearby, and this only delayed the opening of the Dealers' Room about 45 minutes on the first day. The T-shirt was by Cataroo. There was a poster by Gene Catlow (Albert Temple).

Despite the success of ConFurence 9, there was continued criticism of the ConFurence over the Internet afterwards. Criticism of the ConFurence, and of overly pornographic artwork and activities in furry fandom in general, led in September 1998 to the small but vociferous "keep it clean in public" Burned Fur movement which kept up the public complaints against the CF. One complaint was about the lack of any ConFurence 9 publicity in traditional s-f fan and anime fan circles, while Merlino was believed to have promoted it heavily in gay circles. (The ConFurence Committee claimed that it publicized the convention as widely as it could; some circles were more willing to accept the publicity than others. There were also complaints about the Committee's having publicized the convention anywhere outside of furry fandom.) Also, the move next year to the Easter weekend in San Diego, announced at ConFurence 9 as due to the unavailability of any hotels in the Orange County area in January, took many fans by surprise. There was considerable discussion for some time as to whether this would be good or bad for the convention.

Guests of Honor: The five FurryMUCK creators (Ashtoreth, Centaur, Drew Maxwell, Revar, and Shaterri), Carole and Mike Curtis (Shanda Fantasy Arts publishers), Michelle Light (furry artist), Lisanne Norman (s-f author).

Charity: The Deal Whitley scholarship fund.

Chairmen or Organizers: Mark Merlino (Sylys), Rod O'Riley

ConFurence 10: The move to the Easter weekend was generally unpopular, with some fans being unable to attend due to family obligations on the religious holiday. There were also many complaints about the distance of San Diego from the traditional Costa Mesa-Anaheim-Buena Park-Irvine area, and the extremely spread-out Town & Country hotel (fans supposedly got sore feet walking from one event to another). The hotel food was unusually expensive. Attendance shrank by about 400. The ConFurence committee had planned to return to January and the Orange County area as soon as those dates became available at the Orange County hotels again, but the immediate pre-emption of that month by the new Further Confusion created a potential confrontation that popular opinion urged the ConFurence to avoid.

The Filk Song contest was won by Leslie Fish with "Invasion." The 56-page Souvenir Book had a wraparound cover by Gary Lee Seto (Gawain). There were both a ConFurence 10 T-shirt by Rachael Cawley (Cataroo), and a commemorative, non-numbered ConFurence green T-shirt by Ken Sample. The convention was hit with a last-minute ban by the hotel on selling erotica in the Den of Dealers; which was welcomed by many, but caused concern and confusion with some dealers faced with lowered sales, and uncertainty as to whether specific works would be considered erotica by the hotel or not. Publicity of the ban was blamed for some fans' staying home, and for keeping those who did attend on their good behavior. Actually, nothing was banned; dealers just had to keep adult material covered and labeled ADULT. But it did create some worry. Another bad vibe was that, in the wake of lurid press coverage of furry fandom, all attendees and dealers were warned to not cooperate with any press members or camera crews except those accompanied by a convention staff member.

Post-convention criticism increased sharply. Complaints of overly-public sexual displays seemed left over from the Buena Park ConFurences, but the convention committee was now criticized for openly ignoring complaints. Also, the ConFurence had been operating for ten years by this time, and there had been several ConFURence Easts and Anthrocons that had been better-run. Many fans felt that the ConFurence's problems could no longer be blamed on an excusable lack of experience to shield the committee from complaints of incompetence. Shortly after ConFurence 10, at a committee meeting, longtime Director Mark Merlino announced that he and Co-Director Rod O'Riley were stepping down. The meeting voted newsletter editor Darrel Exline (nominated by Rod O'Riley) as the new Director. Merlino sold all rights to the ConFurence to Exline for $1, retaining the leftover Program Books and T-shirts of the previous ConFurences.

Guests of Honor: Mary Hanson-Roberts (artist), Cynthia McQuillan (filksinger).

Charity: The Deal Whitley scholarship fund.

Chairmen or Organizers: Mark Merlino (Sylys), Rod O'Riley

ConFurence 11: New chairman Darrel Exline returned to several old ConFurence traditions. He went back to the old locale just south of Los Angeles, and to a single theme. He revived the ConFurence's formal name of the International Anthropomorphic Convention and Exposition. Exline identified himself as "Owner/Director of The ConFurence Group, and Co-Chair of ConFurence™

11." He also started new traditions. He introduced the "paw on globe" logo (also ™), available as a button or lapel pin; and promoted CritterConDiego 1, a Furry mini-con to be held adjacent to that year's San Diego Comic-Con. He continued the programming policy of leaderless Special Interest Groups. Since the hotel could not or would not provide any Art Show security, the Art Show was set up in a separate inflatable structure behind the hotel, dubbed the "tent Art Show." It was considered overly easy to break into, and was very unpopular. There was a charity auction and other events which raised $4,942 for the medical expenses of Michael-Scot McMurry, who was dying of cancer; McMurry requested that $2,000 of the money raised be directed to Kylen Miles, who had some (unspecified) medical problems. The Filk Song contest was won by Lee Gold with "The Flat Cat Was Cute." The 64-page Souvenir Book had a color front cover by Mitchell Beiro and a back cover by David Bliss. The CF11 T-shirt, illustrating the Furries in Asia theme in color, was by Shannon Stuart. Although Exline did not set any policy on "cleaning up" the convention, he did not deny a rumor that he was a "Burnt Fur" opposed to open displays of gay affection and anything that was "raunchy." This was blamed for a mass boycott by the anti–Burnt Furs. Whatever the real reason was, there was a further drop in attendance.

Guests of Honor: Mitchell Beiro (furry cartoonist), Ben Dunn (Antarctic Press publisher and *Mighty Tiny* writer-artist), Christopher Rowley (s-f author).

Charity: Michael-Scot McMurry's medical expenses ($4,942).

Chairmen or Organizers: Darrel L. Exline, Zsa'nene Klinkler

ConFurence 12: The 2001 ConFurence moved to the Hilton Burbank Airport & Convention Center at Burbank's Bob Hope Airport, the home for ten years of Los Angeles s-f fandom's annual Loscon convention. There was naturally a Fursuit Parade. A memorial was held for furry cartoonist Michael-Scot McMurry, who had just died of cancer on April 4. The Filk Song contest was won by "Don't Draw Them Bigger Than Her Head," by someone who left the contest before the voting was over, and was unknown. A main event on Friday evening was "the wedding of Mitch Beiro and Minerva Mink," with Winnie Woodpecker as the spurned former lover and a WB Lawyer, out to stop the wedding. Despite a lack of controversy this year, attendance continued to decline. The 60-page Souvenir Book had a color front cover by Monika Livingstone and a back cover by Jake Myler; and contained a 14-page guide to the ConFurence 12 Special Awards by Fred Patten. The CF12 T-shirt was by Mike Kazaleh.

The ConFurence inaugurated a new series of annual awards for excellence in anthropomorphic literature and art, with a special award. With 2001 starting a new century, fans were asked in progress reports to vote for the best anthropomorphic motion pictures and TV series of the 20th century, in both live-action and animated forms. Officially, any fan anywhere could request a ballot; in practice, only preregistered ConFurence members voted. The winners (Best Motion Picture (Live Action)—*Who Framed Roger Rabbit?* Best Motion Picture (Animated)—*Fantasia*. Best TV Series (Live Action)—*The Muppet Show*. Best TV Series (Animated)—*Animaniacs*.) received a trophy designed by David Bliss, at a special presentation ceremony.

Guests of Honor: Peter S. Beagle (writer g-o-h; fantasy author), Jymn Magon (writer g-o-h; Disney writer), Monika Livingstone (artist g-o-h; fantasy artist), Mike Kazaleh (artist g-o-h; animator/comic book artist).

Charity: The Exotic Feline Breeding Compound.

Chairmen or Organizers: Darrel L. Exline, Zsa'nene Klinkler

Confurence 2002: The 2002 ConFurence started out as ConFurence 13, but was changed to Confurence 2002 (note the lower-case "f") by Darrel Exline by fiat, over some objections. The attendance continued to decline. The first annual Ursa Major Awards, for excellence in anthropomorphic literature and art, were presented in nine categories. The winners received a certificate drawn by one of that year's artist guests, Roz Gibson. The Filk Contest was won by Martin DeMello with "Furrier

Transforms." The 42-page Souvenir Book had a color front cover by Roz Gibson. The ConFurence 2002 T-shirt was by David Bliss (Rivercoon).

Guests of Honor: Eric Garcia (s-f/mystery author), Roz Gibson, Ed Luena (furry artists).
Chairmen or Organizers: Darrel L. Exline

ConFurence 2003: The capital F was restored, but many fans insisted upon calling it ConFurence 14. Program events were keyed to the Western theme where possible; the annual Ice Cream Social became the Ice Cream Saloon, and the Cabaret Fur-le-Dance "featuring the Return of Omaha Sternberg" was advertised with a 19th-century dance hall-style poster. The second Ursa Major Awards were presented; the winners got a certificate designed by one of the guests-of-honor, Roy Pounds. ConFurence 2003 was the first furry convention to have a Party Floor. Southwest Airlines became an official airline. The Filk Song Contest had two winners; "Coyote Yodel" by Michael Payne for theme, and "Wolfie Shorts" by Ian Martyn (MoogiePower) for audience choice. The 32-page Souvenir Book had a color cover by Dark Natasha. A memorable moment was when about a half-dozen fans were photographing a fursuiter, Scruff E. Coyote, outside the hotel. A squirrel came up, and the photographers instantly focused on the squirrel's incredulous reaction to the fursuiter. It was clear in advance that ConFurence 2003 was not meeting its hotel room block. In an attempt to cover expenses, local fans were offered "The Furry West Homestead Act of CF-2003" of free memberships and some sponsors' perks to take hotel rooms instead of commuting. A large controversy arose when a TV crew from *The Man Show* began to film events and interview fans, in contravention to the custom in furry fandom against press coverage. Darrel Exline was accused of "selling out," but it turned out that the hotel had sold the right to film the convention for the location fee, and the ConFurence never received any of the money. The TV footage was never used.

ConFurence 2003 conbook. Art by Dark Natasha. Used with permission.

This was the final ConFurence. Darrel Exline had insisted on producing the Souvenir Book personally. The rest of the committee learned why when they saw it at the convention with a leading editorial that this was the last ConFurence and they were being discontinued. Strong objections by staffers and other fans were met by Exline's claim that he still owned the ConFurence name, and that any attempt by anyone else to continue the ConFurences would be countered with a legal challenge to that convention's hotel. (Incidentally, this showed that Exline's decision to discontinue the ConFurences had been made before the "disasters" of ConFurence 2003.) Since the ConFurences were never incorporated, Exline had to bear the final loss of the unmet Hotel Room Block personally. He has said that he ended up $60,000 in debt.

Even before ConFurence 2003, the Special Awards Committee had become worried that the Ursa Major Awards, which were intended to be fandom-wide, were being perceived as for ConFurence members only to vote upon. To make them more widespread, the Committee proposed to establish a separate organization to administer them, and to present them at different furry conventions. Exline supported this decision. By the time the ConFurence's cancellation was announced, the Special Awards Committee and its Ursa Major Awards had already become independent as the Anthropomorphic Literature and Arts Association (ALAA).

Guests of Honor: Ruben Avila (furry sculptor), Dark Natasha, Roy D. Pounds, II (furry artists), Theresa Mather (non-furry artist), Leslie Fish (filk singer).

Charity: The Exotic Feline Breeding Compound's Feline Conservation Center.

Chairmen or Organizers: Darrel L. Exline

ConFURence East

ConFURence East was the first furry convention in addition to the ConFurences. They began as Furtasticon 1, but were quickly renamed ConFURence East. They grew out of a minor squabble with s-f fandom's annual Philcons in Philadelphia, but showed the demand by furry fans living east of the Mississippi River for a furry convention that was easier to get to than southern California's ConFurences.

Name & Date	Theme	Location	Attendance
Furtasticon 1 November 18–20, 1994	none	Holiday Inn City Line, Philadelphia, PA	230 (estimated)
ConFURence East October 13–15, 1995	none	Holiday Inn Jetport, Elizabeth, NJ	449
ConFURence East 1996 November 15–17, 1996	none	Holiday Inn Independence, Cleveland, OH	543

Events

Furtasticon 1: Furry fans on the East Coast had come to adopt the annual Philcon s-f convention in Philadelphia in November as home. In 1994, there was a crisis. Some furry fans attempting to enter the Art Show or reserve tables in the Dealers' Room had their applications rejected. The Philcon said it was because their applications were received after both were all out of space; the furry fans claimed anti-furry prejudice. Trish Ny of Cleveland, Ohio, led a movement to pull furry support out of the Philcon and create a new Eastern furry convention. She created Furtasticon 1 (some spelled it FurTasTiCon) on just a couple of months' notice, at the Holiday Inn City Line next door to the Philcon's Adam's Mark Hotel. Attendees came from throughout North America, especially those in the East who could not afford to travel to the ConFurences in Southern California. There was a Furtasticon T-shirt by husband Joseph Ny. Reports were that Furtasticon 1 was a success, but there are no records of what went on there—just that it was so successful that everyone agreed that there should be an annual Eastern North American furry convention. Trish Ny promised to see to it.

Chairmen or Organizers: Susan "Trish" Ny

ConFURence East: The renamed Furtasticon 2 was run by Trish Ny and a committee that seemed to consist mostly of her family, at the Holiday Inn Jetport right by the Newark Liberty International

Airport. Husband Joseph Ny designed ConFURence East's mascot, Carla Cougar. The program more resembled a traditional s-f convention with a strong moderated panel format rather than the ConFurence's more informal Special Interest Groups. The concept of announcing an exact attendance total after the convention instead of just an estimate seemed to startle some fans. The art show included 795 pieces of art; sales were nearly $11,000. An official charity was heavily promoted: the Wolf Park nature study preserve at Battle Ground, Indiana. The convention was covered by both the Sci-Fi Channel (which tried to make ConFURence East look like a gathering of plush animal fetishists) and a radio interview with WBAI 99.5 FM in New York. ConFURence East had a bigger overlap with Eastern U.S. anime fandom than the ConFurence did with West Coast anime fandom. The ANIMEast '95 convention gave ConFURence East a lot of promotion. ConFURence East had noticeably more pets present than a Western ConFurence. There were many evening parties. The 52-page conbook had front and back covers by Vicky Wyman. The T-shirt was by Terrie Smith.

ConFURence East (most fans spelled it Confurence East) was deemed a success in everything but its hotel and neighborhood. The hotel itself was not bad, but its food was highly overpriced; there were no eateries in convenient walking distance, and the hotel management seriously advised everyone to not leave the hotel in the daytime except in groups, and not to go out at night at all. Despite calling out for food being allowed (there was a steady stream of deliveries from pizza and Chinese restaurants), the feeling of being prisoners in a hotel with overpriced food led to the Jetport being dubbed "the Hotel from Hell." There was a popular demand to move to a hotel in a better neighborhood next year.

Guests of Honor: S. Andrew Swann (s-f author), Vicky Wyman (furry artist), E.L.V.I.S. Convention Services.

Charity: Wolf Park ($1,000).

Chairmen or Organizers: Susan "Trish" Ny

ConFURence East 1996: ConFURence East was moved to Chairwoman Trish Ny's home town, in winter (which bemused many Southern California furries by Cleveland's winter snow & ice). It continued organizing a fully programmed convention, with a Dealers' Room ("deluxe" dealers got lunch brought to their tables), an Art Show, an Artists' Alley, an Internet Room, costuming, and the works. Popular furry author Paul Kidd from Western Australia was a guest of honor. There was a tournament of White Wolf's werewolf fantasy card game *Rage*. The dealers' room of fifty tables sold out. The art show had fewer entries (596 pieces), but greater sales ($12,400). In addition to donating all proceeds of the Pet Auction to Wolf Park, there was a raffle for a chance to be "kissed" (licked) by a wolf at the Park's five-day Wolf Behavior Seminar in August 1997. Many attendees carpooled to a local theater for the premiere of Warner Bros.' *Space Jam* that weekend. There was a heavy presence of convention security due to several local fans trying to sneak into the convention without buying a membership. Some attendees were asked to show membership badges, but the security was generally complimented for being low-profile and polite about it. The 24-page conbook had a cover by Terrie Smith. The T-shirt was by Michelle Light.

The second ConFURence East was a success, although many fans complained about the move to Cleveland (too far from the East Coast) and the shift from mid–October to mid–November (which put the convention in the midst of the earliest Cleveland snowfall in thirty years, with foot-high snowdrifts and temperatures in the high 20°–low 30° F range). The cold kept many fans from leaving the hotel to look for cheaper meals, and many of the cartoons drawn at the convention showed freezing furries. Despite the complaints, Trish Ny announced that this hotel would remain the convention's venue for the next several years, and that the convention's name would change to MoreFurCon to avoid confusion with the established ConFurence. However, personal family problems of the Nys over the next few months made this the final ConFURence East. A third annual furry convention, Albany AnthroCon, to be held in Albany, New York, over the Fourth of July weekend starting in 1997, had publicized itself heavily during CF East 96, and most Eastern furry fans were satisfied to go there instead for the better location and time of year.

Guests of Honor: Paul Kidd (furry author), Susan Van Camp (furry artist), White Wolf Game Studios (represented by staff artist Andrew Bates).

Charity: Wolf Park ($3,000).

Chairmen or Organizers: Susan "Trish" Ny

ConFurgence

ConFurgence (CFg) is the renamed MiDFur, Australia's largest furry convention. It was renamed primarily for moving from December to January, rendering the "Melbourne in December" meaning obsolete. The move from hotels to Melbourne's largest convention center also marked a sharp change from the past. The new name was meant to call attention to that. Popular program events repeated each year are the Fursuit Walk, held outdoors near or in the center of Melbourne; the Charity Auction, with a notable guest such as Uncle Kage or 2, the Ranting Gryphon as the auctioneer; a "That Time of Night" late-night talk show featuring CynWolfe; and the evening dance parties. The Program Book covers and T-shirts are generally by the year's artist guests-of-honor.

Name & Date	Theme	Location	Attendance
ConFurgence 2014 January 10–12, 2014	Egyptian Nights	Melbourne Convention and Exhibition Centre, Melbourne, Victoria	544
ConFurgence 2015 January 8–11, 2015	The Dragon Dynasty	The Arrow on Swanston, Melbourne, Victoria	616

Events

ConFurgence 2014: The Fursuit Walks are not counted, but are about 30% to 40% of the total attendance. The 2013 Furry Hall of Fame inductees, made at ConFurgence 2014, were Dark Natasha and Uncle Kage.

Guests of Honor: Tess Garman & Teagan Gavet (Blotch, furry artists), Dark Natasha, LatinVixen (furry artists), Sardyuon (furry performer)

Charity: Siberian Husky Rescue, medical expenses of Sharon Sakai (A$8,550)

Chairmen or Organizers: Pete Smith (CynWolfe)

ConFurgence 2015: The 2014 Furry Hall of Fame inductees, made at ConFurgence 2015, were AlectorFencer and EZwolf.

Guests of Honor: AlectorFencer (furry artist), Wicker (fursuit maker), xodingo

Charity: Save Our Tazzie Devils (A$5,000)

Chairmen or Organizers: Pete Smith (CynWolfe)

ConFurgence 2014 banner. Art by AlectorFencer. Used with permission.

ConFuzzled

Furs in England and Wales began holding house parties and furmeets as early as 1992, with some calling themselves conventions; but ConFuzzled, the first inarguable British furry convention, was organized starting in 2005 by FurbleFox and a committee of BritFurs who felt that it was time for British furry fans to have a regular convention. Organizers from EuroFurence to Further Confusion and other conventions offered advice and help. The ConFuzzled website went online in February 2007, followed by incorporation as ConFuzzled UK, a private non-profit company in March, a forum and FAQ in May, and *ConFuzzled Focus*, a magazine-style newsletter, in October. The permanent mascot from the opening of the website has been Brok the Badger, designed by Josef Zsapka (Tabbie). There has been a full range of panels, workshops, Art Show, Dealers' Den, dances, a Pawpet show, and games.

Name & Date	Theme	Location	Attendance	Parade
ConFuzzled 2008 June 20–23, 2008	Fursuiting	Manchester International Youth Hostel, Manchester, England	136	42
ConFuzzled 2009 May 22–25, 2009	Victorian Era England	Manchester International Youth Hostel, Manchester, England	182	50 (estimated)
ConFuzzled 2010 May 7–10, 2010	Science	Britannia Country House Hotel, Didsbury, Greater Manchester, England	346	100+
ConFuzzled 2011 May 6–9, 2011	The Roaring Twenties	Britannia Country House Hotel, Didsbury, Greater Manchester, England	499	?
ConFuzzled 2012 May 25–28, 2012	Hollywood: The Glitz & the Glamour	Barceló Hinckley Island Hotel, Hinckley, Leicestershire, England	726	?
ConFuzzled 2013 May 30–June 3, 2013	The Middle Ages: A Mediaeval Fayre	Barceló Hinckley Island Hotel, Hinckley, Leicestershire, England	872	?
ConFuzzled 2014 May 23–27, 2014	The World of Tomorrow	Birmingham Hilton Metropole, Birmingham, England	1,079	?
ConFuzzled 2015 May 22–26, 2015	Wonderland	Birmingham Hilton Metropole, Birmingham, England	1,223	?

Events

ConFuzzled 2008: BigBlueFox conducted a cinematic workshop on How To Film Furries. Unique events included the Pub Quiz, the Frankensuit where contestants are given fursuit materials and have one hour to construct a suit, and MotorFurs where attendees show off their vehicles. Memberships were £170. The conbook cover was by Tabbiefox. A T-shirt design contest picked AzraFox's art.

Guests of Honor: Karsten Auchter (BigBlueFox; German furry artist/fursuiter)
Charity: The Badger Trust (£1,610)
Chairmen or Organizers: Mike Francis (FurbleFox)

ConFuzzled 2009: The second ConFuzzled repeated many of the events of the previous year, and added extra gaming events, an anime talk, and a writing workshop. There were over 40 events, including the first UK Pawpet Show, a cartoon workshop led by Tabbiefox, and a talk by Cheetah on how to run a convention. The Pawpet Show featured an original story, "The Great James Mountbatten-

Windsor's Magnificent Zoological Extravaganza; or, The Mancunian Play," with custom-built puppets. The conbook cover was by Spirit Creations, and the T-shirt was by Keovi.

Guests of Honor: Tabbiefox (furry artist), Cheetah (EuroFurence chairman)

Charity: The Badger Trust, Manchester Dogs Home (£2,000)

Chairmen or Organizers: Mike Francis (FurbleFox)

ConFuzzled 2010: The attendees came from 17 different countries. Many events were based on the Science theme, including a talk by a physicist from the Large Hadron Collider. There were Furrylmpics, Fure-okie, and a WikiFur pub quiz contests. The highlight of ConFuzzled 2010 was the charity auction. The opportunity to feed wild cats in a non-public reserve located in Kent went for £550. The final item was a tablecloth that TaniDaReal had drawn a picture upon. Bidding started at £50, and got into a bidding war between Beshon and staffer Colifox. Beshon got it for £2,000. The conbook cover was by Roarey Raccoon, and the T-shirt was by TaniDaReal.

ConFuzzled mascot, Brok the Badger. Art by Skaifox. Used with permission.

Guests of Honor: Tanja Freese (TaniDaReal, German furry artist/fursuiter)

Charity: Wildlife Heritage Foundation (£5,248)

Chairmen or Organizers: Matthew Hood (Matt Lion)

ConFuzzled 2011: The 499 attendees came from 20 countries throughout Europe, Australia, and North America, making ConFuzzled 2011 the second largest (after EuroFurence) furry convention outside the U.S. to that time. The conbook cover was by Nanook123. The T-shirt was by John "The Gneech" Robey, who also did a commemorative mug.

Guests of Honor: John "The Gneech" Robey (furry cartoonist)

Charity: International Otter Survival Fund (£10,000)

Chairmen or Organizers: Matthew Hood (Matt Lion)

ConFuzzled 2012: The ConFuzzled website announced that the new venue was twice as large as the old one, and that the ConFuzzled attendees would enjoy exclusive access. The 726 attendees came from 23 countries, including the previous plus Israel. There was a range of registrations from attending only for £75 to £260 for lodging, meals, the T-shirt, a limited-edition comic book, and all other extras. The conbook cover was by TaniDaReal and the T-shirt was by Rizzorat.

Guests of Honor: Colson Grainger, Mangusu (furry artists, fursuiters/fursuit makers)

Charity: Nuneaton Warwickshire Wildlife Sanctuary (£7,755)

Chairmen or Organizers: Matthew Hood (Matt Lion)

ConFuzzled 2013: ConFuzzled 2013 was extended to five days. The 872 attendees came from 25 countries, including the previous plus New Zealand and the United Arab Emirates. The venue was maxed out, and the nearby Hilton Leicester was designated an overflow hotel, with free transport between hotels. It was announced at the Closing Ceremony that ConFuzzled would move to the larger Birmingham Hilton Metropole for 2014. In addition to the regular registrations, an additional £10 Pet Passport allowed attendees to bring one pet. Due to controversy, attendees were allowed to bring cats without charge. The conbook cover was by Johis, and the T-shirt was by Gabapple.

Guests of Honor: Melissa "Gab" Douglas (furry artist/author), Kyell Gold (furry author)

Charity: STA Ferret Rescue (£11,484)
Chairmen or Organizers: Matthew Hood (Matt Lion)

ConFuzzled 2014: The 1,079 attendees were from 29 countries, including the previous plus Chile, Malaysia, Singapore, and South Africa. Registrations ranged from £70 to £540 for full accommodation in the hotel's de luxe suites including meals and use of the hotel's gym and pool. The conbook cover was by Greevixor, and the T-shirt was by Rick Griffin.
Guests of Honor: Rick Griffin (furry cartoonist), Alexis Rudd (fursuit maker, puppeteer)
Charity: The Cat Survival Trust (£14,265)
Chairmen or Organizers: Matthew Hood (Matt Lion)

ConFuzzled 2015: The theme emphasized exploring "the mysterious and peculiar insanity contained within the works of Lewis Carroll." The conbook cover was by AlectorFencer, and the T-shirt was by Henrieke.
Guests of Honor: Henrieke Goorhuis (Henrieke, furry artist), Jeff "Yak" Minter (games industry)
Charity: Fat Fluffs Rabbit Rescue and Rehome (£13,552)
Chairmen or Organizers: Matthew Hood (Matt Lion)

Conifur Northwest

Conifur Northwest was the first furry convention for the Pacific Northwest area, organized by James Birdsell (Tibo) and Dan Canaan (FlintHoof) of Seattle. Its permanent motto was "Furries in Seattle!," and a permanent policy was that the artist Guest of Honor designed the T-shirt, which was made in three cloth colors for staff, security, and for sale to attendees. When Conifur Northwest was permanently cancelled after 2005, it was replaced by both the short-lived All Fur Fun in Spokane from 2007 to 2009, and by the successful RainFurrest in Seattle from 2007 to 2015.

Name & Date	*Location*	*Attendance*
Conifur Northwest 1998 September 4–7, 1998	SeaTac Clarion Hotel, SeaTac, WA	275 (estimated)
Conifur Northwest 99 October 1–3, 1999	Best Western Executive Inn, Fife, WA	330
Conifur Northwest 2000 November 3–5, 2000	Best Western Executive Inn, Fife, WA	310
Conifur Northwest 2001 October 26–28, 2001	Best Western Executive Inn, Fife, WA	412
Conifur Northwest 2002 October 4–6, 2002	Sheraton Tacoma Convention Center, Tacoma, WA	460
Conifur Northwest 2003 September 26–28, 2003	Sheraton Tacoma Convention Center, Tacoma, WA	523
Conifur Northwest 2004 September 24–26, 2004	Seattle Tacoma Hotel and Convention Center, Tacoma, WA	436
Conifur Northwest 2005 October 21–23, 2005	SeaTac Radisson Airport, SeaTac, WA	525

Events

Conifur Northwest 1998: CN1998 was held in the SeaTac Clarion Hotel in SecTac, Washington, a suburb of Seattle dominated by the Seattle-Tacoma International Airport. The Dealers Room was also the main socializing area. The writers' group of *Tales of the Tai-Pan Universe*, which was edited and published in Seattle, had a strong presence centered around their dealer's table; they also hosted one of the night-time parties. The hotel was memorable for its small size (there was only one room for "clinics," which became the hotel bar at night), and for its staff's inexperience with conventions. The night manager kept stopping fans going at night from one room party to another to ask why they weren't going to sleep. Most attendees were unhappy about the lack of other restaurants within walking distance. The conbook cover was by Diana "Nootka" Vick.

Guests of Honor: Diana Vick (local furry artist)

Charity: None

Chairmen or Organizers: James Birdsall (Tibo); Dan Canaan (FlintHoof)

Conifur Northwest 99: The second Conifur Northwest expanded to two clinic rooms, a much larger Dealer's Den, and an Artists' Alley. The convention tried to hold a Saturday evening Pizza and Movie Event with ordered-in pizzas,

Conifur Northwest 1998 conbook. Art by Diana Vick (Nootka). Used with permission.

but the hotel demanded that the pizzas be supplied by its own kitchen (four slices for $3), which were dreadful. The hotel would not allow any animals larger than ferrets for insurance reasons, which was fine for ConiFur Northwest's two caged ferret mascots, Mayhem & Chaos (Tibo's and FlintHoof's pets), but prevented the convention from holding any exotic animal live-drawing classes as Further Confusion had. A Video Room was run by Phil Bolton, with a Saturday-morning free cereal breakfast. The attendees included Darrel Exline, promoting the "new" ConFurence. The Art Show sales were $13,000+, over double last year's. The highest price was $810 for "Avatar" by Heather Bruton. Attendees were pleased with over a half-dozen eateries within two blocks. Organizers Tibo and FlintHoof talked about incorporating as a non-profit organization, as was becoming common among furry conventions.

Guests of Honor: Jimmy Chin (furry cartoonist and fursuiter)

Charity: None

Chairmen or Organizers: James Birdsall (Tibo); Dan Canaan (FlintHoof)

Conifur Northwest 2000: Attendees were invited to bring their pet ferrets to romp with Mayhem and Chaos. (The hotel required a small pet deposit.) Friday's main event was a Furry Pictionary; Saturday's was the Masquerade. On Saturday night Mitchell Beiro presented his "Midnight Over Minerva" featuring Minerva Mink from WB's TV *Animanacs*. The video program included a bootleg video print of *The Fearless Four*, a German animated feature loosely based on the Brementown Musicians that Warner Bros. (which dubbed it) was suppressing in America; this may have been its only American screening. The convention inaugurated an Ice Cream Social. GoH Roy Pounds, II contributed a different design for each T-shirt, and the front cover to the 36-page conbook.

Guests of Honor: Roy D. Pounds, II (furry artist)

Charity: None
Chairmen or Organizers: James Birdsall (Tibo); Dan Canaan (FlintHoof)

Conifur Northwest 2001: The fourth Conifur Northwest introduced a newsletter, the *Daily Howl*, and a charity. A Charity Auction raised $1,374 for it; donations brought the total to $1,550. Programming was divided into three clinics; writing and artwork, costuming including fursuit making, and social/fan activities. Daytime events included the Charity Auction, a Furry Pictionary, an Artists' Ambush, and a Saturday morning free cereal-&-milk breakfast with Saturday morning cartoons on video, while nighttime events included filk singing, an ice cream social, a Friday night dance and a Saturday Fursuit Beauty Pageant. Max BlackRabbit's cartoon character, Zigzag the zebra-striped skunk, was featured in the convention's artwork. A fourth color of T-shirts was added; green for the Gofurs. The most memorable event was the early-morning fire alarm that required the evacuation of the hotel. Fans, many in pajamas, shivered on the hotel's lawn in freezing weather while the fire department traced the alarm to a burst water heater and flood on the hotel's third floor.
Guests of Honor: Malcolm Earle (Max BlackRabbit; furry artist)
Charity: Washington State Ferret Rescue and Shelter ($1,550)
Chairmen or Organizers: James Birdsall (Tibo); Dan Canaan (FlintHoof)

Conifur Northwest 2002: The program featured old favorites Furry Pictionary, the Friday night dance, Saturday morning free breakfast cereal & Saturday morning TV cartoons, an ice cream social, the Saturday night fursuit masquerade/pageant, a charity auction, and romping with Mayhem & Chaos, the ferret mascots, in their cage in the Dealers Room at any time. A new event was the Fursuit Challenge, where a team of volunteers raced to construct a fursuit of Nootka, the fursuit mascot, before the convention ended. A TV crew from France's ARTE (Association Relative à la Télévision Européenne) cultural network took footage for an eight-minute segment about furries for a children's entertainment program for French and German TV. The move to a larger hotel took Conifur Northwest by surprise! The Best Western Executive Inn went out of business two months before the convention, in August. The hotel was franchised, and the local owner skipped town with all its money. The hotel staff did its best to go out of business in an orderly fashion, including booking Conifur into the larger and usually more expensive Sheraton Tacoma at no increase in price; but Conifur did have to share it with two other conventions and a wedding party. The wedding party and a bankers' convention kept to themselves, but the elementary school hockey players were fascinated by the fursuits and kept asking the furs about their tails and furry ears.

About a week after the convention, *The Stranger*, a free Seattle alternate/entertainment newspaper, published an "exposé" about it by a staffer who had not actually attended. He apparently bribed a hotel employee to tell him about the convention. A report of this on Flayrah drew a dozen outraged comments, but the article was really mild, saying approximately, "I went to a furry convention expecting a lot of wild, kinky sex, but the furries were just weird but boring people."
Guests of Honor: Marci McAdam (furry artist)
Charity: The Washington State Ferret Rescue & Shelter ($1,500, estimated)
Chairmen or Organizers: James Birdsall (Tibo); Dan Canaan (FlintHoof)

Conifur Northwest 2003: Longstanding directors Tibo and FlintHoof stepped down. Tibo became the head of Technical Services. The good news was that Conifur Northwest did not have to share the hotel with another convention this year; the bad news was that, since Conifur did not have the special circumstance of having an old contract to be honored, the Sheraton Tacoma charged its usual rates which were considerably higher. The hotel management was not as friendly as the Best Western's had been; Tibo: "This was the hotel where we discovered why our contract needed to have a clause that the restrooms should remain open and unlocked, for example." The Art Show auction brought $11,000. The *Daily Howl* newsletter was continued. The second Fursuit Challenge, to construct a ferret mascot, was successful. A *Yiff: The Card Game* was played for the first and only time. The 2003 T-shirt was by Grrrwolf.

Guests of Honor: Brent Spotswood (Grrrwolf; furry artist), Chuck Melville (artist/writer)
Charity: Washington State Ferret Rescue and Shelter ($3,011)
Chairmen or Organizers: Shandower

Conifur Northwest 2004: The main events were the Furry Pictionary, the Ice Cream Social, Uncle Kage's Story Hour, and 2, the Ranting Gryphon's rant. The *Daily Howl* newsletter was continued. Many lights were out in the Dealers' Room and the hotel refused to replace them, requiring the con committee to substitute its stage lighting. The T-shirt was by Chad Krueger.

Guests of Honor: Chad Krueger (cartoonist), Edd Vick (s-f fan/furry comic-book publisher)
Charity: Washington Ferret Rescue & Shelter ($2,248)
Chairmen or Organizers: Shandower

Conifur Northwest 2005: Programming included the Art Show, Dealer's Den, and Artists' Alley, Video and Gaming Rooms, the usual clinics, an Ice Cream Social, Fursuit Parade, performances by 2, the Ranting Gryphon and Uncle Kage, the Furry Pictionary, masquerade, dances, etc., and with Mayhem & Chaos. Author Michael Bergey held a reading of his novel, *New Coyote*. The 48-page conbook had a cover by David Hopkins. There was no charity, since the Washington State Ferret Rescue was no longer in existence.

This was the final Conifur Northwest. The Sea-Tac Radisson Airport Hotel was torn down in February 2006. Attempts to find another hotel for 2006 were unsuccessful. In May 2006 FlintHoof announced that the convention was cancelled for 2006 but would return in 2007. However, in February 2007 the Conifur staff donated all of its assets to the new All Fur Fun convention in Spokane, and announced the dissolution of Conifur Northwest for good.

Guests of Honor: David Hopkins (furry internet cartoonist)
Charity: None
Chairmen or Organizers: Dan Caanan (FlintHoof)

CritterConDiego

CritterConDiego was organized by Darrel Exline of The ConFurence Group, as a furry mini-con to complement the Comic-Con International, within easy walking distance of the San Diego Convention Center and on the Comic-Con's bus route. It was deliberately planned for the evening, after the Comic-Con's Dealers' Room was closed for the day. Events included snack food, videos, fursuit dancing, and swimming in the hotel's pool. A dealer's room was also the socializing area. There was no programming; CritterCon Diego was for relaxed socializing, and or furry dealers who did not want to pay the Comic-Con's table prices.

Name & Date	Location	Attendance
CritterConDiego 1 July 21–22, 2000	Holiday Inn on the Bay, San Diego, CA	200 (estimated)
CritterConDiego 2 July 20–21, 2001	Holiday Inn on the Bay, San Diego, CA	240
CritterConDiego 3 August 2–3, 2002	Holiday Inn on the Bay, San Diego, CA	175

Events

CritterConDiego 1: Memberships were only $5 for both evenings, and were not limited to Comic-Con members. There were some preregistrations before the Comic-Con, but mostly Critter

ConDiego was for Comic-Con attendees who came by in the evening and joined at the door. Attendance over the two evenings was about 200.

Chairmen or Organizers: Darrel L. Exline

CritterConDiego 2: CritterConDiego was again "next to" San Diego's Comic-Con International, from 7:00 p.m. to 1:00 a.m. on the two evenings. Chairman Darrel Exline announced in advance that if they could get 260 attendees at the $5 admissions, and sell 40 dealers' tables at $10 each, the convention would break even. They almost made it. There was a miniature Art Show.

Chairmen or Organizers: Darrel L. Exline

CritterConDiego 3: CritterConDiego, as usual, was held during the evening on two days of the Comic-Con International. The hours were changed to 6:00 p.m. to 1:00 a.m. Memberships were $8 with fursuiters getting in free. Tables were now $15.

This was the last CritterConDiego, due to the cancellation of the ConFurence in April 2003, before that year's Comic-Con International.

Chairmen or Organizers: Darrel L. Exline

EAST

EAST (Episches Abfeiern Streunender Tiere), a.k.a. EAST-CON, was formed for East German furs after Tropicon ended. It was decided that, in addition to replacing Tropicon, EAST should gather all the small furmeets in eastern Germany into a youth hostel. The acronym stands for Epic Convention of Stray Animals. EAST has a mascot, Kolja Wostock, a tigerfox who is featured on most EAST posters. There is no Fursuit Parade, but fursuit walks are scheduled in a public area of the towns.

Name & Date	*Theme*	*Location*	*Attendance*	*Furwalk*
EAST 1 September 8–11, 2011	Epic Convention of Stray Animals	Youth hostel Nebra (Unstrut), Sachsen-Anhalt, Germany	37	12 (Nebra)
EAST 2 September 27–30, 2012	Furverance	Youth hostel Falkenstein, Harz Mountains, Germany	57	24 (Wernigerode)
EAST 3 September 19–22, 2013	The Kingdom Far Far Away	Youth hostel Falkenstein, Harz Mountains, Germany	95	39 (Aschersleben town and Zoo)
EAST 4 July 24–27, 2014	Furs in Space	Jugendherberge Dessau-Rosslau, Sachsen-Anhalt, Germany	114	55 (Dessau)
EAST V July 22–26, 2015	The EAST Clinic—Division V	Jugendherberge Dessau-Rosslau, Sachsen-Anhalt, Germany	138	65 (Lutherstadt Wittenberg)

Events

EAST 1: Events included a Sachsen Fur Dance, Summer Outdoor Camping Without Mother (SOCWM), karaoke, an Iron Artist contest, and a game show. The T-shirt was by Konu Eikuku Hentaru.

Chairmen or Organizers: Konu Eikuku Hentaru, LeTigre, Ray, Leu, Shorty

EAST 2: The venue was the Falkenstein youth hostel, about two or three kilometers outside the town. The program was repeated with the addition of a volleyball tournament, a paper chase, an art auction, fursuiting, and more. The T-shirt was by Thearmjing.

Guests of Honor: Changer the Elder
Chairmen or Organizers: Konu Eikuku Hentaru, LeTigre, Ray, Leu, Shorty

EAST 3: The events were repeated. The theme was fairy tales. EAST 3 reached its hostel's maximum attendance. The fursuitwalk was in the town of Aschersleben, with a separate fursuitwalk for charity in the Zoo. The T-shirt was by Kocur (Patrick the Dog).
Guests of Honor: AlectorFencer
Chairmen or Organizers: Konu Eikuku Hentaru, LeTigre, Ray, Leu, Shorty

EAST 4: East 4 moved to the larger Hostel Dessau-Rosslau, a two-story guest house with 150 beds in 39 rooms, about twenty minutes' walk from the town of Dessau in the forests of Saxony-Anhalt. The fursuitwalk was through the town. The T-shirt was by Lizardlars.
Guests of Honor: Furryratchet
Chairmen or Organizers: Konu Eikuku Hentaru, LeTigre, Ray, Leu, toranor, Pawel Lemurr

EAST V: EAST V was extended from 4 to 5 days by popular demand. The medical theme supposed Division 5 within the EAST clinic, a furry hospital. The division specialized in psychiatry. The program included an Art Show and Dealers' Den, a beach volleyball tournament, a fursuitwalk through the streets of Lutherstadt Wittenberg, furdances on Thursday and Saturday, a campfire, a Tropical fursuit singalong, a Dance Dance Revolution contest, and more. There was a fursuit lounge for the furwalkers in the Lutherstadt Wittenberg youth hostel. The T-shirt was by Niuxi.
Guests of Honor: Lizardlars
Chairmen or Organizers: Konu Eikuku Hentaru, LeTigre, Ray, Leu, toranor, Pawel Lemurr

EuroFurence

The EuroFurence was started by German fans who had heard about American fans' ConFurences. They were originally intended to move around all over Europe, but after a couple in other countries, they evolved into an international convention held in Germany, partly due to the legal difficulties in moving across national borders, and partly to other European countries starting their own furry conventions and furmeets. As the EuroFurence has grown, it has moved from a rural farmhouse to the largest hotel in Berlin. There is some concern as to where it can move if it continues to grow.

Name & Date	Theme	Location	Attendance	Parade
EuroFurence June 30–July 3, 1995	none	Gerritt Heitsch's parents' vacation farm, Kaiser-Wilhelm-Koog, Germany	19	none
EuroFurence 2 July 18–22, 1996	none	Rydsskolan college dormitory, Linköping, Sweden	35	none
EuroFurence 3 August 21–24, 1997	none	Freizeitanlage Seeräuber, Bodstedt, Germany	59	none
EuroFurence 4 August 1–5, 1998	none	Ferme de Jean holiday camp, Heeze, the Netherlands	80 (estimated)	none
EuroFurence 5 July 22–25, 1999	none	Juggendorf am Müggelsee youth camp, Berlin, Germany	117	none
EuroFurence 6 August 10–13, 2000	none	Jugendherberge Göttingen, Göttingen, Germany	160	no records kept
EuroFurence 7 July 22–25, 2001	none	Jugendherberge Freusburg youth hostel, Freusburg Castle, Kirchen, Germany	230 (estimated)	no records kept

EuroFurence

Name & Date	Theme	Location	Attendance	Parade
EuroFurence 8 August 15–18, 2002	Furry Intelligence Agency	Jugendherberge Hilders-Oberbernhards youth hostel, Oberbernhards, Germany	260 (estimated)	no records kept
EuroFurence 9 August 21–24, 2003	Cunning Little Vixens	Sportareál Samopše sports center, Středočeský kraj, Czech Republic	165 (estimated)	no records kept
EuroFurence 10 August 26–29, 2004	EFX: The Movie	Jugendherberge Biggesee youth hostel, Olpe, North Rhine-Westphalia, Germany	295	no records kept
EuroFurence XI July 21–24, 2005	Songs of the Old Ages	Nuremburg Castle, Nuremberg, Bavaria, Germany	380	no records kept
EuroFurence XII August 23–27, 2006	The Hounds of Blackwhite Castle	Nuremburg Castle, Nuremberg, Bavaria, Germany	405	no records kept
EuroFurence 13 September 5–9, 2007	The Unlucky Thirteen	Ringberg Resort Hotel, Suhl (in the Thuringian Forest), Germany	585	no records kept
EuroFurence 14 August 27–31, 2008	From Dusk Till Dawn	Ringberg Resort Hotel, Suhl, Germany	777	no records kept
EuroFurence 15 August 26–30, 2009	1001 Arabian Nights	Ringberg Resort Hotel, Suhl, Germany	911	no records kept
EuroFurence 16 September 1–5, 2010	Serengeti	The Maritim Hotel, Magdeburg, Germany	973	216
EuroFurence 17 August 17–21, 2011	Kung Fur Hustle	The Maratim Hotel, Magdeburg, Germany	1,066	no records kept
EuroFurence 18 August 29– September 2, 2012	Animalia Romana	The Maratim Hotel, Magdeburg, Germany	1,232	335
EuroFurence 19 August 21–25, 2013	Aloha Hawaii	The Maratim Hotel, Magdeburg, Germany	1,376	no records kept
EuroFurence 20 August 20–24, 2014	Crime Scene Berlin	The Estrel Hotel, Berlin, Germany	2,015	no records kept
EuroFurence 21 August 19–23, 2015	Greenhouse World	The Estrel Hotel, Berlin, Germany	2,095	no records kept

Events

EuroFurence: The first EuroFurence was organized over the Internet by Tes-Tui-H'ar and unci_narynin as a house party at Heitsch's parents' vacation farm in Kaiser-Wilhelm-Koog, Schleswig-Holstein, Germany (near Hamburg; where the Elbe River flows into the North Sea). Heitsch and Köhler hoped to get ten European fans; they got eighteen, which maxed out Heitsch's parents' farmhouse. The attendees included ten from Germany, five from Britain, and one each from Denmark, Finland, and Sweden. Activities included watching furry videos, drawing in each others' sketchbooks, and a walk in the tidelands of the North Sea. There was a catered meal of potatoes and onion soup. The first EuroFurence had badges, but there was no T-shirt.

Chairmen or Organizers: Gerritt Heitsch (Tes-Tui-H'ar), Tobias Köhler (unci_narynin)

EuroFurence 2: The venue was the Rydsskolan college dormitory in Ryd, a residential neighborhood of Linköping, Sweden used to housing students of Linköping University. The chairman and the rest of the committee were students of the University. The convention was again mostly an informal meet-&-greet of European Internet furries meeting for the first time in person, but attendance almost doubled. Memberships were 300 SEK, with a steep discount to attendees buying and cooking their own meals. (The Rydsskolan dorm had kitchen facilities.) Programming included a martial arts demonstration, sketching, and a trip to Linköping's Kolmården Zoo. There were several furry hall costumes. Thomas Hagenfeldt (Chama) premiered a EuroFurence Hymn. There was a EuroFurence 2 T-shirt by Antti Remes (Nimbl).

Chairmen or Organizers: Martin Gauffin (DivineVixen), Henrik Isacson (Snout)

EuroFurence 3: EuroFurence 3 was supposed to be held in Bingen, Germany, but plans collapsed due to the fan chairman's inexperience. Veteran EuroFurence attendee Cheetah took over and saved EuroFurence 3 at the last minute, but the best venue that he could get with no advance notice was a former GDR youth camp on the Baltic coast at Bodstedt, (former East) Germany. The site was described sarcastically as having "the typical East European charm," but it was the first EuroFurence organized like an American fan convention. Membership was DM80, which included breakfast and dinner every day. The attendees were from eleven countries. The first Art Show and Dealers' Room were set up in the camp gymnasium, the latter with a professional furry dealer: Martin Dudman of United Publications from Britain. A room that could be darkened (and was stifling!) became a video room. Each attendee got a separate photograph taken, and was proclaimed a guest of honor, for publication in a convention final report. There was a "goodie pack" of ConFurence leftovers from Mark Merlino, although the reports do not say whether there was enough for everyone to get something. There were seven entries in a EuroFurence 3 T-shirt contest; the members voted both Thomas Mezösi and Terrie Smith winners. Attendees included the first EuroFurence fursuiter, Skunki. EuroFurence 3 was the first to have an amateurish Program Book; cover artist not credited. The food got good marks, and there was favorable though confused press coverage in the local newspaper, the *Ostsee Zeitung*, which apparently thought that the EuroFurence was a convention of Internet rather than furry fans. (It was both, of course.) At the end of the convention, the attendees took up a collection of DM500 for Cheetah's travel expenses to ConFurence 9, as an expression of thanks for a well-run con. Cheetah even published a detailed financial report after the convention; it made a DM418 profit, which Cheetah turned over to the next year's chairman.

Chairmen or Organizers: Sven Tegethoff (Cheetah) (unofficial)

EuroFurence 4: The site, a holiday camp near Eindhoven, was located by Samarindus, with the assistance of Naros. It was highly unpopular for its communal showers that were constantly backing up and flooding the guest rooms. Attendees had to clean out and dry the site in the middle of the night. The programming included a continuous video room, a Saturday evening barbecue, and a Sunday dealers' den and art show. Fursuiters were concentrated on Monday. A whiteboard was provided for art workshop seminars. A lot of free time was left for visiting tourist attractions around Eindhoven, including the Efteling amusement park and the Beekse Bergen safari park. Attendees were encouraged to bring musical instruments for impromptu jam sessions. The T-shirt contest was a tie between Antti Remes (Nimbl) from Finland (front) and Unicorn from the Netherlands (back), but there was so much controversy over Unicorn's design of a marijuana-smoking skunk with the caption, "Welcome to Holland, Have Some Skunk," that only Unicorn's "Eurofurence IV" title lettering was used on the shirt's back. Unicorn printed his own T-shirts with the whole design and sold them unofficially.

Chairmen or Organizers: Samarindus

EuroFurence 5: The program included a Thursday night relax-around-the-campfire; a Friday Pet Auction and Fur Dance; a Saturday Art Show, Barbecue, and evening Furry Live Music; and author readings, SIG meetings, workshops, and an evening furry video room throughout the convention. EuroFurence 5 ended Sunday early afternoon, with unofficial post-con activities. Aside from the convention activities, EuroFurence 5 was a semi-disaster. It was at the Juggendorf am Müggelsee youth camp in Berlin, Germany—what had been East Berlin, and was still far from West Berlin standards. The cabins were in a poor state, with some attendees almost getting electrocuted by bad wiring in the showers. There were complaints of mice in the cabins and that the mattresses smelled of urine. The camp food was bad. Bad weather (which could not be blamed on the camp) kept attendees from swimming in the popular Müggelsee lake. But the 1999 EuroFurence was the first to have a guest of honor. The 20-page Program Book (in English) had front & back covers by Margaret Carspecken. Memberships were DM135 to April 1 and DM160 at the convention, but so many attendees waited to join at the convention that up to the last day it looked like it would lose considerable money. The T-shirt design contest was won by Richard T. Matheson (FoxSTAR) and Unicorn. An unexpected highlight of the convention was a BSR municipal trash-collection truck driving across the lawn to avoid conventioneers' parked cars along the road, and sinking into the soft ground. The truck was stuck for several hours until a BSR vehicle with a winch could get it out, providing the convention with a popular attraction.

The convention committee was Cheetah, Andreas Jaekel (Tabalon), and Stephan Bartels (Jumpy). Because of the expected financial loss, which the committee would otherwise have been personally responsible for, a group of fans led by Cheetah incorporated earlier in the year as Eurofurence e.V., a social organization to organize Furry events not limited to the EuroFurence. A year later, a 125-minute EuroFurence 5 documentary video was released.

Guest of Honor: Lisanne Norman (s-f author)
Chairmen or Organizers: Sven Tegethoff (Cheetah)

EuroFurence 6: EuroFurence 6 was almost not held due to a lack of suitable venues. Heribert Vogt (Raschkar) found the Göttingen youth hostel in February. The committee was Cheetah (chairman), Jumpy (assistant chairman and cashier), and Tabalon (administrative assistant), operating as Eurofurence e.V. Attendees were urged to preregister to make sure that there would be room for them, since the hostel was limited to 150 guests. The EuroFurence practically filled it, with an attendance of 149. The total attendance, including the committee, was 160. Memberships were DM200. There was no Guest-of-Honor this year. There were 16 entrants in the T-shirt design contest, which was won by Accipiter and Nimbl. Events included the first DoPE (Department of Pawpetry Entertainment) show titled *Lionel Scritchie's Dormitory*, involving four furry hand puppets dancing & singing to (mostly) Dr. Demento records. Part of the show involved two ferrets, Peek and Poke, breaking into a chocolate factory. One of them started throwing miniature chocolate bars into the audience, which retaliated, starting an impromptu chocolate war. The cover of the 24-page Program book was a collaboration between ten fan artists. There was a EuroFurence 2000 poster by Cairyn. The Göttingen youth hostel was popular for being clean and modern, with many shops nearby.

Chairmen or Organizers: Sven Tegethoff (Cheetah)

EuroFurence 7: EuroFurence 7 was the first to have a full furry convention setup and program, with an Art Show, Dealer's Den, a Fursuit Parade, the Pawpet show, a full stage setup, and convention security. The Jugendherberge Freusburg was a youth hostel housed within a 950-year-old castle at Kirchen, in the Rhineland-Palatinate in Germany. Almost half the attendees were from outside Germany. The barbecue and campfire (including amateur music and sing-alongs) were moved up to Thursday night. The program included a fursuit contest, the second DoPE variety show (*Medieval Madness*) themed to the castle, a storytellers' circle, and two new events; an Animal Rights SIG, and a World Tree roleplaying session. There were 29 entries in the T-shirt design contest, which was won by Christian Hefele (SewerRat) and Tanja Freese (Vitani Da Real). The 40-page program book had a cover by Dominik Walter (Xan). The convention broke even financially.

Guests of Honor: Mark Merlino (Sylys Sable; ConFurence founder), Lisanne Norman (Hyperkitty; s-f author), Lee Strom (Chairo; fursuiter, puppeteer, and member of the Further Confusion staff)
Chairmen or Organizers: Sven Tegethoff (Cheetah)

EuroFurence 8: EuroFurence 8 had a full program of panels, workshops, Special Interest Groups, and the first EuroFurence theme. The "Sweet Treats" workshop by Fjordwolf, on how to make tiramisu and cream cakes, was especially popular. There were two Internet Rooms, a Sponsors'

Lounge, and a Fursuit Lounge, in addition to the usual Art Show and Dealers' Den. A frequent shuttle service was set up between the hostel and the nearest DB train station at Fulda, forty kilometers away (a one-hour round trip). The third DoPE puppet show was titled *F.I.A.* around the theme. "The president of the Furry Intelligence Agency decides to remove the perverted subjects from the furry fandom. Especially Poke the sex-crazed big-mouthed ferret is on his list. [...]" There was a round-the-clock Video Room, a Thursday afternoon barbeque, and campfires every night. The closing event was the Saturday night FurDance, with Karsten Auchter (BigBlueFox) and Loewi as DJs. 24 designs were submitted for the T-shirt contest, which was won by Philipp Peteranderl (Silber) and Tanja Freese (Vitani Da Real). The 40-page program book (cover by Dominik Walter/Xan) came in a dark blue folder labeled "Surveillance Report—For your eyes only." Cheetah, Jumpy, and Tabalon were joined on the convention committee by Richard Wagensveld (Watani) and Maik Duismann (Kralle).

Guests of Honor: Dr. Samuel C. Conway (Uncle Kage)

Chairmen or Organizers: Sven Tegethoff (Cheetah)

EuroFurence 9: This was the last EuroFurence held outside Germany, in central Bohemia. The move outside Germany was due to the popular demand to hold it in a different country, to make the EuroFurence more genuinely "European." Again there was no Guest of Honor. Due to its Czech location, Rudolf Těsnohlídek's text and Leoš Janáček's operatic *The Cunning Little Vixen* were emphasized as much as possible. EuroFurence 9 had its usual program, scaled down for the expected lower attendance outside Germany. Martin Dudman from United Publications in England gave a demonstration of its "Tank Vixens" card game. The sports center consisted of four buildings so old that they were unusable, the dining hall, and five new buildings where all events were held. It had facilities for the usual barbeque and evening campfires. The center was plagued by poor technical equipment. Chairman Cheetah was almost electrocuted by the poor grounding of a supporting beam in the main tent at a nighttime show. Uncle Kage coined the word "Czechnology" for it. The fourth DoPE pawpet puppet show was *Ceška Paradisa*. The T-shirt design contest was won by Maja Wrzosek (Bloodhound Omega) and Santi Rowe (Dogz R. Barkin), out of eleven submittals. Tess Garman (Kenket) did the cover of the 24-page program book.

Chairmen or Organizers: Sven Tegethoff (Cheetah)

EuroFurence 10: Many members, including committee members, were hours late in getting to EFX because of a serious accident that closed the Wiehltal Bridge to traffic. The fifth DoPE pawpet show was titled *The Phantom of the Pawpet Show*. The 40-page conbook was the first to feature a wrap-around color cover (by Kenket), and a gallery of all EuroFurence T-shirts, front & back, from EF2 to 10 (EF1 did not have a T-shirt). The T-shirt contest was won by Karoline Baumwolf (Alpha_Ki) and Tanja Freese (TaniDaReal).

Guests of Honor: Timothy Albee (the director/cinematographer of the CGI *Kaze, Ghost Warrior*, the first "feature" to feature a furry)

Chairmen or Organizers: Sven Tegethoff (Cheetah)

EuroFurence XI: EuroFurence XI had 77 sponsors. Because of the 1,000-year-old castle location, there was a larger number than usual of attendees in "medieval" clothing or costumes. The Dealers' Den was renamed the Dealers' Alley due to room constraints. Because of musician GoH Heather Alexander, the programming emphasized musical events, and there was a history of furry music in European fandom in the conbook. The theme was interpreted by puppets in the Pawpet Show, *Songs of the Old Ages*. The first EuroFurence Fursuit Parade and contest was held. The 42-page conbook had a color cover by Timothy Albee. The T-shirt contest was won by Dagmar Pasekova (Olven) and Karoline Baumwolf (Alpha_Ki).

Guests of Honor: Heather Alexander (Celtic musician)

Chairmen or Organizers: Sven Tegethoff (Cheetah)

EuroFurence 12/XII: Cheetah posed this year as the Master of Ceremonies for the Baron of Blackwhite Castle. The attendees again included Uncle Kage and 2, the Ranting Gryphon. Uncle Kage's parents celebrated their 50th wedding anniversary at EuroFurence XII. The Wednesday evening grand opening included a big barbecue. Friday included the fursuit parade and the Art Show auction. The theme was featured in the DoPE Pawpet Show, *The Hounds of Blackwhite Castle*. The 42-page conbook had a front cover by Dark Natasha and a back cover by Dagmar Pasekova (Olven). The T-shirt design contest was won by Olven and TaniDaReal. The EuroFurence staff included twenty "core" members and many volunteers. There was favorable news coverage in the *NordBayern Infonet*.

Guests of Honor: Dark Natasha (furry artist)
Chairmen or Organizers: Sven Tegethoff (Cheetah)

EuroFurence 13: G-o-H Steve Gallacci was unable to attend. There was a Musical G-o-H: Alexander James Adams. EuroFurence 13 initiated a charity. The hotel's convention area was decorated as a Las Vegas-style casino, in keeping with the convention's theme. Events included the traditional Dealers' Den and Art Show, workshops, the Fursuit Parade and Fursuit Dance, a rant by 2, the Ranting Gryphon, a rock concert featuring music composed by furry fans, the DoPE Pawpet puppet show featuring *The Unlucky Thirteen* theme, and "The Fauna Project," a stage event with a fursuited band during which there was an engagement. Uncle Kage conducted the Art Show auction. There was some controversy when EuroFurence 13 banned the erotic *Softpaw Magazine*, specializing in artwork of furry children in risqué poses, from sale in its Dealers' Den. The cover of the Con Book, by Blotch, was selected from four full-color entries by a panel of five judges. The EuroFurence had three articles in local newspapers. The 48-page conbook had a color front cover by Blotch. The T-shirt, commissioned rather than chosen by a contest, was by Olven.

Guests of Honor: Lance Ikegawa (fursuit maker), Steve Gallacci (founder of furry fandom/artist)
Charity: The Waldzoo Offenbach (€1,814)
Chairmen or Organizers: Sven Tegethoff (Cheetah)

EuroFurence 14: EuroFurence 14 was also known as HorrorFurence 14 because of the furry horror theme. Steve Gallacci was named GoH again because he had been unable to attend in 2007. The Ringberg Resort Hotel was filled within three hours after registration opened. The committee hurriedly arranged with the Golden Tulip Hotel to be the convention's overflow hotel, and for a taxi company to provide shuttle service. When the taxi company reneged, the Ringberg Resort Hotel provided a car and convention Security provided volunteer drivers. Numerous American furry notables attended and participated in the events and workshops. The events included Uncle Kage vs. 2, the Ranting Gryphon; a concert by Alexander James Adams; fursuit dances, the Fursuit Parade (no statistics were kept as to how many were in it), and photoshoots; the DoPE Pawpet Show, *Dreamcatchers*; and two charity auctions. Again the 64-page conbook cover was chosen by an Art Contest judged by a panel of judges (Blotch won again, with a wraparound cover), while the commissioned T-shirt was by Herbie Bearclaw. The program book was illustrated in full color. There was coverage of the convention in regional newspapers and TV.

Guests of Honor: Watts Martin (furry author), Steve Gallacci (founder of furry fandom/artist)
Charity: The British National Fox Welfare Society (€3,509.69 [about U.S.$5,200])
Chairmen or Organizers: Sven Tegethoff (Cheetah)

EuroFurence 15: Events included workshops, a Uncle Kage vs. 2 The Ranting Gryphon comedy act, a fursuit dance and the Parade, an Art auction, charity events, and the tenth DoPE (Department of Pawpetry Entertainment) show, *Operation Desert Snow*. The EuroFurence initiated a newszine, *The Daily Eurofurence*, edited by Michael Graf (Luxen). The 68-page conbook, with many full-color pages and double-page spreads illustrating the Arabian Nights theme, had a color front cover by

Angelique Verbeeten (Ashanti) and a back cover by Changer the Elder. There were two write-ups in the *Freies Wort Suhl*.
  Guests of Honor: Jimmy Chin (furry artist/fursuiter), Musical G-o-H Alexander James Adams
  Charity: The Wild Animal Park, Suhl, specifically for the Park's protection of the lynx (€2,938.53 [about $4,225])
  Chairmen or Organizers: Sven Tegithoff (Cheetah)

EuroFurence 16: The EuroFurence moved from its traditional venue of a tourist resort in a castle or small town to a four-star hotel in a large city. The Fursuit Parade left the hotel and marched around the city. In 2010 the EuroFurence passed the ConFurence as the longest-running furry convention. There were attendees from 32 countries. Events included the Dealers' Room and Art Show, workshops and games, a fursuit dance, games, theater, group photo, and a "Stage Fever" fursuit variety show, and the traditional Uncle Kage vs. 2 comedy presentation. The DoPE pawpet show was *Ogwambi*. There were 15 submissions for the conbook color front cover. The commissioned T-shirt was by Blotch. The 72-page program book, with many full-color pages and double-page spreads of the anthropomorphized animal life of the Serengeti, had a front cover by Qzurr and a back cover by Changer the Elder.
  Guests of Honor: Stan Sakai (comic-book creator, letterer)
  Charity: Gnadenhof Emmrich animal sanctuary (€5,771.15 [about $7,442]).
  Chairmen or Organizers: Sven Tegethoff (Cheetah)

EuroFurence 17: The *Bitter Lake* fursuit feature, sponsored by EuroFurence, had its premiere. Uncle Kage's Story Hour replaced the usual Uncle Kage vs. 2, the Ranting Gryphon because 2 could not attend. There was a Kung Fur Chinese martial-arts performance. The DoPE pawpet show was themed to the Year of the Rat. Recurring events included the Big Blue Dance, the Fursuit Parade, dance, and game show, the Art Show and auction, the Dealers Den, and the Dead Dog Party. The Maratim Hotel was booked to maximum capacity. The wraparound program book cover was by Blue_Panther, and the T-shirt by Keto.
  Guests of Honor: Jim Martin (puppeteer)
  Charity: Raubtier- und Exotenasyl e.V. (€8,720.55)
  Chairmen or Organizers: Sven Tegethoff (Cheetah)

EuroFurence 18: Chairman Cheetah, dressed as a Roman emperor, rode to the Coliseum-decorated podium in a chariot pulled by a team of fursuiters to open EuroFurence 18. The 13th DoPE pawpet show was "Pompeii," in keeping with the 2012 Roman Empire theme. There was a "Romans and Wine" wine-tasting. 2, the Ranting Gryphon returned but did a solo standup comedy performance. The 70-page program book wraparound cover and other art, by Dutch furry artist Henrieke Goorhuis, was a furry parody of the Astérix bandes dessinées drawn by Albert Uderzo; she drew Astérix as a fox and Julius Caesar as a leopard. The T-shirt was by TaniDaReal. The Fursuit Parade through Madgeburg coincided with the city's Medieval festival, producing a clash of costumers. The Hotel Maratim was booked out within six days. The EuroFurence Com and hotel allowed groups of three attendees to a room, and the InterCityHotel Magdeburg was designated the overflow hotel.
  Guests of Honor: Peter S. Beagle (s-f author)
  Charity: Far From Fear e.V. (€13,253)
  Chairmen or Organizers: Sven Tegethoff (Cheetah)

EuroFurence 19: There was a Wednesday pre-convention Fursuit Parade at the Magdeburg zoological gardens, with free admission to all fursuit wearers. Many program events were keyed to the Hawaiian theme, including the 14th DoPE pawpet show, "End Tide"; "Furry Legends of Hawaii" with Uncle Kage telling Hawaiian legends featuring animals; and "A Furry Pearl Harbor" which included a screening of the Japanese 1943 animated propaganda featurette *Momotaro no Umiwashi* showing the Imperial Japanese Navy and the Japanese pilots attacking "Devil Island" as funny animals. Other events ranged from the usual Furry dances and workshops to "Flute for Beginners." The 68-page program book was in full color, with a wraparound cover by SilverDeni. The T-shirt artists were Kacey Miyagami and TaniDaReal. The InterCity Hotel Magdeburg was again the official overflow hotel.

Guests of Honor: Warrick Brownlow-Pike, Andy Heath, Iestyn Evans (puppeteers from *Mongrels*)
Charity: Wildtierhilfe Fiel e.V. (€19,307)
Chairmen or Organizers: Sven Tegethoff (Cheetah)

EuroFurence 20: EuroFurence moved to the larger Estrel Hotel in Berlin. It had many of the problems of meeting in a new location; the opening ceremony began two hours late. Chairman Cheetah wore his badges from all twenty EuroFurences. Despite the larger hotel, the increased attendance resulted in many panels being standing room only. The Estrel Hotel was large enough that the Fursuit Parade was kept inside it, marching up & down corridors and stairs and into & out of meeting rooms to cover the entire convention. The 15th DoPE pawpet show was "Keepers of the Light." "Uncle Kage vs. 2" was restored to the program, and 2, the Ranting Gryphon also performed a solo rant. Sardyuon gave a "The Magic World of Sardyuon" fursuited acrobatic performance. Fox Amoore did a live performance of his "Come Find Me" album. There was a "Furs to the '80s" party. The wraparound Program Book cover was by ShinigamiGirl (pencils) and Johis (colors), and the T-shirt by Chibi-Marrow.

Guests of Honor: Kyell Gold (furry author), Ursula Vernon (furry artist/author), Sardyuon, (furry acrobat performer), Sofawolf Press editorial crew (furry publishers)
Charity: Stiftung Fledermaus (€21,081)
Chairmen or Organizers: Sven Tegethoff (Cheetah)

EuroFurence 21: The theme of "Greenhouse World" imagined a future ecologically friendly Berlin inhabited by anthropomorphic animals, who explore in the overgrown ruins of the cities once inhabited by their mysterious "Ancestors." The charity was repeated for the first time, due to flooding and a heavy storm in December 2014–January 2015 that destroyed most of the shelter. The Fursuit Dance was titled "Enter the Arena" and was followed by a new furry music video by EZ Wolf, "Stay As You Are." For the first time in 15 years the Pawpet Show took a break and was replaced by "Pawpet Show—The Story," a history and behind-the-scenes look at the show's preparation. The 70-page program book had a wraparound cover by Kenket (Tess Garman). The T-shirt was by Alpha_Ki.

Guests of Honor: Ned Wilkinson (Rhubarb the Bear), Cosmik (furry musicians)
Charity: Wildtierhilfe Fiel e.V. (€32,000)
Chairmen or Organizers: Sven Tegethoff (Cheetah)

FA: United

FA: United was organized by Shy Matsi and the Northeast Anthropomorphic Association, in collaboration with the Fur Affinity online community (hence the FA name), to establish a new East Coast furry convention following Anthrocon's move from Philadelphia to Pittsburgh. FA: United has always been in New Jersey. It has featured rock bands and rock music. It has often been difficult to distinguish between Fur Affinity the all-year website, and FA: United the annual convention, particularly due to the convention website's emphasis of "Fandoms United" embracing furries, *My Little Pony: Friendship Is Magic* fandom, *Gargoyles* fandom, dragon fandom, and more. The FA: United website boasts "Join FAU for a weekend of cookouts, parties, socializing and more!"

Name & Date	Theme	Location	Attendance	Parade
FA: United August 10–12, 2007		Ramada Newark Airport International Hotel, Newark, NJ	310	25
FA: United 2 August 1–3, 2008	The Power of Rock	Newark Liberty International Airport Marriott Hotel, Newark, NJ	381	26
FA: United Not held in 2009				
FA: United 3 May 28–30, 2010	Gamers United	Marriott's Fairfield Inn & Suites, Mt. Laurel, NJ	510	76
FA: United 4 May 20–22, 2011	Dawn of the Apocalypse	Hotel ML, Mt. Laurel, NJ	531	?
FA: United 5 August 17–19, 2012	Furry Mafia	Hanover Marriott, Whippany, NJ	629	92
FA: United 6 August 16–18, 2013	Applied Sciences	Hanover Marriott, Whippany, NJ	647	121
FA: United 7 August 15–17, 2014	Monster Island	Hanover Marriott, Whippany, NJ	707	142
FA: United 8 September 11–13, 2015	Fandoms United	Hanover Marriott, Whippany, NJ	658	89

Events

FA: United: There were more "founding member" sponsorships than regular sponsorships; the "founding members" received a limited-edition Fur Affinity USB flash drive. There were four featured bands, The Gay Blades, Sikamor Rooney, Zsa Zsa Gabortion, and the Back Alley McBeals, all of which performed free in exchange for unlimited free drinks. The membership bags contained "FA Bucks" which could be redeemed in the Dealers' Room or the convention store. The T-shirt design was by Thazumi on the front and by Sapphire on the back.

Guests of Honor: Tess Garman & Teagan Gavet (Blotch), John Barrett (Roxikat) (furry artists)
Charity: Lakota Wolf Preserve ($1,600)
Chairmen or Organizers: Shy Matsi

FA: United 2: There were three featured bands; Gay Blades, The Press, and Shitty Grape Lollipops. The T-shirt was by Fluke.

Guests of Honor: Fluke (furry artist), SolidAsp
Charity: New Jersey SPCA ($1,820)
Chairmen or Organizers: Shy Matsi

FA: United 3, scheduled for 2009, was not held due to financial problems and committee disagreements. It was rescheduled to 2010.

FA: United 3: Featured musical guests/artists were Matthew Ebel, Joey Pledger (Genki), and Matthew Wayne Davis (2, the Ranting Gryphon); and bands the Tricky Shoes (formerly the "Shitty Grape Lollipops"), A.I. (with DJ Genki), and Calamity Menagerie. The 2009 Ursa Major Awards were presented. The Fender Fursuit (part ferret, part fox; constructed by White Wolf based on a design by K-9 and Dragoneer) debuted at FA: United 3.

Guests of Honor: Jennifer Seng (Spunky, cartoonist), Nekogami (furry artist)
Charity: New Jersey SPCA ($2,458.24)
Chairmen or Organizers: Cray Drygu

FA: United 4: The post–Apocalypse theme was carried out by creating two teams, Survivors and Mutants, who were pitted against each other all weekend through games and other events. By

coincidence, the May 20–22 weekend included May 21, 2011, when Christian radio host Harold Camping was predicting "the Rapture" would happen. Lady Foxglove did both the conbook cover and the T-shirt.
Guests of Honor: John Cole (Kuddlepup, puppeteer), Lynn Hogan (Lady Foxglove, furry artist)
Charity: NJSPCA ($3,544)
Chairmen or Organizers: Dragoneer

FA: United 5: The featured bands were Matthew Ebel and Look Left.
Guests of Honor: Katmomma (furry author/artist/fursuiter), Skulldog (furry artist)
Charity: NJSPCA ($8,076)
Chairmen or Organizers: Dragoneer

FA: United 6: Matthew Ebel and Pepper Coyote were featured rock musicians. FA:U6 debuted a catered pool party.
Guests of Honor: Strype (furry artist), Amber Williams (Miss Mab of *Dan and Mab's Furry Adventures*), Lazarus Long (furry photographer)
Charity: NJSPCA ($10,516)
Chairmen or Organizers: Dragoneer

FA: United 7: Fossil and Colson Grainger had been announced as guests but did not attend. Featured musicians were Fox Amoore, Matthew Ebel, Pepper Coyote, and Myst Xtreme.
Guests of Honor: Macroceli (furry artist, fursuiter), Fox Amoore (furry musician)
Charity: NJSPCA ($8,812)
Chairmen or Organizers: Dragoneer

FA: United 8:
Guests of Honor: Greg Weisman (co-creator of *Gargoyles* TV series), Karine Charlebois (*Gargoyles* comic-book artist), Sophie Cabra (furry artist, fursuiter/maker), Pepper Coyote, Thom Adcox (actor, voice artist for *Gargoyles*)
Charity: NJSPCA (about $7,700)
Chairmen or Organizers: Dragoneer

Fangcon

Fangcon is for Tennessee furs at the center or east of the state, as opposed to Mephit FurMeet in Memphis in the far western end.

Name & Date	Theme	Location	Attendance	Parade
Fangcon 2012 October 26–28, 2012	Musicals	Millenium Maxwell House Hotel, Nashville, TN	201	40
Fangcon 2013 November 1–3, 2013	Carnival/Circus	Holiday Inn Knoxville West–Cedar Bluff Road, Knoxville, TN	231	56
Fangcon 2014 November 7–9, 2014	The 60s	Holiday Inn Knoxville West–Cedar Bluff Road, Knoxville, TN	302	93
Fangcon 2015 October 29– November 2, 2015	Never, Nevfur Land	Holiday Inn Knoxville Downtown, Knoxville, TN	427	137

Events

Fangcon 2012: A Furry Drama Show was a variety show. [Note: Loren McLaughlin has three fursonas; Calamity Coyote, Draconis, and Jugular Jaguar. He has appeared at different conventions as Chairman or Guest-of-Honor under any of the three names.]
  Guests of Honor: Loren McLaughlin (Calamity Cougar, fursuit performer), Ned Wilkinson (Rhubarb the Bear, furry musician), Jugular Jaguar (alternate fursuit of Loren McLaughlin), Artist G-o-H Anna Baker (Wolfaya), Musical G-o-H Husky in Denial
  Charity: Tiger Haven ($1,700+)
  Chairmen or Organizers: Keefur, Jace Inugami

Fangcon 2013: The Furry Drama Show returned.
  Guests of Honor: Heather Luterman (Khyot, furry artist)
  Charity: Tiger Haven ($1,806)
  Chairmen or Organizers: Keefur, Loren McLaughlin (Draconis)

Fangcon 2014: "Extra Events" were programmed on November 6 and 10. Rhubarb the Bear performed. The Furry Drama Show returned. Furry fandom's largest Furry Twister mat, and smallest ball pit, were introduced.
  Guests of Honor: GalaxyOwls, The Frozen Oasis (furry party organizers), Musician G-o-H NIIC the Singing Dog
  Charity: Tiger Haven ($3,600+)
  Chairmen or Organizers: Loren McLaughlin (Draconis), Keefur

Fangcon 2015: A Fangcon fursuit group marched or rode in a makeshift float in the Knoxville Pride Parade on June 20th. The theme was printed in black with "fur" in red, usually followed by "Where you never grow old." The Furry Drama Show and the Twister mat returned. A Furry Elitist level of sponsorship was introduced. A wedding group on the same weekend requested some fursuiters attend for their wedding photos.
  Guests of Honor: Artist G-o-H Tzologist, Writer G-o-H Greg Luterman (Gre7g, husband of Khyot), Musician G-o-H Lucas Raymond (Potoroo, chairman of Camp Feral!), Fursuiter G-o-H Jase Husky
  Charity: Tiger Haven ($2,500)
  Chairmen or Organizers: Loren McLaughlin (Draconis a.k.a. JugularJaguar), Keefur

Feral! *see* **Camp Feral!**

Festival of the Feral *see* **Oklacon**

FinFur Animus

FinFur Animus (FFA) is the convention that FinFur Summer Camp grew into.

Name & Date	Theme	Location	Attendance	Parade
FinFur Animus March 19–23, 2015	Häntien Taisto	Kokoushotelli Gustavelund, Tuusula	124	37

Events

FinFur Animus: The hotel and conference center was about a half-hour by car from Helsinki. There was a (very well made) 7'10" promotional video with English subtitles, featuring fursuiters and furry handpuppets exploring the new hotel. The theme translated as "Clash of Tails," a furry version of

FinFur Animus 2015 conbook front cover. Art by Snowshadow. Used with permission.

George R. R. Martin's *Game of Thrones* fantasy novels; more specifically, their TV adaptation. The conbook front cover was by Snowshadow and the back cover was by Roihu.

Chairmen or Organizers: Santtu Järvi (SlvWolf)

FinFur Summer Camp

Finland's first furry event, at a campground about five hours from Helsinki, was more of a furmeet than a convention, but it was annual, organized, with a website and graphics. It was hosted by the Roolipeliyhdistys FinFur Ry Organization to hold furry events in Finland. It was superseded by a "real" convention, FinFur Animus, in 2015.

Name & Date	Location	Attendance
FinFur Summer Camp 2011 July 1–3, 2011	North Karelia Kittee	54
FinFur Summer Camp 2012 July 11–15, 2012	North Karelia Kittee	59
FinFur Summer Camp 2013 July 17–21, 2013	North Karelia Kittee	70

Events

FinFur Summer Camp 2011: FFSC 2011 was at a summer camp outside the town of Kittee (also spelled Kitee) in North Karelia in eastern Finland, with outdoor BBQs, swimming, a sauna, darts, Frisbee throwing, boating, and husky agility sessions; and indoor board games and a dance with a DJ and smoke machine. A fursuit theater had only a few fursuits. There were banners, badges, plushies, and a program book.

Chairmen or Organizers: Santtu Lake (SlvWolf), Randon, Kisu, Euva

FinFur Summer Camp 2012: FFSC 2012 was increased to four days. It sold out in the first four hours. Events were the same plus a Werewolf Extreme game with special effects, a tree-chopping contest, and a Nose On Fire chili-tasting. There were 12 registered fursuits and two unregistered ones. There were dances on Friday and Saturday nights. The fursuiters were divided into two competing teams. Sponsors got a special illustrated magnet. A beauty-queen-like contest for the Most Popufur was won by Shadow Snow, an Arctic fox fursuiter. The prize was a Popufur sign, a small statuette, and a purple cloak.

Chairmen or Organizers: Santtu Lake (SlvWolf), Randon, Kitty, Euva

FinFur Summer Camp 2013: The program was similar. There was enough demand to upgrade FFSC into a hotel-type convention that FFSC 2014 was cancelled while the organizers planned such an event. This was FinFur Animus in 2015.

Chairmen or Organizers: Santtu Lake (SlvWolf), Randon, Kitty, Euva

FranFurence

FranFurence was intended to be a copy of EuroFurence for French furs. It was only held four times in five years. It disintegrated from the organizers' disappointment after it failed to grow, and its general attitude of the attendees waiting for someone to entertain them rather then participating in it.

Name & Date	Location	Attendance
FranFurence 1 May 1–4, 2003	Home of Ozone Griffox, Chaumes-en-Brie, France	18
FranFurence 2 November 11–14, 2004	Le Domain du Ciran, Ciran, France	30
2005: Not held		
FranFurence 3 April 15–18, 2006	La Hugoire, Chambord, France	37
FranFurence 4 November 23–27, 2007	La Hugoire, Chambord, France	23

Events

FranFurence 1: There were badges, but no conbook until FranFurence 2.
Chairmen or Organizers: Ozone Griffox, Timduru

FranFurence 2: "La convention Furry de FranceFurs." The venue was a "conservatoire de la faune sauvage de Sologne," an estate containing a "castle" (19th-century manor house) surrounded by 3 sq. kilometers of natural park. According to the French-language 16-page conbook, this year's Fran-Furence was based on games and socialization. Events included: (Thursday) opening, snacks, the game *Loups-garoux de Thiercelieux* (a.k.a. *Mafia*), a short film; (Friday) the game *Formula Dé*, a DDR session, presentation of Fursuits, panels, presentation of short films, dance; (Saturday) park promenade, panel, DDR contest, introduction to playacting, playacting; (Sunday) cleaning up, group photo, closing. Practically every event was followed by a meal or snacks. The language of FranFurence was French.
Chairmen or Organizers: Ozone Griffox, Timduru

FranFurence 3: La Hugoire was a large bed-and-breakfast cottage designed for groups of up to 50 weekend vacationers in rural Normandy. The conbook was 16 pages again. "Like last year's, we base this *FranFurence* on amusement and socialization. You will particularly appreciate the buffet from the 10th to the 13th hour…. And we have enlarged the variety of spectacles with, among others, a marionette show, a musical, a LAN party, and a bunch of free-time activities." The cottage featured hiking trails, a ping-pong table, all-terrain bicycles, and a DDR stand. "The schedules will be more-or-less flexible following the success of each event." The Saturday-to-Tuesday program more-or-less followed the previous FranFurence's, with the addition of a PictoFurry competition, a Musicafé, and a Crazy Drawings contest "between four of our best Furry artists." The organizational committee was referred to as the four "Gentle Organizers."
Chairmen or Organizers: Ozone Griffox, Lone_Fox, NightWolf, DeoLoup.

FranFurence 4: This was the final FranFurence. Despite an improved website and a call for greater attendee participation, attendance declined rather than grew, and the participation failed to materialize. Both co-chairmen resigned, and their successors allowed the committee planning Fran-Furence 5 to disintegrate.
Chairmen or Organizers: Ozone Griffox, Rasputch

F3 Convention

F3 Convention, a.k.a. just F3, was the first furry convention in Missouri, as opposed to a campground. It was organized by the Missouri's Furries FurAffinity Group. Its website is notorious for never including full information. The regular chair, Lung Ma, was better known as Dragon Mama.

Name & Date	Theme	Location	Attendance	Parade
F3 Convention 2012 December 14–16, 2012	Escape from the Zoo	Howard Johnson Inn and Convention Center, Springfield, MO	123	?
F3 Convention 2013 December 13–16, 2013	Part Deux: 80s Remixed	Stone Castle Hotel & Convention Center, Branson, MO	55	20
F3 Convention 2014 November 20–23, 2014	Ermagherd! Memes: It C4m3 Fr0m the Intarwebz!1	?	?	
F3 Convention 2015 November 20–22, 2015	Cosplay	Lamplighter Inn & Suites North, Springfield, MO	none	none

Events

F3 Convention 2012: Events were opening and closing ceremonies, a Dealer's Den and Artists' Alley, a charity auction, Fur-Me Poster-Making, a furry drama show, a super-sponsor luncheon, Club Anthro, a Furry Rave, the Fursuit Parade, role-playing games, card and board games, electronic gaming, a Dance Dance Revolution tournament, special-interest meetups, instructional panels, "fursuit first aide," and a 24 hour Anthro Movie Room. Memberships ranged from $30 supporting to a $450 "god level" super-sponsor, and included during the first year only a lifetime membership, ranging from $400 to $1,000 depending upon the registration benefits.
  Guests of Honor: Artist G-o-H Mekala McGaughy (Hazard), Fursuiting G-o-H Calamity Cougar & Bob Burns (Okidoki Coyote)
  Charity: Safari's Interactive Animal Sanctuary ($348)
  Chairmen or Organizers: Lung Ma

F3 Convention 2013: More of the same, plus the Special Guests' performances. $200 was raised for attendee Misora, who lost her house in a tornado.
  Guests of Honor: Bucktown Tiger (furry musician/fursuiter/comedian), Special Guests A Dozen Dead Furs (furry musicians), Tracer Moonshadow (furry comedian), The Furry Drama Show (furry variety show)
  Charity: National Tiger Sanctuary ($821.75), Misora ($200)
  Chairmen or Organizers: Lung Ma

F3 Convention 2014: More of the same. Bound By Fire put on a poi-spinning show.
  Guests of Honor: OzFoxes (Robert & Margaret Carspecken, furry cartoonists/writers), Telephone, Special Guests The Furry Drama Show (furry variety show), Tracer Moonshadow, Bucktown Tiger, Bound By Fire (improve performers)
  Charity:
  Chairmen or Organizers: Lung Ma

F3 Convention 2015: Less than a month before F3 2015, Dragon Mama announced its cancellation due to a lack of support by staffers and her inability to organize F3 single-handedly. She hoped that this was temporary.
  Guests of Honor: Reimina Keishana (Princess Rei, fursuit maker/cosplayer), Margaret Sensanbaugher (Java Meerkat, furry artist/fursuit maker/cosplayer)
  Charity:
  Chairmen or Organizers: Lung Ma

Fur Reality

Fur Reality is a furry convention in Cincinnati, Ohio, for the Cincinnati and northern Kentucky area. It began as a furry track within Cincinnati's older Pandoracon annual s-f convention, but it quickly outgrew the space allotted to it. In 2013 with sponsorship from local Ringtail Café Productions LLC, a comic book and game publishing company, it separated in six weeks into an independent furry convention. Fur Reality is designed as an "immersive" event featuring a story and game. Each Fur Reality is decorated to help attendees feel that they are within the "world/reality" of that convention.

Name & Date	Theme	Location	Attendance	Parade
Fur Reality 2013 October 11–13, 2013	Into the Labyrinth	Hilton Garden Inn Cincinnati/ Sharonville, Sharonville, OH	160	?
Fur Reality 2014 October 10–12, 2014	One with the Machine	Crowne Plaza Cincinnati– Blue Ash, Blue Ash, OH	316	55
Fur Reality 2015 October 9–11, 2015	Viva! Fur Reality	Crowne Plaza Cincinnati– Blue Ash, Blue Ash, OH	382	89

Events

Fur Reality 2013: Since Fur Reality 2013 began within that year's Pandoracon on the same dates, several events were still held at Pandoracon's Atrium Hotel a few miles away. Fur Reality membership was good for admission to Pandoracon; the opposite was not true. Events included the popular "Whose Lion Is It Anyway" improv panel moderated by Alkali Bismuth and SemJay, and a live broadcast of the weekly half-hour *The Dragget Show* podcast.
    Guests of Honor: Alkali Bismuth (fursuiter), Xander the Blue (furry artist)
    Charity: Ohio Alleycat Resource
    Chairmen or Organizers: Jewlz, Reiza, ten others

Fur Reality 2014: FR 2014 moved to a new hotel. Events were those of a typical furry convention.
    Guests of Honor: Alkali Bismuth (fursuiter), Xander the Blue (furry artist), MixedCandy (fursuit makers), Uncle Kage (furry performer, chairman of Anthrocon)
    Charity: Ohio Alleycat Resource ($2,788.46)
    Chairmen or Organizers: The Tak

Fur Reality 2015: The theme was based upon the Mexican Day of the Dead celebrations.
    Guests of Honor: Uncle Kage, Vanderlugt (musician/DJ), Pandez (fursuiter/stand-up comedian), Alkali Bismuth and Xander the Blue (comedy team), Ice TYP (musician)
    Charity: Ohio Alleycat Resource ($3,149.87)
    Chairmen or Organizers: The Tak, Sal

Fur Squared

Fur Squared (originally planned as F²) is a furry convention for the Milwaukee, Wisconsin, area. The Artist Guests-of-Honor do both the conbook covers and the T-shirts.

Name & Date	Theme	Location	Attendance	Parade
Fur Squared 2014 February 28–March 2, 2014	The End is Just the Beginning!	Sheraton Milwaukee Brookfield Hotel, Brookfield, WI	415	101
Fur Squared 2015 February 27–March 1, 2015	Lizards & Labyrinths	Sheraton Milwaukee Brookfield Hotel, Brookfield, WI	555	157

Events

Fur Squared 2014: Since Sema JayHawk was the regular host of *Whose Lion Is It Anyway*, WLIIA was a featured event. Other events included a furry variety show, an open mic variety show, and a live broadcast of the weekly *The Draggit Show* podcast.

Guests of Honor: Sema JayHawk (furry cartoonist/fursuiter/comedian), Artist G-o-H Crazy Corgi
Charity: Humane Animal Welfare Society (HAWS) ($2,100)
Chairmen or Organizers: Alkali Bismuth

Fur Squared 2015: The theme was depicted as a *Dungeons & Dragons*-type fantasy dungeon treasure-hunting adventure.
Guests of Honor: Firr, Artist G-o-H Nyxsiern
Charity: HAWS Waukesha ($8,567.52)
Chairmen or Organizers: Alkali Bismuth

Fur Squared logo. Art by Xander the Blue. Used with permission.

Fur the 'More

Fur the 'More is an annual furry convention for the Baltimore, Maryland, area. It was conceived by the Maryland Furs during the Furstivus convention on December 31, 2011–January 1, 2012. In March 2012 the existing NorthEast Anthropomorphic Association offered to take it on, saving it from having to create its own corporation. After Fur the 'More 2014 it evolved to create its own non-profit corporation, the Mid-Atlantic Anthropomorphic Society. Events are centered around fursuiting and gaming. It is unusual for calling its Dealers' Den the Furry Marketplace. Its mascot is Quoth the Raven, inspired by Edgar Allan Poe's poem "The Raven," Poe being a famous Baltimore author.

Name & Date	Theme	Location	Attendance	Parade
Fur the 'More 2013 April 5–7, 2013	Time Traveler's Party	Hunt Valley Inn, Hunt Valley, MD	473	94
Fur the 'More 2014 March 14–16, 2014	Ninja vs. Pirates	Hunt Valley Inn, Hunt Valley, MD	714	187
Fur the 'More 2015 May 29–31, 2015	Cryptozoology	Sheraton Premiere Hotel, Tyson's Corner, VA	853	215

Events

Fur the 'More 2013: Look Left was a musical guest. The conbook cover artist and T-shirt artist was SolidAsp.
Guests of Honor: Clockwork Creature Studio (fursuit makers), Artist G-o-H SolidAsp
Charity: Frisky's Wildlife & Primate Sanctuary ($2,181.25)
Chairmen or Organizers: Kit Drago

Fur the 'More 2014: There were the standard features of an Art Show, Dealers' Den, panels on fursuit construction, furry art and writing, and dances. "The Chimera Challenge" was a fursuit-construction competition. There was a reading of Poe's work by Sparf, and a flash-fiction contest. Friday night had a "high school prom" dance followed by a "housedance." Matthew Ebel, a musical guest, was featured in the Saturday evening concert. RedCoatCat did both the conbook cover and the T-shirt.
Guests of Honor: John "The Gneech" Robey (furry cartoonist), Tamara Jeanette (Meezer [also RedCoatCat], furry artist)
Charity: Frisky's Wildlife & Primate Sanctuary ($5,600)
Chairmen or Organizers: Kit Drago

Fur the 'More 2015: "The Chimera Challenge," "The Furry Feud," the fursuit dance, and the flash-fiction contests were repeated. A large screen was put up in the hotel's lounge displaying a feed of people's tweets using the con's hashtag. Musical guests included Matthew Ebel, Pepper Coyote, and NIIC the Singing Dog. The conbook cover artist was Windfalcon, and the T-shirt was by Cougari.
 Guests of Honor: Brenda Lyons (Windfalcon, nature artist)
 Charity: Frisky's Wildlife & Primate Sanctuary ($4,550)
 Chairmen or Organizers: Kit Drago

Furbest

Furbest was a one-time event at a hostel in Spain, midway between a furmeet and a convention. It was organized mostly over Facebook and Twitter beginning in March. It did not have any programming beyond informal socializing, but it lasted three days, registered members (called "furbesters") months in advance, and had a cartoon young fox ("el zorrito" or "el zorrete") mascot wearing a dark red FB neckerchief. It and other Spanish furmeets were superseded by the long-range planning beginning February 2016 for Furrnion, to be Spain's first furry convention in January 2017.

Name & Date	*Location*	*Attendance*
Furbest August 14–16, 2015	"Mare de deu de gracia" hostel, Vilareal, Castellón	29

Events

Furbest: Furbest cost €45 for room and meals at the hostel for three days. The hostel maximum was 44, so there was no problem with only 29 members. Attendees received a badge that could be personalized for €2 more. The socializing included wearing fursuits, playing guitars and other musical instruments and singing, and filming videos.
 Chairmen or Organizers: Chugo, Mitsuki-onega, Dalgon, Poliou

FurCoNZ

FurCoNZ, "New Zealand's Furry Convention," is another convention that grew from an annual furmeet hosted in a private residence. The first FurCoNZ was hosted in 2002 by PuppyDog. By 2007 its popularity had outgrown the ability to hold it in private residences, and it changed to a weekend outdoor summer camping/lodge event emphasizing informality "with a Kiwi theme."

While the vast majority of attendees are from New Zealand, it has seen attendees from Australia, U.S., U.K. and even from as far as Sweden. Several FurCoNZ events were even scheduled on back-to-back weekends with Melbourne, Australia's MiDFur, to enable furs to attend both events in one vacation trip. Of the local attendees, the majority of attendees are from the Auckland region. While most FurCoNZ conventions have taken place in the Auckland region, FurCoNZ is not bound to Auckland as its home city, and it has shifted to other locations based on both the Organizer's home location and demand from other furry attendees outside of the Auckland region.

To take advantage of summer season vacations for New Zealand Colleges and Universities, as well as taking advantage of better weather patterns, FurCoNZ was originally run in late-November to mid–December. More recently this has shifted to early–February to avoid conflicts with Christmas vacation periods and also to take advantage of long weekend holidays early in the year (such as Waitangi Day). There is an age limit of 16 for those staying overnight, and 14 for those attending on a day pass for activities. Day pass attendees under 14 must be accompanied by a parent or guardian.

Name & Date	Location	Attendance
FurCoNZ 2007 November 30–December 3, 2007	Kiwanis Camp, Huia, Waitakere, Auckland, NZ	40 (estimated)
FurCoNZ 2008 November 21–24, 2008	Camp Rangi Woods, Pohangina, North Island, NZ	32 (estimated)
FurCoNZ 2009 November 27–30, 2009	"Kokako Lodge," Hunua Ranges Regional Park, Papakura District, Auckland, NZ	58
FurCoNZ 2010 December 10–13, 2010	"Kokako Lodge," Hunua Ranges Regional Park, Papakura District, Auckland, NZ	66
FurCoNZ 2011 December 9–12, 2011	"Kokako Lodge," Hunua Ranges Regional Park, Papakura District, Auckland, NZ	50
FurCoNZ 2012 December 14–17, 2012	Kiwanis Camp, Huia, Waitakere, Auckland, NZ	50
FurCoNZ 2014 February 6–9, 2014	Brookfield Outdoor Education Centre, Wainuiomata, Wellington, NZ	52
FurCoNZ 2015 cancelled		

Events

FurCoNZ 2007: This was the first FurCoNZ convention that was not hosted in a private residence. As with previous furmeets, this convention was run in a "freestyle" manner, where attendees simply gathered and created their own events or entertainment. While accommodation was provided, this event was not catered.

Chairmen or Organizers: Alexander Herbert (Lex Cypher)

FurCoNZ 2008: This was the last "freestyle" FurCoNZ. The site had a central lodge, where most furs gathered for art, games or watching screening of furry-related movies and television shows. While no specific panels or events were timetabled, the outdoor games of "Predator/Prey" and "Sirens," run by Kasper, proved very popular. Cooking meals was a communal event, led by a small number of volunteers.

Chairmen or Organizers: DarthMeow, TrojanCentaur

FurCoNZ 2009: The registration fee of NZ $75 included accommodation and food. FurCoNZ 2009 began to evolve towards a traditional convention by computerizing its registration system, programming its activities, having full catering, organizing dances, and producing badges and a conbook (design by

FurCoNZ 2014 conbook. Art by Nimble. Used with permission.

Blitz, with cover and conbadge art by Kitty-sama). The programming was set around outdoor activities provided by Kokako Lodge instructors.
Chairmen or Organizers: Lyctiger

FurCoNZ 2010: FurCoNZ 2010 cost NZ$85, which included accommodation and meals. There were two streams for the outdoor events, run by Kokako Lodge instructors. These included archery, abseiling, high-ropes course, kayaking and hiking. In an impromptu event a group of attendees, led by Isengrin, built a raft. The raft, christened the "Hunua Ragebeetle," was sailed successfully around the Hunua waterfall pool until it got too close to the falls and was destroyed. Indoor events included board gaming and art. A full A/V room was set up with consoles. There were nightly dances and a "SingStar" (a Playstation 3 karaoke game) event.
Chairmen or Organizers: Lyctiger

FurCoNZ 2011: The registration fee was NZ$94, which again covered accommodation and meals. FurCoNZ 2011 events followed an identical format to FurCoNZ 2010, including a return of the "SingStar" event. It was announced that next year's FurCoNZ would be at a new venue because Kokako Lodge had reached attendance limits. The conbadge art was by Kendra.
Chairmen or Organizers: Lyctiger

FurCoNZ 2012: The NZ$99 registration included accommodations and meals. Unlike previous years at Kokako Lodge, Kiwianis Camp did not have instructed activities. While some activities were timetabled, many of the hikes into the surrounding bush or to the local beach were impromptu. This was also the first FurCoNZ to provide separate and improved accommodations for Sponsors.
Chairmen or Organizers: Lyctiger, DarthMeow

FurCoNZ 2014: The dates of the following FurCoNZ were shifted to February, both to avoid conflicts many attendees had with the Christmas holiday period and to take advantage of a long weekend due to Waitangi Day (a New Zealand national holiday). This stayed within the 2013/2014 summer season (in the Southern Hemisphere). The registration was NZ$119 (or NZ$99 for early registration), and included meals and accommodation. Events included: kayaking (run by Shorty), art room (run by Kendra), digital art panel (run by Dottar), comic challenge (run by Taala and Agheptonygm), Werewolves of the Dark Arts (run by Tobias Amaranth), and a very popular Fursuit building and live duct-tape-dummy demonstration (run by Sparky). Unfortunately several planned outdoor events had to be cancelled due to inclement weather. It was announced that the next FurCoNZ would return to the Auckland Region with the intention to alternate between Auckland and other centers. The conbook was designed by Kendra and Nimble, with featured art by Taala Ruhun.
Chairmen or Organizers: NimbleSquirrel, Kendra

FurCoNZ 2015: The Auckland region organizer, Kamadan (previously known as Lyctiger) resigned for personal reasons and nobody in the region was able to able to replace him. Efforts to arrange an alternate venue in another region were unsuccessful. FurCoNZ 2015 was cancelled, with the announcement that FNZ would return to the Brookfield Outdoor Education Center on February 5–8, 2016. Registration was raised to NZ$125 for full event and NZ$30 for day pass.

FurDU

FurDU (Furry Down Under) was the fourth Australian furry gathering, after MiDFur in Melbourne in 2006, RivFur in Brisbane in July 2007, and FurJAM in Sydney in September 2007. It is arguably the second Australian furry convention, for those who consider RivFur and FurJAM to be only furmeets. It was originally planned for Melbourne, but it was decided to hold it in the Gold

Coast resort area of Queensland. Pre-convention publicity emphasized its affordability; total costs of registration and accommodation were estimated at under A$200.

Name & Date	Theme	Location	Attendance	Parade
FurDU 2010 April 23–25, 2010	The Beach	Vibe Hotel Gold Coast, Surfers Paradise, Queensland	92	
FurDU 2011 April 15–17, 2011	Nightlife	Vibe Hotel Gold Coast, Surfers Paradise, Queensland	150	
FurDU 2012 April 27–29, 2012	Carnival	Watermark Hotel, Surfers Paradise, Queensland	300	
FurDU 2013 April 26–28, 2013	The World of Tomorrow	Outrigger Surfers Paradise, Surfers Paradise, Queensland	352	
FurDU 2014 March 28–30, 2014	Fhloston Paradise	Outrigger Surfers Paradise, Surfers Paradise, Queensland	563	
FurDU 2015 May 1–3, 2015	Jurassic Safari	Outrigger Surfers Paradise, Surfers Paradise, Queensland	490	

Events

FurDU 2010: Planned events were art jams and dealers' tables, a fursuit dance and games, video gaming, karaoke, a barbeque, King Tut Putt-Putt miniature golf, a beach trip, and a visit to Timezone ("the largest Indoor Family Entertainment Centre [FEC] in Australia") for lazertag and bumper cars, and a Dead Dog Dance. The conbook front cover was a collaboration between Wookiee and Oz Kangaroo, and the back cover was by Weasely. The T-shirt was by (and has been each year by) Macroceli.

Chairmen or Organizers: Oz Kangaroo, Flame-Drake, Joeyjoejoe

FurDU 2011: Events were similar but expanded. The Guitar Hero tournament was dropped for lack of interest, and a poker tournament, iron artist contest, and furry game show were added. The convention space was minimal, with attendees encouraged to get out of the hotel and see the Gold Coast's attractions. The conbook (cover by Cooner) emphasized tourist information about the Gold Coast.

Chairmen or Organizers: Oz Kangaroo, Flame-Drake, Joeyjoejoe

FurDU 2012: The program again included dances and games, miniature golf, a beach trip including a Fursuit Beach Walk, a visit to Timezone, and a Dead Dog Dance. New events included a charity, furry chess, a magic show, and an Anthrax comedy act. FurDU 2012 added "special guests" to the convention. Also, the theme began to be emphasized in stage props, decorations, and programming. The conbook cover was by Stu Cat.

Guests of Honor: ActFur on Air (furry podcast), Dustin, Lupie, Anthrax (rock musician, stand-up comedian), Matt Hollywood (rock guitarist)

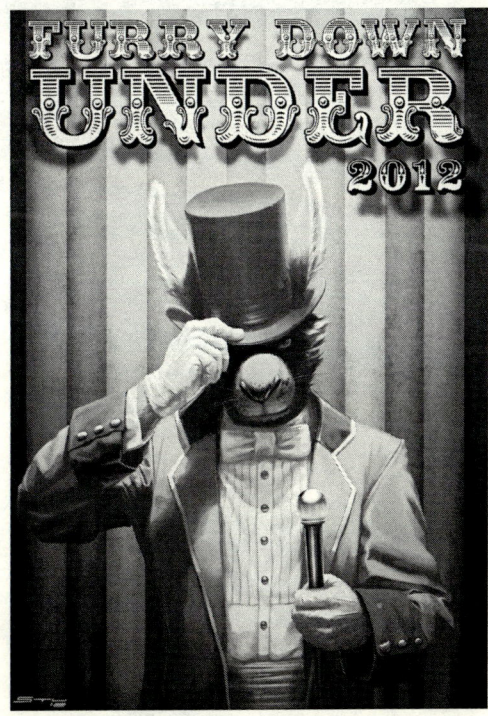

FurDU 2012 conbook. Art by Stu Cat. Used with permission.

Charity: Australia Zoo Wildlife Warriors (no records kept)
Chairmen or Organizers: Oz Kangaroo, FlameDrake, Joeyjoejoe

FurDU 2013: Most events were the same, including the visit to Timezone and the miniature golf. There were separate dances each night and a dance competition. There were two charity shows in addition to the charity auction. The Fursuit Beach Walk was presented as an alternative to other conventions' Fursuit Parades. The conbook cover was again by Stu Cat.
Guests of Honor: Stu Cat, Fox Amoore (furry musician)
Charity: Animal Welfare League of Queesland (A$4,600 [estimate])
Chairmen or Organizers: Oz Kangaroo, FlameDrake, Joeyjoejoe

FurDU 2014: "Fhloston Paradise" is a luxury planet in the s-f film *The Fifth Element*. There was a screening of the movie, which FurDU 2014 was themed around. Fox Amoore gave a charity concert. Events included the usual plus "Who's Fur Is It, Anyway?" The conbook cover was by Stu Cat. Vurt made a sponsor's T-shirt in addition to the regular T-shirt by Macroceli.
Guests of Honor: SilverFox, Fox Amoore (furry musician), Vurt
Charity: Animal Welfare League of Queesland (A$4,296.80)
Chairmen or Organizers: Oz Kangaroo, FlameDrake, Joeyjoejoe

FurDU 2015: There was a sharp drop in attendance, attributed to horrible weather that closed the Gold Coast City and nearby Brisbane airports, cancelling several flights. Due to the weather, outdoor events were cancelled and FurDU 2015 was held in the hotel. Events included the dances and charity events, Fursuit games, charades, comedy shows, and a dance competition. A planned screening of *Jurassic Park* was cancelled due to the studio's withdrawing permission; *Ice Age 3* was shown instead. Stu Cat again did the conbook cover.
Guests of Honor: Jacob Coates (Jay Stoat, Furry author/publisher), Macroceli (furry artist/fursuiter)
Charity: Animal Welfare League of Queesland (A$5,883.60)
Chairmen or Organizers: Oz Kangaroo, FlameDrake, Joeyjoejoe

Fur-Eh!

Ending sentences with "Eh" is a stereotype of Canadians that the furs of Alberta have proudly adopted. Fur-Eh! was proposed by Thallanor Rasmuson in 2010 and first held in 2012. It is a private, not-for-profit event; unincorporated, although that will change. Although Fur-Eh! has the standard events of a furry convention, it also emphasizes unique programming. Its programming features four tracks; for artistry, fursuiting, writing, and a "Go-Kart track." Each year's conbook cover is by that year's guest-of-honor, who is always Canadian. The first year's T-shirt was the Fur-Eh! logo; subsequent T-shirts have also been by the guest-of-honor. Fur-Eh! is known for its merchan-

Fur-Eh! logo. Art by Rei Vagan. Used with permission.

dise/souvenirs, including enameled lapel pins, hockey jerseys, shot glasses and mugs, flasks, T-shirts, keychains, and poker chips.

Name & Date	Theme	Location	Attendance	Parade
Fur-Eh! 2012 May 4–6, 2012	none	Hilton Garden Inn, Edmonton, Alberta	200	40 (estimated)
Fur-Eh! 2013 May 3–5, 2013	The Great Canadian Road Trip	Hilton Garden Inn, Edmonton, Alberta	273	70+
Fur-Eh! 2014 May 2–4, 2014	Pirates of the North Saskatchewan River	Sawredge Inn, Edmonton, Alberta	351	72
Fur-Eh! 2015 May 8–10, 2015	The Wild & Weird West!	Ramada Edmonton Hotel & Conference Centre, Edmonton, Alberta	472	139

Events

Fur-Eh! 2012: There was no official theme, but the convention in general emphasized "Canada." Events included "Drunken Fursuit Construction," "50 Shades of Neigh" (a reading of bad smut; for 18+), and "Dildo or Cactus."
   Guests of Honor: Silent Ravyn (furry artist, fursuit maker)
   Chairmen or Organizers: Fallout Coyote, Dennis Bilyk (Thallanor Rasmuson)

Fur-Eh! 2013: More of the same. The writing track included "Soviet Contraband Smut Factory."
   Guests of Honor: Strawberry Neko (furry artist)
   Chairmen or Organizers: Fallout Coyote, Dennis Bilyk (Thallanor Rasmuson)

Fur-Eh! 2014: Fur-Eh! expanded into the larger Sawredge Inn. The Poutine Social (instead of an ice cream social) was introduced, which sold out in minutes. There were nightly dances, two sessions of Fursuit Games, and panels including "50 Shades of Neigh." There were some minor hotel problems, but the main problem was that Fur-Eh! 2014 was so much larger than expected that it was considered to have outgrown the larger hotel after only one year.
   Guests of Honor: ShinigamiGirl (furry artist)
   Chairmen or Organizers: Fallout Coyote, Dennis Bilyk (Thallanor Rasmuson)

Fur-Eh! 2015: The theme was visualized as "Steampunk Meets the Wild Frontier!" The new hotel & convention center was considered large enough for several years' growth. The Poutine Social was enlarged. New events included the Masquerade & Talent Show, Drunken Fursuit Construction, Cutthroat Art, Poker Tournament, and karaoke singing. Repeated events included nightly dances, the Dance Competition, and Fursuit Games. At the end of Fur-Eh! 2015 a new organizing structure was created with the formation of the Fur-Eh! Organizing Committee to oversee future conventions, including as initial members Thallanor Rasmusson, Maskwa, bcbreakaway, Fallout Coyote, Sierra Racs, and Lucifur Fox.
   Guests of Honor: Strype (furry artist)
   Chairmen or Organizers: Fallout Coyote, Dennis Bilyk (Thallanor Rasmuson)

FurFright

FurFright was a Halloween-themed Anthropomorphic Convention in New England, hosted by Belic Bear and K'gra Leopard. It started as a series of local parties and grew into one of the largest, and longest-running conventions of its kind. In addition to creating many unique events, and hosting

FurFright

popular convention attractions, the convention's focus was on creating a strong sense of family/community, and working to aid animal and environmental causes. The organizers ended the convention following the 2013 event.

Name & Date	Location	Attendance	Parade
FurFright 2003 November 1, 2003	Falcon's Grove, Crystal Lake, Middletown, CT	160+ (estimated)	not recorded
FurFright 2004 October 23–24, 2004	Sheraton Bradley Hotel, Windsor Locks, CT	270	not recorded
FurFright 2005 October 28–30, 2005	Sheraton Bradley Hotel, Windsor Locks, CT	320	not recorded
FurFright 2006 October 20–22, 2006	Sheraton Bradley Hotel, Windsor Locks, CT	515	130
FurFright 2007 October 19–21, 2007	Connecticut Grand Hotel, Waterbury, CT	717	98
FurFright 2008 October 17–19, 2008	Connecticut Grand Hotel, Waterbury, CT	873	146
FurFright 2009 October 16–18, 2009	Holiday Inn, Waterbury, CT	979	not recorded
FurFright 2010 October 29–31, 2010	Crowne Plaza Cromwell, Cromwell, CT	1,284	not recorded
FurFright 2011 October 14–16, 2011	Crowne Plaza Cromwell, Cromwell, CT	1,485	not recorded
FurFright 2012 October 26–28, 2012	Crowne Plaza Cromwell, Cromwell, CT	1,500	321
FurFright 2013 October 25–27, 2013	Crowne Plaza Cromwell, Cromwell, CT	1,500	369

Events

FurFright 2003: FurFright began when the attendance of local parties and barbecues grew beyond capacity. The first FurFright was held at the Falcon's Grove hall in Middletown, CT, and was intended to be a one-off, single day mini-convention that included dances, a masquerade, gaming, a DDR tournament, a dealers' area, and a potluck dinner. The organizers, Belic Bear and K'gra Leopard, expected approximately 50 fans, but welcomed over 160. Public demand for another event led them to register the organization and move into a hotel the following year. The conbook cover was by Robert Denby. There was no T-shirt.

Charities: Animal Haven, Vital Ground ($400)

Chairmen or Organizers: Belic Bear, K'gra Leopard

FurFright 2004: Events and attractions included a masquerade, video/table top gaming rooms, dealers' room, movies, dances, a charity raffle/auction, fursuit parade, fursuit games, panels/classes, a photo shoot, and many other events. Some events and attractions were imaginatively renamed to match the Halloween theme, like the Dealers' Dungeon, Fursuit Massacre, Game Room of Death, Torture Chamber Arcade, Creature Crypt, Movie Morgue, and Headless Hallow. The hotel provided a life-sized horse statue wearing a sombrero (not anthropomorphized). An annual newszine, *The Daily Howl*, made its debut, created and edited by Sedge Hare. Another annual event that originated at FurFright was the "Bucket Brigade," where fursuiters carrying Jack-O-Lantern buckets collected donations for charity. The committee incorporated as FurFright, Inc., a non-profit organization, with Belic Bear & K'gra Leopard serving as co-chairs. FurFright, Inc., reported $8,220 in revenue. The conbook cover was by Quicksilver. The T-shirt was by RedCoatCat.

FurFright 2011 T-shirt. Art by Keto. Used with permission.

Charities: Vital Ground, CATALES ($500)
Chairmen or Organizers: Belic Bear, K'gra Leopard

FurFright 2005: Events and attractions included a Masquerade, video/table top gaming rooms, dealers' room, movies, dances, a charity raffle/auction, fursuit parade, fursuit games, panels/classes, a photo shoot, and many other events. FurFright began the tradition of crowning and Attendee Guest of Honor at Opening Ceremonies, and Koda Bear received that year's honor. FurFright, Inc., reported $12,429 in revenue and $10,214 in expenses. The conbook cover was by Mitsu. The T-shirt was by RedCoatCat.
Charities: Horizon Wings (raptor rehabilitation), ASPCA of Louisiana (to help animals affected by Hurricane Katrina) ($1,059)
Chairmen or Organizers: Belic Bear, K'gra Leopard

FurFright 2006: The Sheraton Bradley Hotel sold out, requiring the Days Inn and Comfort Suites to act as overflow hotels. With more people attending than anticipated, the convention ran out of con books, and had to have additional badges printed. This was the first year FurFright selected Guests of Honor (Stephie "Cybercat" Stone and Taurin Fox). Keeping with their Halloween theme, those purchasing a basic membership registered as Monsters, and sponsor levels included Zombie-

Sponsor, FrankenSponsor, and Casanova FrankenSponsor levels. Northern Wolf from British Columbia, who travelled four days by bus to attend FurFright 2006, was named Attendee Guest-of-Honor. The conbook cover was by Taurin Fox. The T-shirt was by Ivybeth. FurFright, Inc., reported $19,260 in revenue and $11,750 in expenses. The many private but open nighttime room parties included an elaborate one by the Frozen Oasis group (open to attendees over 21) with dancing, live DJ, a laser light show, and an alcoholic bar.

Guests of Honor: Stephie Stone (Cybercat, furry artist), Taurin Fox
Charities: The Endangered Animal Rescue Sanctuary (EARS), Regap of Connecticut ($1,631.64)
Chairmen or Organizers: Belic Bear, K'gra Leopard

FurFright 2007: The attendee guest-of-honor was fursuiter JD Puppy. The convention was almost late in getting set up because of a previous group's Satanic Pajama Party. New events included Friday Furcopalypse (a dinner social and gaming event), The Amazing Broccolini's Dance Party; and the addition of a second "Dead Dog Fursuit Parade" on Sunday night. Returning were popular events such as the Masquerade; Fursuit Massacre (fursuit games); a post-convention Dead Fur Party, and many other events, attractions, and programming. The conbook cover artist was Sara "Caribou" Palmer, and the T-shirt was by Keto. FurFright, Inc., reported $30,401.50 in annual income and $26,426.60 in expenses. The convention got a writeup in the *Hartford Advocate*, "Hell Hath No Furries" (November 1, 2007), that is still cited as an example of very favorable media coverage.

Guests of Honor: Sara Palmer (Caribou, furry artist)
Charity: Moonridge Animal Park ($3,000)
Chairmen or Organizers: Belic Bear, K'gra Leopard

FurFright 2008: Events and attractions included a Masquerade, video/table top gaming rooms, dealers' room, movies, dances, a charity raffle/auction, two fursuit parades, fursuit games, panels/classes, a photo shoot, and many other events. At Opening Ceremonies Nekomon was selected the Attendee Guest of Honor, and the convention began by everyone in attendance forming a conga line and dancing out of the ballroom into convention space (a tradition that would continue each year). The Fursuit Dance Competition made its debut, hosted by Guest Of Honor Beetlejuice. Other events included a Dr. Funkenstein's Furry Dance Party; a concert by Bob Drake's Cabinet Of Curiosities, Masquerade/talent show (with 16 acts, co-emceed by Beetlejuice and Belic); and the Fursuit Massacre (fursuit games). $4,000 was raised for the two charities, and an additional $547.26 was raised for Da-fox, an attendee whose fursuit head was stolen by a hotel guest who was not with the convention. The conbook cover and T-shirt artist was Likeshine. FurFright, Inc., reported $38,538.20 in revenue and $39,591.28 in expenses.

Guests of Honor: Beetlejuice/Mac Dragon (performer of Beetlejuice at Universal park shows), Likeshine (furry artist)
Charities: New Leash On Life, Pays de L'ours ($4,000)
Chairmen or Organizers: Belic Bear, K'gra Leopard

FurFright 2009: In 2009, FurFright began its long-standing relationship with the United States War Dogs Association, a charitable organization run by Veteran Military Dog Handlers who work to honor and aid Military Working Dogs and their human Handlers, past, present, and future. The convention hosted panels and video screenings to help educate their attendees on the plight of these heroic soldiers, and the outpouring of support from FurFright attendees was overwhelming. The War Dogs would become a huge part of the FurFright Community, and synonymous with the convention's identity. The Attendee Guest of Honor was Duncan The Dog. Friday events included the Dealer/Sponsor Dinner, Friday Night Furpacalypse, and Brick Hardmeat's Friday Night Freakout (dance). Saturday events included the Fursuit Parade, a Masquerade showcasing the talents of both attendees and fursuiters alike, and the start of FurFright's annual *Rocky Horror Picture Show Pool Party,* held on a large screen beside the hotel pool. The conbook cover artist was Tod Wills and the

T-shirt was by Ookami Kemono. Issues with poor hotel service led to FurFright relocating to a different hotel the following year.

Guests of Honor: TILT Longtail (fursuiter), Tod Wills (artist, puppeteer)
Charity: United States War Dog Association, Inc. ($7,770)
Chairmen or Organizers: Belic Bear, K'gra Leopard

FurFright 2010: FurFright 2010 was the seventh furry convention to surpass 1,000 attendees. The new venue was much more enthusiastic about the convention, and many hotel staff wore convention t-shirts, ears, and tails. The announced schedule was once again horror-themed. Scheduled events included a "One-Eyed Jacks" blackjack tournament, a "Dead Man's Paw" poker tournament, a rock band tournament; a "Fiendish Sketchoff," "Frightening Figure Drawing"; an *Eye of Argon* reading, "Build a Monster with Science!," and a "Zombie Apocalypse." The *Rocky Horror Picture Show* Pool Party continued, with a second movie (*Jaws*) being added on Friday night. FurFright, Inc., reported $54,081 in revenue (all from memberships), and $32,624 in expenses. The 32-page conbook had a wraparound color cover by Louve and RedCoatCat. Louve did the T-shirt. There was concern that rapidly-growing attendance would diminish the popular intimate, close-knit, community feel of the convention, which led to FurFright officially setting the attendance limit at 1,500 for the 2011 convention.

Guests of Honor: Tamara Jeanette (RedCoatCat, furry artist), Lauren Henderson (Louve, furry artist, fursuiter), Flare Starfire (furry musician)
Charity: United States War Dog Association, Inc. ($12,456.60)
Chairmen or Organizers: Belic Bear, K'gra Leopard

FurFright 2011: Events and attractions included a Masquerade, video/table top gaming rooms, dealers' room, movies, dances, a charity raffle/auction, two fursuit parades, fursuit games, panels/classes, a photo shoot, and many other events. The movie at the Friday Pool Party was *Airplane!*, in honor of Leslie Nielsen. The 32-page program book had a wraparound cover by Keto, who also did the T-shirt. FurFright, Inc., reported $78,745 in revenue (all from memberships), and $99,067 in expenses.

Guests of Honor: Keto (furry artist), JD Puppy (fursuiter)
Charity: United States War Dog Association, Inc. ($12,850.23)
Chairmen or Organizers: Belic Bear, K'gra Leopard

FurFright 2012: Attendance reached the 1,500 limit. The Friday Pool Party movie was *Mystery Science Theater 3000: Prince of Space*. The conbook cover was by guests-of-honor Skulldog and D. Walker. The T-shirt was by Skulldog. FurFright was the first convention to design and offer customized convention-themed hockey jerseys, with Keto's 2011 wolf t-shirt design serving as the logo. The hockey jerseys were supposed to be a limited, single year run, but public demand led the convention to offer them once again the following year. Hurricane Sandy and a second severe storm forced some attendees to leave the convention early on Sunday, causing many to playfully nickname that year's convention "HurriCon." FurFright, Inc., reported $79,605 in revenue (all from memberships), and $60,421 in expenses. Some attendees who harassed the convention staff and Dorsai Irregulars security in the hope of creating controversy later spread false reports on their blogs of serious problems with the way FurFright was run.

Guests of Honor: Skulldog, D. Walker (furry artists)
Charity: United States War Dog Association, Inc. ($15,445.15)
Chairmen or Organizers: Belic Bear, K'gra Leopard

FurFright 2013: Events and attractions included the ever-popular Masquerade, video/table top gaming rooms, dealers' room, movies, dances, a charity raffle/auction, two fursuit parades, fursuit games, panels/classes, a photo shoot, and many other events. The second movie shown at the pool party was *Young Frankenstein*. During Opening Ceremonies Al Bear was crowned the Attendee Guest of Honor, and Trekwolf was honored for his outstanding service to the furry community. FurFright hosted the Fursuit Hockey League (FHL), a group of players, coaches, and fans representing FurFright and Canadian conventions What The Fur? and Furnal Equinox. The FurFright/Boston Bruins defeated the Montreal Canadians in the championship game, 8–2. The convention concluded with a moving video presentation and proposal by JTigerclaw to his fiancé Katalina. The conbook cover artist was Tygurstar. The t-shirt artists were Tygurstar and Wallaby.

Guests of Honor: Wallaby, Tygurstar (furry artists)
Charity: United States War Dog Association, Inc. ($7,942)
Chairmen or Organizers: Belic Bear, K'gra Leopard

On December 1, 2013, Belic Bear and K'gra Leopard announced that they were personally unable to continue organizing FurFright, and brought the convention to a close. The remaining staff, with the aid and blessing of Belic and K'gra, used the former hotel and fanbase to create a new Halloween-themed convention in New England called Furpocalypse.

FurIdaho

FurIdaho, a.k.a. "PotatoCon" (it's the state vegetable), was started in 2012, skipped 2014 due to a lack of funds, and was supposed to return in 2015; but it did not.

Name & Date	*Theme*	*Location*	*Attendance*	*Parade*
FurIdaho 2012 March 23–25, 2012	Good Fur You, Good Fur Idaho!	Boise Hotel and Conference Center, Boise, ID	253	?
FurIdaho 2013 March 8–10, 2013	Furries in Time and Space	Boise Hotel and Conference Center, Boise, ID	?	?
FurIdaho 2014 Not held				

Events

FurIdaho 2012: The FurIdaho logo for the first two years was a map of the state covered with paw-prints and the year in white; purple for 2012 and blue for 2013. The first 150 attendees received a commemorative purple cap with rabbit ears.

Guests of Honor: Kadath, Mokusei Kaze (furry artists), PWN_3, Househead (DJs), Fur What It's Worth (podcast), Fantastic Journeys Publishing, Fine Young Deviants (comedy troupe)
Chairmen or Organizers:

FurIdaho 2013: The theme was specifically *Dr. Who*-centric. FurIdaho 2013 was featured in a slideshow on the *Boise Weekly* website.

Guests of Honor: Fur What It's Worth (podcast), Fine Young Deviants (comedy troupe), Mokusei Kaze (furry artist)
Chairmen or Organizers:

Following FurIdaho 2013, the convention changed organizers. The new organizers cancelled FurIdaho 2014 due to insufficient funds and needing more time to plan for the next convention. However, by 2015 it had not yet returned.

FurJAM

FurJAM is another convention that grew from a fur-meet started in 2004. It was originally like the early MiDFurs and RivFurs; an informal annual occasion for furs in Sydney to socialize while touring the city. In 2007 Flaydramon and Anakaine, the original organizers, lost interest in organizing it again. AussieHusky took it over and made it more formal, by making it a three-day event with specific events. The goal of the convention is for all of the events to either be free, or to have a free alternative. It is between a furmeet and a convention, with an official website, illustrated badges, and usually a T-shirt. Periodic requests to expand FurJAM into a convention in a hotel have been resisted so far, mainly due to the increased costs of booking a hotel.

Name & Date	Location	Attendance
FurJAM 2007 September 21–23, 2007	Sydney, NSW	30 to 60
FurJAM 2008 September 26–28, 2008	Sydney, NSW	60+
FurJAM 2009 September 25–27, 2009	Sydney, NSW	30 to 70
FurJAM 2010 September 24–26, 2010	Sydney, NSW	80 to 100
FurJAM 2011 October 7–9, 2011	Sydney, NSW	100
FurJAM 2012 September 14–16, 2012	Sydney, NSW	120
FurJAM 2013 September 6–8, 2013	Sydney, NSW	100 to 120
FurJAM 2014 September 19–21, 2014	Sydney, NSW	120 to 140
FurJAM 2015 September 18–20, 2015	Sydney, NSW	227

Events

FurJAM 2007: Events included Taronga Zoo, Newtown Food Festival, a tour of The Rocks, and a picnic in the Botanical Gardens with just over 40 attendees. An attempt was made by Timon b, who had been banned from attending by a restraining order because of previous troublemaking, to sabotage its organization by false e-mails.
Chairmen or Organizers: AussieHusky

FurJAM 2008: AussieHusky intended to resign after 2007, but Alexander, the new organizer, did nothing, resulting in AussieHusky taking it back. T-shirts and badges were introduced. Friday was dominated by an evening pub gathering at the Rose in Chippendale; Saturday by an afternoon barbeque and fursuiting in Centennial Park, and an evening at a local movie; and Sunday by lazertag at LazerForce in the morning and an afternoon trip to Manly Harbour to either the Oceanworld aquarium or the WaterWorks. The T-shirt was by DietyOfDooky. FurJAM 2008 was again plagued by Timon b's attempt to sabotage it, by phoning the pub in the event's name to cancel the booking (the pub doublechecked with AussieHusky, who denied it), and telling the local council that the furs at the Centennial Park meet were molesting children (which got the Saturday afternoon activities checked out by a park officer).
Chairmen or Organizers: AussieHusky

FurJAM 2009: AussieHusky redesigned the FurJAM website in early 2009, but technical difficulties required it to be taken down for several months and wiped out all registration information, leading some Sydney furs to believe that FurJAM had been cancelled for that year. Events included ten-pin bowling in Darling Harbour, dinner at Pancakes on the Rocks, a trip to Taronga Zoo and a room party at the University of New South Wales with a DJ, games and art competitions. "Someone" (widely believed to be Timon b) tried unsuccessfully to cancel or change the dates of the events in AussieHusky's name just before the FurJAM. Timon b was seen at the FurJAM on Friday and Saturday nights despite being officially prohibited from attending. There was a brief altercation on Friday night between an attendee and a friend of Timon b.

Chairmen or Organizers: AussieHusky

FurJAM 2010: The events included dinner and drinks in a booked room at the Rose pub on Friday; a Saturday cooked lunch and art jam in Centennial Park, followed by an evening room party at Eastern Suburbs Legion Club featuring dancing, competitions, fursuiting, and a stand-up comedy performance by Anthrax; and Sunday morning laser tag, a scavenger hunt and finally dinner at the Docks Hotel in Darling Harbour. Timon b was refused entry into the Eastern Suburbs Legion Club by the Chairman.

Chairmen or Organizers: Ray Liehm

FurJAM 2011: Events included the usual Friday pub night, BBQ, dance party and scavenger hunt. The pub night moved to the Forresters Hotel in Surry Hills. Shirts for the meet were also available for sale via the FurJAM website.

Chairmen or Organizers: Bane Ranaura, Auri, Foxdale

FurJAM 2012: The Friday night pub event moved to The Occidental, with the second floor function room reserved for attendees. Saturday was the usual afternoon BBQ at Paperback Grove in Centennial Park, and evening activities at the Easter Suburbs Legion Club. Sunday was unscheduled to allow friends to meet and organize their own activities. The events concluded at The Helm Bar on Darling Harbour. There were no T-shirts in 2012.

Chairmen or Organizers: Foxdale, Auri, Enigma, Kat

FurJAM 2013: The Friday night pub event was held again at The Occidental, but the Saturday afternoon BBQ was moved from Centennial Park (in the eastern suburb of Randwick) to Sydney Park (in the suburb of St Peters), and the evening activities moved to Marrickville Bowls Club which was also the venue of the Sunday morning lasertag/bowling meet. The evening pub meet and Closing Ceremony was at the Pyrmont Bridge Hotel. The moves were intended to shorten the travel between the Saturday afternoon BBQ and the Saturday evening and Sunday morning events, which were now only one train station apart, although the unannounced train schedule created minor problems for some. Sunday morning's lasertag or bowling was scheduled opposite the Bronies of NSW's screening of the *Equestria Girls* movie, to present a programming alternative. There were enough calls to transition FurJAM to a regular convention at a hotel that Kat Aclysm issued a formal statement explaining why this was not practical.

Chairmen or Organizers: Foxdale, Kat Aclysm

FurJAM 2014: The Friday evening venue was the Harlequin Inn in Pyrmont, with a BBQ on Saturday morning in Sydney Park. The Saturday evening event was at the Manhattan Superbowl, where people could go bowling or meet downstairs in a privately booked room. Sunday morning was unscheduled to allow attendees to plan their own activities, with the final venue being The Palace Hotel, a pub near the State Capital Theatre. FurJam 2014's attendance was 120 to 140 on Friday and Saturday, shrinking to approximately 40 people attending the Sunday evening venue.

Chairmen or Organizers: Foxdale, Kat Aclysm, Shadow, Sli, Paulfox

FurJAM 2015: The 227 attendance did not include staff or minors who attended the Saturday barbeque under their guardian's membership. Events included a Saturday afternoon barbecue at the park, a Saturday evening dinner and dance on Darling Harbour, and socializing during Sunday. Friday and Sunday evening were just pub meets. The T-shirt was by Ivy/Muttasaur.

Chairmen or Organizers: Kat, Shadow, Foxdale

Furlandia

Furlandia is Oregon's first furry convention (as distinct from a camping event) beginning in 2013. It was organized by the Oregon furry community after several years of their going to Seattle-area furry conventions. After the first year, it was taken in as an activity of RainFurrest's RAIn, Inc., saving it from having to form its own corporation, and making RAIn the first corporation with two annual furry conventions in different cities.

Name & Date	Theme	Location	Attendance	Parade
Furlandia 2013 May 10–12, 2013	Put a Tail on It	University Place Hotel & Conference Center, Portland, OR	280	29
Furlandia 2014 May 23–25, 2014	300 BCE: Furs of the Iron Age	Sheraton Portland Airport Hotel, Portland, OR	348	64
Furlandia 2015 May 22–24, 2015	Adventure on the High Seas	Sheraton Portland Airport Hotel, Portland, OR	463	112

Events

Furlandia 2013: The first Furlandia drew several criticisms of first-convention disorganization: the convention was understaffed; the announced Dealer's Den was not open on the first day; the Fursuit Parade was badly organized and held outside the hotel on an overly-hot day; there were too many programming glitches; there was no place to eat within walking distance. The biggest complaint was that Furlandia was unexpectedly filmed for TV by a Viacommix camera crew for $1,000 donated to Furlandia's charity (which only reached $1,006). The TV filming was only announced at the opening ceremony, so it was unknown before then or to anyone who did not attend the opening ceremony; so the first that many attendees knew of it was when they saw a TV crew filming the convention. Although the cameramen tried to avoid filming anyone who did not give their permission, this still created tension. The footage was never used because the camera crew did not get enough signed clearances, but "us vs. them" rumors were that Viacom considered it "boring" since it did not show any fursuited sex orgies in the halls. The $1,006 charity donation was also challenged as considerably underreported. The committee clarified that that was only the Viacom donation; the total was closer to $2,000. The committee also reported "extreme hostility" by hotel staff toward fursuiters. The 2013 conbook cover was by Tojo the Thief. The T-shirt was by Julie Lane (Bijoux DeFoxxe).

Furlandia logo. Art by Kitsumi. Used with permission.

Guests of Honor: Artist G-o-H Tojo the Thief, Fursuit G-o-H Soki

Charity: Portland PAW Team (about $2,000)

Chairmen or Organizers: Braden Jones (Atso Fox)

Furlandia 2014: The second Furlandia moved to a different hotel. The Art Show was not held. There was a problem with "ghosting"; an estimated 50 to 75 attendees, including several fursuiters, never joined the convention. The T-shirt was in full color on black by Kacey Miyagami, who also did the conbook cover.

Guests of Honor: Artist G-o-H Kacey Miyagami, Fursuit G-o-H NitroShep

Furlaxation

    Charity: none
    Chairmen or Organizers: Shaun Feazle (Triss Winterdusk), Gene Armstrong

Furlandia 2015: Prior to the third Furlandia, there were several complaints from the staff of not enough action by the executive staff, leading to the resignation of chair Triss Winterdusk and the elevation of vice-chair Lumio Draco. Furlandia 2015 started with another 60 to 100 non-members among the attendees, contributing to a large, unruly crowd at the Friday night rave, but tightened badge-checking sharply reduced the "ghosts" by Saturday morning. The cash donation to the charity did not include $1,500 in-kind (volunteer hours). Kitsumi did both the conbook cover and the T-shirt.
    Guests of Honor: Artist G-o-H Kitsumi, Fursuit G-o-H Ognas
    Charity: Animal Aid PDX ($500+)
    Chairmen or Organizers: Lumio Draco

Furlaxation

Furlaxation (FLX) was a furry convention in Columbus, Ohio, from 2012 to 2014. It was organized by Furlaxation, Inc., a furry social and recreation club as distinct from an educational corporation. This permitted it more widespread activities than Morphicon. It self-destructed after FLX 2014; presumably the local furry community felt that Columbus did not need two annual conventions.

Name & Date	Theme	Location	Attendance	Parade
Furlaxation 2012 September 28–30, 2012	Furmageddon	Ramada Plaza Inn and Conference Center, Columbus, OH	241	43
Furlaxation 2013 September 6–8, 2013	Furries in Camelot	Ramada Plaza Inn and Conference Center, Columbus, OH	384	150 (estimated)
Furlaxation 2014 September 12–14, 2014	Murder Mysteries	Ramada Plaza Inn and Conference Center, Columbus, OH	188	60 (estimated)

Events

Furlaxation 2012: The T-shirt was by toboe-chan92.
    Guests of Honor: Randy Fox (Yappy Fox, fursuiter/puppetter), Special G-o-H Uncle Kage
    Charity: ($590.70)
    Chairmen or Organizers: Lightpaws

Furlaxation 2013: The T-shirt was by NekoDorei.
    Guests of Honor: Vermy Fox (furry artist, fursuiter), Revit (fursuiter)
    Chairmen or Organizers: Lightpaws

Furlaxation 2014: A sharp drop in attendance and a small Fursuit Parade was blamed on a lack of publicity, rumors that FLX 2014 had been cancelled, and poor hotel planning. The T-shirt was by Taya. Two weeks after FLX 2014, its hotel was closed by the Board of Health prompted by complaints from the convention. Shortly after that, Lightpaws announced its permanent cancellation due to "conditions of venue, staff professionalism, disastrous ad campaigns, and fandom turnout."
    Guests of Honor: Matthew Wayne Davis (2, the Ranting Gryphon, Furry standup comedian), SyberFox, FirestormSix (furry artist, fursuit maker)
    Chairmen or Organizers: Lightpaws

Furloween

Furloween, held in Orlando, Florida, each Halloween, is a cross between a big dinner & dance party and a furry convention. It is hosted at the Orlando Elk's Lodge by one person, Mach Stormrunner since 2000, but has most of the traditions and accouterments of a furry convention. Furloween has had a mascot, Ozzy Bat, displayed on a Furloween T-shirt and a fursuit, until recently. There has been a Furloween T-shirt since at least 2001. The attendance is not usually recorded. As Furloween has grown, an annual potluck picnic the next day at Blanchard Park has been added. Events outside of the official party have been set up by fans from all over Florida and outside the state, but Stormrunner does not accept responsibility for these.

Name & Date	Theme	Location	Attendance
Furloween 1999 October 30, 1999		Orlando Elk's Lodge, Orlando, FL	87 (estimated)
Furloween 2000 October 21, 2000		Orlando Elk's Lodge, Orlando, FL	?
Furloween 2001 October 27, 2001		Orlando Elk's Lodge, Orlando, FL	?
Furloween 2002 October 19, 2002	The Black Cat Strut!	Orlando Elk's Lodge, Orlando, FL	120+
Furloween 2003 November 1, 2003	Out for Blood!	Orlando Elk's Lodge, Orlando, FL (new address)	?
Furloween 2004 October 30, 2004	A Thief in the Night	Orlando Elk's Lodge, Orlando, FL	?
Furloween 2005 October 29, 2005	Keeps Coming Back	Orlando Elk's Lodge, Orlando, FL	?
Furloween 2006/VIII October 28, 2006	Oh yes, there will be blood paws	Orlando Elk's Lodge, Orlando, FL	?
Furloween IX October 27, 2007	This Spells Trouble	Orlando Elk's Lodge, Orlando, FL	?
Furloween X November 1, 2008	You Can Has Death	Orlando Elk's Lodge, Orlando, FL	?
Furloween 2009 October 24, 2009	?	Orlando Elk's Lodge, Orlando, FL	?
Furloween XII October 30, 2010	Otter B. Dead	Orlando Elk's Lodge, Orlando, FL	148
Furloween 2011/XIII/13 October 29, 2011	Where Nightmares DO Come True	Orlando Elk's Lodge, Orlando, FL	?
Furloween 2012/XIV October 27, 2012	?	Orlando Elk's Lodge, Orlando, FL	?
Furloween 2013 October 19, 2013	?	Orlando Elk's Lodge, Orlando, FL	?
Furloween 2014/15 October 18, 2014	?	Orlando Elk's Lodge, Orlando, FL	?
Furloween 2015 October 24, 2015	?	Orlando Elk's Lodge, Orlando, FL	?

Furloween

Events

Furloween 1999: This was the first general furry Hallow'een party in Orlando, Florida, for the Florida Furs, organized by Herbie Bearclaw because Hallow'een parties at his home had grown too large. He set up a one-evening fully-catered banquet and fursuit dance at the Orlando Elk's Lodge, with a cash bar and a limited number of dealers. It was so much work that he turned it over to Patrick Dowden (Mach Stormrunner) the next year.
 Chairmen or Organizers: Herbie Hamill (Herbie Bearclaw)

Furloween 2000:
 Chairmen or Organizers: Patrick Dowden (Mach Stormrunner)

Furloween 2001: The annual Furloween Party opened with Friday evening dinner at Kanpai Japanese Sushi and Steak House. Saturday began with noon lunch at the Fashion Square Mall food court, next to the Travelodge where participants were advised to stay. After lunch, attendees were advised to hang out at the mall or the Barnes & Noble across the street. The Furloween Party began at 7:00 p.m. at the Elk's Lodge. ($20 for the dinner & dance.) At 2:00 a.m. was the Shutdown Party and the move to the Party Party at the Travelodge. Sunday at noon the unofficial Blanchard Park Party (picnic & games) began, to 5:00 p.m. There was an evening dinner gathering followed by a movie party. RSVPs were required for the Friday and Saturday night dinners. A Furloween T-shirt, white glow-in-the-dark design on black cloth, was provided by Rags.
 Chairmen or Organizers: Patrick Dowden (Mach Stormrunner)

Furloween 2002: The "Fourth Annual Furloween Party" was extended from 7:00 p.m. until 2:00 a.m. It inaugurated an annual theme. [Who did the T-shirt?]
 Chairmen or Organizers: Patrick Dowden (Mach Stormrunner)

Furloween 2003: Furloween 2003 was officially on November 1, 2003; unofficially it stretched from October 31 to November 2. The Saturday night banquet and dance was at the Orlando Elk's Lodge (with a cash bar). Memberships/admission was $20; minors were required to bring a parental consent form. There was also a Friday early evening sushi dinner at the Kanpai Japanese Sushi and Steak House, Saturday lunch at the Fashion Square Mall food court, the Saturday evening Party!, a post–Party party, and a Sunday noon-to-5:00 p.m. picnic at Blanchard Park, followed by a theater group to see *Brother Bear*. The Elk's Lodge had a new address, but the Friday dinner and Saturday lunch were held at the old addresses, at which Mach passed out maps to the new Lodge. Due to the move of the Lodge, attendees staying for the all-night party events were advised to unofficially move from the old Travel Lodge to the closer Colonial Travel Lodge, which gave attendees a discount. The T-shirt by Rags was glow-in-the-dark green on black cloth.

Furloween 2004: Membership/admission was $30. The Furloween dinner and dance Lodge were from 6:00 p.m. to 2:00 a.m. But attendees were required to RSVP by October 24 to ensure admission to the banquet's buffet service, which included carved roast beef and chicken piccata. A cash bar was available to guests over 21. It was recommended that overnight attendees stay at the official Furloween hotel, the Travelodge Orlando Downtown Centroplex. Members staying over to the next day were invited to a potluck picnic at nearby Blanchard Park.
 Chairmen or Organizers: Patrick Dowden (Mach Stormrunner)

Furloween 2005: The dinner and dance lasted from 6:00 p.m. until 2:00 a.m.
 Chairmen or Organizers: Patrick Dowden (Mach Stormrunner)

Furloween 2006/Furloween VIII: Rooms were recommended at the Best Western Orlando East Inn & Suites for those who wanted to arrive early or stay late. Memberships were $30 at the door. As usual, the Furloween featured a fully catered banquet dinner and dance. Attendees were required to RSVP by October 21 to ensure admission to the banquet's buffet service, which included carved roast beef and chicken piccata. A cash bar was available to guests over 21. Two DJs put on a lightshow for a dance. There was a costume contest. Attendees in Fursuits went trick-or-treating afterwards at the Waterford Lakes Town Center mall. The black T-shirt with a glow-in-the-dark design was by Herbie Bearclaw.

Chairmen or Organizers: Patrick Dowden (Mach Stormrunner)

Furloween IX:

Chairmen or Organizers: Patrick Dowden (Mach Stormrunner)

Furloween X: Statistics were kept for Furloween X. 187 attended the evening dinner and party, and 70 to 90 were at the picnic.

Chairmen or Organizers: Patrick Dowden (Mach Stormrunner)

Furloween 2009: Despite the previous year being Furloween X, Furloween 2009 was celebrated as the 10th year "annifursary." Furloween returned to using the year rather than Roman numerals. There was a mix of all previous themes in honor of the tenth anniversary, rather than a new theme.

Chairmen or Organizers: Patrick Dowden (Mach Stormrunner)

Furloween XII: In addition to the usual catered dinner, fursuit dance, and costume contest, there was a murder mystery. There was the usual picnic the next day.

Chairmen or Organizers: Patrick Dowden (Mach Stormrunner)

Furloween 2011:

Chairmen or Organizers: Patrick Dowden (Mach Stormrunner)

Furloween 2012:

Chairmen or Organizers: Patrick Dowden (Mach Stormrunner)

Furloween 2013: A.k.a. Furloween 15. Mach Stormrunner was listed as Party Coordinator, with a staff of 8: Shep Otterpaw, Assistant Party Coordinator; Yappy Fox, Video and Sound; Radix, Web Design/DJ; Urson, Party Patrol; Mek "Stitch," Registration; Kryphos, Badge Design and Printing; DJ Cosmik, Featured DJ; and Wildwolf, Featured DJ.

Chairmen or Organizers: Patrick Dowden (Mach Stormrunner)

Furloween 2014: Cosmik was again a featured D.J.

Chairmen or Organizers: Patrick Dowden (Mach Stormrunner)

Furloween 2015: Cosmik was again a featured D.J.

Chairmen or Organizers: Patrick Dowden (Mach Stormrunner)

Furnal Equinox

Furnal Equinox was named by ShiroTora and promoted as "Toronto's First Furry Convention." It is incorporated as Anthropomorphic Events of Ontario (AEO). It was created to fulfill demand for a furry convention in the Toronto (Canada's largest city) area where no large-scale furry event had previously taken place, other than Camp Feral (a furry camp located three hours to the north). It has become Canada's largest furry convention, and the third-largest outside the United States.

Name & Date	Theme	Location	Attendance	Parade
Furnal Equinox 2010 March 6–7, 2010	Furry Fun and Games	DoubleTree by Hilton-Toronto Airport Hotel, Toronto, Ontario	330	40

Furnal Equinox

Name & Date	Theme	Location	Attendance	Parade
Furnal Equinox 2011 March 11–13, 2011	Wild Magic	DoubleTree by Hilton-Toronto Airport Hotel, Toronto, Ontario	450+	110
Furnal Equinox 2012 March 16–18, 2012	Infurnally Yours	DoubleTree by Hilton-Toronto Airport Hotel, Toronto, Ontario	651	160
Furnal Equinox 2013 March 8–10, 2013	Furries in Uniform	Sheraton Toronto Airport Hotel and Conference Centre, Toronto, Ontario	750+	206
Furnal Equinox 2014 March 7–9, 2014	Circus!	Sheraton Toronto Airport Hotel and Conference Centre, Toronto, Ontario	910+	265
Furnal Equinox 2015 March 13–15, 2015	Furry Arcade	Sheraton Toronto Airport Hotel and Conference Centre, Toronto, Ontario	1,051	285

Events

Furnal Equinox 2010: FE had been organized by a large group over Dan Skunk's Ontario Furries website since July 2008. Despite many resignations and dismissals—Dan Skunk claimed he was treated rudely by staff including the chairman at FE 2010, and was hassled by security—FE 2010 was considered a success. FE started a tradition of inviting two Guests-of-Honour, one from Canada (Bruton) and one from outside Canada. Gaming was played up in keeping with the theme; the committee were "coaches" and attendees were "players." Panels included an animal drawing workshop, a Furry Literature Q & A by Phil Geusz, and a furry history lecture. Reports emphasized that there were "40 Fursuits at the convention," as distinct from the number of fursuits in the Fursuit Parade. Heather Bruton and BushyCat drew the front and back covers of the conbook, with a sports theme. The T-shirt was by Arrowroot. Less than two weeks after the convention, Michael Bard, a leading Canadian furry fan and FE 2010 committee member, died of an unexpected stroke. Much of the FE social followup was dedicated to his memory.

Guests of Honor: Heather Bruton, Rebecca Frey (BushyCat) (furry artists)
Charity: Mississauga Humane Society (C$200)
Chairmen or Organizers: Mike Dickinson (Pakesh De), Blindsight

Furnal Equinox 2011: Furnal Equinox 2011 expanded to three days. Both guests of honor collaborated on the conbook cover and registration badge art. The charity auction included a C$450 commission from ZEN. The eleventh-floor Wolf's Den hospitality suite was introduced for sponsors, members of Ontario Furs, and for receptions by Camp Feral! and What The Fur. An expansion to the hotel's International wing, announced a couple of months before the convention, tripled the floorspace available, enabling FE 2011 to add a larger Dealers' Den, an artist's alley, and a Zoo relaxing area. The conbook front cover was by ZEN and the back cover by FirestormSix, and the T-shirt by Seraph.

Guests of Honor: FirestormSix (fursuit maker), ZEN (furry artist)
Charity: Mississauga Humane Society (C$4,000)
Chairmen or Organizers: Mike Dickinson (Pakesh De), Blindsight

Furnal Equinox 2012: Memberships were C$35 to preregistrants; C$45 at the door. The guests of honor collaborated on all artwork including the conbook cover, T-shirt, badge art, buttons and website artwork, and custom keycards. The Fursuit Parade began outdoors in FE's warmest weather to date (the temperature was almost 20°C, compared to an average of 4°C in mid–March). Sponsors

Furnal Equinox 2012 conbook (mislabeled 2011). Art by Dark Natasha. Used with permission.

received a pizza dinner in the Wolf's Den hospitality suite. The conbook cover was by Dark Natasha, and the T-shirt by Marci McAdam.
  Guests of Honor: Dark Natasha, Marci McAdam (furry artists)
  Charity: Mississauga Humane Society (C$8,000)
  Chairmen or Organizers: Mike Dickinson (Pakesh De), Blindsight

Furnal Equinox 2013: The new hotel offered more rooms and expanded convention facilities, including an expanded Dealers Den and the inaugural Art Show. A Supersponsor level was added to memberships, including an exclusive luncheon, a custom engraved dog tag, and the member's name published in the conbook. The Fursuit Dance Competition was first held (9 entrants). The hotel was sold out. The conbook cover was by RedCoatCat, and the T-shirt by Rukis.
  Guests of Honor: RedCoatCat, Rukis (furry artists)
  Charity: Mississauga Humane Society (C$6,000)
  Chairmen or Organizers: Mike Dickinson (Pakesh De), Blindsight

Furnal Equinox 2014: The first Masquerade was held, with the winners receiving admission to the Costume-Con 32 Masquerade (held in Toronto that year). The Fursuit Dance Competition almost tripled its number of entrants. TaniDa Real created a custom set of her "mood badges" for supersponsors. Bailey Bat and Yuki were married at FE 2014. The conbook cover was by Sandy Schreiber, and the T-shirt by Sabretoothed Ermine. This was the first year the convention had to expand into an overflow hotel, the Marriott Toronto Airport.
  Guests of Honor: Beth Davies (Sabretoothed Ermine), Sandy Schreiber (furry artists)
  Charity: Mississauga Humane Society (C$6,000)
  Chairmen or Organizers: Mike Dickinson (Pakesh De), Blindsight

Furnal Equinox 2015: FE continued to show growth, with the main convention hotel fully selling out by January. The fursuit photobooth moved to a dedicated room. The charitable donation increased, with a "mystery box" selling at the closing ceremonies for C$550. A "logo contest" held in Winter 2015 to rebrand the FE was won by Keianza. The conbook cover was by H0rs3, and the T-shirt by Xenotropis.

Guests of Honor: Xenotropos, H0rs3 (furry artists)
Charity: Mississauga Humane Society (C$9,001)
Chairmen or Organizers: Scani

Furpocalypse

Furpocalypse is the furry Halloween convention in New England that was started as a replacement for the cancelled successful FurFright. As such, it took off running with 1,200 attendees. Its website describes it as "a Halloween-based Anthropomorphic convention in Cromwell, Connecticut, with the goal to raise money for various animal/environmental charities by hosting a sci-fi themed 3-day event for anthropomorphic enthusiasts from all over the world."

Name & Date	Theme	Location	Attendance	Parade
Furpocalypse 2014 October 31–November 2, 2014	It's Alive!	Crowne Plaza Cromwell, Cromwell, CT	1,200	290
Furpocalypse 2015 October 30–November 1, 2015	Dark Carnival Freak Show	Crowne Plaza Cromwell, Cromwell, CT	1,400+	362

Events

Furpocalypse 2014:
Guests of Honor: Likeshine, Painted Dog
Charity: United States War Dog Association, Inc. ($3,807.60)
Chairmen or Organizers: Silver Wolf, Black Wolf, Dark Cougar, Gavin, Lucian

Furpocalypse 2015:
Guests of Honor: Jonathan Vair Duncan (Stigmata), Iggi Eastwind
Charity: United States War Dog Association, Inc. ($5,800)
Chairmen or Organizers: Dark Cougar, SilverWolf, Black Wolf, Lucian

Furry Connection North

Furry Connection North was created for the Detroit-area furs. It was administered by Furry Connection North, Inc., a not-for-profit corporation. Matthew Wayne Davis (2, the Ranting Gryphon) was a local resident and served as Vice-Chair and Director of Programming. FCN's goal was to have a "party" convention. In addition to traditional furry convention features, attendees could sign up at FCN to "Make Your Own Programming." There was an emphasis on games and dances, such as tournaments for poker, pool, Rock Band, Dance Dance Revolution, and open gaming in a video gaming and board gaming room.

Name & Date	Theme	Location	Attendance	Parade
Furry Connection North 2008 April 11–13, 2008	?	Best Western Executive Plaza, Ann Arbor, MI	372	57

Name & Date	Theme	Location	Attendance	Parade
Furry Connection North 2009 April 24–26, 2009	Prohibition	Sheraton Detroit Novi Hotel, Novi, MI	727	156
Furry Convention North 2010 April 9–11, 2010	FCN Rocks the '80s	Sheraton Detroit Novi Hotel, Novi, MI	880	189
Furry Connection North 2011 April 8–10, 2011	Ages of Japan	Sheraton Detroit Novi Hotel, Novi, MI	1,021	238
Furry Connection North 2012 April 13–15, 2012	Top Secret	Sheraton Detroit Novi Hotel, Novi, MI	1,179	230
Furry Connection North 2013 April 12–14, 2013	Mad Science	Sheraton Detroit Novi Hotel, Novi, MI	1,259	272

Events

Furry Connection North 2008: The hotel featured a central atrium with all rooms opening onto it, which added to the party atmosphere. Uncle Kage and 2 gave performances, and the 2 Sense Internet radio show broadcast from the FCN. Friday night DJs were Branwyn, Fizz, and Jibba, and Saturday night's were DJs Oddy and Rok Kaiser, each of whom featured a dance. The Video Room replaced *We're Back: A Dinosaur Story* with *Cats Don't Dance*. There were local micro brews. The Sponsor Lounge had hot dogs, sandwiches, macaroni, meat balls, lasagna, raviolis, candy, cookies and other snacks. A con report said, "I can't say that we always keep it PG-13, but it made for a interesting time."

Guests of Honor: MixedCandy Productions (LatinVixen and Adam Fisher)
Chairmen or Organizers: Gir Tygrin

Furry Connection North 2009: Events included a rant by 2, the Ranting Gryphon and Uncle Kage's Story Hour, fursuit charades, Olympics, and a Furry Variety Show, a Bucktown Tiger Live concert, and Whose Lion Is It, Anyway? (improv). The charity donation was raised in a game of Texas hold 'em poker. The Dorsai Irregulars provided security. The subwoofers of the music setup caused 27 light bulbs and six overhead light fixtures to fall. The conbook cover was by Tracy Butler.

Guests of Honor: Tracy Butler (cartoonist, creator of *Lackadaisy*)
Charity: Paws for a Cause ($280)
Chairmen or Organizers: Gir Tygrin

Furry Connection North 2010: FCN 2010 had a Dealer's Den, an Artist's Alley, and a Sponsor's Lounge, among other features. Events included such games as Furry Charades, Furry Pyramid (tria game show), and a Furry Variety Show. There was an Open Call Puppet Show, a *Method 1* podcast hosted by Nik Vulper & Gir Tygrin, and a Whose Lion Is It, Anyway? improv show. The Fursuit Parade ended outside the hotel where a DeLorean was parked, in keeping with the '80s theme. The hotel staff and convention security were complimented for being polite and friendly. The conbook cover was by Mary Mouse. FCN, Inc., reported $38,402 in revenue and $35,895 in expenses.

Guests of Honor: Mary Minch (Mary Mouse, furry cartoonist), Erin Middendorf (Dingbat, furry artist)
Charity: Humane Society of Huron Valley ($1,000)
Chairmen or Organizers: Gir Tygrin

Furry Connection North 2011: Uncle Kage gave a story hour. There was a Bucktown Tiger Live! Performance, a Furry Variety Show, an Open Call Puppet Show, and "FCN's World Famous Fursuit Games." Panels included one on sushi making. The charity donation included $1,209.70 from the charity table, $325 from the poker tournament, and $1,580 from the charity auction. The conbook cover was by Kacey Miyagami.

Guests of Honor: Kacey Miyagami, Tanja Freese (TaniDaReal) (furry artists), Uncle Kage (furry performer)

Charity: Greyhound Expressions ($5,000)

Chairmen or Organizers: Gir Tygrin

Furry Connection North 2012: Uncle Kage gave a story hour. The $5,000 charity donation included $1,214 in cash, $440 from the poker tournament, $1,975 from the Charity Auction, and $1,371 from FCN, Inc.

Guests of Honor: Scribblefox, Likeshine (furry artists)

Charity: Mutts and Mutts Rescue League ($5,000)

Chairmen or Organizers: Gir Tygrin

Furry Connection North 2013: All minors were banned from FCN 2013 due to the "serious burden" of getting legal parental consents. Uncle Kage's story hour was "Science, Pseudoscience and Outright Crap." Other events were "FCN's World Famous Fursuit Games," Whose Lion Is It, Anyway?, "Will It Freeze? Cryogenic Fun at -320°F!," "Charity Cards Against Humanity, a Look Left Concert, a Fursuit Dance Competition and a Furry Variety Show. The conbook cover was by Lizardbeth.

Guests of Honor: Jill0r, Lis Boriss (Lizardbeth), Karsten Auchter (BigBlueFox)

Charity: Country Cat & City Kitty Cat/Kitten Rescue ($21,299.67)

Chairmen or Organizers: Gir Tygrin

Although FCN 2014 was planned for April 11–13, 2014, FCN 2013 was the final FCN due to the retirement of key senior staff members. Chairman Gir Tygrin announced that to try to replace them "would be unrealistic and would potentially compromise the integrity of the event." FCN's organizers originally planned to hold the event for only five years; they considered the sixth year to be a bonus. The organization's supplies and funds were donated to other events and charities. The cancellation came as a shock to regular attendees since the FCN was very popular, and was incorporated. Basically, despite its popularity with attendees, nobody was willing to become one of the organizers and take on the work of running the FCN.

Furry Fiesta

Furry Fiesta (TFF for Texas Furry Fiesta), in a suburb of Dallas, was founded primarily for Texas furs. It is administered by Dallas Regional Anthropomorphic Meeting Association (D.R.A.M.A.), a 501(c)(7) non-profit governing organization formed in early 2008. Dallas is the home city of FurPlanet Productions, one of the Big Three (as of 2016) furry specialty publishers; and it usually publishes Furry Fiesta's Program Books and other publications.

Name & Date	Theme	Location	Attendance	Parade
Furry Fiesta 2009 February 20–22, 2009	Beginnings	Crowne Plaza Hotel, Addison, TX	542	92
Furry Fiesta 2010 February 19–21, 2010	Space Cowboys	Crowne Plaza Hotel, Addison, TX	779	145
Furry Fiesta 2011 February 25–27, 2011	Disco Infurno	Crowne Plaza Hotel, Addison, TX	1,034	165
Furry Fiesta 2012 February 24–26, 2012	Beyond Thunderdome	Crowne Plaza Hotel, Addison, TX	1,210	244
Furry Fiesta 2013 February 22–24, 2013	The Time-Traveler's Ball	Crowne Plaza Hotel, Addison, TX	1,492	292

Name & Date	Theme	Location	Attendance	Parade
Furry Fiesta 2014 February 21–23, 2014	Heroes & Villains	InterContinental Dallas, Dallas, TX	1,884	325
Furry Fiesta 2015 February 20–22, 2015	Out of the Inkwell: Toon City	InterContinental Dallas, Dallas, TX	2,425	429

Events

Furry Fiesta 2009: The attendance was 542 out of 561 members, with two from New Zealand. There were an Artists' Alley, a Dealers' Den, a Video Room, a Game Room, a Con Suite, and more. The Fursuit Parade, on Saturday evening rather than in the afternoon, was claimed to be the largest for a beginning convention. The opening ceremonies featured the Imperial March from *Star Wars*, played on kazoos. There was a live broadcast of the KnotCast podcast. Sunday events included a Fursuit Rodeo (games in fursuits) including a piñata smashing, keeping up the Texas image. The 52-page conbook had a color front cover by Tiffany Ross. The T-shirt had the TFF logo on the front and a design by Angel Manuel Blanco (Sketch Dalmatian) on the back. TFF 2009 shared its hotel with an orthodontists' convention. Attendees approved of the location, close to many fast-food restaurants.

Guests of Honor: James Robertson (Nexxus, founder of FurNation), Artist G-o-H Tiffany Ross, Musical G-o-H Sub-level 03

Charity: CARE (Center for Animal Research and Education) ($2,700+)

Chairmen or Organizers: Istanbul

Furry Fiesta 2010: Most of the events of the first TFF were repeated. The Pathfinder RPG debuted at the convention. It was covered by the *Dallas Morning News*, and by CBS 11 Dallas, as "Addison Hosting Convention of a Different Beast." The Program Book cover was by Dook. The T-shirt was by Michelle Light.

Guests of Honor: Tigerwolf (wizard of Tigerden Internet Services), Artist G-o-H Michelle Light, Writing G-o-H Kyell Gold

Charity: CARE (Center for Animal Research and Education) ($3,626.86)

Chairmen or Organizers: Istanbul

Furry Fiesta 2011: Friday started slowly, with panels on anatomy for artists, fursuit care, ballroom dance, and "your first furry con." In the evening, the 1970s were celebrated with a live shadow performance of *The Rocky Horror Picture Show*. There were also con essentials like writing and media panels, gaming, dance, and karaoke. Saturday had epic *Magic the Gathering* and *Talisman* gaming, a panel on 1970s culture by furries who experienced it, gaming and writing panels, live podcasting, and a concert by long-time, multi-fandom celebrity Matthew Ebel. Sunday had several panels about moving furry into the real world ("Taking it Pro" and "Using Your Powers for Good," and the first Furry Fiesta Sunday morning tea party, which became an ongoing tradition. The 48-page conbook had a front cover by Megan Giles and a back cover by DocMarcus. The T-shirt was drawn by Megan Giles and colored by Mitch DLG.

Guests of Honor: Lucky Coyote (furry artist, fursuit maker), Artist GoH Megan Giles (Dustmeat)

Charity: CARE (Center for Animal Research and Education) ($4,100)

Chairmen or Organizers: Istanbul

Furry Fiesta 2012: There was a Furry Night Live variety show. There were both a charity auction and a charity poker tournament. There were a separate convention-long Video Room, playing movies, cartoons, and other video programming, and an Internet Room. The attendance of Alex Vance (Khaki Dog), the founder of Bad Dog Books from Amsterdam, was sponsored by FurPlanet Productions. Rhubarb the Bear performed a "one bear" show. The Amber does Dallas group performed "REPO: The Generic Opera." The Program Book cover and T-shirt were by Mary Mouse.

Guests of Honor: Mary E. Minch (Mary Mouse), Kory Bingaman (furry artists, webcomic authors)

Charity: CARE (Center for Animal Research and Education) ($9,067)

Chairmen or Organizers: Glass Ferret

Furry Fiesta 2013: Thursday evening was mostly devoted to social activities. Friday had several meet&greets including a Brony meetup, Derek's Big Cat Sharing Hour, and the Furry Drama Show auditions and rehearsals. Friday evening had Rhubarb the Bear's Maximum fuR&B and the first Werewolf of the Dark Arts session. Saturday had a Piñata Paradox, a Furry Night Live, and several afternoon panels on ballroom dance leading to the evening formal Time Traveler's Ball, and a separate Saturday Night Dance: Till the End of Time. Sunday had a Charity Poker Tournament. It was announced at the Closing Ceremonies that TFF had finally outgrown the Crowne Plaza Hotel, and would move to the larger Intercontinental Dallas next year. Mary Mouse did the Program Book cover again. The T-shirt was by Heather Bruton.

Guests of Honor: Heather Bruton (furry artist), Ciara & Monoyasha (owners of DreamVision Creations, fursuit makers)

Charity: CARE (Center for Animal Research and Education) ($11,750)

Chairmen or Organizers: Path

Furry Fiesta 2014: The new hotel's elevators were strained, and the escalator was inactive. The convention took advantage of it by holding the Fursuit Parade down the inactive escalator—something that was never tried again. There were the usual afternoon panels and evening dancing, including a Friday fencing and swordplay panel for the "Heroes & Villains" theme. There were several demos of the new Mice & Mystics board game. There were book launches of Kyell Gold's *The Mysterious Affair of Giles* and the limited edition hardcover of Alflor Aalto's *The Prince of Knaves*. Friday was heavy on writing panels and workshops. Fox Amoore performed or had panels all three days. The Program Book cover was by Blotch. The T-shirt was outlined by Blotch and colored by Shiva.

Guests of Honor: Tess Garman & Teagan Gavet (Blotch, furry artists), Karsten Auchter (BigBlueFox; German furry videographer/DJ/fursuiter)

Charity: CARE (Center for Animal Research and Education) ($18,532.48)

Chairmen or Organizers: Path

Furry Fiesta 2015: Sanguine Games held a Play Ironclaw with Sanguine Games all three days. The daytime was devoted to panels and workshops, and the evenings to performances, games, concerts, and dances. The International Anthropomorphic Research Project (IARP) held a number of focus groups, including Women in the Fandom, Disabilities in the Fandom, and Artists in the Fandom. Furry DJ Cosmik (from Orlando, Florida) performed dance music throughout the weekend at the first of several conventions (Furry Fiesta, CaliFur, Anthrocon, Megaplex, EuroFurence), usually with his mate Rhubarb the Bear. There was the first official show by Bandthro, furry fandom's rotating-member band led by Fox Amoore. Later, they held an impromptu jazz night in Kempi's, the hotel's basement-level night club. The Program Book cover by Koji was also used for a poster. The T-shirt was by Dingbat.

Food trucks were brought to the hotel as a dining option. This was wildly popular with both the fans and the local business community. A Sunday night ice storm disrupted travel for many departing guests, staff, and the guests-of-honor.

Guests of Honor: Dingbat (furry artist), JD Puppy (fursuiter), Sanguine Games (gaming company)

Charity: CARE (Center for Animal Research and Education) ($17,000)

Chairmen or Organizers: Path

Furry Fiesta held a furmeet mini-convention on July 31–August 1, 2015, Furry Siesta. It was an informal pool party and meetup for fans across Texas, at the Crowne Plaza Addison, the original TFF hotel. 306+ attended. It had a Fursuit Parade led by Haven, the chair of LGBT gaming convention HavenCon, a traditional gaming room, video games, and karaoke. Ruhakana Rugunda, the Prime Minister of Uganda, attending the 12th annual convention of the International Community of Banyakigezi being held at the hotel at the same time, invited several fursuiters to make a brief appearance.

Furry Migration

Furry Migration is a furry convention in Minneapolis, Minnesota, created by Minnesota Furs (MNFurs), a non-profit corporation. It features nightly dances, fursuit games & parade, an artist alley and art show, panels, gaming, room parties, and a photo shoot. The convention's format is similar to that of Minicon, Minneapolis' long-standing s-f convention.

Name & Date	Theme	Location	Attendance	Parade
Furry Migration 2014 September 12–14, 2014	none	Ramada Minneapolis Airport Hotel, Bloomington, MN	543	115
Furry Migration II August 28–30, 2015	Back to Migration II	Hyatt Regency Minneapolis, Minneapolis, MN	701	188

Events

Furry Migration 2014: The first Furry Migration took advantage of Twin City St. Paul's being the home of Sofawolf Press, one of the largest furry fandom specialty publishers, to invite its owner Jeff Eddy and one of its most prominent authors, Kyell Gold as Guests-of-Honor. The program included Iron Artist and Iron Pen competitions to create art or a short story within 24 hours containing required "secret ingredients." There was an "APA at Con" newsletter. The video room featured American and Japanese animated and live-action furry movies and TV series.
  Guests of Honor: Author G-o-H Kyell Gold, Publisher G-o-H Jeff Eddy, Artist G-o-H Foxfeather
  Charity: None
  Chairmen or Organizers: Kellic J. Tiger

Furry Migration II: The charity in Spring Lake Park, MN, is a nonprofit cat & kitten rescue group devoted to catching feral cats, curing any diseases and spaying them, and finding permanent homes for them.
  Guests of Honor: Artist G-o-H Amber Hill (Vantid), Historic G-o-Hs Reed Waller (furry artist, creator of *Omaha, the Cat Dancer*), Ken Fletcher (furry cartoonist, co-creator of *Vootie*)
  Charity: Whisker Rescue ($1,400)
  Chairmen or Organizers: Kellic J. Tiger

Furry Spring Break

Furry Spring Break was intended to be the first "true" annual furry convention in the Deep South, ignoring Furloween which was considered as more of a Halloween party for Orlando-area furs. Despite its success, the first was the only one ever held due to most of its staff starting the rival Pawpet Megaplex the next year.

Name & Date	Location	Attendance
Furry Spring Break March 2–4, 2001	Ramada Resort and Convention Center, Orlando, FL	150

Furry Spring Break: The program included the usual Art Show and Dealers Room, a Pawpet puppet show, fursuit events, a StoryTeller's Circle, two dances ("Ravin' Paws" and "Fursuits and Friends"), a Saturday night banquet followed by a Variety Show, Mitch Beiro's "Midnight over Minerva," and many moderated panels on writing and drawing. The Charity Auction, run by Draconis, brought in $600; it was split between the C.A.R.E. Foundation and the chemotherapy expenses of Carole Curtis, the wife of one of the dealers, Mike Curtis. Unusual events included a Furry Book Swap where members could exchange books, panels hosted by an authorized Teddy Ruxspin representative, and a Wildlife Encounter presentation by the C.A.R.E. Foundation (Creating Animal Respect Education), a Florida wildlife rescue group.

When chairman Matt Henry tried to get a contract from the Ramada for 2002, he found that a group of fans (including several FSB staffers) had already booked it for a rival Pawpet Megaplex for the Orlando area. The FSB 2002 guest-of-honor was to have been s-f author Mercedes Lackey.

Guests of Honor: Phil Morrissey (furry artist)
Charity: C.A.R.E. Foundation ($300); Carole Curtis ($300)
Chairmen or Organizers: Matt Henry

Furry Unlocked

Furry Unlocked was originally named Unthrocon, and has just changed its name. It is the furry convention for Utah. It incorporated in 2013 as Wasatch Regional Anthropomorphic Arts and Entertainment (WRAAE). It has a strong gaming focus, and was unique in not having Guests of Honor, a charity, or a Fursuit Parade until 2015. Its cartoon mascot is Roki, a Utahraptor dinosaur.

Name & Date	Location	Attendance	Parade
Unthrocon 2013 August 30–September 1, 2013	Salt Lake City Radisson Hotel, Salt Lake City, UT	128	none
Unthrocon 2014 October 31–November 2, 2014	Salt Lake City Radisson Hotel, Salt Lake City, UT	212	none
Furry Unlocked 2015 October 30–November 1, 2015	Doubletree Suites, Salt Lake City, UT	252	55

Events

2012: In 2012 a sort of "convention preview" party was held, called tongue-in-cheek "Unthrocon," for those who couldn't attend Anthrocon that weekend. One ballroom at the Salt Lake City Sheraton hotel, one day (June 16, 2012), as many events as could be made work in the space. About 50 people showed up, which was considered as good enough to plan a con. It was started by Barnaby (formerly Overzen) and Tenax Raccoon. Damon Husky and Markaroo later volunteered to help. The party's attendees were polled in early 2013 and found to really want a convention with social spaces, gaming (a favorite), and dealers/artists. This helped set the stage for future years by focusing on what brought out the most attendees. The moniker "The Un-con" was coined as a play on the unofficial name of Unthrocon, and the convention's doing away with low-return traditional con aspects such as guests of honor, con books, art show, etc., was approved.

Unthrocon 2013: Gold-level preregistrants received a personalized dice bag and a full set of roleplaying dice. Many games, some modified for the furry setting, could be checked out during the convention. There were a Dealers' Den, fursuit group photo shoots, and dances. The T-shirt was by Lil Chu. There was no official chairman, but Barnaby filled the leadership role. Other core convention leadership included Tugs, Tenax, Damon Husky, Digi Dragon, and Markaroo.

Chairmen or Organizers: Barnaby

In late October 2013, Tenax, Tugs, Digi Dragon, Damon, and Markaroo incorporated Wasatch Regional Anthropomorphic Arts and Entertainment (d.b.a. WRAAE), a nonprofit chartered with putting on a yearly Utah furry convention with longer term goals of also providing support and programs back to the local furry community. Barnaby stepped down from convention staff/leadership to handle the fursuiting activities aspect of the convention.

Unthrocon 2014: It was moved to Halloween weekend (October 31–November 2, 2014) for cost reasons and as a great way to introduce locals to the furry fandom. There was more of everything.

Furry Unlocked 2015 logo. Art by RokiRed. Used with permission.

The 212 attendees included over 50 fursuiters. There were more dealers. Events included dances on Friday and Saturday nights, a Fursuit Dance Competition and a Medieval Dance Class, and both fursuit games and video game tournaments. Rabbit Valley, the furry specialty publisher, gave classes on furry writing. Gold preregistrations also received a personalized embroidered pillowcase. The T-shirt was by Lil Chu. This was the first year operated by WRAAE with a convention chair, Zato Bull, assisted by convention leadership including Tugs, Roochi, Digi, Damon, Tenax, Brighton, and Markaroo.

Chairmen or Organizers: Zato Bull

Furry Unlocked 2015: It was announced in January 2015 that Unthrocon would change its name to Furry Unlocked. Reasons were that it officially established a unique name and ended "Unthrocon," which had begun as a joke meaning "not Anthrocon" but was too often mistaken as "Anthrocon"; it was too hard to spell and was meaningless; and participants wanted a name identifying it instantly as a furry fandom activity. Furry Unlocked meant "an opportunity to unlock your inner furry." Competing local (non-furry) conventions necessitated a change in venue to the Salt Lake City Doubletree Suites. Attendance increased to 252 (the maximum allowed by the fire marshalls was 250) with tickets selling out by Saturday afternoon. A Fursuit Parade and a charity were added. The T-shirt was by Lil Chu. Zato started out the year as convention chair, but he moved out of state for work obligations, so the role transitioned to Klik. Klik's con staff included Tugs, Tenax, Lyrick, Roochi, Damon, Kuragari, Koru, Keagos, and Markaroo.

Charity: Best Friends Animal Society ($400+)

Chairmen or Organizers: Klik

On December 13, 2015, Furry Unlocked's parent organization, WRAAE, voted to cease operations and dissolve in March 31, 2016, citing its inability "to find anyone interested in and qualified for the business side of running a convention, and after four years and thousands of hours and tens of thousands of dollars, it was deemed that continuing to organize and host a convention in Salt Lake was no longer fungible." Unofficial reasons included the establishment of competing conventions such as Biggest Little Fur Con in nearby Reno, Nevada; Arizona Fur Con in Phoenix, Arizona; and a ComicCon in Salt Lake City; and the growth of Rocky Mountain Fur Con in Denver.

Furry Weekend Atlanta

Furry Weekend Atlanta grew out of social gatherings held at the homes of Atlanta-area furs over many years. The idea of holding a convention was first raised in 2001. Serious planning began in August 2003. The name was based on the older Anime Weekend Atlanta. The FWA was originally held around St. Valentine's Day, and often reflected this, until it was moved to mid–March in 2009. As of 2015, it is the fourth largest furry fan convention. FWA has had no conbook; it has a poster drawn by the guest of honor instead.

Name & Date	Theme	Location	Attendance	Parade
Furry Weekend Atlanta 2004 February 13–15, 2004		Holiday Inn Atlanta Airport-North Hotel, Atlanta, GA	270	20
Furry Weekend Atlanta 2005 February 11–13, 2005		Holiday Inn Atlanta Airport, Atlanta, GA	500 (estimated)	38
Furry Weekend Atlanta 2006 February 17–19, 2006		Holiday Inn Atlanta Airport, Atlanta, GA	563	56
Furry Weekend Atlanta 2007 February 16–18, 2007		Sheraton Gateway Atlanta Airport Hotel, Atlanta, GA	762	101
Furry Weekend Atlanta 2008 February 15–17, 2008		Sheraton Gateway Atlanta Airport Hotel, Atlanta, GA	1,046	165
Furry Weekend Atlanta 2009 March 19–22, 2009	Safari	Hilton Atlanta Hotel, Atlanta, GA	1,371	201
Furry Weekend Atlanta 2010 March 25–28, 2010	Carnival	Hilton Atlanta Hotel, Atlanta, GA	1,561	194
Furry Weekend Atlanta 2011 March 17–21, 2011	Furries in Wonderland	Hilton Atlanta Hotel, Atlanta, GA	1,621	?
Furry Weekend Atlanta 2012 March 15–19, 2012	Furries at the Moulin Rouge	Hilton Atlanta Hotel, Atlanta, GA	1,902	366
Furry Weekend Atlanta 2013 March 14–17, 2013	Still in Love	Westin Peachtree Plaza, Atlanta, GA	2,396	380 (estimated)
Furry Weekend Atlanta 2014 March 20–23, 2014	Furry University Shangri La:	Westin Peachtree Plaza, Atlanta, GA	2,488	415 (estimated)
Furry Weekend Atlanta 2015 April 9–12, 2015	The Furgotten Orient	Westin Peachtree Plaza, Atlanta, GA	3,252	700+

Events

Furry Weekend Atlanta 2004: The convention, centered around Valentine's Day, grew out of several years of informal fur-meets at furs' homes around Atlanta, Georgia. Planned events included anime, regular movie, and game rooms; an Art Show and Dealers' Den; an Artist Alley and a Headless Lounge; a Friday night poker tournament; Saturday afternoon Fursuit Masquerade and Parade, a Magic the Gathering tournament, Saturday evening improve and 2, the Ranting Gryphon's rant, and late-night dance with a DJ; and Sunday fursuit games and a DDR competition. There were panels and workshops on furry writing, fursuit construction, creating a furry web comic strip, furries in anime, and more.

Guests of Honor: LatinVixen (artist/fursuiter)
Chairmen or Organizers: Tiger Paw

Furry Weekend Atlanta 2005: The staff wore black jerseys with red and white highlights.
Guests of Honor: Jessica Maia Albee (Jessie T. Wolf), Fel (furry artists)

Charity: Ellijay Wildlife Rehabilitation Sanctuary (almost $3,000)
Chairmen or Organizers: Tiger Paw

Furry Weekend Atlanta 2006: The staff wore red and white jerseys with white text. The Frozen Oasis group hosted its first big adult (open to attendees of 21 and older) room party with dances, a DJ, a laser light show, and an alcoholic bar.
Guests of Honor: Bill Holbrook (comic-strip cartoonist), Matt Burt (Gunmouth, furry artist)
Charity: Ellijay Wildlife Rehabilitation Sanctuary (almost $4,000)
Chairmen or Organizers: Tiger Paw

Furry Weekend Atlanta 2007: The hotel sold out all rooms. The staff jersey was purple & black with white text; there were 45 committee and staff members. Activities included concerts by Critical Fail and Sub-level 03 on Friday and Saturday nights; three days of fursuit games; evening dances with the first hour of each dance for fursuiters; a rant by 2, the Ranting Gryphon; an Art Show auction conducted by Uncle Kage (who did NOT give a Story Hour here); and a Saturday night Texas hold 'em poker game conducted by Tiger Fox. A memorial service was held for fursuiter Kimberfox, who died of cancer earlier that month. A Video Game Room had heavy security to guard against theft of an Xbox 360 and a Wii. Frozen Oasis hosted a big room party. On Saturday night, a heavily-drunken fan who had been ejected from several room parties tried to commit suicide by jumping down a hotel staircase and getting stuck in the railings. There were several witnesses, and both the police and an ambulance were called. This gave rise to a following year of jokes and cartoons about "Tumbles the Stairdragon." "Tumbles" reappeared at FWA2008 to publicly apologize and to show that he was no longer drinking.
Guests of Honor: Strider Orion and Daria McGrain (artists)
Charity: Conservator's Center, Inc.
Chairmen or Organizers: Tiger Paw

Furry Weekend Atlanta 2008: Events included various panels, workshops, games, and dances, a Critical Fail concert, a Chocolate Fondue social, a Charity No Limit Texas Hold'em Tournament, a rant by 2, the Ranting Gryphon, a Matthew Ebel (Hali of Firpine) musical concert, a Furry Variety Show, and a big Video Gaming Room. A large inflatable obstacle course was set up outside the hotel. Furry Weekend Atlanta, Inc., reported $37,938 in revenue and $24,094 in expenses.
Guests of Honor: Bonk (furry artist), TILT Longtail (fursuiter)
Charity: Conservator's Center, Inc. ($5,001)
Chairmen or Organizers: Tiger Paw

Furry Weekend Atlanta 2009: FWA 2009 became the fifth furry convention to top a thousand attendees. It moved from the Sheraton Gateway to the much larger Hilton Atlanta Hotel, the location of Dragon*Con and much closer to the airport. However, the move required the FWA to give up its traditional Valentine's Day dates due to the new hotel's already being booked. The move from mid–February to mid–March meant better weather, and the abandonment of the Valentine theme. The Safari theme was emphasized. The Conservators' Center brought four servals to the FWA.
Guests of Honor: Lis Boriss (Lizardbeth, furry artist), Matthew Ebel (Hali of Firpine, musician)
Charity: Conservators' Center, Inc. ($5,054)
Chairmen or Organizers: Tiger Paw

Furry Weekend Atlanta 2010: FWA 2010 added a Rock Band tournament, with a new sound system and a flying truss from the ceiling to accommodate the bands. The charity donation included $880 from a poker tournament.
Guests of Honor: Kami Cheetah
Charity: Conservators' Center, Inc. ($4,600+)
Chairmen or Organizers: Tiger Paw

Furry Weekend Atlanta 2011:
 Guests of Honor: Lacy, CloudPouncer (fursuit making team), Rusty Shakleford (Zhivago D, furry artist)
 Charity: Conservators' Center, Inc. ($8,000+)
 Chairmen or Organizers: Tiger Paw

Furry Weekend Atlanta 2012: The programming included a poker tournament that added $1,440 to the charity donation.
 Guests of Honor: Kyell Gold (furry author), Rukis (furry artist, author)
 Charity: Conservators' Center, Inc. ($18,000+)
 Chairmen or Organizers: Tiger Paw

Furry Weekend Atlanta 2013: The FWA moved to the larger downtown Westin hotel. Its 70 floors led to its nickname of ElevatorCon. The Fursuit Parade included an honor guard, led by a fursuiter holding a U.S. flag, of three EMTs holding a photograph of Lemonade Coyote (Timothy McCormick), a popular fursuiter and EMT who was killed in a traffic accident the previous month.
 Guests of Honor: Jimmy Chin (furry cartoonist, fursuiter), Hillary Renee Luetkemeyer (Hibbary, furry artist)
 Charity: Conservators' Center, Inc.
 Chairmen or Organizers: Tiger Paw

Furry Weekend Atlanta 2014: On October 13, 2013, FWA sponsored the GeorgiaFurs' fursuit-intensive float in the Atlanta Pride Parade and Party. At FWA 2014, the Fursuit Dance competition was broadcast online, and was watched by an estimated 7,000+ people.
 Guests of Honor: Lauren Henderson (Louvelex, a.k.a. Louve, furry artist, fursuiter)
 Charity: Conservators' Center, Inc. ($20,000)
 Chairmen or Organizers: Tiger Paw

Furry Weekend Atlanta 2015: Silverfox5213 drew a poster.
 Guests of Honor: Princess Rei (furry artist), Silverfox5213 (Malay furry artist)
 Charity: Conservators' Center, Inc. ($28,000)
 Chairmen or Organizers: Tiger Paw

Furry Weekend Holland

Furry Weekend Holland began as a furmeet in the northern Netherlands in 2010, and grew into a social convention in 2012. Although arguably still a furmeet, its size, number of staff, hotel setting, and annual schedule qualify it as a convention. Attendance is not automatic; attendees must pre-register and be approved by the organizers.

Name & Date	*Location*	*Attendance*
Furry Weekend Holland 2012 March 30–April 1, 2012	Tweehek (Groups Accommodation), Wesdorp, Drente, Netherlands	57+
Furry Weekend Holland 2013 March 15–18, 2013	The Labyrinth, Sleen, Drenthe, Netherlands	84
Furry Weekend Holland 2014 March 28–31, 2014	The Labyrinth, Sleen, Drenthe, Netherlands	80
Furry Weekend Holland 2015 March 27–30, 2015	The Labyrinth, Sleen, Drenthe, Netherlands	81

Events

Furry Weekend Holland 2012: FWH 2012 featured socializing with friends, good food, and fursuiting.
Chairmen or Organizers: Sithy, Okill

Furry Weekend Holland 2013: The same.
Chairmen or Organizers: Okill, Sithy

Furry Weekend Holland 2014: The same.
Chairmen or Organizers: Okill, Sithy

Furry Weekend Holland 2015: The same. Registration was €150.
Chairmen or Organizers: Okill, Sithy

FurryCon

FurryCon was a Swedish convention held in 2009. It was primarily a social event, but it did last for three days, included about 30 staff, had a few dealers, and included two fursuiters. It was considered a success, but was not repeated.

Name & Date	Location	Attendance
FurryCon September 18–20, 2009	A social meeting area next to a café, Karlstad	110

Events

FurryCon: Drugs including alcohol were not allowed, and adult material was restricted. The attendees shared a dormitory in a nearby gymnasium (senior high school). The organizers took the name of Spots and Stripes (SAS). There were originally two co-chairs, Ringo and Kirrow, but due to disagreements, Ringo dropped out before the convention. Memberships were 150 SEK with dormitory access, 100 SEK without, and 50 SEK for one-day attendance. Events and included fursuit bowling, a combined dealers'/video game area, a drawing area, movies, an ear tail construction workshop, and a charity raffle.
Charity: Djurskyddet Karlstad [Karlstad Animal Welfare] (1,181 SEK [about $170])
Chairmen or Organizers: Kirrow

FurryCon

FurryCon began as a supposed one-time-only convention; the Furry End of the World Convention in Rochester, New York, to take advantage of the popular Mayan End-of-the-World prediction in 2012. The world didn't end, and Rochester furry fans—especially the convention's organizer—discovered that they liked having an annual convention. FurryCon, for 21+ attendees, is permanently organized by Chairman Soron, operating as the Kanouse Entertainment Group. Each FurryCon has included a Friday night Frozen Oasis party, hosted by Soron and Etheras. In June 2014, the U.S. Patent and Trademark Office only allowed Soron to register the FurryCon service mark and name with a specific disclaimer of the use of the term "furry con" as exclusive.

Name & Date	Theme	Location	Attendance
Furry End of the World Convention December 20–23, 2012		Radisson Riverside Rochester, Rochester, NY	278

FurryCon

Name & Date	Theme	Location	Attendance
Game of Con Chairs Cancelled for 2013			
FurryCon 2014 May 8–11, 2014	A Game of Con Chairs Season One: A Winner Is Coming	Radisson Riverside Rochester, Rochester, NY	313
FurryCon 2015 May 21–25, 2015	A Game of Con Chairs Season Two: War Is Coming	Radisson Riverside Rochester, Rochester, NY	294

Events

Furry End of the World Convention: It was billed as "The Last Furry Convention Ever!!" and "Where Will You Be on 12.21.2012?" (the end of the world according to the "prophecy." There were no Guests of Honor or traditional charity, although $1,200 was raised for Wolfgem's medical expenses. (Gemily West, Wolfgem, was seriously injured and her furry boyfriend killed by a drunk driver while walking their dogs on July 16, 2012.) There was a 36-page "The Wasteland Survival Guide." The singular convention was so popular that it was announced that it would be followed in December 2013 by Furry CON(spiracy), but this was cancelled. When it was resumed for 2014, it was quite different.

Chairmen or Organizers: Soron

FurryCon 2014: FurryCon 2014 was billed as Game of Con Chairs: Season 1, the first in a series of three themed as an elaborate furry version of George R. R. Martin's "Game of Thrones" fantasy novels (and its TV spinoff). Costumes, convention decorations (including elaborate coats-of-arms), staff roleplaying, and five Guests of Honor (as honorary House leaders) were announced. The ruling House was House Bearathon (motto: "Ours is the Furry," leader fursuiter Foxwell). The other Houses were House Lyonstare ("Hear Us Roar!," Draconis and Keefur); House Bark ("Bark Bark Bark Bark Bark," Kyle McCarthy); House Taurgaryen ("Two Sets of Claws and Four Paws," Roxikat); and House Foxish ("Cuteness is Power," Etheras). At the closing ceremony, SomaCat of House Taurgaryen was declared the winner and next year's honorary Chairman ("Paw of the King"). Other events: 1st, 2nd, and 3rd place were awarded in a Magic the Gathering tournament, a poker tournament, five video game tournaments, six fursuit games, a costume competition, and a dance contest. And the Frozen Oasis Party. The 40-page conbook was titled "The Lineages and Histories of the Seven Fandoms." (Soron was officially "Soron, of House Bearathon, First of His Name, King of the Anthros and the First Furs, Lord of the Seven Fandoms, and Protector of the Realm.")

Guests of Honor: see above
Chairmen or Organizers: Paw of the King Soron

FurryCon 2015: The Houses and House Leaders/G-o-Hs were House Avarryn ("Soar as High as Honor," Temperance); House Bark ("Never Send a Dog to Do a Fox's Job," Hixbi Fox); and Houses Lyonstare and Foxish returning. Lord Aerun Wolfsong of House Bark was the winner. There was a 46-page conbook. It was announced that 2016's theme would be A Game of Con Chairs Season 3: The Final Season, with the motto "Vengeance Is Coming." Nobody knew what would become of FurryCon next.

Guests of Honor: see above
Chairmen or Organizers: Paw of the King Soron

Top: Anthrocon T-shirt (art by TaniDaReal, used with permission). *Bottom:* Arizona Fur Con 2013 conbook (art by Myenia, used with permission).

EuroFurence XVIII conbook (art by Henrieke Goorhuis, used with permission).

Left and middle: Zampacon mascots, Dante and Beatrice (art by Aledon Rex and Hologram, used with permission). *Right:* EAST V logo (art by Greykitty & Konu, used with permission).

Japan Meeting of Furries 2014 poster (art by anonymous, used with permission).

Philippine Anthro Festival 2015 poster (art by JAZcabungcai, used with permission).

Camp Feral! 2010 Survival Guide (art by Blotch, used with permission).

Left: Furry Weekend Atlanta 2015 poster (art by Silverfox5213, used with permission). *Right:* Furry Fiesta 2015 poster, mislabeled 2014 (art by Koji, used with permission).

Gdakon 2014 banner (art by Fuckie, used with permission).

Top: Furry Connection North 2011 Conbook (art by Kacey Miyagami, used with permission). *Bottom, left:* Infurnity banner (art by Zilvan, used with permission). *Bottom, right:* Kemocon poster (art by J.O., used with permission).

ZodiaCon 2013 poster (art by Mikairu, used with permission).

FurryLah

FurryLah (FL!) was advertised as "Singapore's first Furry convention, held this year end right in Sunny Singapore on her 2015 Jubilee year running from November 28th to 29th. The convention will bring you the best of the furry fandom right here in Singapore with fusion of local Singaporean twists here lah!"

Name & Date	Location	Attendance
FurryLah November 28–29, 2015	Bayview Hotel Singapore	30

Events

FurryLah: The first day of FL! ran from 8:30 in the morning when registration began to the Closing Ceremony at 5:00 p.m. The program was held in the Bayview Main Stage hall. The schedule included Opening Ceremony, a half-hour "My First Furcon" panel, a one-hour "Icebreaker," a one-hour "AnthroAsia" panel, a one-hour lunch break, a one-hour "Creative PawPads" special interest group, a half-hour "Art Jam Wall Scrawl," a half-hour "Meet the Fursuiters," a half-hour "Fursuit Photoshoot," a one-hour "Vee's Fursuit Games," and the Closing Ceremony. There was a separate Dealers Den. The second day "(Sunday) 29th Nov will comprise of a Fursuit walk at Suntec City shopping center and convention center and a concurrent visit to the annual Anime Festival Asia (AFA). Tickets to AFA are not included in the convention registration fees."

The panels showed that FL! had the support of the AnthroAsia online group. Several Southeast Asian furry fans attended both FL! in Singapore in November and FURUM in Kuala Lumpur the next month. Those who could afford to also went to Thai Tails, the first Thai furry convention, in Bangkok on January 30, 2016 (or 2559—Thailand uses the Buddhist calendar).

Chairmen or Organizers: Krado, Gale, Gyro Wolf

FurryLah! 2015 poster. Art by FL! Committee. Used with permission.

Furs Upon Malaysia (FURUM)

Furs Upon Malaysia is a furry convention for **Malaysian** fans in Kuala Lumpur, the capital. It was created after several years of Malaysia's furry meets in conjunction with Comic Fiesta, an anime/comics convention held annually since 2002 with an attendance of over 30,000 in 2012. "Apa khabar 'bulu-bulu' (furries) sekalian! [translates to 'How's every furry doing?']. Do you always drool all over yourself, seeing your fur-iends attending countless furry conventions? Do you also secretly weep in front of your screen looking at the tons of photos during and after those conventions?

Furs Upon Malaysia banner. Art by fatdrake. Used with permission.

If the answer is yes, don't worry! We're with you. This year, we'll be bringing a part of the furry convention experience to Malaysia! All are welcome to FURUM [FURs Upon Malaysia]." It has two cute cartoon mascots: Slappy the Tiger and Sunny the Bear.

Name & Date	Theme	Location	Attendance	Parade
Furs Upon Maylasia December 19–20, 2015	Cuti-cuti Maylasia	Mines Wellness Hotel, Kuala Lumpur	86	23

Events

Furs Upon Malaysia [2015]: The convention was held alongside Comic Fiesta at the neighboring Mines International Exhibition and Convention Center, a 15-minute drive from the Kuala Lumpur city center. The Guest of Honor (GoH) for the convention was Silverfox5213, a famous Malaysian furry artist with an international presence. Attendees were required to register by November 18. The attendance was almost triple the expected attendance of 30. Besides Malaysian fans, there were attendees from the Philippines, Singapore, Thailand, and the U.S. Attendees (RM 30) received their choice of a Slappy or Sunny illustrated badge, and a goodie bag with a mascot 3D papercraft, custom candy box by fatdrake (containing a piece of candy and a button badge designed by the GoH), and a A4 poster of the mascots. Sponsors (RM 90) received the above plus a customized badge with their fursona's photo, and a T-shirt (done by the GoH as well). Malaysian furry art ("Artis Buatan Malaysia" in Malay) was emphasized with most of the artwork contributed by local furry artists. The Fursuit Parade walked from the FURUM hotel to the main entrance of the Comic Fiesta. There were furcon introduction panels, icebreakers, video games and board game sessions, individual and group photography sessions, a painting workshop by Guest of Honor Silverfox5213, and demonstration of papercraft by fatdrake. The closing ceremony included a free commission by the GoH as a mystery gift during the lucky draw session.

Guests of Honor: Silverfox5213 (furry artist)
Chairmen or Organizers: CTWolf with Dapiko Dapaw, FatDrake, Foster Cole, and Marvin Raptor

Furstivus

Furstivus was a one-time-only furry convention organized in Philadelphia by SkippyFox to celebrate the 2012 New Year, since the traditional New Year's Furry Ball furmeet (since 2005) was not held that year. After the event, SkippyFox allowed the Furstivus.com domain to expire and returned to the New Year's Furry Ball.

Name & Date
Furstivus
December 30, 2011–January 1, 2012

Location
Crowne Plaza Philadelphia West,
Philadelphia, PA

Attendance
238

Parade
45

Furstivus was "a holiday furry convention" with a full convention format of a website, a Dealers' Den, a Fursuit Parade, panels and games, live music, a charity, a conbook with a cover by Herbie Bearclaw, and a T-shirt by Crystal Gafford (Kittrel). It mimicked the Festivus parody holiday of TV scriptwriter Dan O'Keefe with an "Airing of Grievances" and "Feats of Strength," furry-themed.

Charity: Child's Play ($3,243)
Chairmen or Organizers: SkippyFox

Furstivus T-shirt. Art by Crystal Gafford (Kittrel). Used with permission.

— Furstock —

Poland's Furstock is not really a furry convention, since it takes place unofficially amidst the July-August Przystanek Woodstock at Kostrzyn nad Odrą, the largest open-air music festival in Europe. But due to its multi-day length and its size, it is closer to a convention than a furmeet. It is organized by members of the Polfurs group who pitch their tents together in a circle, creating a furry mini-colony with power generators, laptops, floodlighting, cooking equipment, etc., within the music festival. The furs both participate in the general activities, and have their own furry events. All attendance totals are estimates, due to the constant wandering in & out of non-furry festival attendees. There are few or no fursuits, but there is a Polfurs pawprint flag.

Name & Date	*Attendance*	*Name & Date*	*Attendance*
Furstock 2005 August 5–6, 2005	6	Furstock 2011 August 4–6, 2011	40
Furstock 2006 July 28–29, 2006	12	Furstock 2012 August 2–4, 2012	40
Furstock 2007 August 3–4, 2007	26	Furstock 2013 August 1–3, 2013	45
Furstock 2008 August 1–3, 2008	40	Furstock 2014 July 31–August 2, 2014	45
Furstock 2009 July 31–August 2, 2009	45	Furstock 2015 July 30–August 1, 2015	About 45
Furstock 2010 July 30–August 1, 2010	40		

Furtastic

Furtastic is the first Danish furry convention. It is small, limited to fifty furs in an outdoor, rustic setting. The T-shirt each year is by EvilKitty3.

Name & Date	Theme	Location	Attendance
Furtastic 1 July 8–10, 2011	none	"Tyvdalhøj," a scout cabin outside Aalborg	29
Furtastic 2 July 12–15, 2012	none	"Tyvdalhøj," a scout cabin outside Aalborg	26
Furtastic 3 July 4–7, 2013	none	"Tyvdalhøj," a scout cabin outside Aalborg	31
Furtastic 4 July 10–13, 2014	none	Olufsborg camp, Hundslund, Jutland	42
Furtastic 5 July 22–25, 2015	Music of the Wild	Olufsborg camp, Hundslund, Jutland	51

Furtastic 4 T-shirt. Art by EvilKitty3. Used with permission.

Events

Furtastic 1: Furtastic was organized around New Year's of 2010, but due to other furry events in Denmark planned for that year, it was postponed until 2011. It met at a scout camp in the midst of a wooded area outside Aalborg, with accommodation for 60 people. The informal program emphasized indoor board and card games such as "Ottie's Adventure," and reading furry comics and books; and outdoor social activities and relaxing under the trees. A bar tent was available. There were a Saturday trip into Aalborg, a BBQ, a group photograph, an art auction, and an evening party with dancing. There were 3 fursuiters.
Chairmen or Organizers: Peter Schytte (Terril)

Furtastic 2: Furtastic 2 was the same. There were 5 fursuiters.
Chairmen or Organizers: Peter Schytte (Terril)

Furtastic 3: "Ottie's Adventure," evening dancing, and the art auction became regular events. The dancing became a fursuit dance with the growing number of fursuits. There was an emphasis on hiking, but it was not a theme.
Chairmen or Organizers: Peter Schytte (Terril)

Furtastic 4: Furtastic 4 moved to a better new camp closer to the sea. There was free WiFi.
Chairmen or Organizers: Peter Schytte (Terril)

Furtastic 5: The Olufsborg camp was popular, but the attendance of 51 was the camp's maximum. A discussion was held whether to move to a larger camp, or to remain at Olufsborg with 51 as the attendance limit.
Chairmen or Organizers: Peter Schytte (Terril)

Furtasticon *see* ConFURence East

Further Confusion

Further Confusion was created in 1999 in the San Francisco Bay area when the ConFurence moved its traditional late January dates to April, creating an opening for a new January convention.

Name & Date	Theme	Location	Attendance	Parade
Further Confusion 1999 January 14–17, 1999	Paws Across the Bay	Westin Santa Clara, Santa Clara, CA	691	no records
Further Confusion 2000 January 27–30, 2000	FCY2K	San Mateo Marriott, San Mateo, CA	982	no records
Further Confusion 2001 January 25–28, 2001	A Furry Odyssey	San Mateo Marriott, San Mateo, CA	1,114	no records
Further Confusion 2002 January 24–27, 2002	Further Confusion University	San Mateo Marriott, San Mateo, CA	1,137	no records
Further Confusion 2003 January 23–27, 2003	Furries in Wonderland	DoubleTree by Hilton—San Jose Hotel	1,201	no records
Further Confusion 2004 January 22–26, 2004	The Great Outdoors	DoubleTree by Hilton—San Jose Hotel	1,411	125
Further Confusion 2005 January 13–17, 2005	Furries of the Nile	DoubleTree by Hilton—San Jose Hotel	1,712	no records
Further Confusion 2006 January 19–23, 2006	Renfair: A Knight's Tail	DoubleTree by Hilton—San Jose Hotel	1,911	208

Name & Date	Theme	Location	Attendance	Parade
Further Confusion 2007 January 18–22, 2007	Fur Your Eyes Only	DoubleTree by Hilton—San Jose Hotel	2,062	287
Further Confusion 2008; FCX January 24–28, 2008	The Fur East	DoubleTree by Hilton—San Jose Hotel	2,423	380(?)
Further Confusion 2009 January 22–26, 2009	Surf Safari	DoubleTree by Hilton—San Jose Hotel	2,587	530
Further Confusion 2010 January 21–25, 2010	Gold Rush	Fairmont San Jose, San Jose, CA	2,770	487
Further Confusion 2011 January 13–17, 2011	Furries Gone Wild!	Fairmont San Jose, San Jose, CA	2,801	477
Further Confusion 2012 January 12–16, 2012	The Infurmary	San Jose Convention Center, Marriott and Hilton Hotels, San Jose, CA	3,021	458
Further Confusion 2013 January 17–21, 2013	Furbidden Planet—A Retro Sci-Fi Adventure	San Jose Convention Center, Marriott and Hilton Hotels, San Jose, CA	3,380	560
Further Confusion 2014 January 16–20, 2014	Further Confusion vs. the World: An Adventure in Comics & Gaming	San Jose Convention Center, Marriott and Hilton Hotels, San Jose, CA	3,560	643
Further Confusion 2015 January 15–19, 2015	London Fog: A Victorian Murder Mystery	San Jose Convention Center, Marriott and Hilton Hotels, San Jose, CA	3,527	643

Events

Further Confusion 1999: Further Confusion was technically run by Anthropomorphic Arts and Education, Inc., a not-for-profit corporation incorporated primarily to organize Further Confusion. FC 2000 published FC 1999's financial report, which listed $45,500 in revenue, from $27,390 in memberships and $18,110 in donations. Expenditures included $3,500 to the charities, a pass-on to FC 2000 for its initial expenses, and the remainder to the parent AAE, Inc., for its expenses and to sponsor other charity events. There were panels, workshops, costuming presentations (fursuits), a masquerade, exotic animal life-drawing classes, and evening dances, both DJd and with a live band, the Purple Nurple Live! There were an Art Show and Dealers' Room. The Dealers' Room of 39 tables sold out and a Dealers' Annex of nine more tables was added on the second floor. (The dealers there complained of being overlooked.) FC 1999 started a tradition of giving attendees a blank transparent badge holder with just their names, and letting them choose which of six miniature color Badge Art paintings to put in it. The 64-page conbook had a color cover by Ken Mitchroney. The T-shirt was by Chris McKinley.

Guests of Honor: Ed Kline (fursuit maker), Ken Mitchroney (cartoonist), Michael H. Payne (furry author)

Charities: The Coyote Point Museum, Therapy Pets ($3,500)

Chairmen or Organizers: Brent Edwards (Chip Unicorn), Peter Torkelson (WhiteFire)

Further Confusion 2000: Memberships were $35 at the door. The program was again in s-f convention format with moderated panels, and workshops on art and fursuit making. The Dealers Room sold out. Anthropomorphic Arts and Education, Inc., reported $79,523 in revenue, mostly from memberships and donations. The Art Show and auction made $35,570.88, and reported that all checks to artists were sent out within a month after the convention. The 60-page Program Book

Further Confusion logo. Art by Foofers (Phil Burgess). Used with permission.

had a color front cover by John Nunnemacher, and a back cover by Frank Gembeck, Jr. The FCY2K T-shirt was by Baron Engel.

Guests of Honor: C. J. Cherryh, Jane Fancher (s-f authors), Shawn Keller (animator), John Nunnemacher (furry cartoonist), Karen Prell (Henson Productions performer), Mike Quinn (Pixar puppeteer)

Charity: Cartoon Art Museum, Friends of the Sea Otter ($3,000 each)

Chairmen or Organizers: Peter Torkelson (WhiteFire)

Further Confusion 2001: FC 2001 became the third furry convention to top 1,000 attendees. Thursday was left unprogrammed for socializing; the convention officially began when the Dealers Room opened on Friday. A programming highlight was a life-drawing class featuring exotic animals from an ocelot and a serval to large snakes and a rose cockatoo hungry for affection; brought by the Barry Kirshner Foundation. (An advantage to the San Mateo Marriott was that it was about the only hotel that would allow large animals.) There was a puppet musical dramatization of the song, "The Thing." Several s-f authors were speakers, including Poul and Karen Anderson. Cheetah and several other German fans were present to promote EuroFurence 7 later that year. There were Pawpet Shows on Friday and Sunday. Saturday featured an Iron Artist competition, the Masquerade, and Uncle Kage's Story Hour. There was a convention-long Video Room. There were all the daytime programming events and nighttime parties of a large s-f convention. The 68-page conbook had a wraparound color cover by Christina "Smudge" Hanson. The FC 2001 T-shirt by Frank Gembeck featured a white glow-in-the-dark design on black. AAE, Inc., reported total revenue of $83,690, with $37,554.08 from the Art Show. The weather was horrible, isolating fans in the hotel. It was so bad that many flights to San Francisco International Airport were cancelled or diverted to another airport miles away, requiring fans who had expected to take the free bus from the San Francisco airport to the hotel to make a long and expensive taxi trip instead. The main problem, and a bad one, was with overcrowding. On the last day of the convention, the committee went to the Dealers Room to take table reservations for FC 2002. So many people signed up for tables so quickly that the 2002 Dealers Room was seriously oversold before anyone realized it, with several major 2001 dealers not yet signed up at all. The committee took full responsibility for the error, which most attendees felt was of the "it could have happened to anyone" nature. Unfortunately, FC was already under contract to hold the 2002 convention in the San Mateo Marriott, so moving to a larger hotel was not an option.

Guests of Honor: Diane Duane, Peter Morwood (husband-wife s-f authors), Christina Hanson (furry artist), David Shapiro (Felorin), Talzhemir (creators of *Furcadia*)

Charities: The Oakland Zoo, The Barry R. Kirshner Wildlife Foundation ($3,620 each)

Chairmen or Organizers: Peter Torkelson (WhiteFire)

Further Confusion 2002: In keeping with the FCU theme, programming tracks were "Academic" for Writing & Literature, Art & Graphic Design, Costuming & Performance Arts, the Winter Masquerade, and Science, and "Extracurricular Activities" for Social Events, Dances, and Tournaments, including Iron Artist and a Rapid Fiction Writing Contest. All the convention committee took academic titles; the chairman was the "chancellor." This was the first year of the Critterlympics, featuring teams of fursuiters competing in simple sports. The 48-page Program Book included three blank pages for college yearbook-type autographs and cartoons, and a wraparound color cover by Malathar. An Artist Passport booklet was available to collect eleven featured furry artists' rubber-stamped "admissions." The T-shirt was by Paf! AAE, Inc., reported $90,832 in revenue. This was the first FC since the 9/11 Event, and many attendees who flew to San Mateo complained about the increased airfares and the hassle of airport security. It was unknown if this affected attendance. Last year's charities again brought exotic animals for a packed life-drawing class. The Barry Kirshner Foundation brought a white tiger cub, a spider monkey, a fennec, and several others. German fan Ronald Klemp (Cairyn) brought an English edition of his furry *Khiray of the River* novel (in three volumes); it sold out.

Guests of Honor: David Brin (s-f author), Dave Feiten (animator/Disney Imagineer), and Kevin Palivec (Malathar) (dragon artist)

Charities: Tiger Touch University Retreat, The Comic Book Legal Defense Fund ($2,600 each)

Chairmen or Organizers: Leon Horne (MitRa)

Further Confusion 2003: The convention committee took the name of the Head Madhatters. The convention's website featured "The Red Queen's Art Gallery," with theme illustrations added weekly; and the newsletter was "Rabbit Tracks." AAE, Inc., reported $126,907 in revenue and $114,883 in expenses. The 64-page Program Book had a color front cover by Jonas Silver and a back cover by Grant Freckleton.

Guests of Honor: Karen Anderson (s-f author/fan), Toby Bluth (animator)

Charities: Pets Are Wonderful Support (PAWS), The Seymour Marine Discovery Center ($3,000 each)

Chairmen or Organizers: Lee Strom (Chairo), Michael Sawyer (Aetobatus)

Further Confusion 2004: There was a chaotic variety of registration lines that had some fans standing in line for 15 or 20 minutes before they found that they were in the wrong line. There was an Internet Lounge. There were nine programming tracks. The third year of Critterlympics had 48 fursuiters in six teams competing in four events: a baseball relay, a shooting gallery, musical chairs, and a dogsled race. The DoubleTree Hotel would not allow exotic animals for life-drawing classes, but it did allow pets; the pets present included a 25' albino python, three wolves, and numerous large dogs such as huskies and dobermans. (There were many jokes that the wolves, which mostly slept, were better-behaved than the fans.) Art Show sales were approximately $60,000, due mainly to a non-stop bidding war between Lance Rund and David Cooksey (Flint Otterhall) for one painting, "Eyes of the Night" by Christy Grandjean (Goldenwolf). Rund got it for $10,000. There were flyers for 17 furry conventions and fur-meets around North America and Europe. There was considerable criticism when the Art Show and the Dealers Room closed on Sunday, a day before the end of the convention. The committee explained that Monday was not a holiday, and most artists and dealers had to leave early for their regular jobs. AAE, Inc., reported $134,923 in revenue and expenses of $87,606. The 60-page Program Book had a color front cover by Grant Freckleton.

Guests of Honor: Heather Alexander (musician), Grant Freckleton, Larry Niven (s-f author)

Charities: Bay Area Bears/Good Bears of the World, The Exotic Feline Breeding Compound ($5,000 each)

Chairmen or Organizers: Michael Sawyer (Aetobatus)

Further Confusion 2005: Events included an Iron Artist competition, a fursuit dance, a concert with Heather Alexander and Uffington Horse, a fursuit masquerade, a Furries on the Nile dance with DJs Genki and BigBlueFox, a rant by 2, the Ranting Gryphon, a screening of *Kaze, Ghost Warrior*, a Furry Variety Show, and a "A Dynasty of Sound" dance with DJs Rigel and Croc. The convention was used as a "talking point" by The Rush Limbaugh Show. AAE, Inc., reported $133,745 in income and $98,021 in expenses. The 52-page Program Book had a color front cover by Walter Crane, and a back cover by Katherine Dinger. The T-shirt was by Jace.

Guests of Honor: Walter Crane (comic-book artist), Alan Dean Foster (s-f author), Musical G-o-H Uffington Horse (Celtic folk rock band)
Charities: Therapy Pets, Friends of Lulu ($5,000 each)
Chairmen or Organizers: Peter Torkelson (WhiteFire)

Further Confusion 2006: There were ten tracks of programming: Art, Business, Filking, Fursuiting, Puppetry, Science, Social, Species, Tech, and Writing. Six colored "badges" were available for members. Although there were 208 in the Fursuit Parade, there were an estimated 250+ at the convention. AAE, Inc., reported $128,265 in revenue and $98,922 in expenses. The 52-page color Program Book had a color front cover by Eric Elliott and a back cover by Starfinder. The T-shirt was by Jonas and Ocelot.

Guests of Honor: Eric Elliott (artist), Jane Lindskold (s-f author)
Charities: Wildlife Companions and the Comic Book Legal Defense Fund ($15,000)
Chairmen or Organizers: Jason Thomas (Loran Skunky)

Further Confusion 2007: FC 2007 became the second furry convention to top 2,000 attendees. Memberships were $50 at the door, $15 of which was a tax-deductible donation to AAE, Inc. FC2007 kept particularly good statistics: there were a Dealers' Den, an Iron Artist contest, dances, 137 panels covering writing to furry spirituality to fursuit construction. A Masquerade presented prizes in six categories. Art Show sales and auctions brought in $53,881. The 6th Critterlympics was hosted by Brian Hagen (Penh Gwyn). The two charities received donations of $8,000 each. AAE, Inc., reported $136,018 in revenue and $113,574 in expenses. The 56-page Program Book had a color front cover by Baron Engel and a back cover by Smudge. The T-shirt was by Jonas. Frozen Oasis hosted a party.

Guests of Honor: Baron Engel (artist), Jerry Pournelle (s-f author), Sub-level 03 (musical group)
Charities: Golden State Greyhound Adoption, and Stanislaus Wildlife Care Center ($16,000)
Chairmen or Organizers: Laura Cherry (Squirrel)

Further Confusion 2008: Since this was the tenth Further Confusion, the abbreviation FCX was popular. FCX maintained an active presence on Second Life, with the Further Confusion ClubHouse in Critter Valley. It rained for most of FCX, forcing cancellation of the outdoor Critterlympics. Some of the events included Taiko drum performers, Iron Artist, and a Furry Night Live. The Video Game Room had an impressive number of games. There were many dances, including a DDR tournament. FCX followed the previous year's EuroFurence's lead in banning the erotic *Softpaw Magazine* from the convention. The 60-page full-color conbook had a wraparound color cover by Moira Hahn. The T-shirt was by Phillip Burgess (Foofers). There were many calls in convention reports and forums for a larger hotel. Art Show sales were $52,068. AAE, Inc., reported $158,494 in income and $135,664 in expenses.

Guests of Honor: Moira Hahn (artist), Dave Barclay (puppeteer). Alexander James Adams was a special musical guest.
Charities: The House Rabbit Society, Rattie Ratz, Wildcare ($22,000)
Chairmen or Organizers: Chris Bartlett (Bos'n C. Otter)

Further Confusion 2009: Events included a presentation on Guide Dogs for the Blind, a history of surfing, a hula performance by the Ka Hale o Ku'u Hoaloha Hula troupe, the 8th annual Critterlympics, tournaments of DDR, Guitar Hero rock bands, FMCL@FC cribbage, and Texas Hold 'Em poker, and several puppet skits and improv. Art Show sales were $43,541. AAE, Inc., reported $159,596 in revenue and $143,590 in expenses. The 60-page Program Book had a color front cover by Jeff Pidgeon and a back cover by Silent Ravyn. The T-shirt was by Khranos. (Kipper also did a T-shirt that was printed but was not the official shirt.) After the convention, several attendees reported that their credit cards had been charged double during transmissions at the hotel. This was apparently caused by equipment malfunction rather than fraud. Patrick Reed (Furp), a fursuiter and veteran staffer at Further Confusion, Rocket City FurMeet, Califur, Anthrocon, FurFright, and Midwest FurFest, was killed by a drunk driver less than a month after FC2009. Almost all the attendees' convention reports included a tribute to him.

Guests of Honor: Jeff Pidgeon (animator), Anita Coulter (puppeteer), Clare Bell (s-f author)
Charities: The Mountain Lion Foundation ($5,000), Guide Dogs for the Blind ($10,000)
Chairmen or Organizers: Jeremy Doran (Frysco)

Further Confusion 2010: Attendees missed the DoubleTree Hotel, but there was general agreement that the larger Fairmont Hotel was superior and friendlier, not counting an incident in November 2009 when several early hotel registrants reported unexpected early charges. The Gold Rush theme was carried out in FC 2010s cartoon mascot of Chuck, a cat gold miner (the plastic room keys showed Chuck trying to get into his room), and inclusion in the registration packets of a drinking skin and bags of pyrites (fool's gold). A few attendees got certificates redeemable for real gold. Main events included the Fursuit Parade, the Masquerade, and Furry Night Live. Art Show sales were $40,502. AAE, Inc., reported $173,363 in revenue and $170,491 in expenses. The 60-page Program Book had a wraparound color cover by T. Lewis. The T-shirt was by Kipper Otter.

Guests of Honor: Michael Fry & T. Lewis (writer & artist of *Over the Hedge* newspaper comic strip), Sofawolf Press (furry publisher), Ursula Vernon (fantasy author/artist)
Charities: Therapy Pets ($7,000), Guide Dogs for the Blind ($2,000), NARF Animal Rescue ($7,500), Best Friends—Haiti Fund ($1,614) ($18,114 total)
Chairmen or Organizers: Jason Thomas (Loran Skunky)

Further Confusion 2011: G-o-H Paul Kidd from Australia could not attend due to inability to enter the U.S. The conbook cover artist was Blotch, and the T-shirt artist was Khranos.

Guests of Honor: Tess Garman & Teagan Gavet (Blotch, furry artists), Paul Kidd (furry author)
Charities: Greater California German Shepherd Rescue, Wildlife Education & Rehabilitation Center, House Rabbit Society ($8,000)
Chairmen or Organizers: Mike Baker (Vandrav)

Further Confusion 2012: The 46-page program book had a wraparound cover by Khranos. The T-shirt was by Blotch.

Guests of Honor: E. E. Knight (s-f author), Matthew Ebel (musician)
Charities: Town Cats of Morgan Hill; 13th St. Cats ($7,000)
Chairmen or Organizers: Chris Bartlett (Bos'n C. Otter)

Further Confusion 2013: The hotel was overbooked, and several attendees had to share a room with several others. The 44-page program book had both covers by Mitti. The conbook cover and T-shirt were by Margaret Trauth (Egypt Urnash). After the convention, the parent AAE, Inc., held a contest during June and July to select a new Further Confusion logo, to replace the one used since 1999. The winner was Foofers (a.k.a. Helvetica Bold, real name Phil Burgess) with a design showing the silhouettes of a dog, dragon, and cat, in white above the word "FurCon."

Guests of Honor: Ursula Vernon (fantasy author/artist), Chris Savino (writer, animator)
Charities: Cat House on the Kings, Little Blue Society ($10,000; $5,000 to each)
Chairmen or Organizers: Sean Wally (SmackJackal)

Further Confusion 2014: There was a presentation to celebrate the 25th anniversary of furry conventions. The conbook cover was a collaboration between Lauren Kelsey (Latte) & Chris Torres. The T-shirt artist was Mitti. The Clean Room Contest was adopted from Midwest FurFest, with slight changes in the rules. Instead of three rooms getting free weekends, there are a first prize from each of FC's two hotels of three room nights credited back to the reservation maker by the hotels; a second prize of one night credited back to the reservation maker; and a third prize of a $30 credit.
    Guests of Honor: Mitti (furry artist), Chris Torres (PRguitarman; creator of internet memes, webcomics)
    Charities: Digital Game Museum ($9,000)
    Chairmen or Organizers: Vincent Cardinale (Berg Polarbear)

Further Confusion 2015: For the first time, attendance shrank slightly. The 36-page program book had a wraparound cover by CrookedWolf. The T-shirt was by Farore Nightclaw. The illustrated membership badge was by Savannah Horrocks.
    Guests of Honor: Warrick Brownlow-Pike, Andy J. Heath (puppeteers from *Mongrels*)
    Charities: Rocket Dog Rescue ($6,000)
    Chairmen or Organizers: Jeff Bowman (Dax Wildsong)

FURUM *see* **Furs Upon Maylasia (FURUM)**

FurVention

FurVention is a furry convention in Liverpool, England, U.K.

Name & Date	Theme	Location	Attendance
FurVention 2015 January 23–26, 2015	Boot Up the Systems!	The Aloft Hotel, Liverpool, England	64

Events

FurVention 2015: The original hotel cancelled due to renovations in December 2014. Fortunately, the committee was able to find a new hotel quickly at lower prices.
    Guests of Honor: CoLD SToRAGE (professional musician)
    Charity: Cancer Research U.K. (£100)
    Chairmen or Organizers: Fang, Medosai

FurWAG

FurWAG stands for Furry Western Australia Gathering. It is the annual furry convention for Perth, Western Australia. It is operated as a subsidiary of Australian Fandom Conventions (the same organization that runs ConFurgence). The FurWAG logo was chosen in a contest won by Cameron Dadd (Cormack), who received a lifetime membership.

Name & Date	Theme	Location	Attendance
FurWAG 2013 October 4–6, 2013	The Maiden Voyage	Rendezvous Studio Hotel, Perth, Western Australia	137
FurWAG 2014 October 3–5, 2014	FurWAG 3000	ibis Styles Hotel, Perth, Western Australia	177

Name & Date	Theme	Location	Attendance
FurWAG 2015 October 2–4, 2015	Monster Ball	ibis Styles Hotel, Perth, Western Australia	170

Events

FurWAG 2013: 2013 saw the Maiden Voyage of Perth's first furry convention under chairman Darky Gryphon. The "Maiden Voyage" theme emphasized pirates. The convention was a lively affair, featuring a performance by renowned Perth sword swallower Matty Blade, fursuit games, a pub quiz, a photoshoot with animals from the yearly charity Native Animal Rescue, a charity auction, and various other panels and events. FurWAG's 2013 special guests were local Perth author Paul Kidd and artist EngineFace from Geraldton in WA's midwest. 2013 saw the first performance at FurWAG by fight choreographers Rebel Empire Workshops, who have performed at each FurWAG opening ceremony. The conbook cover and T-shirt were both by Toulouse.

Guests of Honor: Paul Kidd (furry author), Engineface (furry artist)
Charity: Native Animal Rescue (A$4,800)
Chairmen or Organizers: Louise Cocks (Flye), Darky Gryphon

FurWAG 2014: FurWAG's second year saw a relocation to a larger venue at the ibis Styles in Northbridge. The theme of "FurWAG 3000" was introduced in the futuristic space travel-themed convention announcements throughout the preceding year, and followed up with fiction published in the conbook and website. The convention aimed to raise money for Painted Dog Conservation Inc., and did so through events such as a charity concert by guest of honor Amadhia Albee, pub quiz and charity auction. Attendees also enjoyed events including a fursuit walk, panels, fursuit games, dance workshop with guest of honor Blu the Dragon, dance parties, karaoke, and more. The conbook cover and T-shirt were both by Amadhia.

Guests of Honor: Amadhia Albee (furry artist), Blu the Dragon (furry dancer)
Charity: Painted Dog Conservation, Inc. (A$5,000)
Chairmen or Organizers: Darky

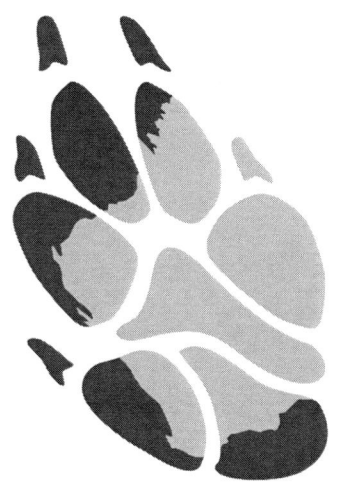

FurWAG logo. Art by Cormack (Cameron Dadd). Used with permission.

FurWAG 2015: The Monster Ball was the theme of FurWAG's third year, and with it came an increased focus on decoration of the venue. The convention welcomed Australian artist Muttasaur as its guest of honor, and its charity fundraising efforts were in aid of AMRRIC (Animal Management in Rural and Remote Indigenous Communities). For the first time, FurWAG included events on a Friday morning, bringing the convention to a full three days in duration. Attendees enjoyed a wide range of events such as a fursuit walk, art show, fight choreography workshop with Rebel Empire, dance parties, and the innovative new Fursuit Life Drawing panel, where human models were replaced by fursuiters. The conbook cover and T-shirt were both by Muttasaur.

Guests of Honor: Ivy Ianieri (Muttasaur, furry artist)
Charity: Animal Management in Rural and Remote Indigenous Communities (AMRRIC) (A$4,500)
Chairmen or Organizers: Louise Cocks (Flye)

FurWanted

FurWanted is a Wild West-themed furry event at the Pullman City simulated Western town ("Die Lebende Westernstadt") in

Eging am See, Bavaria, Germany. It grew out of visits to Pullman City by German furs beginning in 2010. By 2013 FurWanted I was organized (the "Wanted" being a common feature of Wild West sheriff's posters). Western-styled fursuits are encouraged, although photos of past FurWanteds show mostly non-fursuiters with a few canid fursuiters with Western stetsons, vests, sheriff's badges, and bandanas or Indian feather headdresses, and a few large dogs. Besides Pullman City's Big Al's "Wild Arrows" shooting gallery, horseback riding, Black Bison Saloon, "Mexikanisches Restaurant," and other Western-themed events and locales, there are a fursuit dance in the Main Street, fursuit horseback riding, and a poker tournament.

Name & Date	Theme	Attendance
FurWanted I July 12–14, 2013		30
FurWanted II July 10–13, 2014		45
FurWanted III July 8–12, 2015	Pirates of the Caribbean	25

Events

FurWanted I:
Guests of Honor:
Chairmen or Organizers: Darcus (Klaus Montjan), Shade

FurWanted II: The illustrated member badge art was by Zilven.
Guests of Honor:
Chairmen or Organizers: Darcus (Klaus Montjan), Shade

FurWanted III: The third FurWanted mixed the Western fursuiters with those dressed in Disney's *Pirates of the Caribbean* motif. The member badge art was by Ifus.
Guests of Honor: TheKarelia (furry artist/fursuit maker)
Chairmen or Organizers: Darcus (Klaus Montjan), Shade

Futerkon

Futerkon is the replacement for Futrzakon. It differs from the previous convention with a new organizational team, and in involving the attendees to interact and come to know each other, while still having fun with old friends. There are still many contests, discussion groups, panels, tournaments, and workshops.

In addition to the Futerkon and Gdakon conventions, there is an annual FENEK New Year's celebration/furmeet in Warsaw each year, and several spontaneously-organized furmeets of around 10 to 20 furs in smaller towns like Wroclaw, Lodz, Krakow, Gdansk or Katowice.

Name & Date	Theme	Location	Attendance
Futerkon 2012 August 8–11, 2012	The End Is Near…	Training and Recreation Centre Dzierzazna, Dzierzazna, Poland	85
Futerkon 2013 August 7–10, 2013	Wild West with a Splash of Steampunk	Training and Recreation Centre Dzierzazna, Dzierzazna, Poland	93
Futerkon 2014 August 20–23, 2014	All That Jazz— Chicago in 1920s	Municipal Cultural Center, Dzierzazna, Poland	100
Futerkon 2015 August 5–8, 2015	Sci-Fi Soap Opera	Sport and Recreation Center Wawrzkowizna, Wawrzkowizna, Poland	105

Events

Futerkon 2012: Dzierzazna is located in the center of Poland, near Lodz. All attendees received a badge, conbook, T-shirt, advertising leash, patch, and small wooden pendant with the Futerkon emblem. The program was divided into two parts; the general program, and a themed story. The general program included a Wednesday campfire and karaoke session, Thursday shooting and drawing workshops, an after-dinner charity auction and dancing, Friday presentations, a group photo, and a documentary movie about the abandoned Chernobyl zone. For the story, all attendees were divided into two factions, the Syndicate and the Cartel (with flags), and assigned competing quests to find a lost blueprint: "The future is in your paws!" Solaxe and Kyubi did the conbook cover. The T-shirt was by Gusto.
  Guests of Honor: CamashRed, Solaxe (Scottish and Polish furry artists)
  Charity: Bernardyn Foundation for Polish lynx (2,100 zł [estimated])
  Chairmen or Organizers: Kyubi

Futerkon 2013: The translation of the charity is the Unwanted and Forgotten Foundation, for abandoned pets. KocurKotka and Kyubi did the conbook cover. Solaxe did the T-shirt.
  Guests of Honor: CamashRed
  Charity: Fundacja Niechciane i Zapomniane (2,300 zł [estimated])
  Chairmen or Organizers: Kyubi, Kot, Gravedigger, Pasterz, Blajn

Futerkon 2014: Kyubi did the conbook cover. Hufnaar did the T-shirt.
  Guests of Honor: none
  Charity: Łódź Animal shelter (2,500 zł [estimated])
  Chairmen or Organizers: Kyubi

Futerkon 2015: The charity was the "Sanctuary Under Dog Angel" Foundation. Titash and Kyubi did the conbook cover. Ritka did the T-shirt.
  Guests of Honor: Titash (furry cartoonist, fursuiter)
  Charity: Azyl Pod Psim Aniołem
  Chairmen or Organizers: Kyubi

Futrzakon

Futrzakon means Furry Convention (Futrzak + Konwent) in Polish. The first Futrzakon was organized by Polish fans via www.polfurs.org.

Name & Date	Theme	Location	Attendance
Futrzakon 1 September 26–28, 2008		The Dzierżązna community center near Łódź	37
Futrzakon 2 August 13–16, 2009		The Dzierżązna community center near Łódź	50+
Futrzakon 3 August 11–14, 2010	Colorful 70s	The Dzierżązna community center near Łódź	77
Futrzakon 4 August 10–16, 2011	?	Wawrzkowizna, central Poland	?

Events

Futrzakon 1: Events included a large evening bonfire around which the attendees were encouraged to get to know each other, a movie-making workshop, an art competition, LARPs, RPG sessions, a volleyball tournament, workshops, and games. T-shirts were provided by Leniwiec.

Charity: The WWF's "Save the European Lynx" Fund (1,380 zł [about $430])
Chairmen or Organizers: Ryan Blackpaw, Kudłaty

Futrzakon 2: The Futrzakon was increased from two to three days by popular demand. The attendance of 50 was the total that the community center would accept as three-day guests; there were many more attendees that visited during the day. Activities included Bonfire/Socializing, Tai-Chi, Furry Soccer and Volleyball, Water Fights, Jenga Workshop, DDR and karaoke competitions, the charity auction, an Art competition, a "Movie" workshop, "Who wants to be a Millionaire" game, and The Dance, including many additional minor competitions such as "Name that Melody." Kyubi and Ryan Blackpaw were responsible for the official con T-shirts. Like the previous year, the shirts had a simple sign with the name of the convention.
Charity: The WWF's "Save the European Lynx" Fund (1,810 zł [about $645])
Chairmen or Organizers: Ryan Blackpaw

Futrzakon 3: Futrzakon 3 events included a charity auction, karaoke contest, DDR contest, archery competition, volleyball/basketball games, the bonfire socializing, tai chi, and a drawing contest. The "Logo Futrzakonu 3" was by Polish artists Edi and Nerevar.
Charity: World Wide Fund for Nature
Chairmen or Organizers: Kyubi

Futrzakon 4: Wawrzkowizna is an isolated modern hotel in central Poland specializing in weekend vacations and school trips featuring sylvan nature activities, and small business conventions in a rustic setting.

After Futrzakon 4, all three 2011 organizers redesigned the convention so extensively that it was cancelled and started over as Futerkon 2012.
Charity:
Chairmen or Organizers: Kyubi, Kot, Gravedigger

Gateway FurMeet

GateWay FurMeet (GFM) is a furry convention in St. Louis, Missouri. Its cartoon mascot is Clyde, a Clydesdale horse.

Name & Date	Theme	Location	Attendance	Parade
Gateway FurMeet 2014 April 18–20, 2014	Gateway to the West	Hampton Inn-Gateway Arch, St. Louis, MO	211	62
Gateway FurMeet 2015 May 8–10, 2015	Clydezilla	Lumière Place Casino & Hotels, St. Louis, MO	223	50

Events

Gateway FurMeet 2014: GFM 2014 almost did not happen. It was originally announced for The Millennium Hotel, but on November 21, 2013, it was announced that that hotel was closing in January. A new hotel was secured in December 2013. The theme emphasized the *Wild Wild West* TV series, with Clyde as a cowboy horse. There were panels on character creation and art. Activities included fursuit games, tabletop gaming, and nightly dancing. Fursuiters took a trip to the Arch and interacted with the public. PeacePaw Yoye did the conbook front cover. Kappy did the back cover, which was also used as that year's website banner. The T-shirt was by YellowBronco.
Guests of Honor: PeacePaw Yote (furry artist/fursuiter)
Charity: Stray Rescue of St. Louis ($1,455)
Chairmen or Organizers: Kiara Shiba

Gateway FurMeet 2014 conbook back cover. Art by Kappy. Used with permission.

Gateway FurMeet 2015: The events included panels on art and fursuit construction. There were fursuit games and nightly dancing. A game room included console games. There was a midnight matinee. Going out and exploring the city was encouraged. The conbook cover and T-shirt were both by Clawshawt.
  Guests of Honor: Clawshawt (furry artist/animator)
  Charity: Five Acres Animal Shelter ($2,051)
  Chairmen or Organizers: Kiara Shiba

Gdakon

Gdakon, "Gdański konwent furry," began as a furmeet in Raksha's apartment in Gdańsk, Poland in 2007. By 2011 it grew into a convention. It is considered Poland's complement to Futrzakon (later Futercon) as a Western-style convention in a hotel, at the opposite time of the year, and on the Polish coast rather than in mid-country. There is not a Western-style Fursuit Parade as much as a fursuit walk about the city. Gdakon, a combination of Gdańsk and konwent, sounds like "gdakanie" (a hen's clucking), which furry artists drew as Gdakon 2011's cartoon mascot. She quickly evolved into Gdakonek, a gryphon who became the official mascot. Gdakonek has been interpreted by different artists, but is little-used today. The Gdakon website has different Easter Eggs each year. Gdakon works closely with foreign conventions and furgroups like SachenFurs to organize its events.

Name & Date	Theme	Location	Attendance
Gdakon 2011 January 27–30, 2011	Hawaii	Hostel Bursztynek, Gdańsk	44
Gdakon 2012 February 23–26, 2012	Medieval Times	Hostel Bursztynek, Gdańsk	59
Gdakon 2013 February 14–17, 2013	Vikings	Hostel Bursztynek, Gdańsk	74

Name & Date	Theme	Location	Attendance
Gdakon 2014 February 20–23, 2014	Horrors	Hotel Amber, Gdańsk	121
Gdakon 2015 March 5–8, 2015	The Jungle	Hotel Amber, Gdańsk	157

Events

Gdakon 2011: The hotel was in the city center.
Chairmen or Organizers: Raksha, Kunako

Gdakon 2012: Gdakon 2012 introduced evening furdances to Poland, with lighting equipment provided by SachenFurs. They have since become a favorite program event. The first furdance brought complaints from non-fan guests in the Hostel Bursztynek who wanted to sleep, but they were bribed with alcohol to let the furdance continue. A bus brought the attendees to the start of the fursuit walk.
Chairmen or Organizers: Pablo, Kudlaty, Raksha

Gdakon 2013: Gdakon 2013 introduced an annual "Program Book," beginning as a one-page flyer. There was an official Gdakon image of a fox and wolves partying that was used on posters put up all over. A lottery was also introduced, to draw the attendees into the program activities a little more.
Chairmen or Organizers: Pablo, Kudlaty, Raksha

Gdakon 2014: Gdakon moved to a larger hotel further from the city center. The first choice for the new hotel seemed to go smoothly, but at the signing of the contract, at the last moment, the hotel raised its price to an unacceptable level. The organizers, in a panic, got the manager of the Hotel Amber to sign an acceptable deal on the evening (after hours, but the hotel manager was glad to get such a large convention) of the same day.
Chairmen or Organizers: Pablo, Kudlaty, Raksha, Fuckie, Bakus

Gdakon 2015: The top (3rd) floor of the Hotel Amber was turned into a Party Floor. Some attendees did not come to any programmed events but just partied all convention long. The organizers tried to get some genuine non-Christian shamans to come to Gdakon, but failed. It was agreed to extend future Gdakons for one day longer.
Chairmen or Organizers: Pablo, Kudlaty, Raksha, Fuckie, Bakus, Arashi

Golden Leaves Con

The GLC is an autumn-themed convention for Swiss and German 18+ furs in the Swiss Alpine countryside. The attendees enjoy the Alpine setting, a furdance, a heated outdoor pool, a torch walk, a cocktail night, and a game show. The meals are heavy on Swiss cheese fondue and local dishes. The cartoon mascot is a squirrel wearing an Alpine hat.

Name & Date	Theme	Location	Attendance
Golden Leaves Con 2010 November 4–7, 2010		Baselbieter Chinderhus, Langenbruk, Switzerland	42
Golden Leaves Con 2011 November 3–6, 2011		Baselbieter Chinderhus, Langenbruk, Switzerland	42
Golden Leaves Con 2012 November 15–18, 2012		Baselbieter Chinderhus, Langenbruk, Switzerland	42
Golden Leaves Con 2013 November 14–17, 2013		Gruppenhaus Bärgsunne, above Lake Thun, Bernese Oberland, Switzerland	82

Name & Date	Theme	Location	Attendance
Golden Leaves Con 5 November 13–16, 2014		Gruppenhaus C'est la Vie, Hasliberg, Switzerland	134
Golden Leaves Con 6 October 29–November 1, 2015		Gruppenhaus C'est la Vie, Hasliberg, Switzerland	140

Events

Golden Leaves Con 2010: The Baselbieter Chinderhus was a resort inn isolated in the Alpine countryside. The 42 attendees fully booked its facilities. The first three GLCs there were limited in attendance to the inn's 42-person capacity. (GLC 2013 moved to a larger resort.) More than 600 photographs posted online showed several pet cats and large dogs but only two fursuiters. There was a white-on-black T-shirt by EosFoxx of a squirrel peeking out from a bed of ferns.

Chairmen or Organizers: Michael Graf (Luxen), MafunDi, Avalon, Nikko, Christoph Kellner (KingTaibu)

Golden Leaves Con 2011: The T-shirt was by EosFoxx.
Chairmen or Organizers: Michael Graf (Luxen), MafunDi, Avalon, Nikko, Christoph Kellner (KingTaibu), Dominik Fahrni (naut), Fendracus

Golden Leaves Con 2012: The T-shirt was by Anatoliba.
Chairmen or Organizers: Michael Graf (Luxen), MafunDi, Avalon, Nikko, Dominik Fahrni (naut), Fendracus

Golden Leaves Con 2013: The move to a larger lodge permitted raising the attendance limit. It quickly filled, with newer registrants placed on a Waiting List. The T-shirt was by Henrieke. A poster showed a photograph of a hedgehog in a teacup.
Chairmen or Organizers: Michael Graf (Luxen), MafunDi, Avalon, Dominik Fahrni (naut), Fendracus, Elwetika, Dragi P, IsaacFox

Golden Leaves Con 5: The official name was Golden Leaves Con 5, but everyone called it Golden Leaves Con 2014. There were three customized lanyards. The attendance limit was raised, and it was still booked out. The T-shirt was by EosFoxx.
Chairmen or Organizers: Michael Graf (Luxen), MafunDi, Avalon, Dominik Fahrni (naut), Fendracus, Elwetika, Dragi P, Garra, AlectorFencer, Jürgen, Koltas, Daszh, IsaacFox

Golden Leaves Con 6: GLC 6 took advantage of being over the Halloween weekend in its spooky theme. The attendance limit was raised to 140. Dogs (presumably large) were permitted upon arrangement with the organization team. The website said, "The 'Gruppenhaus C'est la Vie' is located in the Bernese Alps, right next to the Reuti cable car station. […] The house offers a big terrace with a panorama view. As we do not have any direct neighbors and we are renting the whole place, privacy is guaranteed. […] Of course, we will bring back the hot outdoor pool, genuine Swiss cheese fondue, a small Dealers' Den, a fursuit-friendly disco and a great many other nightmarish contraptions."
Chairmen or Organizers: Michael Graf (Luxen), MafunDi

Great Lakes Fur Con

Great Lakes Fur Con (GLFC) is a furry convention in Grand Rapids, Michigan. It was started in December 2012 at a furry bowling meet in Grand Rapids when Lamper Fox (fursuiter) proposed starting a local furry convention. A committee was formed during 2013. GLFC is unique in having two charities each year, one long-term and one for the year.

Name & Date	Theme	Location	Attendance	Parade
Great Lakes Fur Con 2014 February 7–9, 2014	404: Theme Not Found	Ramada Plaza Grand Rapids, Grand Rapids, MI	264	76
Great Lakes Fur Con 2015 May 22–24, 2015	Back Through the Wardrobe	Holiday Inn Express & Suites Grand Rapids South, Grand Rapids, MI	323	105

Events

Great Lakes Fur Con 2014:

Guests of Honor: Rei Meerkat (furry artist, fursuiter), OMGSparky (fursuiter)

Charity: Long-term, Crash's Landing and Big Sid's Sanctuary; short-term, Paws With A Cause (PAWS)

Chairmen or Organizers: Lamper Fox

Great Lakes Fur Con 2015:

Guests of Honor: Tyzin (fursuiter), Rebecca Sharpe (Sharpe19, fursuit maker)

Charity: Long-term, Crash's Landing and Big Sid's Sanctuary ($3,816.02)

Chairmen or Organizers: Lamper Fox

Great Lakes Fur Con 2014 poster. Art by Birty. Used with permission.

H-Con

H for Hesse, Germany. It's an "old time" tiny furry convention in a rented guest house in a rustic location between the cities of Frankfurt and Heidelberg, with either no staff or all attendees as part of the staff. Everyone is expected to bring and share food, and to participate in whatever is going on. As a result, attendance is limited. There is at least one T-shirt. The traditional logo is a triangular yellow traffic sign with an individualized black image. Despite most signage being in English, the language of H-Con is German.

Name & Date	Theme	Location	Attendance
H-Con 1 October 2–3, 2005	The Forgotten Tails	Scharbach/Odenwald	45
H-Con 2 September 29–October 2, 2006	The Tails on Fire	Scharbach/Odenwald	53
H-Con 3 October 4–7, 2007	Tails from the Twilight World	Scharbach/Odenwald	56
H-Con 4 October 2–5, 2008	and the Temple of Tails	Scharbach/Odenwald	50

H-Con

Name & Date	Theme	Location	Attendance
H-Con 5 October 1–4, 2009	Tails from the Ashes	Stromberg (RP)	45
H-Con 6 September 30–October 3, 2010	Tailbusters	Bühl-Neusatzeck	59
H-Con 7 September 29–October 2, 2011	Where No Tail Has Gone Before	Bühl-Neusatzeck	59
H-Con 8 October 3–7, 2012	Wild Tails West	Bühl-Neusatzeck	58
H-Con 9 October 9–13, 2013	The Sorcerer's Nine Tails	The Petershof near Erbach/Erbuch	62
H-Con 10 October 1–5, 2014	X-Tails	The Petershof near Erbach/Erbuch	61
H-Con 11 September 30–October 4, 2015	The Curse of the Black Tail	The Petershof near Erbach/Erbuch	64

Events

H-Con 1: The logo featured a snarling Doberman's head. Registration was €70.
Chairmen or Organizers: Markus Kalkbrenner (Atalon the Deer), Sven Schumacher (Bobcat)

H-Con 2: The logo featured a dragon looking with horror at its tail on fire. Registration increased to €80. A "Dead Dog Night" after-party was held on October 2–3.
Chairmen or Organizers: Markus Kalkbrenner (Atalon the Deer), Sven Schumacher (Bobcat)

H-Con 3: The logo featured a raccoon warrior's head. Registration was €87. Activities included flying radio-controlled helicopters and making an amateur movie. 1,070 kilograms of food and drink were consumed. A "Dead Dog Night" after-party followed on October 7–8.
Chairmen or Organizers: Markus Kalkbrenner (Atalon the Deer), Sven Schumacher (Bobcat)

H-Con 4: The logo featured a snarling sabertooth's head. Registration was €90. The T-shirt showed a classic temple whose roof was being supported with difficulty by various furs.
Chairmen or Organizers: Markus Kalkbrenner (Atalon the Deer), Sven Schumacher (Bobcat), Heiko Stangel (Wolffire)

H-Con 5: Due to issues with the former site, the con was moved. The logo featured an anthro wolf's head rising from a fire. Registration was €90.
Chairmen or Organizers: Heiko Stangel (Wolffire)

H-Con 7 T-shirt front. Art by Meo. Used with permission.

H-Con 6: H-Con was moved again to a larger site near Bühl in the Black Forest. More furs from Switzerland participated. The limit was raised to 60 by popular demand. The logo showed a bushy foxtail being zapped by the Ghostbusters' photon pack. Registration was €90. There were two T-shirts.
Chairmen or Organizers: Heiko Stangel (Wolffire)

H-Con 7: The logo showed a lion's tail between the stars. Registration was €90. Activities had a strong sci-fi content. The T-shirt showed two furry *Star Trek* themes, front and back.
Chairmen or Organizers: Heiko Stangel (Wolffire)

H-Con 8: The logo showed a Stetson-hatted fox head superimposed on a sheriff's badge. Registration was €95.
Chairmen or Organizers: Heiko Stangel (Wolffire)

H-Con 9: The venue was a rented guest house in the forested valley of Odenwald Mümling, with a limit of 60 people. Dogs were allowed with prior arrangement. The logo showed a stylized fox wizard's head. Registration was €95. There were two T-shirts.
Chairmen or Organizers: Heiko Stangel (Wolffire)

H-Con 10: The logo showed an X superimposed on a target, similar to that of *The X-Files*. Registration was €95. There were two T-shirts, one with an official-looking emblem: "Department of the X-Tails. Furry Bureau of Investigation."
Chairmen or Organizers: Heiko Stangel (Wolffire)

H-Con 11: The logo showed a pirate-hatted parrot. Registration was €95.
Chairmen or Organizers: Heiko Stangel (Wolffire)

Ibercamp

Ibercamp was a short-lived Spanish outdoor camp similar to Canada's Camp Feral! and Brazil's Abando.

Name & Date	Theme	Location	Attendance
Ibercamp 2012 November 24–25, 2012	Animales a Raudales	Sierra de Mariola "parque natural," Salem, Valencia, Spain	24
Ibercamp 2013 October 11–13, 2013	none	Camp outside Almedijar, Castellón, Spain	30 (estimated)

Events

Ibercamp 2012: Ibercamp 2012 was at a camp in the mountains outside Salem. The theme translated as "Unleashed." Registration was €75 and included all meals. It opened on September 3 and was supposed to be open until October 15, but the 24-person limit was sold out within 24 hours. Activities included tournament games, karaoke singing, hiking, and a bar. The Ibercamp website featured a comic strip by furry artist RayFkm.
Chairmen or Organizers: Alex Vixgeck

Ibercamp 2013:
Chairmen or Organizers: Alex Vixgeck
Ibercamp 2014 was announced for October 10–12 but was cancelled. On March 6, 2015, it was announced that Ibercamp was permanently cancelled.

IndyFurCon

The iFC is administered by the Indiana fur group WhoozFur, Inc., a not-for-profit corporation. The first iFC was promoted as an opportunity for Midwestern furs to socialize in the "downtime" between nearby conventions.

The two iFC mascots do not have names, but the cardinal is Indiana's state bird and the buffalo (bison) appears on Indiana's state seal. The guest of honor is always an artist who draws that year's conbook cover, T-shirt, membership badges, etc.

Name & Date	Theme	Location	Attendance	Parade
IndyFurCon 2010 August 13–15, 2010	Tropical, Furry, Fun!	Hilton Indianapolis North, Indianapolis, IN	350	62
IndyFurCon 2011 August 12–14, 2011	Furries of the Lost Ark	Hilton Indianapolis North, Indianapolis, IN	369	75
IndyFurCon 2012 August 10–12, 2012	FURS IN SPACE!	Sheraton Indianapolis Hotel at Keystone Crossing, Indianapolis, IN	482	110
IndyFurCon 2013 August 9–11, 2013	Back to School!	Sheraton Indianapolis Hotel at Keystone Crossing, Indianapolis, IN	560	110
IndyFurCon 2014 August 29–31, 2014	Storybook Villains	Sheraton Indianapolis Hotel at Keystone Crossing, Indianapolis, IN	527	147
IndyFurCon 2015 August 14–16, 2015	As seen on TV!	Indianapolis Marriott East, Indianapolis, IN	735	223

Events

IndyFurCon 2010: Uncle Kage, 2, the Ranting Gryphon, and Bucktown Tiger provided informal entertainment. The T-shirt was by DBruin (Devious Bruin).
  Guests of Honor: Jeff Beedon (DBruin, furry artist)
  Charity: Exotic Feline Rescue Center ($1,150)
  Chairmen or Organizers: Tora NightProwler

IndyFurCon 2011: Uncle Kage, 2, the Ranting Gryphon, and Bucktown Tiger returned, as did Whose Lion Is It, Anyway?, and an Art Show was added to the program. SamJay, who could not attend, participated via webcam. Tincrash and Leasara got married on Saturday night.
  Guests of Honor: Noel Melendez (Tincrash, furry artist)
  Charity: Southside Animal Shelter ($1,212)
  Chairmen or Organizers: Tora NightProwler

IndyFurCon 2012: Uncle Kage was on the program.
  Guests of Honor: Alkali Bismuth (fursuiter), Fursuit of Honor Skroy, Featured Artist Chris B. Critter
  Charity: Southside Animal Shelter ($2,500)
  Chairmen or Organizers: Tora NightProwler

IndyFurCon 2013: Panels were renamed Homerooms for the Back to School! theme. Bravo designed a school crest. Twitch Da Woof and his band, Furry Punk Rock Massacre, held an hour-long fursuit concert. Uncle Kage, 2, the Ranting Gryphon, and Bucktown Tiger again performed.
  Guests of Honor: Bravo (furry artist), Fursuit G-o-H Twitch Da Woof
  Charity: Southside Animal Shelter ($2,455)
  Chairmen or Organizers: Roxas

IndyFurCon mascots. Art by poppawolf. Used with permission.

IndyFurCon 2014:
  Guests of Honor: Kim (Bloodhound, furry artist)
  Charity: Southside Animal Shelter ($6,000+)
  Chairmen or Organizers: Roxas

IndyFurCon 2015:
  Guests of Honor: Lyenuv (furry artist)
  Charity: Southside Animal Shelter ($8,048)
  Chairmen or Organizers: Pandez Panda

Infurnity

This was the first furry convention held in Taipei, as opposed to informal furmeets. The illustrated logo by Zilven was captioned "Taiwan Furry Convention."

Name & Date	Theme	Location	Attendance
Infurnity October 31, 2015	Halloween	No. 33, Ln 279, Fuxing South Road, Da'an District, Taipei	62

Events

Registration was closed on June 16 to ensure that the venue was not overcrowded. Attendees received an illustrated plastic membership badge, convention book, button, and logoed paper bag. Sponsors received the above plus a poster, sticker, and T-shirt. Events included many small games, for which points were awarded, including wearing the best costume showing the Halloween theme; and a short tutorial for fursuit beginners. The game points could be exchanged for the convention souvenirs given to the sponsors. There were 34 fursuiters including three from Japan and one from Thailand; a group photo was taken of them. Many items, mostly original artwork, were donated for

a ticketed charity raffle. The Japan Meeting of Furries convention in Toyohashi on January 8–10, 2016 was promoted. All conbook art was by J. C.
   Charity: Animal Rescue Team TAIWAN (7,250 NT)
   Chairmen or Organizers: J. C.

Japan Meeting of Furries

The Japan Meeting of Furries was created during 2012, and was held in January 2013, to be Japan's first Western-style furry convention in a hotel; outside of Tokyo but still on the main island of Honshu.

Name & Date	Theme	Location	Attendance
Japan Meeting of Furries 2013 January 12–13, 2013	none	Sunroute Hikone, Hikone, Shiga	100 (estimated)
Japan Meeting of Furries 2014 January 11–12, 2014	The Fifty-Three Stations of the Tōkaidō	Loisir Hotel, Toyohashi, Aichi	232
Japan Meeting of Furries 2015 January 10–11, 2015	The Gunman at Sunset	Loisir Hotel, Toyohashi, Aichi	408

Events

Japan Meeting of Furries 2013: The first convention was a test to see if there was enough support to hold a convention. There were no theme, guests, or a charity. There were no Dealers' Den or Artists' Lounge; it was felt that those who wanted to buy or sell art, books, or fanzines would attend one of the Comikets that specialize in that. There were events on stage and a fursuit group photo, workshops and seminars on acting, art, fursuit making, and more. There was no changing area as at other Japanese furry conventions; fursuiters were advised to change in their hotel rooms. But there was a headless lounge. The Program Book cover was by Aoino Broome.
   Chairmen or Organizers: Yusuke Kurita (Kriske)

Japan Meeting of Furries 2014: The previous events were repeated. There were attendees from Japan, Thailand, Hong Kong, and the U.K. The artist of the Program Book cover was anonymous.
   Guests of Honor: Yuko Asami (manga author; wife of the artist)
   Charity: Japan Guide Dog Association (¥9,000)
   Chairmen or Organizers: Yusuke Kurita (Kriske)

Japan Meeting of Furries 2015: *The Gunman at Sunset* is the Japanese title of the Italian Western movie *For a Few Dollars More/Once Upon a Time in the West*. The theme is bilingual in Japanese and English, starting this year. Besdes individual registration badges, there were illustrated badges in English for "Artist" and "I Speak English" indicating those appropriate. The Program Book cover was by Maito Utsuke.
   Guests of Honor: Akira Himekawa (manga artist duo)
   Charity: Toyohashi Zoo & Botanical Park (¥262,950)
   Chairmen or Organizers: Yusuke Kurita (Kriske)

Kemocon

Kemocon, from the Japanese *kemono* (animal; beast), is the successor of TransFur. It is organized more like a traditional furry convention, although it still began as an introduction of furry fandom to the general public. It has evolved to be more like a Western furry convention.

Name & Date	Theme	Location	Attendance
Kemocon 1 November 30, 2008	none	Exhibition room 4F, Kawasaki City Industrial Promotion Hall, Kanagawa Prefecture, Tokyo	180+
Kemocon 2 November 28, 2009	none	Exhibition room 4F, Kawasaki City Industrial Promotion Hall, Kanagawa Prefecture, Tokyo	220
Kemocon 3 November 20, 2010	none	Exhibition rooms 1F and 4F, Kawasaki City Industrial Promotion Hall, Kanagawa Prefecture, Tokyo	390+
Kemocon 4 November 19, 2011	none	Sumida Industrial Center, Sumida, Tokyo	412+
Kemocon 5 December 1, 2012	none	Sumida Industrial Center, Sumida, Tokyo	420+
Kemocon 6 December 7, 2013	none	Sumida Industrial Center, Sumida, Tokyo	420
Kemocon 7 November 22–23, 2014	none	Kazusa Academia Hall, Kisarazu, Chiba Prefecture	380 (estimated)
Kemocon 8 November 21–22, 2015	Music	Kazusa Academia Hall, Kisarazu, Chiba Prefecture	380

Events

Kemocon 1: Kemocon 1 was organized more like a traditional furry convention with a program. The admission was ¥1,000. 10:30 a.m., doors open. 11:00 a.m., opening ceremony and opening of dressing room to dress in fursuits. Noon, Fursuit Parade and introduction of characters. 1:00 p.m., fursuit group photo. 2:00 p.m., Kigurumi quiz. 3:00 p.m., dance party. 5:00 p.m., closing ceremony and opening of dressing room to undress from fursuits. 6:00 p.m., closing of exhibition room. There were about 50 fursuits in the group photo.

Chairmen or Organizers: KemoConProject (Muddyfox, Altia, Ryoga, OTK, PANJA!, Leon)

Kemocon 2: There were no memberships, but there was a ¥1,000 admission. 11:00 a.m., doors open. 11:30 a.m., opening ceremony and changing into fursuits for entrance parade. 11:45 a.m., rock-scissors-paper tournament. 12:15 p.m., introduction to fursuit characters (on overhead projector). 12:45 p.m., Fursuit Parade of characters. 1:15 p.m., group photo of fursuits. 1:30 p.m., free time (socializing and lunch). 2:30 p.m., musical chairs. 3:10 p.m., dance party. 4:10 p.m., free time (relaxing after the dance). 4:40 p.m., lottery. 5:10 p.m., closing ceremony and opening of dressing room to change out of fursuits. 6:00 p.m., room closed. There were almost 60 fursuits in the group photo.

Chairmen or Organizers: KemoConProject (Muddyfox, Altia, Ryoga, OTK, PANJA!, Leon)

Kemocon 3: Due to the growing size, Room 1F was added. Kemocon 3 lasted from 11:00 a.m. to 6:00 p.m. There were no memberships, but there was ¥1,000 admission, children free. In addition to the organizers, there was a staff of 7 and 25 volunteers. Attendees received a Program Book. Events included: 11:00 a.m., doors open and dressing in fursuits. Noon, group photo. 12:30 p.m., opening ceremony. 12:40 p.m., egg race. 1:40 p.m., "Kemocon on Stage." 3:00 p.m., dance party. 4:30 p.m., lottery. 5:00 p.m., closing ceremony and changing out of fursuits. 6:00 p.m., rooms cleared. The fursuit group photo had over 75 fursuits. A terrace outside of Room 4F was used for individual photos.

Chairmen or Organizers: KemoConProject (Muddyfox, Altia, Ryoga, OTK, PANJA!, Leon)

Kemocon 4:
Chairmen or Organizers:

Kemocon 5: The attendees included 160 fursuiters in the group photograph.
Chairmen or Organizers:

Kemocon 6:
Chairmen or Organizers:

Kemocon 7:
Chairmen or Organizers:

Kemocon 8: Kemocon 8 was declared a brother convention of CaliFur.11. CaliFur's 2015 theme was Anime Kemono, emphasizing Japanese animation featuring anthropomorphic animals. The KemoCon Project helped organize it. Photographs showed about 100 fursuiters.
Chairmen or Organizers:

Kemono Square

Kemono Square, or Shizuoka Kemono Square, is located in Shizuoka city, about halfway between Tokyo and Nagoya on Japan's main Honshu island. Shizuoka is the fifth largest city in Japan, and offers Japanese furs a venue outside of Tokyo. In English, it is literally Animal or Beast Square, but it is translated by Japanese furs as Furry Square. It was organized by Eixin in 2012. It is a one-day gathering from 10:00 a.m. to 7:00 p.m. (19:00) for furs to socialize, play board games, billiards, and music, a voluntary gift exchange (gifts costing about ¥1,000 are recommended), and wear fursuits for a group photograph, followed by a large catered buffet dinner from 7:00 to 9:00 p.m. (19:00 to 21:00). A fursuit dressing room/headless lounge is available. Individual video recording and photographing is permitted, although caution is requested with dangerous props such as swords. Memberships (more properly admission) are ¥2,000 for the daytime event; ¥5,000 including the dinner. Registering in advance is recommended to allow planning for the furry staff. It is an all-ages event with alcohol and tobacco banned. The fursuit group photo shows 50 to 75 fursuits. For out-of-town furs, the Higashi Shizuoka Station is the nearest train stop, and staying at the Tokinosumika Hotel is recommended. There is a list of nearby eateries.

Name & Date	*Location*	*Attendance*
Kemono Square 1 December 22, 2012	6F Conference Hall, "Granship" Shizuoka Convention & Arts Center, Shizuoka	40
Kemono Square 2 August 31, 2013	6F Conference Hall, "Granship" Shizuoka Convention & Arts Center, Shizuoka	83
Kemono Square 3 June 7, 2014	6F Conference Hall, "Granship" Shizuoka Convention & Arts Center, Shizuoka	107
Kemono Square 4 June 6, 2015	6F Conference Hall, "Granship" Shizuoka Convention & Arts Center, Shizuoka	179

Events

Kemono Square 1:

Kemono Square 2:

Kemono Square 3: A performance stage with a microphone was added. The costumed juggler Glacier Mr. Juggling Dragon began appearing. Statistics were 107 daytime attendance including 72 fursuiters, and 61 dinner participants.

Kemono Square 4: Glacier Mr. Juggling Dragon performed again.

KharCon

KharCon, in Kharkiv, Ukraine, has been in the news in relation to the political unrest, rioting, and outright civil war in Ukraine since 2012. On January 28, 2014, a representative of KharCon 8.5 was quoted in Kharkiv's news that furries are apolitical, and would not let the fighting deter them from holding the KharCon from January 31 through February 2. But despite this, KharCon remains a furmeet. Held every few months (several times a year) since October 2012, KharCon is a three-day event with an attendance of about 20, held at a changing private residence for a headquarters. It features fursuit walks through Kharkiv, furry films, games, singing, a raffle, a nightly sauna, sometimes a barbecue, and lots of food. Most of the ₴500 registration fee (about $57) goes to buying food for KharCon's meals. It's informal fun, but it's not a convention.

Kigukemo

Kigukemo is a semi-annual convention held each Summer and Winter in Nagoya, Aichi Prefecture, Japan since 2011. It is like most Japanese furry conventions; a one-day opportunity to meet other Japanese furs and to show off fursuits, and a show-and-tell for the general public. It is always held at the 4th floor conference rooms of the Nagoya SME Promotion Center, although it has expanded from one to three conference rooms as Kigukemo has grown. Kigukemo is a portmanteau word, from kigurumi (commercial animal pajamas; loose full-body animal pajamas with animal headpieces that expose only the wearer's face) and kemono = animal.

Name & Date	Location	Attendance
Kigukemo 1 January 22, 2011	4th floor Conference Room(s), Nagoya SME Promotion Center, Chikusa-ku, Nagoya, Japan	?
Kigukemo 2 June 4, 2011	4th floor Conference Room(s), Nagoya SME Promotion Center, Chikusa-ku, Nagoya, Japan	?
Kigukemo 3 January 7, 2012	4th floor Conference Room(s), Nagoya SME Promotion Center, Chikusa-ku, Nagoya, Japan	?
Kigukemo 4 August 4, 2012	4th floor Conference Room(s), Nagoya SME Promotion Center, Chikusa-ku, Nagoya, Japan	?
Kigukemo 5 February 2, 2013	4th floor Conference Room(s), Nagoya SME Promotion Center, Chikusa-ku, Nagoya, Japan	?
Kigukemo 6 July 13, 2013	4th floor Conference Room(s), Nagoya SME Promotion Center, Chikusa-ku, Nagoya, Japan	?
Kigukemo 7 February 1, 2014	4th floor Conference Room(s), Nagoya SME Promotion Center, Chikusa-ku, Nagoya, Japan	?
Kigukemo 8 August 23, 2014	4th floor Conference Room(s), Nagoya SME Promotion Center, Chikusa-ku, Nagoya, Japan	?
Kigukemo 9 March 7, 2015	4th floor Conference Room(s), Nagoya SME Promotion Center, Chikusa-ku, Nagoya, Japan	?
Kigukemo 10 August 29, 2015	4th floor Conference Room(s), Nagoya SME Promotion Center, Chikusa-ku, Nagoya, Japan	?

Events

The Nagoya SME Promotion Center is a five-minute walk from the nearest train station, Fukiage Station No. 5. Admission was free to Kigukemo 1 and 2; ¥500 to Kigukemo 3, and has been ¥1,000 since. Pre-registration is advised, but walk-ins and the public are welcome. Kigukemo has expanded from a single conference room at Kigukemos 1 to 3, to two rooms at Kigukemos 4 to 6, and three rooms since. The traditional schedule has grown from 13:00 to 21:30 (1:00 to 9:30 p.m.) to 9:00 to 20:30 (9:00 a.m. to 8:30 p.m.), and now includes doors opening and fursuit changing (some professional clothiers are usually present to make hasty one-day fursuits on the spot, for a fee), opening ceremonies an hour later, a group photograph in the mid-afternoon to evening, a public lecture about two hours before un-fursuiting begins, un-fursuiting an hour before the Center closes, overlapping the closing ceremony a half hour before the Center closes.

Maltese Fur-Con

Maltese Fur-Con (usually referred to as "The Maltese Fur-Con") is a furry convention centered around a mystery drama event; a *crime noir* milieu with fursuits. The title is a reference to Dashiell Hammet's classic *The Maltese Falcon*, which introduced private eye Sam Spade. The convention offers both traditional furry convention events, and a role-playing murder mystery game with clues for those who wish to participate.

Name & Date	Theme	Location	Attendance	Fursuit Parade
Maltese Fur-Con (2014) August 1–3, 2014	Film Noir	Boston Logan Hilton Hotel, Boston, MA	197	28

Maltese Fur-Con 2014 kickstarter page. Art by Maltese Fur-Con Committee. Used with permission.

Name & Date	Theme	Location	Attendance	Fursuit Parade
Maltese Fur-Con (2015) August 14–16, 2015	The Weird West	Embassy Suites, Waltham, MA	not held	

Events

Maltese Fur-Con (2014): The Maltese Fur-Con created and promoted the Boston Furries Meet-up Group "as a way for local furs to more easily find meetings in and around Boston and all of Massachusetts." The theme was dramatized in an artifact called "The Maltese Pigeon" and its three, jewel-encrusted eggs, which surfaced from time to time in various eras of history as a parody and homage to Hammet's tale. A trophy company was commissioned to create a Maltese Pigeon statuette. There were also promotional police badges for sponsors. G-o-H Betsy Beaver did the conbook cover. A T-shirt featured the con logo on the front and con information on the back.

Guests of Honor: Betsy Nichols (Betsy Beaver, furry and animation artist)
Charity: United States War Dogs, Inc. ($247.81)
Chairmen or Organizers: Rourke Danyals (Rourkie)

Maltese Fur-Con (2015): The theme was a furry version of weird tales from the wild west, similar to the *Wild Wild West* TV series or the roleplaying game Deadlands, with F.O.X. Agents assigned by Mission Central in "Headquarters" in the Wild West era to investigate a supernatural incident in a town that time seemed to forget. The plot of the weekend centered around 3 families in a dispute over a lost gold mine. The theme featured receiving periodic clues. However, in June 2015, MFC announced its cancellation due to less than half of the previous year's attendance preregistering, resulting in insufficient funds to prepare the convention. It was not known whether MFC would be held in the future.

Guests of Honor: Spitfire Jackal
Charity: United States War Dogs, Inc.
Chairmen or Organizers: Rourke Danyals (Rourkie)

The Maltese Fur-Con *see* Maltese Fur-Con

Megaplex

Megaplex (originally Pawpet Megaplex) took over from Furry Spring Break as the first full-scale furry convention in the South. Despite its controversial and confrontational beginnings, it has settled down to become one of the more successful annual conventions.

Name & Date	Theme	Location	Attendance	Parade
Pawpet Megaplex March 8–10, 2002	none	Ramada Resort and Convention Center, Orlando, FL	126	none
Pawpet Megaplex 2 March 21–23, 2003	none	Sheraton Studio City Resort, Orlando, FL	197	none
Megaplex 3 March 19–21, 2004	none	Sheraton Studio City Resort, Orlando, FL	357	23
Megaplex 4 March 11–13, 2005	Road Trip	Sheraton World Resort, Orlando, FL	387	32
Megaplex 5 March 17–19, 2006	The Horror! Saluting B-movies, especially the great horror flicks	Sheraton World Resort, Orlando, FL	257	41

Megaplex

Name & Date	Theme	Location	Parade	
Magaplex 6 March 2–4, 2007	Game Shows	Wyndham Jacksonville Riverwalk, Jacksonville, FL	185	31
Megaplex 7 March 28–30, 2008	Comic Books: Heroes & Villains	Wyndham Jacksonville Riverwalk, Jacksonville, FL	255	45
Megaplex 8 July 24–26, 2009	Toyland! Christmas in July	Radisson WorldGate Resort Orlando Hotel, West Kissimmee, FL	425	78
Megaplex 9 July 23–25, 2010	Mad, Mad Science!	Radisson WorldGate Resort Orlando Hotel, West Kissimmee, FL	410	80
Megaplex 10 July 29–31, 2011	Retro Arcade	Radisson WorldGate Resort Orlando Hotel, West Kissimmee, FL	553	86
Megaplex XI July 27–29, 2012	Turn Back the Gears!	Radisson WorldGate Resort Orlando Hotel, West Kissimmee, FL	625	142
Megaplex XII July 26–28, 2013	Rocking at the Hop	Orlando Airport Marriott Lakeside, Orlando, FL	821	185
Megaplex XIII July 25–27, 2014	The Candy Factory	Orlando Airport Marriott Lakeside, Orlando, FL	1,281	320
Megaplex XIV July 31–August 2, 2015	Cops & Robbers	Orlando Airport Marriott Lakeside, Orlando, FL	1,472	359

Events

Pawpet Megaplex: The Ramada was the same hotel that would not give Matt Henry a contract for Furry Spring Break 2. It was organized by Pawpet Live Experiences, Inc. (PLEx), which incorporated only two months earlier. (Due to the hurry to incorporate before the convention, PLEx chose to incorporate as a faster for-profit corporation, although it promised to be run on a not-for-profit basis.) Although the panels and other events were very similar to those of other furry conventions, PLEx heavily promoted itself as "The very first ever Funny Animal Convention," focusing on "independent and amature [sic] entertainment through the use of Funny Animals." There was an emphasis on puppet shows. There was a headless room for fursuiters. The publicity promised a movie room showing appropriate features, a gaming room, improvisational comedy seminars, "rollercoaster and theme park trips," seminars on how to draw and animate Funny Animals on a computer, and more. "It will be a weekend packed full of GOOD CLEAN FUN!" The implied slur against other furry conventions resulted in considerable criticism—some said "vitriol"—from some established furry fans. The conbook cover was by Herbie Bearclaw.

Charity: The C.A.R.E. Foundation for abandoned pets
Chairmen or Organizers: Karl F. Meyers (Carl Fox)

Pawpet Megaplex 2: The new hotel was closer to Universal City Florida. There was a policy of, "This is totally a news, press and media free event," banning any reporters. A guest-of-honor was added. The program included Uncle Kage's Story Hour, a rant by 2, the Ranting Gryphon, variety shows, a magic act, a Fursuit Parade, a C.A.R.E. Foundation presentation that included a Florida panther, and a MegaPlex Puppet Parade and lots of Pawpet puppet performances. The Charity Auction was conducted by Uncle Kage. There were dances on all three evenings. The Toxic Audio five-person singing group appeared on the program. PLEx conducted a vigorous campaign during 2002 to combat the negative publicity that it was denying that it was a furry convention. The emphasis on it being a Funny Animal convention was dropped, but PLEx continued its claim to being "GOOD CLEAN FUN." The conbook cover was by Susan Rankin.

Guests of Honor: Susan Rankin (furry cartoonist)
Charity: The C.A.R.E. Foundation for abandoned pets
Chairmen or Organizers: Karl F. Meyers (Carl Fox)

Megaplex 2013 poster. Art by Tirrel. Used with permission.

Megaplex 3: The "Pawpet" was dropped from the convention's name as implying too much puppet programming, although the resulting MP3 abbreviation, alluding to digital audio recording, was taken advantage of in the convention's publications. Informal gatherings of fursuiters began to be organized into a Fursuit Parade. The program again included Uncle Kage's Story Hour, and a live animal presentation by the C.A.R.E. Foundation, followed by a charity auction conducted by Uncle Kage. Programming encouraged the members to take part in the puppeteering, costuming and fursuiting (called "mascoting"), Variety Show performing, and dancing, secure in the knowledge that no press or TV would be allowed into the convention to record it. The Toxic Audio singing group returned. The conbook cover was by Erika Leigh "Chilly" Rosengarten.
    Guests of Honor: MST3K's Trace Beaulieu, a puppeteer.
    Charity: The C.A.R.E. Foundation
    Chairmen or Organizers: Karl F. Meyers (Carl Fox)

Megaplex 4: The hotel was next to the SeaWorld Orlando theme park. The events included a C.A.R.E. Foundation live animal demonstration, the charity auction for the C.A.R.E. Foundation, lots of dances and improv comedy shows, a fursuit construction demonstration, and karaoke singing. The amount of the charity donation began to be recorded. A "Potpourri of Puppets" for children to demonstrate their puppetry was held Sunday night. There was no formal Dealers' Room; a number of tables were set up in an Artist Alley on a first-come claim basis for attendees to use as they wished. The only qualification was that no art drawn or sold could be above a PG rating. Drawing instruction seminars were also scheduled for the room. The theme was illustrated in the convention's emblem of a "Megaplex 4" highway sign. The conbook cover was by Erika Leigh "Chilly" Rosengarten.
    Guests of Honor: John Kennedy (puppeteer)
    Charities: The C.A.R.E. Foundation ($2,210)
    Chairmen or Organizers: Karl F. Meyers (Carl Fox)

Megaplex 5: The programming included performances by Uncle Kage and 2, the Ranting Gryphon, fursuit games, and a screening/performance of *The Rocky Horror Picture Show*. The first Megaplex T-shirt was made, with art by Brian Reynolds who also did the conbook front cover. Some attendees complained that the hotel was not efficient; the Megaplex was sharing the hotel with other conventions and tourists, and the Megaplex rooms were very spread out. "I really wish the 2 rooms we booked had been in the same building." This was at least partially due to the fact that the Sheraton World Resort Hotel was due to be sold to another hotel chain. It was known that the new management would raise prices so much that it would not be feasible for the Megaplex to continue meeting there. Presumably the staff was unsure whether they would still be employed by the new management, and the outgoing management was not motivated to correct any problems. The conbook back cover was by Terry "Mouse" Sender.
    Guests of Honor: Brian Reynolds (video game artist), 4:2:5 (a capella musical group)
    Charity: The C.A.R.E. Foundation ($3,100.40)
    Chairmen or Organizers: Karl F. Meyers (Carl Fox)

Megaplex 6: Megaplex left Orlando because the Megaplex's previous hotels all doubled or tripled their rates, and the Megaplex had to leave Orlando to remain affordable. The attendance drop was blamed on the Megaplex's closeness to FWA2007. There were rumors just before the convention that the move to Jacksonville &/or the closeness to FWA2007 had caused its cancellation, but it met as advertised. Events included a Gong Show variety show, "Whose Line Is It, Anyway?," "Family Feud," a convention-long mystery event, the ever-popular 2, the Ranting Gryphon and Uncle Kage, a dance DJ'd by DJ Rory, lots of Fursuiting and Pawpet panels and workshops, and a late-night live performance of *The Rocky Horror Picture Show*. One attendee donated $900 to the C.A.R.E. charity. The conbook cover and T-shirt were by Mike Kazaleh.

Guests of Honor: Mike Kazaleh (animator & comic-book artist)
Charities: The C.A.R.E. Foundation ($2,825)
Chairmen or Organizers: Karl F. Meyers (Carl Fox)

Megaplex 7: Beginning at Megaplex 7, the convention relaxed its "good, clean fun" image to that comparable to other furry conventions. A Megaplex 7 mascot was created; MegaPanther. Events included games and dances, a rant by 2, the Ranting Gryphon and Uncle Kage's Story Hour, an Art Track, a Puppet Track, and a concert by Hali. Convention chairman Carl Fox announced that he was stepping down. The conbook front cover was by Adam Wan, and the back cover by Steve Martin. The T-shirt was by Adam Wan.

Guests of Honor: Adam Wan (fan artist), with Matthew Ebel (Hali of Firpine) as a Special Musical Guest
Charities: The C.A.R.E. Foundation ($1,185)
Chairmen or Organizers: Karl F. Myers (Carl Fox)

Megaplex 8: Megaplex returned to the Orlando area after two years in Jacksonville, and moved from March to late July to get better hotel rates and by popular demand to increase the time-gap from the growing Furry Weekend Atlanta. The return was immediately reflected by a sharp increase in attendance. A lounge area, The Lair, was added next to the Dealers' Den (a separate room) as the hub of the convention space, and the Artists' Alley tables were moved there. MegaPanther was so popular at Megaplex 7 that he returned as the permanent Megaplex mascot, renamed Pounce the Panther. BigBlueFox hosted an all-night "Dance till Dawn" DJ rave from Saturday until Sunday morning. Matthew Ebel gave a concert, and there was a performance by Bucktown Tiger. Other events included repeats of the Funday Pawpet Show, *The Rocky Horror Picture Show* led by Matthew Ebel as Dr. Frank N. Furter, "Fursuit Deal or Big Deal" and "Family Feud," a rant by 2, the Ranting Gryphon, and fursuit games. Tastings, a wine bar adjacent to the hotel, hosted The Funday Pawpet Show. The conbook cover was by Herbie Bearclaw. BigBlueFox did the T-shirt.

Guests of Honor: Karsten Auchter (BigBlueFox; German furry artist/fursuiter)
Charities: The C.A.R.E. Foundation ($1,500)
Chairmen or Organizers: John Cole (KP or Kuddlepup)

Megaplex 9: Events included a concert by Matthew "Hali of Firpine" Ebel, the Funday Pawpet Show, a Fursuit Game Show, a photo shoot, and individual fursuit games, a C.A.R.E. animal presentation, the Charity Auction, a furry variety show, a WTF Improv Theater, an all-night dance with DJ BigBlueFox, a *Rocky Horror Picture Show* screening, and off-site fursuit outings to a bowling alley and a mini-golf course. G-o-h Paul Zaloom performed his Paul Zaloom's Puppet Show, a one-man Punch-&-Judy-style event. The conbook had an uncredited front cover and an advertisement on the back cover. Herbie Bearclaw did the T-shirt.

Guests of Honor: Paul Zaloom (actor, puppeteer)
Charity: The C.A.R.E. Foundation ($2,928)
Chairmen or Organizers: John Cole (KP or Kuddlepup), Randy Fox (Yappy SlyFox)

Megaplex 10: There were two Fursuit Parades. The regular afternoon one had 86 fursuiters, and the second Late Night one had 64. The conbook cover was by Blitz Wolfang. The T-shirt was by Chad Krueger.

Guests of Honor: Chad Krueger (artist)
Charity: The C.A.R.E. Foundation ($1,368)
Chairmen or Organizers: John Cole (KP or Kuddlepup), Randy Fox (Yappy SlyFox)

Megaplex XI: "Turn Back the Gears!" was a furry steampunk theme. There were 69 video games; attendees were advised to "save your quarters." Events included a Florida Furries Meet & Greet,

The Funday Pawpet Show, a Matthew Ebel concert, karaoke singing, fursuit games, Uncle Kage's Story Hour, a scavenger hunt, a dance competition, and a dessert social & pool party. Rhubarb the Bear gave a musical performance, "Julie Bunny Must Die!" There was a wedding, and off-site fursuit bowling. The conbook cover was by Crashheart Otter. The T-shirt was by Herbie Bearclaw.

Guests of Honor: Ron Schneider (EPCOT Center's "Dreamfinder), Noel MacNeal (puppetter)
Charity: The C.A.R.E. Foundation ($4,257)
Chairmen or Organizers: John Cole (KP or Kuddlepup), Randy Fox (Yappy SlyFox)

Megaplex XII: Fox Amoore hosted a live rock concert. Megaplex rented an entire bowling alley for pre-convention early arrivals, for exclusive use at no charge by attendees including fursuiters. Rhubarb the Bear gave a musical theatrical performance, "Fosgate: Ferret Loan Officer." There was a free dessert social with key lime pie, cheesecake, and chocolate cake with ice cream. The T-shirt was by Tirrel, who did the 44-page conbook front cover. The back cover was an advertisement with art by TaniDaReal.

Guests of Honor: Fox Amoore (furry musician), Tirrel (furry artist)
Charity: The C.A.R.E. Foundation ($4,038)
Chairmen or Organizers: John Cole (KP or Kuddlepup), Randy Fox (Yappy SlyFox)

Megaplex XIII: There were two Fursuit Parades; the main one on Saturday that had 320 fursuits, and one on Sunday with 76 fursuits. Other events included a C.A.R.E. presentation besides the charity auction, dances, karaoke, a Story Hour created by audience suggestions illustrated by several quick-draw artists, Uncle Kage's Story Hour, a charity poker tournament, art, puppet, and fursuit tutorials, musical performances by Pepper Coyote, Rhubarb the Bear, Bucktown Tiger, and Husky In Denial, and the off-site furry bowling. Mary Mouse's conbook cover (44 pages) illustrated The Candy Factory theme. The T-shirt was by TaniDaReal.

Guests of Honor: Mary E. Minch (Mary Mouse), Tanja Freese (TaniDaReal) (furry cartoonists)
Charity: The C.A.R.E. Foundation ($10,696.98)
Chairmen or Organizers: John Cole (KP or Kuddlepup), Randy Fox (Yappy SlyFox)

Megaplex XIV: Events included a C.A.R.E. "Meet the Animals" presentation, an in-depth presentation and demonstration of laser entertainment by Fizz Otter, dance parties, fursuit games, a 2-hour Funday Pawpet puppetry show, art/fursuit/puppetry tutorials, musical performances, Uncle Kage's Story Hour, panels such as "World Culture and History in Furry Writing," a tribute to "furries who are no longer with us," and the traditional off-site furry bowling. G-o-H FableFire cancelled three days before the convention due to illness, but she did the 42-page conbook cover and T-shirt art.

Guests of Honor: FableFire, Fizz Otter (furry artists)
Charity: The C.A.R.E. Foundation ($8,260.23)
Chairmen or Organizers: John Cole (KP or Kuddlepup), Randy Fox (Yappy SlyFox)

Mephit FurMeet

Mephit FurMeet was so-named because it was held in the Memphis, Tennessee, area. The Mephit name promptly gave it its skunk mascot.

Name & Date	Theme	Location	Attendance	Parade
Mephit FurMeet 1 August 29–September 3, 1997	?	Howard Johnson Inn, Memphis, TN	68	?
Mephit FurMeet 2 September 4–7, 1998	?	Holiday Inn Select Memphis East, Memphis, TN	188	?

Name & Date	Theme	Location	Attendance	Parade
Mephit FurMeet 3 September 3–6, 1999	?	Holiday Inn Select Memphis East, Memphis, TN	288	?
Mephit FurMeet 2000 September 1–4, 2000	?	Holiday Inn Select Memphis East, Memphis, TN	405	?
Mephit FurMeet 2001 August 31–Sept. 3, 2001	?	Holiday Inn Select Hotel, Memphis International Airport, Memphis, TN	362	?
Mephit FurMeet 6 August 30–Sept. 2, 2002	?	Holiday Inn Select Hotel, Memphis International Airport, Memphis, TN	392	?
Mephit FurMeet 7 August 29–Sept. 1, 2003	Seventh Silly Skunkie Symposium	Holiday Inn Select Hotel, Memphis International Airport, Memphis, TN	420	?
Mephit FurMeet 8 September 3–6, 2004	Earn Your Stripes!	Holiday Inn Select Hotel, Memphis International Airport, Memphis, TN	502	70
Mephit FurMeet 9 September 2–4, 2005	Nine Lives, Baby!	Holiday Inn Select Hotel, Memphis International Airport, Memphis, TN	601	?
Mephit FurMeet X September 1–3, 2006	?	Holiday Inn Select Hotel, Memphis International Airport, Memphis, TN	630	?
Mephit FurMeet 11 August 31–Sept. 2, 2007	In 2007 Comes 11	Holiday Inn Select Hotel, Memphis International Airport, Memphis, TN	630 (est.)	94
Mephit FurMeet 12 August 29–31, 2008	Office Space	Holiday Inn Select Hotel, Memphis International Airport, Memphis, TN	650 (est.)	96
Mephit FurMeet 13 September 4–6, 2009	Murder Mystery	Holiday Inn Select Hotel, Memphis International Airport, Memphis, TN	550 (est.)	84
Mephit Furmeet 14 September 3–5, 2010	Welcome Home to Where the Wild Things Are—Southern Style	Whispering Woods Hotel & Conference Center, Olive Branch, MS	600	90 (est.)
Mephit FurMeet 15 September 2–4, 2011	Under Construction	Whispering Woods Hotel & Conference Center, Olive Branch, MS	546	?
Mephit FurMeet 16 August 31–Sept. 2, 2012	Year of the Skunk	Whispering Woods Hotel & Conference Center, Olive Branch, MS	548	96
Mephit FurMeet 17 August 30–Sept. 1, 2013	A Trip to the Zoo	Whispering Woods Hotel & Conference Center, Olive Branch, MS	478	108
Mephit FurMeet 2014 August 28–31, 2014	A Night at the B-Movies	Whispering Woods Hotel & Conference Center, Olive Branch, MS	455	107
Mephit FurMeet 2015 September 4–6, 2015	Steampunk Skunk	Whispering Woods Hotel & Conference Center, Olive Branch, MS	432	99

Events

Mephit FurMeet 1: Mephit Furmeet became the second furry convention to be held on a holiday weekend; Labor Day. It grew out of a prior furry fan pizza party at the apartment of GrowlTiger. The permanent mascot was a cartoon skunk, and the permanent motto was "Welcome home." The attendees all used fursona names. GrowlTiger had expected only a larger fur-meet pizza party; when the event grew larger than that, Mike and Carole Curtis helped rent a second room for an impromptu Dealers' Den. There were some fursuits. An annual T-shirt design contest was started; this first one was won by Loran Skunky.
Chairmen or Organizers: GrowlTiger

Mephit FurMeet 2: The committee incorporated as the Mid-South and Tennessee Anthropomorphic Arts Association (MST3A), a non-profit organization "created to foster and promote the appreciation of anthropomorphic arts, literature and culture." Attendance more than doubled. The MFM had its first guest-of-honor. There were opening and closing ceremonies, Special Interest Group panels, a larger Dealers' Den, and a Saturday night dance. Despite this, GrowlTiger says that the first three MFMs were basically fur-meets and not conventions, because of their friendly, informal nature. The T-shirt design vote was won by Joe Rosales.
Guests of Honor: Bill Holbrook (newspaper/Internet cartoonist)
Chairmen or Organizers: GrowlTiger

Mephit FurMeet 3: There were panels and SIG groups, opening/closing ceremonies, a much larger dealer area, and a Saturday night dance. The T-shirt design contest was won by Brian McPherson.
Guests of Honor: Radio Comix (Pat Duke and Elin Winckler, publishers, and staff artist Joe Rosales)
Chairmen or Organizers: GrowlTiger

Mephit FurMeet 2000: The name change from Memphis FurMeet 4 was due to the replacement of GrowlTiger by Kodian as chairman. The T-shirt design contest was won by Herbie Hamill (Herbie Bearclaw). After the convention, scenes from it appeared in the 2002 80-minute documentary *Fans and Freaks*, directed by two Nashville-area filmmakers.
Guests of Honor: Dave Braun (Plonq; short story writer)
Chairmen or Organizers: Kodian

Mephit FurMeet 2001: Uncle Kage attended as "The Great Unknown Furry." A new committee was introduced for the next year, including a new chairman, Christopher Roth (TygerCowboy). The annual T-shirt design contest was won by Gideon Artwolf. The conbook cover was by S. "Aloha" Cardozo.
Guests of Honor: Tigerwolf of Tigerden Internet Services (Major George Nemayer, a retired USAF Major in real life)
Charity: Tiger Haven ($8,000+)
Chairmen or Organizers: Kodian

Mephit FurMeet 6: There were a Dealer's Room, an Artists' Alley, and an auction. Programming was divided into tracks. There were a Furry Puppet Track, a Spirituality Track, a Gaming/Roleplay Track, a GreyMuzzle Track, a Fursuit Track, and tracks for Art and Writing. The T-shirt design contest (required features: the convention name or MFM, the year 2002 or "6," a skunk theme not to exceed PG, and black-&-white line art) was won by Steve Dark. About half of the convention space was unexpectedly requisitioned by the Transportation Security Administration. Phil Geusz says, "There were black screens and sheets draped everywhere, and here and there men with AR-15's poised to shoot anyone who might try to step beyond them. This made for probably the strangest con atmosphere in fandom history."

Guests of Honor: Odis Holcomb (Ryngs Raccoon, furry artist/fursuiter)
Charity: Tiger Haven ($7,000+)
Chairmen or Organizers: Christopher Roth (TygerCowboy)

Mephit FurMeet 7: A memorial dinner was held to honor David Neff (TV Dave), a broadcast journalist who had covered furry fandom before he died of diabetes in Saudi Arabia while covering the Iraq War. The T-shirt design contest was won by Jodi Tong (J3T), with the back by Jaden Heartdancer, selected by chairman TygerCowboy.
Guests of Honor: Loriana Vixen (artist/fursuiter)
Charity: Tiger Haven ($7,000+)
Chairmen or Organizers: Christopher Roth (TygerCowboy)

Mephit FurMeet 8: Some attendees insisted the attendance was considerably higher than the official 502. MFM8 claimed several records broken: 112 sponsor and super sponsor badges issued; 70 fursuiters in the parade; 132 pizzas consumed on Saturday night; and over $15,000 raised for the Tiger Haven sanctuary. The T-shirt design contest was won by Jodi "J3T" Tong, and director/chairman TygerCowboy selected the design of Philip Eggerding (Cirrel) for the back. The convention published a cookbook, *Put a Tiger at Your Table*, of recipes contributed by the committee and members; all proceeds above the publication costs were donated to Tiger Haven.
Guests of Honor: Rog Minotaur (furry artist), "with special guest in concert: Sub-level 03"
Charity: Tiger Haven ($15,000+)
Chairmen or Organizers: Christopher Roth (TygerCowboy)

Mephit FurMeet 9: The hotel was filled with refugees from Hurricane Katrina on August 29–30. The attendees donated both money and resources to the refugees. Chairman TygerCowboy reported the total funds raised for charity were $16,600, including $12,600 raised for Tiger Haven and $4,000 raised for the American Red Cross. Some convention attendees also banded together to raise $3,000 for another attendee who lost their car due to the events surrounding the hurricane and subsequent flooding. The 36-page conbook had multiple black-&-white covers printed from losing T-shirt art. The T-shirt design contest was won by Cirrel, with the back chosen by TygerCowboy by Diana Kellogg (White Wolf). There was also a separate staff T-shirt by J3T. The traditional Hospitality Room was called the Horsebrutality Suite. Almost two weeks after the convention, there was a long and condescending article about it in the *Memphis Flyer*, emphasizing the freaky fursuits and not mentioning the help given to the hurricane refugees.
Guests of Honor: John "The Gneech" Robey (furry cartoonist)
Charities: Tiger Haven; the American Red Cross ($16,600)
Chairmen or Organizers: Christopher Roth (TygerCowboy)

Mephit FurMeet X: The 630 attendance did not include the convention staff. Decade level SuperSponsors received a jacket with art by Ursula Husted. Friday night White Wolf was married (for real) in a well-attended ceremony. Saturday noon was the Fursuit Parade. Sunday night was an Ice Cream Social. There were lots of late-night parties with balloons. MFMX had 200+ pizzas delivered during the convention. The T-shirt design contest was won by Evol Otter; the back was by Dustin Friend (Bauske Destad), chosen by chairman TygerCowboy. The staff T-shirt design was won by J3T. The 48-page conbook again had multiple black-&-white covers, printed from losing T-shirt art. Frozen Oasis hosted a room party. An attendee, Joseph Wilson (Canis Claxis), was banned for life from the convention for inappropriate behavior toward a female member. There was a protest against the convention by a church group in front of the hotel during the Furry Masquerade, but they were ordered off by the Memphis police.
Guests of Honor: Jodi Tong (J3T)
Charity: Tiger Haven ($12,121.02)
Chairmen or Organizers: Christopher Roth (TygerCowboy)

Mephit FurMeet 11: The T-shirt design contest was won by Carissa St. Clair (CrssaFox); chairman TygerCowboy chose the design by Laschita Whelan for the back. TygerCowboy also officiated at a "pawfasting" between Susan Foxx (Butterscotch Vixen) and Spectra Vixen. Two other attendees got engaged (and later married) during the Friday night karaoke. The 44-page conbook had a front cover by Laschita Whelan. Frozen Oasis hosted a room party with lounge music, card games, and Jaspian dressed in a real Las Vegas show costume, for the "Viva Las Vegas" theme.
  Guests of Honor: Jim Lane (furry author)
  Charity: Tiger Haven ($9,000+)
  Chairmen or Organizers: Christopher Roth (TygerCowboy)

Mephit FurMeet 12: There were the usual Artist Alley, Dealer's Den, Video Room, Internet Room, and Fursuit Lounge. Scheduled events included a puppet show, Writers' and Fursuit Meet & Greets, drawing/painting workshops, the Masquerade, fursuit games, furry Idol Karaoke, dances, a 9:00 p.m.–1:00 a.m. room set up for "open mike" comedians/artists/musicians with refreshments, gaming, and more. The annual T-shirt design contest (front) was won by Rayen Wolffe and Nihaler, while the back chosen by chairman TygerCowboy was by Diana Kellogg (White Wolf). The convention staff T-shirt design chosen by the staff was by Philip Eggerding (Cirrel).
  Guests of Honor: Jon Albers (PandaGuy, fursuiter)
  Charity: Tiger Haven ($10,000+)
  Chairmen or Organizers: Christopher Roth (TygerCowboy)

Mephit FurMeet 13: Features and events were similar to the previous year's. There were a Saturday evening ice cream social, a KWKAT Internet Radio Broadcast, and a SubLevel 3 concert. There were Special Interest Groups as specialized as Rails and Tails, for furs who either work for railroads (museum or regular) or enjoy model railroading. The T-shirt contest winner (for the front) was Blackfrost. TygerCowboy chose Oldfreek's design for the back. The staff's choice for the staff T-shirt was Cirrel's design. At the closing ceremony, it was announced that the MFM would move to the Whispering Woods Hotel & Conference Center in Olive Branch, Mississippi, just across the state line.
  Guests of Honor: Isfacat (furry comedian)
  Charity: Tiger Haven ($5,472)
  Chairmen or Organizers: Christopher Roth (TygerCowboy)

Mephit FurMeet 14: Features and events were similar to those of previous years. They included a Pizza Feed, a masquerade, "Wielder's Moments" (comedy performance), "Saturday Night Zoo" (5-hour dance), and an Ice Cream Social. The 32-page conbook had a front cover by Charles Ettinger. The T-shirt contest winner (for the front) was Charles Ettinger. TygerCowboy chose Pavel Kompaniet's (Wolfy-Nail) design for the back. The staff's choice for the staff T-shirt was Mari's design.
  Guests of Honor: Tiffany Byers (Razzek; furry cartoonist)
  Charity: Tiger Haven ($6,289)
  Chairmen or Organizers: Christopher Roth (TygerCowboy)

Mephit FurMeet 15: The winner of the popular vote for the front of the T-shirt was Growly. The director's choice for the back of the shirt was Rust Rat. The staff's choice for the staff T-shirt was slashersivi. At the closing ceremony, at least $300 was raised for the charity in addition to the $14,059.
  Guests of Honor: Bucktown Tiger
  Charity: Tiger Haven ($14,059)
  Chairmen or Organizers: Christopher Roth (TygerCowboy)

Mephit FurMeet 16: The winner of the popular vote for the front of the T-shirt was Tavi Munk. The director's choice for the back of the shirt was Felpur.Samael. The staff's choice for the staff

T-shirt was Wolfaya. The conbook cover was by Holcomb II. Tiger Haven received over $6,300 at its table in addition to the con donation. Just after the closing ceremony, there was a tornado warning and the tornado was visible from the hotel, which lost power for two hours.
Guests of Honor: Tiger Haven, the charity, was made the guest of honor
Charity: Tiger Haven ($7,191)
Chairmen or Organizers: Christopher Roth (TygerCowboy)

Mephit FurMeet 17: The winner of the popular vote for the front of the T-shirt was Coon Spoon. The director's choice for the back of the shirt was Tavi Munk. The staff's choice for the staff T-shirt was Wolf Pup Wielder.
Guests of Honor: Wolf Pup Wielder
Charity: Tiger Haven (about $7,200)
Chairmen or Organizers: Christopher Roth (TygerCowboy)

Mephit FurMeet 2014: The winner of the popular vote for the front of the T-shirt was Becky A. The director's choice for the back of the shirt was Mary Mae Smith. The staff's choice for the staff T-shirt was Tavi Munk. The conbook cover was uncredited.
Guests of Honor: Floe
Charity: Tiger Haven ($7,300)
Chairmen or Organizers: Christopher Roth (TygerCowboy)

Mephit FurMeet 2015:
Guests of Honor: Doc Bolt
Charity: Tiger Haven ($5,405)
Chairmen or Organizers: Christopher Roth (TygerCowboy)

Mephit MiniCon

The Mephit MiniCon was the second furry convention created in Europe, and the first whose language is other than English. Today it is the third largest furry convention in Europe. Since 2006 it has been at the Jugendherberge Freusburg youth hostel in Freusburg castle, and has filled the castle to its 200 attendee capacity. It has a high Swiss attendance in addition to German. It is incorporated in Germany as FurCon e.V. It shares some equipment with EuroFurence.

Name & Date	Theme	Location	Attendance
Mephit MiniCon May 1–3, 1998	?	Andreas Schulmayer's apartment, Rüsselsheim, Hesse	18
Mephit MiniCon 2 ?, 1999	?	Falken Jugendheim, Seeheim	28
Mephit MiniCon 3 ?, 2000	?	Falken Jugendheim, Seeheim	35
Mephit MiniCon 4 April 26–29, 2001	A Furry Odyssey	Falken Jugendheim, Seeheim	43
Mephit MiniCon 5 April 25–28, 2002	Ye Olde and Furry Myths	Turner- und Jugendheim Loreley e.V. youth hostel, Lorelei Rock, Sankt Goarshausen	65
Mephit MiniCon 6 May 1–4, 2003	A "Tail" from Ancient Times	Turner- und Jugendheim Loreley e.V. youth hostel, Lorelei Rock, Sankt Goarshausen	100 (estimated)
Mephit MiniCon 7 May 6–9, 2004	The Phantom of the MMC	Turner- und Jugendheim Loreley e.V. youth hostel, Lorelei Rock, Sankt Goarshausen	100 (estimated)
Mephit MiniCon 8 May 19–22, 2005	Unendlichkeit	Turner- und Jugendheim Loreley e.V. youth hostel, Lorelei Rock, Sankt Goarshausen	140

Mephit MiniCon

Name & Date	Theme	Location	Attendance
Mephit MiniCon 9 May 4–7, 2006	Märchen	Jugendherberge Freusburg youth hostel, Freusburg Castle, Kirchen	200 (estimated)
Mephit MiniCon 10 May 17–20, 2007	Project Evolution	Jugendherberge Freusburg youth hostel, Freusburg Castle, Kirchen	200 (estimated)
Mephit MiniCon 11 May 8–11, 2008	Spiegelwelten	Jugendherberge Freusburg youth hostel, Freusburg Castle, Kirchen	200 (estimated)
Mephit MiniCon 12 April 30–May 3, 2009	Voll auf die Zwölf	Jugendherberge Freusburg youth hostel, Freusburg Castle, Kirchen	200 (estimated)
Mephit MiniCon 13 May 13–16, 2010	Steampunk	Jugendherberge Freusburg youth hostel, Freusburg Castle, Kirchen	200 (estimated)
Mephit MiniCon 14 April 28–May 1, 2011	Friedhof der Kuscheltiere	Jugendherberge Freusburg youth hostel, Freusburg Castle, Kirchen	200 (estimated)
Mephit MiniCon 15 May 17–20, 2012	Versunkene Welten	Jugendherberge Freusburg youth hostel, Freusburg Castle, Kirchen	200 (estimated)
Mephit MiniCon 16 May 9–12, 2013	Fahrendes Volk	Jugendherberge Freusburg youth hostel, Freusburg Castle, Kirchen	200 (estimated)
Mephit MiniCon 17 May 1–4, 2014	Loony Lodge	Jugendherberge Freusburg youth hostel, Freusburg Castle, Kirchen	200 (estimated)
Mephit MiniCon 18 April 30–May 3, 2015	Finally 18!	Jugendherberge Freusburg youth hostel, Freusburg Castle, Kirchen	200 (estimated)

Events

Mephit MiniCon: The 18 attendees of the first MMC were personally invited by H'Lven. Despite the informal beginning, it had a website. The gathering led to a more formal convention that is today the third largest furry convention in Europe, and the first whose "official" language is not English.
   Chairmen or Organizers: Andreas Schulmayer (H'Lven)

Mephit MiniCon 2: H'Lven moved the MMC from his apartment to a youth hostel in Seeheim, near Frankfort.
   Chairmen or Organizers: Andreas Schulmayer (H'Lven)

Mephit MiniCon 3: It was also called Mephit MiniCon 2K.
   Chairmen or Organizers: Andreas Schulmayer (H'Lven)

Mephit MiniCon 4: There was an Art Show and Dealers' Den, and afternoon SIGs on How to do Fursuits, Bondage, and Mascot Acting and Interacting. Videos were shown in the evenings. Attendance rose to 40, which was past the comfortable limit of the site. Attendees had to cook their own meals. The 8-page conbooklet had a cover by Anbessa and illustrations by Cairyn. All agreed that a larger site was needed for the future.
   Chairmen or Organizers: Andreas Schulmayer (H'Lven)

Mephit MiniCon 5: Sankt Goarshausen was a popular tourist town on the Rhine. There was an Art Show and Dealers' Den. Afternoon SIGs (in German) were on applying computer animation technology in animal behavioral research, and the reintroduction of wolves in Montana, U.S. There was a RPG gathering. BigBlueFox became MMC's "resident DJ" from 2002 onward. Videos were shown in the evenings. The 16-page conbooklet cover was by Cairyn.
   Chairmen or Organizers: Andreas Schulmayer (H'Lven)

Mephit MiniCon 6: There was an Art Show and Dealers' Den. Afternoon SIGs (in German) were on Relation-Ships? ("Beziehungs-Weise?"), Furries in the Media, Furries and Online Role Playing,

The Wolves—They are among us!, and Fursuit Basics. Videos were shown in the evenings. The 16-page conbooklet had a cover by TaniDaReal and illustrations by several members. The T-shirt was by Alpha_Ki. Both showed sexy skunk-girls.

Chairmen or Organizers: Andreas Schulmayer (H'Lven)

Mephit MiniCon 7: The "Phantom" was a reference to H'Lven, who was unable to organize the MMC for the first time. There were the usual Art Show and Dealers' Den. There was a SIG on Bondage. Tyger gave a reading. A BBQ and Frisbee playing were scheduled, "weather permitting" (it rained a lot). Videos were shown in the evenings. A T-shirt contest had two themes; "Skunks On Vacation/Lazy Skunks," and "You are the kittens, aren't you?," by TaniDa Real and Nimrais. The 20-page conbooklet cover was by Alpha_Ki. Both T-shirts and conbook cover were white on black.

Chairmen or Organizers: Matthias Chrzonsz (somewolf)

Mephit MiniCon 8: The theme meant Infinity. The registration fee was €88. The T-shirt design contest was won by Blue_Panther, who also did the conbook cover; both in orange on black, but without the skunk-girl visual theme. H'Lven organized the MMC under the title of "Chair Skunk."

Chairmen or Organizers: Andreas Schulmeyer (H'Lven)

Mephit MiniCon 9: The MMC moved to the larger Jugendherberge Freusburg youth hostel in Freusburg Castle, Kirchen. This was the locale of EuroFurence 7 in 2001. The attendance was estimated by the 200 limit of the castle/youth hostel, which was sold out. The program included informal socializing around the usual Dealers' Den, Art Show, BBQ/Campfire, and Video Room. The T-shirt design contest was won again by Blue_Panther. The back of the T-shirt (full color on black) was by Maja Wrzosek (Bloodhound Omega). The conbook had a full-color cover, the front by Bloodhound Omega and the back by Marion Fischer (EosFoxx); without skunk-girls.

Chairmen or Organizers: Andreas Schulmayer (H'Lven)

Mephit MiniCon 10: The registration fee was €110. A guest of honor was added. There were the Art Show and Dealers' Den. A new addition was the MMC Café; a room in the castle's basement where attendees could relax, socialize, and drink coffee. SIGs were held on Making Stone Fetishes (this was also a SIG for the next two years), and Storytelling. Videos were shown in the evening. Khaosdog did a color wraparound cover for the 20-page conbooklet, and the T-shirt. The membership badge was designed by Marion Fischer (EosFoxx). Attendees came from six countries.

Guests of Honor: Saskia Lemke (Khaosdog, furry artist).
Chairmen or Organizers: Matthias Chrzonsz (somewolf)

Mephit MiniCon 11: The theme was translated as Mirror Worlds. The planned program included an Art Show and auction, a Dealers' Den, a Furdance, a Café, and (weather permitting) a BBQ. The conbook had a wraparound color cover by Bloodhound Omega and EosFoxx. There were complaints that the registration (€110) had grown too expensive, and that it automatically included the commissioned T-shirt by Akeyla, Bloodhound Omega, and EosFoxx whether the attendee wanted it or not.

Chairmen or Organizers: Matthias Chrzonsz (somewolf)

Mephit MiniCon 12: Attendees were notified that the youth hostel's management had stopped allowing attendees to bring their dogs with them. The theme was a pun on this being the 12th MMC, and the German expression "voll auf die 12" ("right in the kisser"). The registration fee was raised to €115. There were the usual Art Show, Dealers' Den, and MMC Café. Events included a brunch, group photo, barbecue, and jam session. The evening videos featured the German humorous s-f *Ijon Tichy: Raumpilot* TV series, loosely based on Stanisław Lem's *The Star Diaries* stories. The 16-page conbooklet had a color wraparound cover by AlectorFencer, and a color centerfold by Pan Hesekiel-Shiroi. The T-shirt was by Nelena. The two MMC badges were designed by Titana; one "for the Carnivores" and one "for the VEGGIES" (but the same design).

Guests of Honor: AlectorFencer.
Chairmen or Organizers: Matthias Chrzonsz (somewolf)

Mephit MiniCon 13: The conbook wraparound color cover was by PatriX. The T-shirt was by Magus Lupus. The two grillmarken (membership badges) were by Titana; "for the Carnivores" showing a dragon grilling a steak (on a red background), and "Vegetarier" showing the same dragon grilling a carrot (on a green background).
Chairmen or Organizers: Matthias Chrzonsz (somewolf)

Mephit MiniCon 14: The theme was translated as Pet Sematery. The registration fee was raised to €120. The conbook wraparound color cover was by Twice. The T-shirt was by Titana. The two full-color grillmarken (membership badges) were by Anatoliba, with totally different art but continuing the "fleisch" and "vegetarier" themes.
Chairmen or Organizers: Matthias Chrzonsz (somewolf)

Mephit MiniCon 15: The theme was translated as Lost World. The conbook wraparound color cover was by Pan Hesekiel-Shiroi. The T-shirt was by Khaosdog. The two grillmarken (membership badges) were by AlectorFencer.
Guests of Honor: Special guest Michaela Frech (Pan Hesekiel-Shiroi, furry artist)
Chairmen or Organizers: Matthias Chrzonsz (somewolf)

Mephit MiniCon 16: The theme was translated as Vagrants. The con fee was €125. The conbook had a wraparound color cover by Akeyla and a T-shirt by Serena. The two grillmarken (membership badges) were by Shex.
Chairmen or Organizers: Matthias Chrzonsz (somewolf)

Mephit MiniCon 17: The conbook had a wraparound color cover by Shex and a T-shirt by Sethaa. The two grillmarken (membership badges) were by Windmelodie.
Chairmen or Organizers: Management, Matthias Chrzonsz (somewolf), KayJay

Mephit MiniCon 18: The con fee was €140.
Chairwoman: Sarah Paulus (Pegasus)

MiDFur

The Melbourne in December Fur Meet (MiDFur) began in 1999 as a weekend house party that included a dinner get together, a walk on a Saturday morning through the Melbourne shops, an artjam in a local home, a barbeque in the Saturday evening, compilation of the December issue of *South Fur Lands*, Australia's premiere furry fanzine on the Sunday afternoon, and watching various videos in the evening. The furmeet grew slowly due to promotion on the OzFurry network and the SA (South Australia) Furs discussion forum. In 2006 that year's chairman, furry artist Scrapper, arranged it more formally and with a plushie theme. MiDFur was the first Australian furmeet to evolve into a convention. The numbering of MiDFur's previous furmeets was continued. It was the third furmeet in 2006 to graduate into a convention, after the Western Pennsylvania Furry Weekend and RBW.

Name & Date	Theme	Location	Attendance Parade
MiDFur 2006 December 15–17, 2006	Plushies		55 (estimated)
MiDFur 2007 December 14–16, 2007	none		127

Name & Date	Theme	Location	Attendance	Parade
MiDFur X December 12–15, 2008	none	Victoria Hotel, Melbourne, Victoria	177	
MiDFur 11 December 3–6, 2009	At the Movies	Rydges Hotel, Melbourne, Victoria	247	
MiDFur 12 December 2–5, 2010	Heroes and Villains	Rydges on Swanson Hotel, Melbourne, Victoria	339	
Rescheduled from December 2011 to January 2012				
MiDFur 13 January 4–7, 2012	Tails from the Crypt	The Arrow on Swanston, Melbourne, Victoria	399	
MiDFur 2012 December 4–8, 2012	The Furry Apocalypse Cometh	The Arrow on Swanston, Melbourne, Victoria	474	

Events

MiDFur 2006: MiDFur 2006 was also known as MiDFur 8. Members were encouraged to wear ears and a tail if not full fursuits, and to carry a plushie. It began with a Friday evening dinner at the Café Retro, met at 9:00 a.m. on Saturday at Federation Square for breakfast and an all-day City Walkabout ending with a group going to the movie *Eragon*, and began Sunday at 10:00 a.m. at Federation Square for more walking and stopping at restaurants, or for those who wanted, the all-day *South Fur Lands* assembly at Scrapper's home. Prizes were awarded for various categories of plushies. Two different MiDFur 2006 T-shirts were available. There were still no conbooks or need to register to attend. MiDFurs 2006 and 2007 are considered more furmeets than real conventions.

Chairmen or Organizers: Scrapper (furry artist)

MiDFur 2007: Attendance for the whole weekend was about 88, and at the Friday night dinner alone was 127. It began on Friday at 7:00 p.m. at Sophia's Pizza Restaurant that was overcrowded with more people than the organizers expected. Saturday began with 8:30 a.m. breakfast at the Australia on Collins restaurant, a 10:00 a.m. choice of a walking tour of Melbourne or an all-day wine & cheese tour, 2:00 p.m. Fursuiting & Art Jam in Federation Square, a 5:00 p.m. barbeque dinner, and 8:15 p.m. Laser Skirmish at the Box Hill Darkzone; but rain during most of the day cut down attendance. Sunday began with a morning tour of the craft markets in Luna Park, an afternoon lunch at Noble Park, and a party at Scrapper's home from 3:00 to midnight including the binding of *South Fur Lands*, furry games, and an evening backyard screening of *Bee Movie*. It was at MiDFur 2007 that it was decided to turn the furmeet into a full convention. T-shirts with art by MistyStriker, hoodies, and lanyards were for sale.

Chairmen or Organizers: Scrapper

MiDFur X: This was considered the first MiDFur to be a convention rather than an elaborate furmeet. It was publicized throughout Australia, not just to those in Melbourne furry fandom. Events included the usual furry convention Dealers' Den and Art Show, panels and workshops, a trip to the Eureka Tower Sky Deck and to the Melbourne Zoo, two dinners, and a gala ball. The organizers incorporated as the Australian Furry Association (AUSFA), and inaugurated the annual AUSFA Furry Hall of Fame, to honor notable contributors to the development of furry fandom. The first induction, at MiDFur X, was of furry author Bernard Doove (Chakat Goldfur) and of the Anthrocon convention; the latter accepted by longstanding Anthrocon chairman Uncle Kage. The T-shirt was by Blotch. There was controversy due to the delayed charity donation until June 2009.

Guests of Honor: Matthew Wayne Davis (2, the Ranting Gryphon), Dr. Samuel Conway (Uncle Kage), Paul Kidd (furry author), Zaen Kreecha (makeup artist)

Charity: The RSPCA (A$3,840 [about $3,540])

Chairmen or Organizers: Pete Smith (ArcticPete)

MiDFur 2012 poster. Art by Blotch. Used with permission.

MiDFur 11: MiDFur 11 was the first with an official theme: At the Movies. It carried out the movie theme by decorating the convention area with furry mockups of movie posters, film strips, and movie equipment. Tim Albee could not attend due to illness, so he was replaced as a G-o-H by Australian filmmakers Stephan Elliott (winner of the Fido Award in 2008 for best performance by a dog, for *Easy Virtue*) and Sheridan Jobbins. A Surprise G-o-H turned out to be Uncle Kage, who joined 2, the Ranting Gryphon in a charity comedy performance that raised A$840 of the charity donation. A Hollywood-style Gala Ball with red carpet was held. 2, the Ranting Gryphon and Paul Kidd were inducted into the AUSFA's Furry Hall of Fame. MiDFur 11 received positive coverage in *The Age*. (Pete Smith changed his fursona from ArcticPete to CynWolfe.)
  Guests of Honor: Matthew Wayne Davis (2, the Ranting Gryphon), Tim Albee
  Charity: The Lort Smith Animal Hospital (A$5,705 [about $5,260])
  Chairmen or Organizers: Pete Smith (CynWolfe)

MiDFur 12: MiDFur created promotion including a trailer and a video. The committee in addition to CynWolfe included Kyle, Foxy Malone, Ben Raven, StephenQuoll, Rubah Fox, StarShadow, Goldfur, Kraden, Carnival, and Iceleron. Event highlights were: Friday, opening ceremony and dance party, a Wacom demonstration, a Madman anime arena (Madman is a major Australian licensee of anime), ACTfur podcast, separate under-18 and over-18 dance parties; Saturday, a fursuit photoshoot, talent show, Furry Hall of Fame induction (Stan Sakai, BigBlueFox, Jenner, and CynWolfe), evening dance party; Sunday, Fursuit Parade and games, a charity comedy performance with Uncle Kage and "Anthrax the blue collar blue heeler," charity auction, closing ceremony and dance party. There were many panels and fursuit workshops throughout the convention. The hotel had a pool deck that was a popular socializing area, and for poker games and artjams.
  Guests of Honor: Stan Sakai (comic-book creator, letterer), Karsten Auchter (BigBlueFox; German furry artist/fursuiter)
  Charity: Lost Dogs Home (A$7,771)
  Chairmen or Organizers: Pete Smith (CynWolfe)

MiDFur 13: The MiDFur Board was unable to book a hotel during December 2011 and had to settle for January 2012. Also, December was an unpopular month with university students because of exams. MiDFur 2012 was held in December 2012 as usual, making 2012 the only year with two MiD-Furs. The 399 attendance was only one less than the hotel's 400 limit. A video presentation was made of the 2011 Furry Hall of Fame inductee, Fred Patten, who was wheelchair-bound in Los Angeles.
  Guests of Honor: Jason Smith (Jibba FoxCoon, furry dancer), Tanja Freese (TaniDaReal), Matthew Wayne Davis (2, the Ranting Gryphon, furry standup comedian), Karsten Auchter (BigBlueFox, furry artist, fursuiter, DJ)
  Charity: Lost Dogs Home (A$8,050)
  Chairmen or Organizers: Pete Smith (CynWolfe)

MiDFur 2012: The convention was expanded from four to five days to commemorate its fifth anniversary. Almost all previous Guests of Honor attended. The Furry Hall of Fame inductees were furry specialty publisher Sofawolf Press (accepted by staffers Tim Susman and Mark Brown), and Steve Gallacci. Blotch designed the first MiDFur T-shirt. The first DVD recording was made of Anthrax, a local furry musician and standup comedian.
  Guests of Honor: Blotch (furry artist), Uncle Kage, 2, the Ranting Gryphon, Dark Natasha, Paul Kidd, Karsten Auchter (BigBlueFox), Timothy Albee
  Charity: Dingo Discovery Centre (A$15,200)
  Chairmen or Organizers: Pete Smith (CynWolfe)

Following MiDFur 2012, it was announced that the convention would move to January, from a hotel to a convention center, and would change its name to ConFurgence. This was due to the unpopularity of December with university students, the need to find a larger venue, and the dissatisfaction of some Melbourne furry fans who felt that their informal furmeet had been co-opted. With the permanent move from December, the MiDFur name was no longer applicable, and was returned to the fans who wished to continue it as a small, informal furmeet. See ConFurgence for the continuation of MiDFur as a convention.

Midwest FurFest

Midwest FurFest (MFF) was created to be the Chicago-area, Thanksgiving-time furry convention. It grew out of Chicago's annual June s-f convention, DucKon, when Robert C. King (who coined the word "fursuit") persuaded DucKon 3 in 1994 to add a furry track to its programming. By DucKon 8 in 1999, it was estimated that furry fandom had grown to about a quarter to a third of DucKon's attendance and programming. Furry fandom could not ask Duckon to expand the furry programming, so the furry fans, led by Robert C. King and Jim Doolittle (Aureth), decided to create a separate furry convention. They started by incorporating as Midwest Furry Fandom, Inc. The DucKon staff provided considerable aid in helping them get started. The MFF staff decided to standardize at the opposite end of the year and picked the weekend before Thanksgiving.

Name & Date	Theme	Location	Attendance	Parade
Midwest FurFest 2000 November 17–19, 2000	none	Sheraton Arlington Park, Arlington Heights	388	38
Midwest FurFest 2001 November 16–18, 2001	none	Sheraton Arlington Park, Arlington Heights	513	55 (estimated)
Midwest FurFest 2002 November 22–24, 2002	none	Hyatt Regency Woodfield, Schaumberg	685	75 (estimated)
Midwest FurFest 2003 November 21–23, 2003	none	Hyatt Regency Woodfield, Schaumberg	800 (estimated)	100 (estimated)
Midwest FurFest 2004 November 19–21, 2004	Around the World in 80 Days	Hyatt Regency Woodfield, Schaumberg	986	130 (estimated)
Midwest FurFest 2005 November 18–20, 2005	Whodunnit? It's a Mystery	Hyatt Regency Woodfield, Schaumberg	1,066	150 (estimated)
Midwest FurFest 2006 November 17–19, 2006	County Fair	Hyatt Regency Woodfield, Schaumberg	1,422	213
Midwest FurFest 2007 November 16–18, 2007	Critters On The High Seas	Hyatt Regency Woodfield, Schaumberg	1,690	287
Midwest FurFest 2008 November 21–23, 2008	North to Alaska	Westin Chicago North Shore, Wheeling	1,992	358
Midwest FurFest 2009 November 20–22, 2009	Ten Years of Midwest FurFest	Westin Chicago North Shore, Wheeling	2,040	357
Midwest FurFest 2010 November 19–21, 2010	Chicago Blues	Hyatt Regency O'Hare, Rosemont	2,285	413
Midwest FurFest 2011 November 18–20, 2011	Route 66	Hyatt Regency O'Hare, Rosemont	2,600	574
Midwest FurFest 2012 November 16–18, 2012	It Came from TV	Hyatt Regency O'Hare, Rosemont	3,216	743
Midwest FurFest 2013 November 22–24, 2013	Pirates of Lake Michigan	Hyatt Regency O'Hare, Rosemont	3,904	972
Midwest FurFest 2014 December 5–7, 2014	Holidays in the City	Hyatt Regency O'Hare, Rosemont	4,571	1,132

Midwest FurFest

Midwest FurFest 2015 conbook. Art by Ifus. Used with permission.

Name & Date	Theme	Location	Attendance	Parade
Midwest FurFest 2015 December 4–6, 2015	Midwest FurFest!	Hyatt Regency O'Hare, Rosemont	5,606	1,378

Events

Midwest FurFest 2000: Midwest FurFest 2000 was deliberately a close copy of the DucKon. It was in the same hotel (corporately renamed that year), had many of the same staffers as DucKon's furry track, and was organized along s-f convention lines. There were eight programming tracks, for Arts & Literature, Fandom, Furry Tech, Fursuiting, Gaming, Kids, Special Events, and Spirituality. There were the usual Art Show, Artist's Alley, and Dealers Den. The programming copied DucKon's Friday night Furry Variety Show and Saturday night dance. There was a big production on Saturday of the Pawpet Theater, whose lead puppeteer, Steve Plunkett, was instrumental in getting MFF started as a separate convention. There were two T-shirts; one by Margaret Carspecken showing a raccoon girl on a tire swing, and one by Derrick Dasenbrock showing a group of furries on a tractor. Phil Geusz says, "[S]ome of the early MFF's for a period of several years shared a hotel with a National Guard unit. While many expected friction, the two groups quickly became best friends and came to actively look forward to sharing the building for a weekend. Invariably, there were tailed uniforms walking about by Sunday." Tom Brady says, "Really, it was an incidental thing. We were in two separate areas of the hotel so with the exception of the lobby and the sleeping rooms there wasn't really any clash of the groups. When we moved in 2002 we left the National Guard group behind."

Guests of Honor: Robert & Margaret Carspecken (furry writer/artists), Derrick Dasenbrock (cartoonist), Rapid T. Rabbit (Richard Concepcion) of the *Rapid T. Rabbit and Friends* cable TV program.

Charities: Wolf Park, Valley of the Kings Sanctuary & Retreat for large felines, Chicago House anti–HIV and AIDS ($3,522).

Chairmen or Organizers: Robert C. King

Midwest FurFest 2001: The three programming tracks were named Constructed Fuzziness, Gaming, and Lifestyle and Spirituality. There were an Art Show, a Thursday night mixer in the Con Suite, several Pawpet Shows, a Charity Auction with Uncle Kage as the auctioneer, a Furry Variety Show, and a performance by 2, the Ranting Gryphon. The hotel was considered stuffed to capacity. The MFF 2001 T-shirt was by Jessica Willard.

Guests of Honor: Mary Hanson-Roberts (furry artist), Matt J. McCullar (furry author), and Jessica Willard (Ginger) (furry artist).

Charity: Animals for Awareness ($6,800).

Chairmen or Organizers: Robert C. King

Midwest FurFest 2002: The new hotel was very popular, both for its larger size and its nearness to the Woodfield Mall with many cheap restaurants. There were 85 hours of programming in eight rooms, including a tail making workshop, a Dance Dance Revolution tournament, a charity auction, a Saturday night dance, and a Sunday night Dead Dog Dance. The Furry Variety Show remained in its traditional timeslot of midnight Friday, as it had since DucKon days. The T-shirt was by DBruin.

Guests of Honor: David C. Simpson (furry cartoonist), Ursula Husted (furry artist), Ysengrin Werewolf of Wolf Studios/Haunted Verdun Manor.

Charity: Animals for Awareness ($6,088).

Chairmen or Organizers: Jim Doolittle (Aureth)

Midwest FurFest 2003: MFF 2003 was a full fan convention with eight tracks of programming, an Art Show, a Dealers Room, and so on. Mary Jo Pehl of *Mystery Science Theater 3000* appeared. At the end of the convention, chairman Aureth announced his resignation and introduced next year's chairman, Dan Hauschild (Takaza J. Wolf). The T-shirt was by Thomas K. Dye. A MFF 2003 DVD of photos from the convention was produced for sale.

Guests of Honor: Jeff Beedon (D'Bruin), Thomas K. Dye (furry artists), M. C. A. Hogarth (furry author).
Charity: Animals for Awareness ($6,500).
Chairmen or Organizers: Jim Doolittle (Aureth)

Midwest FurFest 2004: There were 140 hours of programming in eight rooms. Highlights included increased programming in the gaming room, a fursuit construction workshop, gaming with the Guests of Honor, and several panels being held in the Hyatt Woodfield's outdoor tent. Part of the charity donation was from a special comedy show featuring Uncle Kage and 2, the Ranting Gryphon together. The T-shirt was a collaboration between David Gilbert, Scribblefox, and Ursula Vernon.
Guests of Honor: David Gilbert (newspaper cartoonist), Ursula Vernon (fantasy artist), Jared Ledger (ScribbleFox) (furry artist/fursuiter).
Charity: Furry Friends Foundation ($7,000).
Chairmen or Organizers: Dan Hauschild (Takaza J. Wolf)

Midwest FurFest 2005: MFF 2005 became the fourth furry convention to top a thousand attendees. Attendees included 2, the Ranting Gryphon, Uncle Kage, and Laurence Parry (GreenReaper), there to promote WikiFur. The mystery theme included killing as many of the notable attendees as possible. The Funday Pawpet Show was hosted by Babs Bunny and her friend, Timothy Rabbit. There was a fire alarm on Saturday evening that briefly interrupted the disco dance. There were both a convention T-shirt and a sponsor's T-shirt, by Tincrash and Kenket.
Guests of Honor: Gene Breshears (furry author), Tess Garman (Kenket), Noel Melendez (Tincrash) (furry artists).
Charity: Wildlife in Need ($6,800).
Chairmen or Organizers: Dan Hauschild (Takaza J. Wolf)

Midwest FurFest 2006: Thursday night registration was combined with the Thursday night mixer, which included both an ice cream buffet and a cotton candy machine. A large number of attendees came on Friday and Saturday nights, after registration was closed; they were given temporary badges that they exchanged for regular badges the next morning. The 213 participants in the Fursuit Parade was believed to be a record. The $13,048.96 charity donation included $5,570 from the charity auction. The T-shirt was by Jen "Spunky" Seng.
Guests of Honor: Heather Luterman (Kyoht) (furry artist), Steven Scharff (WhiteyFawks) (fursuit maker), Jen Seng (Spunky) (cartoonist).
Charity: Safe Haven Wildlife Refuge ($13,048.96).
Chairmen or Organizers: Paul Lester (Linnaeus)

Midwest FurFest 2007: Events included Iron Artist, Whose Lion Is It Anyway?, Figure Drawing (human and fursuit), and a "High Seas Fashion Show." Although all convention reports were favorable, there were some complaints of arrogant Security and too much/too open drinking. As with previous conventions at the Hyatt Regency Woodfield, MFF 2007 shared the hotel with a Japanese airline flight crew, who were bemused by the furry antics.
Guests of Honor: Erika Rosengarten (Chilly; illustrator), Jill0r (artist/costumer), Will Sanborn (furry author).
Charity: Flint Creek Wildlife Rehabilitation ($15,193).
Chairmen or Organizers: Paul Lester (Linnaeus)

Midwest FurFest 2008: There was a rant by 2, the Ranting Gryphon. Uncle Kage held his Story Hour, and was the auctioneer for the Art Show and the Charity Auction. There were numerous fursuit events and workshops. Art Show statistics were 1,066 works entered by 68 artists; 524 pieces sold, with 53 going to art auction; for total sales of $22,928. The 62-page conbook had a wraparound color cover by Darcy Sowers. The T-shirt was by Foxfeather. On the first night of the convention, a fire alarm (caused by someone smoking in a non-smoking room) forced the evacuation of the hotel into 28° F weather. The hotel hot tub was shut down by someone having sex in it. On Friday, a fire alarm (caused by someone opening a fire sprinkler relief valve in the stairwell) forced the evacuation of the hotel into 28° F weather. The hotel required that all relief valves in the stairwell of the 16-floor building be under constant watch to prevent a recurrence. This required 24-hour coverage from six locations to have sight of all of the valves. In what came to be known as "Stairwell Appreciation Duty," Every Midwest FurFest staff member stepped up to each take at least one two-hour shift sitting on a desk chair in the stairwell. Once word (quietly) got out that help was needed, staff members from Anthrocon, DucKon, Windycon, the Dorsai Irregulars, and several other furry conventions volunteered to help. The convention was able to meet the hotel's request for full coverage until Monday morning. In order to prevent attendees from opening any valves that year or the following year (which was already contracted), the convention was forced to use the excuse that the fire alarm was caused by someone smoking in the stairwell and that was why 24-hour surveillance was needed.

Guests of Honor: Darcy and Matt Sowers (furry comic strip artist & writer), Lucky the Evil Dog (fursuit performer), Foxfeather R. Zenkova (artist).

Charity: Rainbow Animal Assisted Therapy ($15,000).

Chairmen or Organizers: Tom Brady (Duncan da Husky)

Midwest FurFest 2009: MFF 2009 became the third furry convention with over two thousand attendees. There were so many Sponsors and Anniversary Sponsors that MFF 2009 ran out of gifts for them and declined further signups. In addition to the amount raised at the Charity Auction, the Charity Poker Tournament (won by Jaggers Pawtucket) donated $700, and a benefit by Uncle Kage and 2, the Ranting Gryphon raised $773. The Art Show included 1,129 pieces by 81 artists, bringing $16,302. An experimental theatrical event, *Too Much Light Makes The Baby Go Blind*, was a success and continued to be a staple of the convention. It was announced that the MFF had outgrown its hotel, and would be moving to a larger hotel next year. The T-shirt was by Ursula Vernon. In addition, there was an embroidered polo shirt with art by Jen Seng.

Guests of Honor: All of the Guests of Honor from the first nine years.

Charity: Kane Area Rehabilitation and Education for Wildlife ($12,799).

Chairmen or Organizers: Tom Brady (Duncan da Husky)

Midwest FurFest 2010: The new hotel, the Hyatt Regency O'Hare, very convenient to Chicago's O'Hare International Airport, was quite popular. Although the majority of the convention opened at the usual times, because of space conflicts with another group (something that would continue to be a thorn in the convention's side for several years) the A/V crew had to work late into the night to have the Main Stage ready for opening ceremonies at noon on Friday, and Con Suite was not able to open until 5 p.m. Friday. Kipper Otter did the T-shirt.

Guests of Honor: Amber Hill (Vantid, furry artist), Alexis Rudd (The Blue Hyena, furry puppeteer, fursuit maker), Kipper Otter (furry artist, fursuit maker, California ferret activist).

Charity: Castaway Pet Rescue, Inc. ($11,300).

Chairmen or Organizers: Dan Hauschild (Takaza J. Wolf)

Midwest FurFest 2011: MFF 2011 continued to take advantage of the facilities at the Hyatt Regency O'Hare, hosting a Shiny Sponsors Reception in Ventana's, a rotating former restaurant at the very top of the hotel. The Charity Auction raised $6,000 and Midwest Furry Fandom, Inc., the parent corporation for Midwest FurFest, added another $12,500 to the donation. At the end of the convention, the chairman duties were handed off to Toby Murono (Perro). Also, it was announced that the convention would be staying at the Hyatt Regency O'Hare at least through 2015.

Guests of Honor: Rick Griffin (furry cartoonist); Thornwolf (furry artist)
Charity: Lake County Animal Education and Rescue ($19,574.79)
Chairmen or Organizers: Dan Hauschild (Takaza J. Wolf)

Midwest FurFest 2012: With its 2012 convention attendance of 3,216, Midwest FurFest became the world's second-largest furry convention. This year was notable for two things: Midwest FurFest was able to make the largest donation to its charity ever, aided by the $8,500 that was placed in their donation jars over the course of the weekend (including a single donation of $1,000). More importantly, it was calculated that with this year's donation the total of donations to charities by all furry conventions exceeded the $1,000,000 mark.

Guests of Honor: FirestormSix (furry artist), Melita Curphy (Miss Monster; furry artist), Jennifer Miller (Nambroth; artist)
Charity: Felines & Canines ($40,500+)
Chairmen or Organizers: Toby Murono (Perro)

Midwest FurFest 2013: The second (2013) ALAA Hall of Fame honorees, those characters, people, books, or films that helped to mold furry fandom, were announced at a presentation ceremony: the novella *Animal Farm* by George Orwell; the novel *The Pride of Chanur* by C. J. Cherryh; and the 1973 theatrical feature *Robin Hood* by the Walt Disney Studios. After the convention, it was determined that it required so much function space and had so many attendees that the only way for the convention to succeed was to move to a date where it did not conflict with another large group. After consideration of many possibilities, the decision was made to move from the traditional weekend before Thanksgiving to the first weekend in December.

Beginning with MFF 2013, the MFF committee has arranged with its hotel to hold a Clean Room Contest. Basically the hotel chambermaids report to their management which attendees' rooms are kept the cleanest, with dirty bed linens and towels placed neatly by the door, and all trash placed into provided trash bags. The hotel management reports to the MFF Committee. The prizes are a free weekend (three room nights) for the three cleanest rooms. This has been announced on the Hyatt Regency O'Hare's Facebook page and Twitter account. It has been very popular with the hotel managements and their housekeeping staffs, and has been copied with some modifications by Further Confusion beginning in 2014.

Guests of Honor: Chibi-Marrow (furry illustrator), Lindsey Bristow (Silver Huskywolf; fursuit maker), Sonderjen (artist)
Charity: One Tail at a Time ($28,000+)
Chairmen or Organizers: Toby Murono (Perro)

Midwest FurFest 2014: The convention was held later than usual due to scheduling conflicts with the hotel. The program book wraparound cover by Sabretoothed Ermine won that year's Ursa Major Award for Best Published Illustration. Just after midnight Sunday morning, the release of chlorine gas on the 8th and 9th floors resulted in the evacuation of several thousand guests in the hotel, and the hospital examination of 19 people. Police investigated it as a deliberate attack. TV news footage of the early morning evacuation of people still in fursuits caused one TV commenter to break into uncontrollable laughter, and the *San Diego Union-Tribune* reported it as "Gas leak evacuates 'furry' convention; lets world in on giant animal costume subculture" and talked about "outing" furry fandom, implying that the chlorine gas had been an accident, and that the furry convention had been trying to hide itself from the public.

Despite the disruption, the convention leadership decided that the best way to respond was to continue the convention programming as scheduled, a decision that was welcomed by the attendees. After the convention, the quick and level-headed response of the convention staff was praised on social media.

Guests of Honor: Lacy and CloudPouncer (fursuit makers), Novadog, Beth Davies (Sabretoothed Ermine; furry artist)
  Charity: Critter Camp Exotic Pet Sanctuary ($31,445.93)
  Chairmen or Organizers: Toby Murono (Perro)

Midwest FurFest 2015: MFF 2015 adopted a new logo of a stylized raccoon mask and tail, designed by Codex. It had over 250 staff members and over 50 on-site volunteers. There was a noticeable police presence, in case of anything like the previous year's chlorine gas incident (there was not). The traditional Con Suite was renamed the FurFest Lounge, creating confusion with the Fursuiters' Lounge. The charity auction included a $5,500 bid for a Blackhawks-signed charity hockey stick. A Charity Poker game, won by Rio Tanuki, raised $2,440. The performance group The Neo-Futurists presented "Too Much Light Makes the Baby Go Blind." The presentation of the fourth (2015) ALAA Hall of Fame honorees, to those characters, people, books, or films that helped to mold furry fandom, was announced: Hayao Miyazaki, the movie *The Secret of NIMH*, and Walt Kelly. The 52-page conbook wraparound cover was by Ifus. There were three T-shirts; a general one by Mahrkale, a sponsor's T-shirt by Ifus, and a gofurs' shirt by Yonoa.
  Guests of Honor: Stephanie Johnson (Ifus, furry artist/fursuit maker), M. Schaefer (Mahrkale; furry artist), Yonoa (fursuit maker)
  Charity: Save-A-Vet ($62,020.71)
  Chairmen or Organizers: Tim Wood (Woody)

Morphicon

Morphicon in Columbus, Ohio, has grown from an informal gathering of Columbus-area furry fans into an annual convention.

Name & Date	Theme	Location	Attendance	Parade
Morphicon 0 June 21, 2003	The Zeroth Iteration	Sharon Woods Park, Columbus, OH	60 (estimated)	
Morphicon 2004 June 25–27, 2004	In the Beginning	Clarion Hotel, Columbus, OH	115	
Morphicon 2005 May 6–8, 2005	Growing Pains	Radisson Hotel, Columbus, OH	158	
Morphicon 2006 May 5–7, 2006	The Food Chain	Radisson Hotel, Columbus, OH	187	
Morphicon 2007 May 18–20, 2007	Technofurs	Radisson Hotel, Columbus, OH	245	31
Morphicon 2008 May 16–18, 2008	Hooray for Furrywood!	Columbus-Worthington Holiday Inn, Worthington, OH	275	26
Morphicon 2009 May 15–17, 2009	Inner City Critters	Columbus-Worthington Holiday Inn, Worthington, OH	307	43
Morphicon 2010 May 13–16, 2010	Furry State Fair	Columbus-Worthington Holiday Inn, Worthington, OH	275	34
Morphicon 2011 May 12–15, 2011	Furries in Wonderland	Columbus-Worthington Holiday Inn, Worthington, OH	307	48
Morphicon 2012 May 3–6, 2012	Fables and Furry-tails	Columbus-Worthington Holiday Inn, Worthington, OH	302	41
Morphicon 2013 May 2–5, 2013	Furries Around the World	Columbus-Worthington Holiday Inn, Worthington, OH	297	48

Morphicon

Name & Date	Theme	Location	Attendance	Parade
Morphicon 2014 May 1–4, 2014	Howls, Growls, and Things Afoul: A Furrightenly Good Time	Columbus-Worthington Holiday Inn, Worthington, OH	317	61
Morphicon 2015 April 30–May 3, 2015	Retro Gaming	Columbus-Worthington Holiday Inn, Worthington, OH	342	74

Events

Morphicon 0: In February 2003, furry fans in Columbus who gathered for a dinner outing and theater party to see *The Lion King* talked about starting an annual convention. Morphicon 0, four months later, was an all-day picnic at Sharon Woods Park on the north side of Columbus, Ohio, organized by Trixie Wolf and Jewel to see if there were enough furs in the Columbus area to hold an annual convention. It would not qualify as a convention except that it gave rise to one.

Chairmen or Organizers: Trixie Wolf; Michael Pinnegar (Jewel)

Morphicon 2004: Morphicon 2004 was considered by many as the first "real Morphicon." The organizers incorporated as the Morphicon Corporation, a not-for-profit corporation. The three days of the convention were called Foxday, Satyrday, and Skunkday. There were panels themed for spirituality, puppeteering, and costuming. There were a furry variety show, a work-in-progress puppet version of *Little Shop of Horrors*, and a judged Masquerade with awards. The program book cover was by Mark Merlino. The T-shirt was by Babs Bunny.

Guests of Honor: Mark Merlino (furry convention founder), Eric W. Schwartz (early furry video creator)

Charity: Animal Adoption Foundation (AAF) ($351)

Chairmen or Organizers: Trixie Wolf

Morphicon 2005: The toys and gaming area had a slot machine that paid tickets for the charity raffle. A Macro Rampage allowed fursuiters to stomp on toy Japanese soldiers and a toy Tokyo. The lack of a fursuit/headless lounge was criticized. An AnthroCar parked just outside the hotel was heavily graffitied all through the con. The T-shirt competition was won by Karen Kling and Lisa Sample. The program book cover was by Lisa Sample.

Guests of Honor: Mike & Carole Curtis (Shanda Fantasy Arts), Richard Thatcher (SFA staffer), NeoGeen (furry artist)

Charity: Animal Adoption Foundation (AAF) ($844)

Chairmen or Organizers: Trixie Wolf

Morphicon 2006: The announced schedule was: Meet the Guests sessions, a convention-long Fluxx tourney, Dances all three days, Friday Masquerade, a midnight AstronoFurs meeting outside for stargazing ("Telescopes and binoculars will be set up to show you the highlights of the heavens in early May and amature [sic] astronomers will be on hand to help you find the constellations visible in the Spring Sky."), a Saturday furry variety show and Atomic Hour of Comedy, a late-evening unstructured Art Schmooze ("If you come, you must draw. No idlers."), and Sunday puppetry building, judging, and performance. There were many animal-themed panels and Special Interest Groups. The T-shirt competition was won by Kitt Foxx. The runner-up, Candy Dewalt, did the program book cover. The Frozen Oasis group hosted a big room party.

Guests of Honor: Bill Holbrook (comic-strip artist), Candy and Ryan Dewalt (Trixi and Tet) (husband & wife furry cartoonists)

Charity: Ferrets Unlimited Rescue Services (FURS) ($566)

Chairmen or Organizers: Trixie Wolf

Morphicon

Morphicon 2007: The dubbing of the Morphicon into Fursday, Foxday, Satyrday, and Skunkday continued. There were panels and workshops. Performance was encouraged, with many furry variety shows, an Atomic Hour of Comedy, puppet shows, and several Atomic (Battle, Feast, Party) of DOOM!s. The hotel was remodeling, so the scheduled movie/video room was turned into the SIG room, which was more popular due to many well-attended SIGs on mature themes that would not have fit into the old SIG room. An unofficial movie room took place on Friday night thanks to someone with a laptop and access to many videos. The T-shirt competition was won by Chris B. Critter. The runner-up, Firehazard, did the program book cover. Frozen Oasis hosted a big room party. On Sunday, a giant Nerf battle was held in the hotel's main conference room. Someone dubbed Patches (no real name or fursona known, but much discussed and reviled in con reports afterwards) in a falling-apart fursuit wandered around the hallways for the entire Morphicon without joining, forcing himself on others and creeping out attendees so much that there were 25 formal complaints about him.
   Guests of Honor: Steve Plunkett (puppeteer), Kitt Foxx (fursuiter), Summer Jackel (artist)
   Charity: Ferrets Unlimited Rescue Services (FURS) ($1,000)
   Chairmen or Organizers: Craig E. Smith (Max Goof, Max DeGroot)

Morphicon 2008: The planned schedule was: Fursday evening, open gaming & Dealers' setup; Foxday, opening ceremonies, ears & tail worpshop, G-o-Hs presentations, Looney Labs game demos, Atomic Chess Match of Doom, Furry Writers of Ohio, cake decorating contest, Dr. Strangefur game, Masquerade, puppet show, Dance 'til U Die!; Satyrday, Duct Tape Dummies workshop, Hot Lead, Cold Wine, and Furrywood game, Spectacle of Doom; Skunkday, puppetry, Fursuit Parade, Atomic Feast, Battle, & Party of DOOM! There were panels and SIGs throughout the convention. Morphicon 2008 presented the 2007 Ursa Major Awards. The Fursuit Parade had 26 fursuiters, although more fursuiters were at the convention. There were an Art Show, Dealers' Den, and Movie Room throughout the convention. The T-shirt was by Mary Mouse. Frozen Oasis hosted a room party.
   Guests of Honor: D. C. Simpson (cartoonist), Malcolm Earle (Max Black Rabbit, furry artist)
   Charity: Ferrets Unlimited Rescue Services (FURS) ($2,000)
   Chairmen or Organizers: Craig E. Smith (Max Goof, Max DeGroot)

Morphicon 2009: Chairman Jewel streaked for the charity, raising $265. The T-shirt art was by Korth, with lettering by Joey-Poey. The Program Book cover was by Joey-Poey and Monster-Chan. Frozen Oasis hosted a room party with Bucktown Tiger as a DJ.
   Guests of Honor: Joey-Poey (graffiti artist), Bucktown Tiger (furry musician/comedian)
   Charity: Ferrets Unlimited Rescue Services (FURS) ($1,400)
   Chairmen or Organizers: Michael Pinnegar (Jewel)

Morphicon 2010: Events included a Spectacle of Doom furry variety show, an Atomic Comedy Hour of Doom, a Friday night Fursuit Masquerade with both a construction judging and a presentation judging, and a cake decoration contest. "Through Fox's Eyes," a short documentary film on furries by Eric Risher (Ash), was premiered with screenings and a talk by Ash on Friday, Saturday, and Sunday. The T-shirt competition got 154 entries, and was won by Pavia Mostyn (PMoss) with 66 votes. The runner-up was Shinji with 47 votes. PMoss also did the Program Book cover. Frozen Oasis hosted a room party Friday night themed to the movie *The Imaginarium of Doctor Parnassus*.
   Guests of Honor: Victoria Borah Bloom (Bumblebee), Bard Bloom (Floki), Rhys Bloom (Mothra) (World Tree creators)
   Charity: Ferrets Unlimited Rescue Services (FURS) ($1,050)
   Chairmen or Organizers: Michael Pinnegar (Jewel)

Morphicon 2011: Roxikat and Flinters collaborated on the Program Book cover. The 2010 Ursa Major Awards were presented.

Guests of Honor: John Barrett (Roxikat), Dan Canaan (Flinters) (furry cartoonists)
Charity: Ferrets Unlimited Rescue Services (FURS) ($1,400)
Chairmen or Organizers: Michael Pinnegar (Jewel)

Morphicon 2012: The Program Book cover was by Sigil.
Guests of Honor: Sigil (furry artist), Alan Loewen (Heavy Horse, furry author)
Charity: Ferrets Unlimited Rescue Services (FURS) ($1,800)
Chairmen or Organizers: Michael Pinnegar (Jewel)

Morphicon 2013: The T-shirt was by Shinji. The Program Book cover was by P. Moss.
Guests of Honor: Pavia Mostyn (P. Moss), Shawntae Howard (furry artists)
Charity: Ferrets Unlimited Rescue Services (FURS) ($3,287.55)
Chairmen or Organizers: Snap

Morphicon 2014: The T-shirt was by Nut-Case.
Guests of Honor: Krahnos, Fossil the Undead Anthrosaur Artist (furry artists)
Charity: Ferrets Unlimited Rescue Services (FURS) ($1,764)
Chairmen or Organizers: Snap

Morphicon 2015: The convention theme focused on 8-bit gaming. The Fursday-Foxday-Satyrday-Skunkday names were continued. The Headless Lounge for fursuiters was named the Robespierre Room, and the social area was the Zoo. The 2014 Ursa Major Awards were presented. The T-shirt design was by liiix. The Program Book cover was by Skulldog.
Guests of Honor: Skulldog (furry artist), Koh (furry musician)
Charity: Happy Hearts Feline Rescue ($1,528.72)
Chairmen or Organizers: Snap

Following Morphicon 2015, the convention and its non-profit corporation changed their name to AnthrOhio, to reflect changes in staff and to better distinguish themselves from Power Morphicon, a convention of *Mighty Morphin Power Rangers* fans.

Motor City Furry Con

Motor City Furry Con was created as a replacement for the discontinued Furry Connection North, Detroit's annual furry convention. MCFC advertised itself as "same time and hotel as FCN." As such, it began as the largest "first convention" ever, even though it was restricted to 18+ adults only. Some confusion has been created by its incorporated name, Motor City Furry Con, LLC, since most fans refer to it as "Fur Con" despite its official name.

Name & Date	Theme	Location	Attendance	Parade
Motor City Furry Con 2014 April 11–13, 2014	Under Construction	Sheraton Detroit Novi Hotel, Novi, MI	967	248
Motor City Furry Con 2015 March 27–29, 2015	Down on the Farm	Sheraton Detroit Novi Hotel, Novi, MI	1,028	?

Events

Motor City Furry Con 2014: There was no conbook, but Danji did the T-shirt and badge art.
Guests of Honor: Danji, Firestorm Six Studios
Charity: K-9 Stray Rescue League ($7,000)
Chairmen or Organizers: Indy

Motor City Furry Con 2015: Lucky did the conbook cover and a sketch of the T-shirt design. The finished T-shirt art was by Neon Slushie.

Guests of Honor: TILT Longtail (fursuiter), Don't Hug Cacti Studios (fursuit makers)
Charity: Happy Hearts Feline Rescue ($8,000)
Chairmen or Organizers: Indy

NordicFuzzCon

Although there were previous individual furry conventions in Sweden such as EuroFurence 2, NordicFuzzCon (NFC) is Sweden's first annual furry convention, intended for all Nordic furry fans. It is the largest Nordic furry convention, and one of the largest in Europe. It originated in a two-day furmeet in Stockholm in Spring 2012 that included a fursuit walk around Old Town (Gamla Stan). It was so popular that it was decided to expand it into a full convention.

Name & Date	Theme	Location	Attendance	Parade
NordicFuzzCon 2013 March 28–31, 2013	Vikings vs. Pirates	Quality Hotel Winn Haninge, Stockholm	175	see below
NordicFuzzCon 2014 February 27–March 2, 2014	A Steampunk Murder Mystery	Quality Hotel Winn Haninge, Stockholm	271	75
NordicFuzzCon 2015 February 26–March 1, 2015	Scandinavian Folklore: The Enchanted Forest	Utsikten Meetings, Nynäshamn	393	109

Events

NordicFuzzCon 2013: A cartoon mascot was introduced in precon publicity: Mausie, a little black mouse with a blue bow on his tail (originally a plushie made by Nienna, belonging to Trax). Attendees were from 15 countries, over half from Sweden with the rest from Norway, the U.K., Finland, the Czech Republic, and others. Events included an art show and dealers' den, a video gaming room, a Music Café, fursuit charades and games, Cards Against Humanity, a charity auction, Once Upon a Fuzz, dances, and a Dead Dog Party. The guests-of-honor hosted panels on furry history. The theme was emphasized in a vikings-vs.-pirates treasure hunt. Due to icy weather, the outdoors Fursuit Parade was cancelled; instead, 51 fursuiters joined in a conga line around the hotel lobby. It was considered overly strenuous and was not repeated. The conbook wraparound cover was by Greevixor. There were 9 staffers. Only a staff T-shirt was printed, due to underestimation of the demand from the attendees for a souvenir T-shirt.

Guests of Honor: Martin Gauffin (DivineVixen), Henrik Isacson (Snout) (early European furs, co-chairmen of EuroFurence 2 in 1996)
Charity: Södertälje Katthem (30,000 SEK)
Chairmen or Organizers: Trax, NewEinstein

NordicFuzzCon 2014: The Music Café, and fursuit charades and games were repeated. A charity concert, an ice cream social, fur-e-oke singing, and a "Furries Got Talent" talent show were added. The video game room was enlarged. The charity was The Animals' Island, a wildlife rescue organization. The weather was good enough that the fursuit group photograph was held outdoors; the walk from the convention to the group photograph was considered the Fursuit Parade, displaying the fursuits to the public. There were 75 fursuits in the Fursuit Parade, but 126 at the convention. A Fursuit Zoo was held at the hotel after the photograph where the fursuiters and non-fursuit-wearing attendees could mix. The treasure hunt was replaced by a murder mystery to be solved. An "Eat Sweden" event was added. "Grandville and the Anthropomorphic Tradition" was one of several

NordicFuzzCon 2014 conbook. Art by saitenyo. Used with permission.

panels hosted by g-o-h Brian Talbot, the creator of the *Grandville* series. The conbook wraparound cover was by saitenyo. A T-shirt for attendees was added. There were 24 staffers. The hotel sold its own furry steampunk beer, which had a cartoon label drawn by the hotel staff, in the bar.
Guests of Honor: Bryan Talbot (comic book artist)
Charity: Djurens Ö (57,408 SEK)
Chairmen or Organizers: Trax, NewEinstein

NordicFuzzCon 2015: There were attendees from 23 countries (24 if the Åland Islands are considered as separate from Finland, which some people do). There were again many more fursuiters than the 109 in the Parade; 184 total. The opening ceremonies featured a Mausie fursuiter. The Music Café, fursuit charades and games, ice cream social, and talent show were repeated once again. The videogame room was enlarged again. There was a screening of *Bitter Lake*, the fursuit movie by g-o-h EZwolf. The charity, a dog re-homing society, presented a dog show. The conbook wraparound cover was a collaboration by EosFoxx and Keovi. There were 46 staffers.
Guests of Honor: Marion Fischer (EosFoxx; furry artist), EZwolf (furry cinematographer/fursuiter)
Charity: Hittehund (53,675 SEK)
Chairmen or Organizers: Trax, NewEinstein

Oklacon

Oklacon, beginning as Festival of the Feral and held at Oklahoma's Roman Nose State Park, was the first U.S. annual furry outdoor convention, inspired by Canada's Camp Feral! Its motto is: "World's Largest Outdoor Furcon."

Oklacon

Name & Date	Theme	Location	Attendance
Festival of the Feral October 31–November 2, 2003	none	Roman Nose State Park, Watonga, OK	47
Oklacon 2004 October 28–31, 2004	!	Roman Nose State Park, Watonga, OK	117
Oklacon 2005 October 27–30, 2005	Inner Animal	Roman Nose State Park, Watonga, OK	63
Oklacon 2006 October 27–29, 2006	Ruffin' It	Roman Nose State Park, Watonga, OK	128 (estimated)
Oklacon 2007 October 25–29, 2007	Oklacon V—V for Vermin	Roman Nose State Park, Watonga, OK	283
Oklacon 2008 October 23–27, 2008	Mark of the Beast	Roman Nose State Park, Watonga, OK	223
Oklacon 2009 October 22–26, 2009	The Seven Furry Sins	Roman Nose State Park, Watonga, OK	241
Oklacon 2010 October 27–November 1, 2010	The Great Depression	Roman Nose State Park, Watonga, OK	273
Oklacon 2011 October 19–24, 2011	A Stitch in Time Saves 9	Roman Nose State Park, Watonga, OK	300
Oklacon 2012 October 17–22, 2012	It Came from Planet X!	Roman Nose State Park, Watonga, OK	344
Oklacon 2013 October 24–27, 2013	Let the Games Begin!	Roman Nose State Park, Watonga, OK	352
Oklacon 2014 October 23–26, 2014	The Good, the Bad, and the Furry!	Roman Nose State Park, Watonga, OK	291

Events

Festival of the Feral 2003: The Park featured two small lakes, a mess hall, a dining hall, several A frame cabins for sixteen campers each, a few cottages for those willing to pay for more privacy, a small amphitheater, a fire pit, and other amenities. An Artist Gallery was set up in the dining hall. Events included a Polar Bear swim at the Three Springs swimming pool at dawn, dances, miniature golf, more dances, and nighttime socializing around the fire pit. On Saturday night a local band, Sub-Level 3, played at the fire pit. The T-shirt contest was won by Windpaw Coyote. The rules for the annual T-shirt contest were: "The submittal must relate to the theme. Grand prize Winner will receive a free T-shirt with their artwork featured on it, Guest of Honor status for next year's con, and Attending level membership for this year's convention. Second place Winner will have their art featured on this year's convention book cover and an Attendance level membership for this year's convention. ⊠Third place Winner will have their art on the back of the convention book along with a $10 discount for this year's convention." There were no theme or charity.

Festival of the Feral was intended to be an annual event, and it had emphasized on its website that it was in no way connected to Camp Feral! in Ontario, but in early 2004 Camp Feral! formally objected to the name as being too similar, and asked Festival of the Feral to change theirs. They chose Oklacon.

Guests of Honor: Bucky Boy (furry artist), Nexxus (webmaster of FurNation)
Chairmen or Organizers: Arc

Oklacon 2004: Due to Camp Feral!'s demand that the Festival of the Feral change its name, the organizers not only did so to Oklacon, but incorporated as the Oklahoma Association of Anthropomorphic Arts, Inc., a not-for-profit membership organization. A delegation from Camp Feral! attended to establish friendly relations. In addition to the usual outdoor activities and Furry workshops, Jakebe conducted a morning meditation session, and Mark Merlino (Sylys Sable) led a panel on "The History of Fur." There was a "24 Hour Super Mega Scavenger Hunt." Safari's Interactive Animal Sanctuary was announced as the Oklacon's permanent charity. The Charity Auction was held in the Park's central multipurpose building, the Turkey Roost. There was also a Charity Poker Game, and donations from Art Show sales were added to the overall donation to the animal sanctuary. Oklacon 2004 was a "press-free" event. The T-shirt contest was won by Equus.

Oklacon logo. Art by BlueOtter. Used with permission.

Guests of Honor: Matthew Wayne Davis (2, the Ranting Gryphon), D'Bruin (furry artist), Windpaw Coyote (the winner of the previous year's T-shirt contest)
Charity: Safari's Interactive Animal Sanctuary ($1,650)
Chairmen or Organizers: Horses' Ghost, the band manager of Sub-level 03 and first president of OAAA, Inc.

Oklacon 2005: Wamndog won the Scavenger Hunt. The T-shirt contest was won by Lightfoot Kyohti.
Guests of Honor: Jakebe (furry stand-up comedian), Lightfoot Kyohti (furry artist)
Charity: Safari's Interactive Animal Sanctuary ($4,000)
Chairmen or Organizers: Darkmoor

Oklacon 2006: Lightfoot Kyohti was also the Camp Cook. Memberships were $18, which was all donated to the charity. The programming included nighttime campfire gatherings and DJ-led songfests. A preregistered member drawing was won by Starwind, who got a T-shirt and other goodies. The T-shirt design contest was won by EbonyTigress.
Guests of Honor: Christy Grandjean (Goldenwolf), Lightfoot Kyohti (Furry artists)
Charity: Safari's Interactive Animal Sanctuary ($2,300)
Chairmen or Organizers: BlueOtter

Oklacon 2007: Oklacon was increased to five days. Aside from the campground activities and games, events in the Turkey Roost main building included the Dealers' Den, Art Show, and Artists Alley; a Thursday night barbecue and singing around the campfire; Friday volleyball and croquet games, an evening chili dinner and Fursuit Dance, charity poker, two dances (Hanging With Heros! and Groovin' With Genki!) emceed by DJs Heros and Genki!, and a midnight Howl at the Moon; Saturday Biscuit Breakfast, Fursuit Bocce Ball game, Guest of Honor Luncheon, Animal Demonstration by SIAS, spaghetti dinner, and more nighttime dances; and Sunday closing activities. The T-shirt was by Blotch.
Guests of Honor: Tess Garman & Teagan Gavet (Blotch), Sheryn Brown (Ebony Tigress) (furry artists)
Charity: Safari's Interactive Animal Sanctuary ($5,277)
Chairmen or Organizers: Draconis

Oklacon 2008: Events besides the outdoor activities in the Turkey Roost center included the Dealers' Den and Artists' Alley, a Sub-level 03 concert, a charity poker tournament, a presentation of several wild animals including a bobcat by the charity, and dances. Several members brought large dogs, and one brought a young kangaroo. The Oklacon 2008 T-shirt was by Oddy Redwing.

Oklacon

Guests of Honor: Oz Kangaroo (artist, fursuiter), Jeff Goode (TV writer)
Charity: Safari's Interactive Animal Sanctuary ($4,700)
Chairmen or Organizers: Wolff (a member of Sub-level 03), Durango Dingo

Oklacon 2009: The organizing group changed from the Oklahoma Association of Anthropomorphic Arts, Inc., to Fuzzy Productions, LLC. Oklacon 2009 featured the usual outdoor/camping events. The T-shirt was by Stephanie de la Loba.
Guests of Honor: Stephanie de la Loba Negra (furry artist), Ringtail Café (furry comic book; the creators thereof)
Charity: Safari's Interactive Animal Sanctuary ($3,200)
Chairmen or Organizers: BlueOtter, Cutepuppy, Horses' Ghost, Pardus, Wolff

Oklacon 2010: The theme of the 1930s Depression was a change from the usual horror and Hallowe'en themes. Events besides the outdoor activities included a fursuit dance, and Charity Auction and Poker. The donation jar collected $1,326. Balto drew a promotional poster.
Guests of Honor: Albert C. Peña (Balto, furry cartoonist), KnotCast (furry podcast)
Charity: Safari's Interactive Animal Sanctuary ($5,365 + a Canadian $5 bill)
Chairmen or Organizers: BlueOtter, Cutepuppy, Horses' Ghost, Pardus, Wolff

Oklacon 2011: Oklacon 2011 was considered especially successful due to increased attendance, lots of events, and more relaxed security. A goal of $6,000 for charity set during the Opening Ceremonies was surpassed through charity poker, a special Super Sponsor Soiree event, and a collection taken at the Closing Ceremonies. Harvest the Husky, a committee member, broke his arm at the beginning of the convention and was taken to Oklahoma City for surgery, resulting in his becoming a major topic of conversation throughout the con as "Stumbles the Hill Husky." Oklacon and Furry Fiesta formed a partnership to offer a dual-convention discounted membership rate.
Guests of Honor: Myenia (furry artist), Bucktown Tiger (furry musician)
Charity: Safari's Interactive Animal Sanctuary ($8,193.88)
Chairmen or Organizers: BlueOtter, Cutepuppy, Horses' Ghost, Pardus, Wolff, and over two dozen others

Oklacon 2012:
Guests of Honor: Ugly Little Monster (furry horror artist), Kyell Gold (furry author)
Charity: Safari's Interactive Animal Sanctuary ($9,250)
Chairmen or Organizers: BlueOtter, Horses' Ghost, Pardus, Wolff, and almost a dozen others

Oklacon 2013: The theme was role-playing games.
Guests of Honor: Vantid (furry artist)
Charity: Safari's Interactive Animal Sanctuary ($4,675)
Chairmen or Organizers: BlueOtter and many others

Oklacon 2014:
Guests of Honor: Kimzie, Laken SteelJaw (furry artist, fursuiter)
Charity: Safari's Interactive Animal Sanctuary ($4,280)
Chairmen or Organizers: BlueOtter, Dizmis, Lykourgos, over a dozen others

Unfortunately, Oklacon 2014 was the last Oklacon. Oklacon 2015 was scheduled for October 29–November 1, 2015, with the theme of "The Legend of the Black Coyote." But the inappropriate, lewd, and illegal behavior of three first-time attendees at Oklacon 2014 resulted in Roman Nose State Park's cancelling Oklacon's application for 2015, and Oklacon's being blacklisted from moving to any other Oklahoma state park.

Pacific Anthropomorphics Weekend

Pacific Anthropomorphics Weekend (PAW), a.k.a. Pacific Anthro Weekend, PacAnthro, and PAWcon, is a second furry convention for the San Francisco Bay area, but smaller and more relaxed than the full-scale Further Confusion. It is supported by the Bay Area Furries mailing list. It features socializing, fursuit games and dancing. There is both a Fursuit Parade and a group photograph. Incorporation as Pacific Anthropomorphics League is pending. Its emblem is a black pawprint over a turquoise map of California.

Name & Date	Theme	Location	Attendance	Parade
Pacific Anthropomorphics Weekend 2014 November 14–16, 2014	none	San Jose Garden Airport Hotel, San Jose, CA	213	45
Pacific Anthropomorphics Weekend 2015 October 30–November 1, 2015	Survival of the Furriest	Doubletree By Hilton Hotel San Jose, San Jose, CA	310	76

Events

Pacific Anthropomorphics Weekend 2014: The new PAWcon was advertised as a "PAW-raiser" furry fall fundraiser to help build awareness and launch a full-scale weekend event in 2015. It was initially controversial, accused by some as competing against the established Further Confusion rather than being a complement to it; but the controversy had mostly died away by convention time. There were complaints of inadequate signage, and of new organization team inexperience. But since it was advertised as informal and relaxed, most attendees felt that it went off well enough, and was worth supporting for the future. Furry Night Live, "The Greatest Show in Fur," hosted a room party. There was no conbook. The T-shirt featured a paw supplied from clip art by the manufacturer, and the name of the convention.

Guests of Honor: NeonBunny (fursuit DJ), Bucker Fuskyote (fursuit musician), Cohn Jonner, Raid Zero, Ikkuma

Chairmen or Organizers: Spike Crutcher (Idylwild Fox)

Pacific Anthropomorphics Weekend 2015: A charity was added. The conbook cover and T-shirt were both by EmptySet.

Guests of Honor: Pepper Coyote (furry musician), WhiteyFawkes (fursuit/corporate mascot maker)

Charity: Wildlife Companions ($2,325)

Chairmen or Organizers: Spike Crutcher (Idylwild Fox)

PawFur *see* **Biggest Little Fur Con**

Pawpet Megaplex *see* **Megaplex**

Philippine Anthro Festival

Philippine Anthro Festival (PHAnthroFest) is a one-day convention in Manila. It was first proposed by Tooth Less in February 2013.

Name & Date	Theme	Location	Attendance
Philippine Anthro Festival 2014 May 17, 2014	Adventure Awaits	SM Megatrade Conference Center, SM Megamall, Metro Manila	134

Name & Date	Theme	Location	Attendance
Philippine Anthro Festival 2015 October 17, 2015		SM Megatrade Conference Center, SM Megamall, Metro Manila	103

Events

Philippine Anthro Festival 2014: The Festival was first planned to be held in a hotel, but it was felt that neither the organizers nor attendees would be able to afford a hotel. Several events were also scaled back; for example, a planned dance competition was replaced by a dance workshop when not enough attendees knew how to dance. Participants got a pet dog blanket. There were 9 fursuiters. Uncle Kage did not attend but addressed via Skype (but was interrupted by technical problems). DJ Rei Takamaya hosted a furry rave. A Fureedom Wall was set up where attendees could write whatever they liked.

Guests of Honor: Uncle Kage
Chairmen or Organizers: Xyrus Chase, Tooth Less

Philippine Anthro Festival 2015: The 2015 poster showing a fox waving a sword was by John Razel M. Cabungcai (JAZcabungcai).
Guests of Honor: none
Chairmen or Organizers: Tooth Less, Xyrus Chase, KC Cabug-os, Benjamin Sia, Jaime Honrado

RainFurrest

RainFurrest was created to replace the Conifur Northwest by Gene Armstrong and Trap Winters in Seattle, at the same time that All Fur Fun was created in Spokane for the same purpose. RainFurrest had its act together and succeeded where All Fur Fun faded away after three years. After the first RainFurrest, it was incorporated as Rainfurrest Anthropomorphics International (RAIn). RainFurrest is known for its particularly strong furry literary emphasis, with writers' workshops, author readings, panels featuring at least one of the furry specialty publishers, and (since 2011) an original furry anthology. However, due to attendee misbehavior at RainFurrest 2015, its hotel cancelled its contract. As of press time, RAIn had briefly accepted an offer to move RainFurrest 2016 to the Spokane Convention Center before announcing its cancellation for 2016 and hope to come back in the future.

RAIn is a non-profit group which "exists primarily for the purpose of holding events to facilitate education in anthropomorphic literature, art and culture, and to facilitate the donation of funds to non-profit institutions that the board decides are worthy." RAIn filed for 501(c)(3) status in January 2013, which was achieved in January 2016.

Name & Date	Theme	Location	Attendance	Parade
RainFurrest 2007 August 24–26, 2007		Holiday Inn Seattle-Sea-Tac Airport Hotel, Seattle, WA	370	41
RainFurrest 2008 September 26–28, 2008	Flight	Seattle Airport Marriott Hotel, Seattle, WA	599	89
RainFurrest 2009 September 18–20, 2009	Zombie Attack	Seattle Airport Marriott Hotel, Seattle, WA	905	159
RainFurrest 2010 September 24–26, 2010	Furst on the Moon	Seattle Airport Marriott Hotel, Seattle, WA	1,045	184
RainFurrest 2011 September 22–25, 2011	Furry Camping	Hilton Seattle Airport & Conference Center, Seattle, WA	1,420	378

Name & Date	Theme	Location	Attendance	Parade
RainFurrest 2012 September 27–30, 2012	Warehouse Furteen	Hilton Seattle Airport & Conference Center, Seattle, WA	1,705	517
RainFurrest 2013 September 26–29, 2013	Dancing in the Moonlight	Hilton Seattle Airport & Conference Center, Seattle, WA	2,202	487
RainFurrest 2014 September 25–28, 2014	Cyberpunk: Fur Meets Chrome	Hilton Seattle Airport & Conference Center, Seattle, WA	2,586	504
RainFurrest 2015 September 24–27, 2015	Swords and Sorcery	Hilton Seattle Airport & Conference Center, Seattle, WA	2,704	492

Events

RainFurrest 2007: The Masquerade only had three entries. There were numerous panels and workshops, but the guest-of-honor dinner ($35) had notably poor food even by hotel poor food standards. The convention sold out the hotel by a few days before it started. The T-shirt was by Monika Livingstone. There was no theme, but one was retroactively assigned: The Rainforest.

Guests of Honor: Artist G-o-H Monika Livingstone, Fan G-o-H Dennis Avner (Stalking Cat), Writer G-o-H Phil Geusz, Musical G-o-H Alexander James Adams

Charity: The Sarvey Wildlife Center (almost $1,000)

Chairmen or Organizers: Gene Armstrong, Tank Winters (Trapa)

RainFurrest 2008: Registered member received airplane-style metal wings pins; brass for regular members, silver for patrons, and gold for members who were real pilots. Events included a Fursuit Masquerade, a Pet Auction, a Plushie Costume Contest, an Ice Cream Social, workshops, gaming, and dances. WerePuppy did the T-shirt. The hotel staff was reported as very friendly. This was unofficially considered "RainFurrest I," with the previous year's as either "RainFurrest 0" or "a beta test."

Guests of Honor: Mark Brill (WerePuppy) (furry artist)

Charity: The Ferret Rescue Society ($1,000+)

Chairmen or Organizers: Tank Winters (Trapa)

RainFurrest 2009: RainFurrest 2009 had a Dealers Den, an Art Show, a large Fursuit Lounge, a Gaming Room with a DDR tournament, a Sponsor/Patron Lounge, a three-day writers' workshop, and many panels and other workshops. Events included a zombie game, the Fursuit Parade, the Ice Cream Social, a plushie costume contest, a Variety Show, the Guest of Honor dinner, a rant by 2, the Ranting Gryphon, a concert by Alexander James Adams, and dances with four DJs. The 42-page conbook had a wraparound color cover by Farore Nightclaw. The T-shirt was also by Farore Nightclaw.

Guests of Honor: Farore Nightclaw (furry artist), Adam Riggs (Nicodemus, fursuiter), Special G-o-H Matthew Wayne Davis (2, the Ranting Gryphon), Alexander James Adams, Kyell Gold

Charity: Critter Care Wildlife Society ($536.78)

Chairmen or Organizers: North

RainFurrest 2010: In 2010, RainFurrest became the sixth convention to surpass 1,000 attendees. The "Furst on the Moon" theme was emphasized in a program throughout the convention of landing a fur on the Moon and returning him or her safely to fandom. The fur was revealed by Dr. Werner von Wolfenstein to be a Cosmofur Siberian Husky of the Sovipaw Air Force. In addition to the Charity Auction, there were tip jars in the con store with the faces of con staffers Gene, Aloha, North, and Trapa. All donations went to the charity, and the jar getting the most donations got its staffer hit in the face with a pie by the volunteer who worked the most during the con. Other events included a plushie costume contest, a Second Life social, a live model workshop, a furry high tea, and a Graveyard

RainFurrest

Greg book celebration with his first novel. DragonDyne Publishing launched its new game, *Neverwhen*. Kyell Gold held a writing workshop. The T-shirt was by Balto.

Guests of Honor: Artist G-o-H Albert C. Peña (Balto), Fursuiter G-o-H Kodi, Writer G-o-H Graveyard Greg

Charity: Northwest Wildlife Rehabilitation Center ($3,000+)

Chairmen or Organizers: North

RainFurrest 2011: RainFurrest's first annual charity anthology went on sale: *Stories of Camp RainFurrest*, printed by FurPlanet Productions; a 108-page trade paperback with 11 donated short stories for $10 with all proceeds donated to that year's charity. TaniDaReal drew both the conbook cover and the T-shirt.

Guests of Honor: Artist G-o-H Tanja Freese (TaniDaReal), Writing G-o-H Alan Dean Foster, Fursuit G-o-H Deanna Larsson (Beetlecat), Artist Special Guest Astolpho

Charity: Love A Mutt Pet Rescue ($4,000+)

Chairmen or Organizers: Loial

RainFurrest 2012: The presentation of the first (2012) ALAA Hall of Fame honorees, to those characters, people, books, or films that helped to mold furry fandom, was announced: Bugs Bunny; Walt Disney; and the novel *Watership Down* by Richard Adams. RainFurrest's second annual charity anthology was *Tails of a Clockwork World*, 119 pages/eight donated stories with all sales going to the charity. YamiBliss drew both the conbook cover and the T-shirt.

Guests of Honor: Artist G-o-H Jeffrey Camion (YamiBliss), Writing G-o-H Elizabeth Ann Scarborough, Fursuit G-o-H Sara Howard (Matrices)

Charity: Rabbit Meadows Sanctuary & Adoption Center ($2,500+)

Chairmen or Organizers: Gene Armstrong

RainFurrest 2013: RainFurrest 2013 was the fifth furry convention to surpass 2,000 attendees. Its third annual charity anthology was *Dancing in the Moonlight*, 77 pages/five donated stories with all sales going to the charity. Soulscape drew both the conbook cover and the T-shirt.

Guests of Honor: Artist G-o-H Thea Reven (Soulscape), Fursuit G-o-H Temperance, Writing G-o-H FurPlanet Productions, Fandom G-o-H Fred Patten (in absentia), Writing Special Guest Phil Geusz

Charity: The Clouded Leopard Project ($6,454.17)

Chairmen or Organizers: Aloha

RainFurrest 2014: The presentation of the third (2014) ALAA Hall of Fame honorees, to those characters, people, books, or films that helped to mold furry fandom, was announced: Carl Barks; the novel *Charlotte's Web* by E. B. White; and Osamu Tezuka. RainFurrest's fourth annual charity anthology was *Furtual Horizons; A Rainfurrest Anthology*, 264 pages/eleven donated stories with all sales going to the charity. The 48-page wraparound Program Book cover was by Egypt Urnash, who also did the T-shirt.

Guests of Honor: Writing G-o-H Kyell Gold, Artist G-o-H Margaret Trauth (Egypt Urnash), Music G-o-H Jared Clark (Pepper Coyote), Fursuit G-o-H Croc

Charity: Cougar Mountain Zoological Park ($7,000)

Chairmen or Organizers: Cerb

RainFurrest 2015: The Dealers' Room was booked to capacity early. Instead of putting later applicants on a waiting list as usual, the committee held a juried judging of all applicants. This resulted in some long-time dealers being rejected and some first-time dealers being accepted, which resulted in some loud complaints. There were two 2015 charity anthologies; *A Menagerie of Heroes* for PG-13 stories, 322 pages/fourteen donated stories, and *Naughty Sexy Furry Writing: Enter at Your Own*

Risk for NC-17 stories, 124 pages/six donated stories. Jan did both the conbook cover and the T-shirt.

There was much unfavorable publicity from the perception that the RF committee discriminated against veteran fans in favor of promoting a "youth" atmosphere. Whether true or not, there were multiple examples of flamboyant drunken and other inappropriate public behavior from new teenage attendees, including severe hotel vandalism; enough to result in the RainFurrest's hotel since 2011 revoking their contract and forcing the planned RainFurrest 2016's cancellation.

Guests of Honor: Artist G-o-H Jan, Writing G-o-H Renee Carter Hall (Poetigress), Fursuit G-o-H RedHyena

Charity: Cougar Mountain Zoological Park ($10,000+)

Chairmen or Organizers: Rex Wolf

RBW

RBW started in 1998 as a Christmas banquet for the LondonFurs. By 2006 it had grown so large that chairman Rapido turned it into a formal boat excursion on the Thames, originally called the London Boat Party. RBW stood for Red, Blue & White.

Name & Date	Theme	Location	Attendance
RBW 2006 December 3, 2006	?	The Theodore Bullfrog pub; MV *Erasmus*, River Thames, London, England, U.K.	85 (estimated)
RBW 2007 December 1–2, 2007	Furs in Black	The Calico Bar pub, Royal National Hotel, London, England, U.K. in the daytime, the Golden Jubilee boat party on the River Thames on Saturday night	242
RBW 2008 November 27–30, 2008	Masters of Alchemy	The Royal National Hotel, Russell Square, London; and the Saturday evening boat trip up and down the Thames on the MV *Erasmus*	290
RBW 2009 October 30–November 1, 2009	Good Vibrations	The Britannia International Hotel, Canary Wharf, London; and the Saturday evening boat trip up and down the Thames on the MV *Erasmus*	226
RBW 2010 November 5–7, 2010	Space Cowboys	The Britannia International Hotel, Canary Wharf, London; and the Saturday evening boat trip up and down the Thames on the MV *Erasmus*	216

Events

RBW 2006: The boat party aboard the MV *Erasmus*, one of the largest party boats on the Thames, began after the traditional LondonFur Christmas meet at The Theodore Bullfrog pub. The entertainment included music and a rant by 2, the Ranting Gryphon.

Guests of Honor: Matthew Wayne Davis (2, the Ranting Gryphon)

Chairmen or Organizers: Rapido

RBW 2007: The attendance included 197 on the boat party. American furry notables included Timothy Albee, Steve Gallacci, Lance Ikegawa, and Uncle Kage. The events included Saturday morning and afternoon workshops and games (including the Fursuit Commonwealth Games), the Saturday evening boat party including a late night rant by 2, the Ranting Gryphon, and a 11:30 p.m. Fursuit Walk; and a Sunday afternoon fursuit performance, a Treasure Hunt, and the Charity

Auction. The donation to the charity included both the auction and a percentage of the convention store sales. The late night boat party was reported as highly enjoyable despite a very choppy river. The boat returned to the wrong pier, requiring the partygoers (some in fursuits) to walk back to the hotel.

Guests of Honor: Matthew Wayne Davis (2, the Ranting Gryphon) (Entertainment Track), Fatkraken (Fursuiting Track), Cassandra Gunn (Ultraviolet) (Art Track)
Charity: Mammal Trust UK (£1,331.23)
Chairmen or Organizers: Rapido

RBW 2008: The fursuiting events went well, but non-fursuiting events at the hotel were described as disorganized and chaotic. The boat party was a success, despite having its pickup location changed at the last moment. The hotel staff was described as uncooperative and surly, and the hotel had many non-fan guests who complained about the fursuits. RBW 2008 operated at a loss that was covered by private donations.

Guests of Honor: Timduru (fursuiter), ZEN (artist), Sven Tegethoff (Cheetah, EuroFurence chair)
Charity: The Wildfowl and Wetlands Trust (£1,100 estimated)
Chairmen or Organizers: Rapido

RBW 2009: The convention's acronym was officially changed from Red, Blue & White to Rather Brilliant Weekend. It featured 33 events (unnamed).

Guests of Honor: None, but "Specially invited attendees" were Markus Kalkbrenner (Atalon Deer, fursuiter), Fatkraken (fursuit maker), KaputOtter (furry artist), and Sketchkat (furry artist/fursuiter)
Charity: UK Wolf Conservation Trust (£1,868.45)
Chairmen or Organizers: Robert Barnes (tryst_fel_cath), kittiah

RBW 2010: This was the final RBW. Due to the competition of other Britfur events, it was announced in February 2011 that the convention part of RBW was being cancelled but that the boat party would remain. In July it was announced that the MV *Erasmus* was not available for late October or November. After that, the organizers became involved in other activities.

Guests of Honor: None
Charity: Sled Dog Welfare (£6,396.90)
Chairmen or Organizers: Robert Barnes (tryst_fel_cath), kittiah

RivFur

This was a furmeet that brought all Brisbane's Furry fans together in a semi-convention setting. The name refers to the Brisbane River that flows through the city. It grew into a full convention, shifting to a hotel venue in 2012 and adopting the RSPCA as its charity; but after RivFur 2014, it returned to an informal furmeet.

Name & Date	Theme	Location	Attendance
RivFur 2007 July 6–9, 2007		Brisbane, Queensland	30 to 40 (estimated)
RivFur 2008 July 4–6, 2008		Brisbane, Queensland	40 to 50 (estimated)
RivFur 2009 July 17–19, 2009		Brisbane, Queensland	50+
RivFur 2010 July 9–11, 2010		Brisbane, Queensland	50+

Name & Date	Theme	Location	Attendance
RivFur 2011 July 8–10, 2011		Brisbane, Queensland	90+
RivFur 2012 June 29–July 1, 2012		Brisbane, Queensland	~150
RivFur 2013 August 2–5, 2013		Mercure Hotel, Brisbane, Queensland	170+
RivFur 2014 August 8–10, 2014	Retro Gaming	Hotel Grand Chancellor, Brisbane, Queensland	~200

Events

RivFur 2007: RivFur 2007 registered attendees got customized chibi badges. The planned itinerary included a Friday late afternoon barbecue at South Bank Piazza, attending an evening screening of the *Transformers* movie at South Bank Cinemas; a Saturday morning trip to the Australia Zoo, a 6:30 p.m. dinner at Southside RSL, Mount Gravatt; Sunday morning free for socializing or mini-golf, an evening laser tag tournament at a local arcade; and a Monday morning chocolate making class, and afternoon bowling. Those who attended in tails or full fursuits were said to be popular with tourists and children. The T-shirt was by MistyStriker.

Chairmen or Organizers: FlameDrake, Christine Cupit (Foxy Malone), Nikita Wolfpaw

RivFur 2008: Events included a Friday evening barbeque at South Bank Piazza, Saturday morning trip to Movie World and evening FurBall game at Mansfield Tavern, and Sunday morning Scavenger Hunt at Brisbane City Botanical Gardens and evening Laser Tag/pizza party again at Woolloongabba Laserforce. The Saturday evening at Mansfield Tavern was the site of fursuit events and dances. FlameDrake provided tokens at the Laserforce so furry fans could play for free. Periods between scheduled events were left free for socializing and visiting Brisbane tourist sites in groups. Registered members received a customized ID card. The T-shirt was by Rose Quoll.

Chairmen or Organizers: FlameDrake, Christine Cupit (Foxy Malone), Nikita Wolfpaw

RivFur 2009: RivFur 2009 began on the 17th (Friday) with a 6:00 p.m. barbeque at South Bank Piazza; continued on Saturday at 11:00 a.m. with a choice between indoor rockclimbing at Rock-Sports or a visit to the Sciencentre at the Queensland Museum, and a 7:00 p.m. FurBall at Mansfield Tavern; and ended on Sunday with a 10:00 a.m. trip to Dreamworld. Registered attendees got custom keyrings by Mistystriker and Bingo Dingo. The T-shirt was by Bingo Dingo.

Chairmen or Organizers: Christine Cupit (Foxy Malone), Nikita Wolfpaw

RivFur 2010: RivFur 2010 attendees who registered early got a personalized chibi badge of their fursona drawn and colored by Mistystriker and Bingo Dingo. It began with a Friday 5:00 p.m. choice of a barbeque or picnic at South Bank Piazza, followed by a movie at South Bank Cinemas (most went to *Despicable Me*); Saturday noon, a choice between indoor rockclimbing at RockSports or a scavenger hunt at the Brisbane Botanical Gardens, and 6:00 p.m. FurBall at Mansfield Tavern; and Sunday 10:00 a.m. trip to Seaworld. The T-shirt was by Nikita Hyena.

Chairmen or Organizers: Christine Cupit (Foxy Malone), Nikita Wolfpaw

RivFur 2011: Registered attendees got customized chibi badges. RivFur 2011 featured a meet & greet at South Bank Parklands on Friday; a Saturday morning meeting at New Farm Park and Furball along the river in the afternoon; and a Sunday meeting at Alma Park Zoo, ending with a RivFur Bowling Night at the Chemside Hyper Bowl. The T-shirt was by KazzyCaboodles.

Chairmen or Organizers: Kiba Swiftpaw, MistyStriker

RivFur 2012: RivFur 2012 featured a meet & greet at South Bank Parklands, the Fursuit Walk, and a movie on Friday; Laser Tag and Furball on the Brisbane River on Saturday, and on Sunday a choice

RivFur banner. Art by Jonas Pride. Used with permission.

of a Lan Party or a day at New Farm Park with an art jam, fursuit games, and a Nerf war, ending in the evening at the Strike Wintergarden bowling center.
   Chairmen or Organizers: MistyStriker, Jet Dingo

RivFur 2013: RivFur expanded into a full-scale convention in a hotel, with guests, a charity, and a program. A charity auction was held on Sunday.
   Guests of Honor: Drakon Vectarus, Tevionbee (furry artists), Sabre McCullough, Kendal (furry hypnotists), B& From RivFur (furry band)
   Charity: RSPCA (A$4,250)
   Chairmen or Organizers: Jet Dingo

RivFur 2014: The Guest of Honour was dropped. Sponsors got 3D printed Nintendo cartridges. The T-shirt was by TriggerFox.
   Charity: Second Chance Cat Rescue (~A$3,000)
   Chairmen or Organizers: Kiba Swiftpaw
   After RivFur 2014, it was decided to return RivFur to its informal furmeet format. The RivFur website was closed.

Rocket City FurMeet

RCFM was the idea of Brody Catsmouth. KO and furry fans in Huntsville calling themselves the North Alabama Regional Furs incorporated as Rocket City FurMeet, Inc., a nonprofit social and recreational club intended as a furry convention in Huntsville, Alabama. They chose the Rocket City name since Huntsville was known for astronautical activities thanks to its closeness to the U.S. Space and Rocket Center, Marshall Space Flight Center, and Redstone Arsenal.

Name & Date	Theme	Location	Attendance	Parade
Rocket City FurMeet 2003 May 23–25, 2003		Radisson Suite Hotel Huntsville, Huntsville, AL	103	6 (estimated)

Name & Date	Theme	Location	Attendance	Parade
Rocket City Furmeet 2004 May 28–30, 2004		Radisson Suite Hotel Huntsville, Huntsville, AL	140	14 (estimated)
Rocket City FurMeet 2005 May 27–29, 2005	Furries…. In …. Space…	Radisson Suite Hotel Huntsville, Huntsville, AL	202	?
Rocket City FurMeet 2006 May 26–28, 2006	The 4th Dimension	Radisson Suite Hotel Huntsville, Huntsville, AL	229	?
Rocket City FurMeet 2007 May 25–27, 2007	Sci-Five	Radisson Suite Hotel Huntsville, Huntsville, AL	332	43
Rocket City FurMeet 2008 May 23–25, 2008	Deep Six	Radisson Suite Hotel Huntsville, Huntsville, AL	352	58 (estimated)
Rocket City FurMeet 2009 May 22–24, 2009	Magnificent Seven	Embassy Suites, Huntsville, AL	355	?
Rocket City FurMeet 2010 May 28–30, 2010	Lucky 8	Embassy Suites, Huntsville, AL	328	?
Rocket City FurMeet 2011 May 27–29, 2011	Dressed to the Nines	Embassy Suites, Huntsville, AL	302	43
Rocket City FurMeet 2012 May 25–27, 2012	Decades	Hilton Garden Inn, Huntsville, AL	242	?
Rocket City Furmeet 2013 cancelled				

Events

Rocket City FurMeet 2003: The convention included a well-stocked Con Suite that was the main socializing area, and small Dealers' Room and Artists' Alley. There was a Video Room. The hotel pool was popular. The 2003 Worldcon hosted a party Saturday night. The conbook cover and the regular members' T-shirt was by Oldfreek. The sponsors' T-shirt, "The Stone Age," was designed by HavocFox. RCFM 2003 was covered in *The Southern Fandom Confederation Bulletin*, August 2003, in a brief report that summarized it from a s-f point of view as, "They seemed an insular group but friendly enough." (Neither Rocket City FurMeet, Inc., nor the North Alabama Regional Furs were included in the *Bulletin*'s long list of s-f, fantasy, anime, comic-book, and other fan clubs in the Southern/old Confederate States area.) Brody Catsmouth was officially listed as Co-Chair for many years because RCFM was originally his idea, but he was seldom more than one of the convention committee.

Guests of Honor: Bill Holbrook (comic strip cartoonist)
Charity: Parenting Children of a Different Species (PCDS) ($500 estimated)
Chairmen or Organizers: Kevin Omel (KO)

Rocket City FurMeet 2004: The convention was also known as RCFM 2.0. A "Wheel of Blame" was introduced which had every RCFM staffer's name on it. It was spun during the opening ceremonies, and whoever "won" received all the blame for everything that went wrong during the convention. A second spin during the closing ceremonies allocated the blame for everything to go wrong for the committee until the next convention. The 2004 "winners" were Spirituality Leader Yotewah Californicus for "Staff Member X" during RCFM 2004, and Security head Alexander Katz for afterwards. Programming was heavily fursuit related. The conbook cover was by Setsu-P. The sponsors' T-shirt, "The Egyptians," was by HavocFox.

Guests of Honor: Jim Groat (furry cartoonist), TygerCowboy (the Mephit Furmeet chairman)
Charity: Parenting Children of a Different Species (PCDS) ($1,000+)
Chairmen or Organizers: Alexander Katz, Kevin Omel (KO)

Rocket City FurMeet 2005: The convention was also known as RCFM Pi. Babs Bunny was a panelist-of-honor. The Wheel of Blame spin resulted in staffers Flain Falcon and Fyrefang/Brody Catsmouth being declared responsible for everything that went wrong at the convention and after it, respectively. The programming was extended to Sunday evening. This was the first RCFM with performances by 2, the Ranting Gryphon, Sub-level 03, and the Critical Fail rock band. The conbook cover was again by Setsu-P. The sponsors' T-shirt, "Greek/Roman/Classical," was by HavocFox.
   Guests of Honor: Matthew Wayne Davis (2, the Ranting Gryphon), StickDevil (furry artist)
   Charity: Parenting Children of a Different Species (PCDS) ($1,200+)
   Chairmen or Organizers: Alexander Katz, Kevin Omel (KO)

Rocket City FurMeet 2006: "The 4th Dimension" just meant that this was the 4th Rocky Mountain FurMeet. The committee members picked by the Wheel of Blame were Raczoon for whatever went wrong during the convention, and Raczoon with Vincent VanLeopard for the year afterwards. RCFM 2006 hosted the presentation of the 2005 Ursa Major Awards. The conbook had a front cover by Aura Moser and a back cover by Setsu-P. The sponsors' T-shirt, "The Dark Ages/Fantasy" (silver ink on maroon), was by Setsu-P.
   Guests of Honor: Aura Moser (artist/fursuiter), Sub-level 03 (furry band). Panelist G-o-H: Santa Fox (fursuiter/puppeteer). Special G-o-H: Andrew Muchtler (Kinky Turtle)
   Charity: Parenting Children of a Different Species (PCDS) ($1,364)
   Chairmen or Organizers: KO ("head cat"); co-chair: Brody Catsmouth

Rocket City FurMeet 2007: The convention had a sci-fi theme. The panelist-of-honor was fursuiter Commander Kitsune. The Wheel of Blame staffers were Santa Fox and Brody Catsmouth. The Hospitality Suite kept all attendees well-fed. Some non-fan public lewd activity in the hotel led to Master of Security Alexander Katz warning against it at the opening ceremony. At the closing ceremony, TallyHawk was made a lifetime member for his various contributions. Five-year RCFM veterans were acknowledged. The conbook cover was by Margaret Carspecken.
   Guests of Honor: AnimeCat (fursuiter), Robert & Margaret Carspecken (furry writer/artists), Jeff Goode (TV writer)
   Charity: Parenting Children of a Different Species (PCDS) ($1,768)
   Chairmen or Organizers: Kevin Omel (KO)

Rocket City Fur Meet 2008: RCFM 2008 had a nautical theme. At the opening ceremonies, a drawing was held of all the registered members to select a Mystery-Guest-of-Honor; the winner was Furry DJ Sabrina Bear. The Wheel of Blame committee members were Jayrith during the convention and Kinyin afterwards. Events included Second Life activities, Crimson Mist and Critical Fail concerts, and dances on each night. The conbook cover and T-shirt were by WerePuppy. This was the final year that Santa Fox ran the Fursuiting Track.
   Guests of Honor: Mark Brill (WerePuppy, fantasy artist), Lionel Vogt (Solion) (fursuiter). The panelist-guest-of-honor was Eltee Statosky of Second Life
   Charity: Parenting Children of a Different Species (PCDS) ($3,536)
   Chairmen or Organizers: Kevin Omel (KO)

Rocket City Fur Meet 2009: RCFM 2009 had a Western theme. The Wheel of Blame selected Brody Catsmouth as responsible for whatever went wrong during the convention, and Bunny Halberd for whatever went wrong afterward. The Mystery G-o-H, an attendee chosen by a drawing during Opening Ceremonies, was Leo Lovely. A planned Fursuiter G-o-H, Joecifur, was forced to cancel just before the convention. There were a Variety Show, a Crimson Mist musical performance, a Second Life programming track, and dances. Most fursuiters congregated on the bridge from the hotel over the street. The conbook cover and T-shirt were by Sue Deer.
   Guests of Honor: Susan Rankin (Sue Deer, furry cartoonist), Special G-o-H Tinintri (furry artist)

Charity: Parenting Children of a Different Species (PCDS) ($2,162.12)

Chairmen or Organizers: Kevin Omel (KO)

Rocket City Fur Meet 2010: Rocket City FurMeet 2010 was also known as RCFM Lucky 8. The Wheel of Blame selected Sabrina Bear as Staff Member X during the convention and Corsi as Staff Member X for the year after it. Bucktown Tiger, Kawazu, Crimson Mist, and Buck Riley performed musical acts. Isfacat did a comedy routine. There were dances. The conbook cover was by XianJaguar.

Guests of Honor: Robert C. King (furry conrunner/fursuiter), XianJaguar (furry artist)

Charity: Parenting Children of a Different Species (PCDS) ($2,488)

Chairmen or Organizers: Brody Catsmouth

Rocket City FurMeet 2011: RCFM 2011 was also known as RCFM Dressed to the Nines. Featured events included a musical solo by Bucktown Tiger and a trio by Crimson Mist; a comedy by Isfacat; and a Furry Formal dance. The conbook cover was by Kyoht. The T-shirt was by Scape Goat.

Rocket City Fur Meet 2006 sponsors' T-shirt. Art by Setsu-P. Used with permission.

Guests of Honor: Heather Lutermann (Kyoht, artist), Scape Goat (fursuiter)

Charity: Parenting Children of a Different Species (PCDS) ($2,257.05)

Chairmen or Organizers: Brody Catsmouth

Rocket City FurMeet 2012: RCFM 2012 had a Tenth Anniversary theme. Events included "Bucktown Tiger Sets Up Shop" (fursuit keyboard musical performance), "Crart Jam," "Fossil's Livefeed" (guest of honor drawing and talking while broadcasting), "Furry Variety Show," "KO's Cappucchino," "Iron Artist," Friday Evening Dance, Saturday Evening Pizza Feed, and Saturday night formal dance.

Guests of Honor: Fossil, the Undead Anthrosaur Artist

Charity: Parenting Children of a Different Species (PCDS) ($2,000)

Chairmen or Organizers: Shirokuma

Rocket City FurMeet 2013/2014: RCFM 2013, a.k.a. RCFM The Eleventh Hour, was never held. It was scheduled for June 14–16, 2013 at the Four Points by Sheraton Hotel at the Huntsville Airport. However, the hotel was owned by the Transportation Security Administration, and after it was too late to find another hotel, RCFM was told that wearing fursuits would not be allowed. RCFM was postponed until 2014 and rescheduled for June 13–15, 2014 at the Amberley Suites Hotel in Decatur, AL. However, in January that hotel underwent extensive damage due to a burst pipe. RCFM was notified in April that the hotel would be closed through the summer; again too late to get another

hotel. Faced with cancellation for a second year in a row, RCFM was postponed indefinitely but not expected to be revived.
 Guests of Honor (intended): Rick Griffin (furry cartoonist)
 Charity (intended): Parenting Children of a Different Species
 Chairmen or Organizers (intended): Kevin Omel (KO)

Rocky Mountain Fur Con

RMFC was started as a convention for furry fans in the Rocky Mountain area, and Denver, CO in particular. It is unique in having a bandana as well as a T-shirt.

Name & Date	Theme	Location	Attendance	Parade
Rocky Mountain Fur Con 2007 June 1–3, 2007	Are You Wild Enough?	Denver Adam's Mark Hotel, Denver, CO	236	20
Rocky Mountain Fur Con 2008 May 23–25, 2008	The Urban Wilderness	Hyatt Regency Hotel, Denver, CO	319	40
Rocky Mountain Fur Con 2009 August 7–9, 2009	A Wild Night on the Town	Crowne Plaza Hotel, Denver, CO	400	54
Rocky Mountain Fur Con 2010 August 6–8, 2010	The Wild West	DoubleTree Hotel Denver, Denver, CO	526	71
Rocky Mountain Fur Con 2011 August 12–14, 2011	I Need a Hero!	DoubleTree Hotel Denver, Denver, CO	643	101
Rocky Mountain Fur Con 2012 August 10–12, 2012	The Furry Apocalypse	DoubleTree Hotel Denver, Denver, CO	863	200
Rocky Mountain Fur Con 2013 August 2–4, 2013	Lucky 13!	DoubleTree Hotel Denver, Denver, CO	1,006	190
Rocky Mountain Fur Con 2014 August 8–10, 2014	14ers!	Marriott Denver Tech Center, Denver, CO	1,354	303
Rocky Mountain Fur Con 2015 August 7–9, 2015	Game Shows!	Marriott Denver Tech Center, Denver, CO	1,640	382

Events

Rocky Mountain Fur Con 2007: The convention committee incorporated as the Mid-America Anthropomorphics and Arts Corporation. The hotel was next door to Denver's 16th Street Mall, and the Fursuit Parade was held outside the hotel in the Mall; the first furcon Fursuit Parade to be held outside its hotel. Goldenwolf did the conbook cover and T-shirt, but not the bandana.
 Guests of Honor: Christy Grandjean (Goldenwolf), Dark Natasha, Michelle Light (furry artists)
 Charity: Rocky Mountain Raptor Program (not recorded)
 Chairmen or Organizers: Kahuki Lairu

Rocky Mountain Fur Con 2008: Some events were held around the Urban Wilderness theme, such as a panel on graffiti art. The convention failed to meet its hotel room block and owed $25,000, which was gradually paid off, partly through donations. Erika Leigh R (front) and Blotch (back) did the conbook cover, Erika Leigh R did the T-shirt, and the bandana designer was not credited.
 Guests of Honor: Tess Garman & Teagan Gavet (Blotch, furry artists), LatinVixen (fursuiter)
 Charity: Wolf Sanctuary (not recorded)
 Chairmen or Organizers: Kahuki Lairu

Rocky Mountain Fur Con 2009: The attendance included 54 fursuiters. Although the attendees generally liked the hotel, most felt that a larger hotel was needed; especially one that did not require crossing the parking garage to get to the Dealers' Den. Sorin (front) and Keihound (back) did the conbook cover, Sorin did the T-shirt, and the bandana designer was not credited.

Guests of Honor: Keihound (furry artist), Jared Ledger (ScribbleFox) (furry artist/fursuiter)
Charity: The Denver Zoo (not recorded)
Chairmen or Organizers: Sorin Kat

Rocky Mountain Fur Con 2010: The DoubleTree Hotel was popular enough to become the RMFC's venue through 2013. In addition to traditional furry convention activities, there were three events featuring Nerf toy weapons: a High Noon Quick-Draw Competition, a Free-for-All City Shootout, and a Team Death-match. The conbook had a wraparound color cover by Heather Bruton, and Blotch did both the T-shirt and bandana. While the hotel did not have any other events, a nearby little league soccer tournament resulted in many juvenile soccer players staying in the hotel, causing some minor friction between high-spirited kids and fursuiters.

Rocky Mountain Fur Con 2015 Game Shows logo. Art by Sari NeoChaos. Used with permission.

Guests of Honor: Heather Bruton (furry artist), Lucky Coyote (fursuiter and co-founder of the Don't Hug Cacti Studios custom fursuit company), Matthew Wayne Davis (2, the Ranting Gryphon)
Charity: Front Range Equine Rescue ($480)
Chairmen or Organizers: Sorin Kat

Rocky Mountain Fur Con 2011: The theme focused on costumed superheroes. Noben did the conbook cover, and Rukis did both the T-shirt and bandana.

Guests of Honor: Kyell Gold (furry author), Rukis (furry artist/author)
Charity: Freedom Service Dogs ($1,200+)
Chairmen or Organizers: Sorin Kat

Rocky Mountain Fur Con 2012: Idess did the conbook cover, David Hopkins did the T-shirt, and Rukis did the bandana.

Guests of Honor: David Hopkins (furry author, cartoonist), Syber (fursuit maker)
Charity: Freedom Service Dogs ($2,500)
Chairmen or Organizers: Sorin Kat

Rocky Mountain Fur Con 2013: The theme was originally announced as casino life in the 1920s, but was revised to the 1950s. Rock Erekson (RKTDWG) did the conbook cover, Idess did the T-shirt, and Dark Natasha did the bandana.

Guests of Honor: M. "Idess" Sherwood (Idess, furry artist), Midori (fursuiter), Matthew Wayne Davis (2, the Ranting Gryphon, furry stand-up comedian)
Charity: Freedom Service Dogs ($3,588.09)
Chairmen or Organizers: Sorin Kat

Rocky Mountain Fur Con 2014: RCFM 2014 moved to a larger hotel. The theme revolved around mountaineering in the 54 peaks in the Rockies over 14,000 feet high. True Blue did the conbook cover, ShinigamiGirl did the T-shirt, and Sidian did the bandana.
  Guests of Honor: ShinigamiGirl (furry artist), WhiteyFawks (fursuit maker)
  Charity: Freedom Service Dogs ($5,500)
  Chairmen or Organizers: Sorin Kat

Rocky Mountain Fur Con 2015: It was announced that the game-show theme would feature "Trivial Fursuit." Sparky Nekomi did the conbook cover, Zhivago did the T-shirt, and Mataeus DeVailo did the bandana.
  Guests of Honor: Fursuit G-o-H Phoenix Wolf, Visual Arts G-o-H Rusty Shakleford (Zhivago)
  Charity: Freedom Service Dogs ($2,974.88)
  Chairmen or Organizers: Sorin Kat

Ruhrcon

Ruhrcon was created in 2009 as a local convention at a hostel in a wilderness area in the Ruhr valley in northwestern Germany.

Name & Date	Theme	Location	Attendance Parade
Ruhrcon 2009 April 3–5, 2009	Die Anfanger (beginnings)	"Naturfreundehaus Ebberg," Schwerte, North Rhine-Westphalia	85
Ruhrcon 2010 April 1–4, 2010	v2.0.10	"Naturfreundehaus Ebberg," Schwerte, North Rhine-Westphalia	79
Ruhrcon 2011 April 7–10, 2011	Time Is Running Out!	"Naturfreundehaus Ebberg," Schwerte, North Rhine-Westphalia	79
Ruhrcon 2012 Planned but cancelled			
Ruhrcon 2013 Not held			
Ruhrcon 2014 Not held			
Ruhrcon 2015 April 16–19, 2015	Das Leben ist kein Ponyhof	"Naturfreundehaus Ebberg," Schwerte, North Rhine-Westphalia	77

Events

Ruhrcon 2009: The first Ruhrcon was organized as a cozy gathering in a two-story public meeting hostel in Schwerte, a small town near Dortmund, in the heart of the Ruhr forest. Meals were provided by the hostel. Activities included a fursuit show, a fur dance, a photo shoot, a Pawpet SIG, and a small dealer's den; as well as outdoor hiking and a nighttime bonfire. Ruhrcon has never had a souvenir conbook. A two-month contest for a T-shirt was won by Revaivwra, with the second-place design by Lily Night Road used for the con badges. Due to limited parking in Schwerte, attendees were asked to plan car pools from Dortmund.
  Chairmen or Organizers: Saber, Saturios, Luschhoernchen, Orci, AkiFox, Neo, Tristan

Ruhrcon 2010: Ruhrcon 2010 was planned as a repeat of the first year. The winner of the T-shirt contest was Twice, who was unable to attend. The member badge art was by Royal-Pain-In-The-Ass.
  Chairmen or Organizers: Neo, Saber, Luschhoernchen, Orci, AkiFox

Ruhrcon 2011: The activities were similar. The T-shirt was by Mekki. The member badge art was by Fahrstuhl.
Chairmen or Organizers: Saber, Neo, AkiFox

Ruhrcon 2015: The activities were similar. The slogan was a German saying meaning "Life ain't easy." It was developed as a Viking theme. A group photograph was taken by Orci in a meadow against a forest bandground, showing 14 fursuiters. The T-shirt art was by TeR, and the badge art was by Natoli.
Chairmen or Organizers: Saber, Neo, AkiFox

RusCon *see* RusFURence

RusFURence

The RusCon, later renamed RusFURrence or RusFURence, is a convention for Russian fans in or near Moscow. It is held in January or February, originally because it originated as a birthday party then, later both because it is a student holiday period, and because late January-early February at the height of a Russian winter is the most convenient time to find convention facilities available.

Name & Date	Theme	Location	Attendance
RusCon 1 February 26, 1999		Apartment of Paul Kopeikin, Moscow	6
RusCon 2000 January 2–3, 2000		Apartment of Paul Kopeikin, Moscow	8
RusCon 2001 January 4–7, 2001		"Our Arbat" cultural center, Moscow	23
RusCon 2002 January 4–6, 2002		"Our Arbat" cultural center, Moscow	41
RusCon 2003 January 9–12, 2003		Zvenigorodskiy boarding house, Moscow	30 (estimated)
RusFURrence 2004 January 15–18, 2004		Zvenigorodskiy boarding house, Moscow	25 members, 16 guests
RusFURrence 2005 January 31–February 6, 2005		Zvenigorodskiy boarding house, Moscow	60–70 (estimated)
RusFURrence 2006 January 30–February 5, 2006		Zvenigorodskiy boarding house, Moscow	101
RusFURrence 2007 January 29–February 4, 2007		Moskviich (Moscovite) recreation center, Moscow	106
RusFURrence 2008 January 28–February 3, 2008		Zvenigorodskiy boarding house, Moscow	116
RusFURrence 2009 January 28–February 1, 2009		Holiday boarding house "Rus," near Moscow	140+
RusFURrence 2010 January 26–31, 2010		Malahovka boarding house, near Moscow	197
RusFURrence 2011 February 1–6, 2011		Zvenigorodskiy boarding house, Moscow	200 (estimated)
RusFURrence 2012 January 31–February 5, 2012		Zvenigorodskiy boarding house, Moscow	245

RusFURence

Name & Date	Theme	Location	Attendance
RusFURrence 2013 February 5–10, 2013	Horror Castle	Avantel Club Istra, near Moscow	196
RusFURrence 2014 February 5–9, 2014	The Wild West	Zvenigorodskiy boarding house, Moscow	204
RusFURrence 2015 February 4–8, 2015	Back to the USSR	Zvenigorodskiy boarding house, Moscow	202

Events

RusCon 1: The first RusCon was actually the birthday party of Paul Kopeikin (Ukiwa the cheetah) at his home in Moscow. There were 6 attendees, all fans of Disney's *The Lion King* more than of furry fandom in general. Since Ukiwa had already been holding furry house parties, this would not count as a convention; except that Russian furry fandom considers it as the first of the RusCons or RusFURrences that have grown into a regular convention.
  Host: Paul Kopeikin (Ukiwa)

RusCon 2000: The highlight was the presence of Molly, a lioness, and a leopard, tame animals rented by the attendees from a circus. The attendees cuddled with Molly and took photographs with the leopard.
  Host: Paul Kopeikin (Ukiwa)

RusCon 2001: RusCon grew from a one- or two-day fur-meet in a private apartment to a four-day convention in a rented basement meeting hall (described as "stuffy") of the cultural center, "Our Arbat," in the Arbat district in central Moscow near the Smolensk metro station. A banner saying "Furry TLK Party" in English was mounted over one of the center's arches. Cubby demonstrated karate on the first day, and balloons bearing the TLK logo were inflated. By Friday (the second day), most attendees were present. The Russian furs were almost all Internet fans who had never met in person, so the day was spent in socializing and drawing in sketchbooks. On Saturday, Ivan Martynov (Marty) used an old piano and music synthesizer to play everything from music from *The Last Unicorn* and *The Lion King* (of course) to the old Soviet national anthem. Later in the afternoon, a female reporter, Nastya, from *Radio Russia* arrived to conduct interviews about what furry fandom is all about. (However, later the *Express* newspaper reprinted the photographs without permission in a made-up story making fun of furry fandom.) On the last day, two fans arrived from Kharkov. Two professional musicians came and played music from *The Lion King*. The final event was a presentation of three boxes of snack foods for everyone to help themselves. Then the convention was over and everyone went home, except for those who stayed to clean up the hall as was required.
  Chairmen or Organizers: Vadim Dyatlenko (Justin), Sergei Zubkov (Cubby)

RusCon 2002: The organizers, Chairman Skar, Vice-Chairman Justin, and Treasurer SimBa, were from the *The Lion King* subgroup of Russian furry fandom. RusCon 2002 was promoted over the Internet, and its dates were voted upon. The Arbat district of Moscow was promoted for being a tourist attraction for its many fast-food restaurants and its proximity to the Kremlin and other historic buildings. Memberships were the ruble equivalent of U.S.$15. The attendance was mostly from Moscow, but some were from other Russian and Ukrainian cities, and one each from Canada and the U.S. The main activity was the socializing of the furry Internet fans who could only get together on this occasion. There were fans from throughout Russia. Marty played music again. Dmitry Prokhorov (Black Lion) brought a carful of computers and audio-visual equipment, and the convention was well-documented photographically for a video CD.
  Chairmen or Organizers: Sergei Atamanov (Skar)

RusFURence 2015 website banner. Art by Lingrimm. Used with permission.

RusCon 2003: The Zvenigorodskiy boarding house is 35 km. outside of Moscow, "in a calm Russian woodland." The RusCon website said that "15°C or 20°C below zero is usual." The boarding house rooms offered (with some differences): 1 sleeping bed, refrigerator, TV-set, table, chair, extra chair-bed, wardrobe, bedside-table, reading lamp, combined lavatory, loggia. Sergei Atamanov (Skar) said in his convention report, "There are no words to describe how much nicer, more comfortable and more fun to hang out in a comfortable suburban boarding house, away from the bustle of the big city. [...] We had only to eat three times a day, to make forays into nature, to make a row of 3 nights, sleep till noon, absorb insane quantities of beer and constantly shock the local population with their tails :)." The move to the boarding house was arranged by Black Lion, and the expenses were largely paid by supersponsors Blake and Beast. The other two members of the staff were Vice-Chairman SimBa and Treasurer Ukiwa.

Chairmen or Organizers: Black Lion

RusFURrence 2004: The informal convention was formalized under the RusFURrence name. The first program events were organized. The organizers were again Chairman Black Lion, Vice-Chairman SimBa, and Treasurer (really, everything else) Ukiwa.

Chairmen or Organizers: Black Lion

RusFURence 2005: Events included a theatrical production directed by Black Lion and Black Wolf, scripted by "all artists together," music events, DDR dancing, etc. Most events were planned and run by the Orgateam, with little participation from the attendees. It was hard to tell the attendance because participants had the option of staying at the rooming house for two, four, or six nights. The first RusFURrence T-shirt was introduced, by Martin Wolf. This was the first RusFURrence with any fursuiters; two Ukranian fans, Basil Lion and Simplewolf.

Chairmen or Organizers: Black Lion, SimBa, and Ukiwa

RusFURrence 2006: The boarding house was on the outskirts of Moscow, allowing for a rural re-laxicon. Again the Orgateam planned and organized all of the events. The theatrical production was directed and scripted by Jagu. This year's and future T-shirts were by Wolfy Nail, Omega the Lioness, and others.

Chairmen or Organizers: Black Wolf (not Lion), SimBa, Ukiwa

RusFURrence 2007: The first two days were for informal socializing; the other four days were programmed. Attendees could join for two, four, or six days. All attendees stayed at a nearby hotel. In 2007 an animal mascot was added to RusFURrence; 2007's was the fox. There were problems with the Moskviich center. It was the recreation center of the FSB, the Russian FBI, and the center of it was off-limits to the public. There were many small rooms, none really large enough for the whole convention. It was several buildings rather than one large one. This was not a problem in summer, but in the midst of a Russian winter, nobody wanted to have to cross from one building to another. Some buildings were too warm; others were too cold.

Chairmen or Organizers: Black Wolf. SimBa was Vice-Chairman, and Tingriel, the wife of Black Wolf, was the third member of the orgateam.

RusFURrence 2008: The RusFURrence returned to the Zvenigorod boarding house where all events were in one large building. Members could pay from 3,800 rubles to 13,800 rubles, depending on how many days they were staying, and whether they wanted a private room or a shared room. A wider variety of program events was held, including furry games, guess-the-melody, snow games such as a snow battle and building a snow furry, telling humorous stories, a DDR competition, table tennis competitions, how-to-draw classes, a contest of teams given a subject and creating a skit in ten minutes, a Fursuit competition, a Karaoke competition, and so on. There was a Dealers' Den. There was a meeting of the writers of *ARFI (Art Russian Furry Initiative)*, a Russian furry magazine. The animal mascot was the wolf. A third fursuit joined Basil Lion and Simplewolf; WinFox, also from the Ukraine.

Chairmen or Organizers: Black Wolf, with SimBa as Vice-Chairman, and Tingriel again

RusFURrence 2009: The boarding house was in Aksakovo village, 18 kilometers outside Moscow. Two buses were provided from the Timirjazevskaja metro station in Moscow to the venue. The convention booked the entire boarding house, so there was nobody else to complain about too much noise. Registration was 169, but estimates of attendance was only 140+. There was an Art Show. The program was largely the same as the previous year's, with some additions from the EuroFurence. (SimBa had attended the previous year's EuroFurence.) The first amateur film contest and first Dealers' Den were held. 2009's animal mascots were the spotted cats: snow leopards, cheetahs, etc. There were around ten fursuits. There was considerable trouble with the Rus boarding house. It was owned by a big factory that used it mostly as a summer resort for its employees. The hotel management did not care for the extra work of catering to fans in the winter, even if they paid extra, so the basic attitude was, "Go away!" They did the next year.

Chairmen or Organizers: Black Wolf, SimBa, and Tingriel as usual, plus Nexion as Hotel Liaison. (SimBa would change his name to Dimonius by 2011.)

RusFURrence 2010: The Malahovka boarding house was 12 kilometers from Moscow. It was chosen by Nexion, and when SimBa objected to it, Nexion fired him from the committee. According to SimBa, most scheduled program events were up to five hours late, and most attendees got food poisoning. The animal mascot was the lion. There were 15 fursuiters.

Chairmen or Organizers: Nexion, with Black Wolf as Vice Chairman, Tingriel, and a much larger staff

RusFURrence 2011: RusFURence 2011 returned to the Zvenigorodskiy boarding house. Advance announcements said that attendees could choose to stay from 2 to 5 days, making their arrangements directly with the boarding house. The approximately 200 attendees ranged from 2 to 5-day boarding house guests, plus single-day attendees, and non-fan boarding house residents who joined the convention. The animal mascot was the lynx. The T-shirt was by Koul.

Chairmen or Organizers: Dimonius, Leo Leopard, Klyk, Taffka, Faert

RusFURrence 2012: Early arrival on January 30 was available. A lottery held among preregistrants for a free membership was won by LeoMearido. The 240 attendees included 145 full-time fans (2 to 5 days) and 95 single-day participants. The animal mascots were foxes from opposite sides of the world: the desert fennec and the polar fox. There were about 95 fursuiters. New features included a furry bar and a room for fursuiters. A security team was introduced. The conbook cover was by Sauron.

Chairmen or Organizers: Dimonius, Leo Leopard, Klyk, Taffka, Faert

RusFURrence 2013: The RusFURrence experimented with the Aventel hotel, 55 kilometers from Moscow in a forest. Attendees were booked into a single wing of the hotel. The first Guest of Honor and theme were added. The animal mascot was the bat. The 196 attendees included about 96 members and 100 guests. The conbook cover was by Mephitis. The T-shirt was by Orphen Sirius.

Guests of Honor: Alex Vance (furry publisher)
Chairmen or Organizers: Taffka, Llanowar, Dimonius, Faert, Black Wolf, Jar, Mash

RusFURrence 2014: The convention returned to the Zvenigorodskiy boarding house again, this time large enough to book the entire facility. Early arrival was again available. There were about 85 fursuits. The Guest of Honor and theme were repeated, and the charity of Western furry conventions was added. The hotel was renamed Furville for the Wild West theme, with Coyote Marty as the villain—the coyote was the animal mascot. The 204 attendees included 150 guests. The conbook cover was by SilverFox.

Guests of Honor: Fox Amoore (furry musician)
Charity: Lion Guardians (₽ 35,427.50)
Chairmen or Organizers: Llanowar, Taffka, Dimonius, BlackLion, Leo Leopard

RusFURence 2015: The official Anglization of the convention was simplified from RusFURrence to RusFURence. The animal mascot was a Soviet-style bear. The 202 attendees also included about 150 guests. Instead of a Fursuit Parade, a "Winter Shenanigans" video was made of all (or most) of the fursuiters at the convention cavorting outdoors in the snow. The conbook cover was by Qzurr.

Guests of Honor: Qzurr (furry artist)
Charity: Cheetah Conservation Fund (₽ 28,000)
Chairmen or Organizers: Blacklion, Fleki, Leo Leopard, KlyK

ScotiaCon

ScotiaCon (pronounced "Sko-sha-con") is technically a U.K. furry convention but with a proud Scottish identity. It was incorporated in June 2010 as ScotiaCon UK Ltd., a private non-profit company. It was originally planned to take place around Easter 2010, but ThrashWolf, the chairman, had to postpone it for personal reasons. It was first held in July 2011 in Inverness, and has become the leading furry event in Scotland. The permanent cartoon mascot is Wallace, an anthromorphized Scottish terrier named after William Wallace, wearing a superhero-like costume based upon the Scottish flag.

Name & Date	Theme	Location	Attendance
ScotiaCon 2011 July 15–17, 2011	none	Ramada Jarvis Hotel, Inverness, Scotland	50 (estimated)
ScotiaCon 2012 July 27–30, 2012	Keep Calm and Sing Along!	Mercure Inverness Hotel, Inverness, Scotland	100
ScotiaCon 2013 August 2–5, 2013	Science…. Fiction!	Mercure Inverness Hotel, Inverness, Scotland	89

ScotiaCon

Name & Date	Theme	Location	Attendance
ScotiaCon 2014 November 7–9, 2014	Superheroes and Villains	Mercure Livingston Hotel, Livingston, Scotland	105
ScotiaCon 2015 November 6–8, 2015	Apocalypse!	Mercure Livingston Hotel, Livingston, Scotland	152

Events

ScotiaCon 2011: Although ScotiaCon 2011 did not have a formal theme, it was devoted to Scotland and Scottish culture. A poster advertised "City-Centre location—In the midst of the Highlands—Hotel with gym and pool—Close to Loch Ness." Registration was £65 for attendance and the conbook, or £95 for those plus the T-shirt and a print. Events included a science talk, charades, a Highland Fur Games, the "Furry-vision Song Contest," and "Eat Scotland" (a chance to sample Scottish delicacies such as Cullen skink, haggis, and deep-fried Mars bars), as well as the usual fursuit walk, dances, and charity auction. There was not a charity or a Fursuit Parade, but there were about a dozen fursuits present. Hotel staff wore tails and joined the singing. There were fursuit billiards, and an official huge Convention Cake for all attendees. The conbook covers and T-shirt were by Tsaiwolf.

Guests of Honor: Fox Amoore (furry composer), Fatkraken (fursuit maker)
Chairmen or Organizers: Blackwolf, Smirnoff

ScotiaCon 2012: The events were similar. A charity was added. The conbook cover was by Nimrais. The T-shirt was by Kaji.

Guests of Honor: Kaji, Nimrais (a couple; furry artists)
Charity: Highland Tiger: The Scottish Wildcat (£2,080)
Chairmen or Organizers: Blackwolf, Smirnoff

ScotiaCon 2013: The events were similar. The conbook cover was by TaniDaReal. The T-shirt was by Spiritraptor.

ScotiaCon mascot, Wallace. Art by Booshie. Used with permission.

Guests of Honor: Tanja Freese (TaniDaReal, furry artist), Richard Nightpaw (fursuiter, vice-chairman of EuroFurence)
Charity: Hounds for Heroes (£615.85)
Chairmen or Organizers: Blackwolf, Smirnoff

ScotiaCon 2014: SC 2014 moved from Inverness to a larger hotel in Livingston, and from July/August to November to avoid summer crowds and to get better hotel prices. The events were similar. The conbook cover was by Kneezle (front) and Rachex (back). The T-shirt was by FatCorgiOnyx.

Guests of Honor: Blackkrystal (furry artist/fursuit maker)
Charity: World Horse Welfare (£655.81)
Chairmen or Organizers: Silverfoxwolf, Ceilfox, Graafen Blackpaw

ScotiaCon 2015: The events were similar. The conbook cover was designed by Heartlilly and Booshie. The 2015 T-shirt design was by Syber.
  Guests of Honor: Kerijiano (furry artist/fursuit maker)
  Charity: Scottish Owl Centre (£2,089.40)
  Chairmen or Organizers: Silverfoxwolf, Ceilfox, Graafen Blackpaw

Texas Furry Con

Texas Furry Con, originally called Texas Fur Con, was a single event held in Austin. It was organized by a single fan, Kuro-Kai, with the sponsorship of Shiner Bock beer, brewed by the Spoetzl Brewery in nearby Shiner, Texas. It was originally announced as Texas Fur Con until February 2004, but due to Further Confusion's trademarking the term "fur con," it changed Fur to Furry. Although considered successful, Kuro-Kai was unable to continue organizing the convention due to health issues, and nobody else took it over. Continued discussion of it among Texan furry fans was one of the influences leading to Furry Fiesta in 2009.

Name & Date	Location	Attendance
Texas Furry Con March 19–20, 2004	Holiday Inn Express, Austin	400 (estimated)

Events

Texas Furry Con: There was a small dealers room for artisans (self-made furry merchandise) and a few panels. A major event was a Furcadia game, widely publicized as giving fans of the game the chance to meet in person. There was a charity barbecue on the second day. The convention was "heavily invaded" by activists of the Something Awful website (organized in 2003), known for satirical or mocking attacks on furry fandom; but nothing ontoward happened beyond its members wearing "AnthroGoons: Fags, Fat, and so many Whores" T-shirts, and posting several insulting con reports later. The convention staff forced several notorious Something Awful members led by Vorpal Bunny to sign an agreement to not post anything against the convention on the Internet, which the signers ignored as soon as the convention was over.
  Charity: National Fish and Wildlife's Save the Tiger fund ($5,000)
  Chairmen or Organizers: Aisha Rolentaes (Kuro-Kai)

Texas Furry Fiesta *see* **Furry Fiesta**

TransFur

TransFur was the first Japanese furry convention.

Name & Date	Location	Attendance
TransFur 1 May 7, 2005	BumB sports and culture hotel, Kawasaki Prefecture, Tokyo	90 (estimated)
TransFur 2 December 3, 2005	Kawasaki City Industrial Promotion Hall, Kanagawa Prefecture, Tokyo	120 (estimated)
TransFur 3 May 4, 2006	Exhibition room 4F, Kawasaki City Industrial Promotion Hall, Kanagawa prefecture, Tokyo	170 (estimated)
TransFur 4 December 3, 2006	Exhibition room 4F, Kawasaki City Industrial Promotion Hall, Kanagawa prefecture, Tokyo	170+

Name & Date	Location	Attendance
TransFur 5 December 15, 2007	Exhibition room 4F, Kawasaki City Industrial Promotion Hall, Kanagawa prefecture, Tokyo	180+

Events

TransFur 1: There were no memberships, no admission was charged, and the public was welcome to come in. TransFur was primarily for socializing and to introduce the public to fursuits. There were about 30 fursuits, but no Fursuit Parade. TransFur was the first furry convention to be held twice a year, generally in the Spring and Winter. No chairmen or organizers were recorded.

TransFur 2

TransFur 3

TransFur 4: The attendance included a larger number of women than before. There were about 50 fursuiters in the group photograph.

TransFur 5: The attendance included 47 fursuiters. This was the final TransFur, due to the organizers giving it up. It was replaced by Kemocon the next year.

Tropicon

Tropicon was a small convention in Berlin from 2006 to 2009, on Entenwall Island in the midst of an arbor settlement in Köpenick. The site included a main building, two smaller outbuildings, a grassy area with a large communal tent, a smaller pavilion tent that was used as the Fursuit Lounge, and a small dock that linked the island to the opposite shore by two small boats. Tropicon 2010 was planned for July 15–18, but was cancelled due to the management's converting the island into a nature preserve. Tropicon was replaced by EAST in 2011.

Name & Date	Attendance
Tropicon 2006 July 14–16, 2006	16
Tropicon 2007 July 27–29, 2007	18
Tropicon 2008 July 18–20, 2008	18
Tropicon 2009 July 3–5, 2009	25

Events

Tropicon 2006: Activities included archery, table tennis, and throwing cups.
Chairmen or Organizers: Konu Yoshikawa (Konu Eikuku Hentaru), LeTigre

Tropicon 2007: Activities were the same.
Chairmen or Organizers: Konu Yoshikawa (Konu Eikuku Hentaru), LeTigre

Tropicon 2008: Activities were the same. "Tropical Fursuit Games" were planned, but were rained out.
Chairmen or Organizers: Konu Yoshikawa (Konu Eikuku Hentaru), LeTigre

Tropicon 2009: "Tropical Fursuit Games" were again rained out. A party was held in the communal tent instead.
Chairmen or Organizers: Konu Yoshikawa (Konu Eikuku Hentaru), LeTigre

UkrMiniFurka *see* **WUFF**

Unthrocon *see* **Furry Unlocked**

UralFurence

UralFurence, or UralFurentsiya, is held in Yekaterinburg, the largest city in the Ural Mountain district (Sverdlovsk Oblast) of Russia. It is designed for "the community of artists, animators, writers, costume designers, and just fans of anthropomorphic creatures." There are two mascots; an anthropomorphic Russian bear for the European part of Russia, and an anthropomorphic Siberian sable for the Asiatic part of Russia.

Name & Date	Theme	Location	Attendance
UralFurence 2015 November 6–9, 2015	?	"Recreational Trubnik," Kurganova village	122

Events

UralFurence 2015. The age limit was 16, unlike the RusFurence age limit of 18. Attendees were required to register in advance; 122 did so. Only one mascot was used this year; Nadezhda the sable, drawn as a white sable wearing a dark green scarf with a black pawprint by saint-yves. For attendees who did not drive or take a taxi, a "mikrofurobus" took attendees from a monument at the train station at Yekaterinburg to the venue, the "Recreational Trubnik" just outside the village of Kurganova, an hour to 1½ hour's drive away. Events included scheduled meals, an opening and closing ceremony, indoor and outdoor games including playing musical instruments, a clay pigeon shooting tournament won by Steele, Licorice Monster, and Kunava, the wearing of fursuits, and a Saturday night disco dance. There were 5 fursuiters. Souvenirs for sale included a T-shirt and a magnet showing the mascot, both illustrated by Darya Alexandrova. UralFurence 2015 was the first furry convention in Russia that did not allow any alcohol.

Chairmen or Organizers: Will King, Alex King, WLF the dragon, PhoenixTV, Xen Wirder

VancouFur

VancouFur was the first furry convention on Canada's West Coast. It grew from a demand for Vancouver's Howloween furmeet (started in 2002) to grow into a full-scale hotel convention. Beginning in its second year, VancouFur has featured a Community Spotlight for talent from the British Columbia, Alberta, and Northern Washington furry communities. A unique feature of VancouFur is its character cakes made for the guests-of-honor by Temrin, often with figure decorations by Julie Julien.

Name & Date	Theme	Location	Attendance	Parade
VancouFur 2012 March 9–11, 2012	Great White North	Executive Suites Hotel & Conference Centre, Burnaby, BC	347	73
VancouFur 2013 March 1–3, 2013	Rocks and Rails	Executive Suites Hotel & Conference Centre, Burnaby, BC	484	78
VancouFur 2014 February 27–March 2, 2014	Gateway to the Pacific	Executive Suites Hotel & Conference Centre, Burnaby, BC	600	123
VancouFur 2015 March 5–8, 2015	Gangsters & Gumshoes	Executive Suites Hotel & Conference Centre, Burnaby, BC	724	141

Events

VancouFur 2012: The first VancouFur was planned from Spring 2011. The 347 attendees came from as far away as Poland. The conbook wraparound color cover was a collaboration by Davecko, Temrin, Soulscape, and Apoxon, and the T-shirt was by Scribble fox. There was local newspaper and TV coverage.
  Guests of Honor: Thumper (fursuiter/musician/DJ)
  Charity: BC Siberian Husky Club (C$350 to C$400)
  Chairmen or Organizers: Coal Silvermuzzle, Aphinity, Tank Winters (Trapa)

VancouFur 2013: The Rocks & Rails theme emphasized British Columbia's railroad and mining industries. Convention signage around the hotel showed railway crossing signals. The Community Spotlight was begun. The VancouFur chairman was elected by popular vote. The conbook color cover was a collaboration by Apoxon, Chelsey Bueckert, Davecko, Temrin, Soulscape, and Weremagnus. The T-shirt was by Weremagnus.
  Guests of Honor: Jana Stout (Maly), Jon DiFrancesco (Jondi), Omekin Lutz (furry artists, the three owners of Con*Tact Caffeine)
  Charity: BC Siberian Husky Club (C$1,275)
  Chairmen or Organizers: Akonite

VancouFur 2014: The theme emphasized the cultures around the Pacific Ocean. The Community Spotlight featured artist Davecko and DJ Tigon. Fox Amoore was guest musician. The conbook wraparound color cover, showing the theme, was a collaboration by Apoxon, Chelsey Bueckert (MYSTIQE), Davecko, Temrin, Thea Reven (Soulscape), Amanda Kadatz (Weremagnus), Onnanoko, and Nancy Andrews (ICEBANSHEE). The T-shirt was by Davecko.
  Guests of Honor: Ami McKim (BlooFox), Wolever Wuff (fursuit makers)
  Charity: Vancouver Orphan Kitten Rescue Association (VOKRA) (C$1,700)
  Chairmen or Organizers: Akonite, Medlar

VancouFur 2015: The Community Spotlight featured Shay Duval (Rhari, furry artist, fursuiter, & committee member). The VF2015 conbook cover illustrating the Gangsters & Gumshoes film noir theme was a collaborative artistic effort between Seylyn, Rhari, Razzy, Temrin, and Soulscape. The T-shirt was by Seylyn. At the closing ceremonies, it was announced that VancouFur would move to the larger Executive Plaza Airport Hotel in Richmond, BC.
  Guests of Honor: Seylyn (furry artist, fursuit performer), Fursuit G-o-H Razzy Lee, DJ G-o-H Akonite
  Charity: Vancouver Orphan Kitten Rescue Association (VOKRA) (C$1,600)
  Chairmen or Organizers: Tank Winters (Trapa), Cekuba

—— Western Pennsylvania Furry Weekend ——

The Western Pennsylvania Furry Weekend was a convention that grew from a fur-meet. Pittsburgh's furry fans had held Fall and Spring Fur-be-ques since 2001. The Spring Fur-be-ques were considered a prelude to the Anthrocon in Philadelphia. By 2004 and 2005 they were adding guests-of-honor and publications. With the move of the Anthrocon to Pittsburgh in July 2006, it was decided to turn the Fur-be-ques into a full mini-convention for fall or early winter. The permanent motto is "Fur and Fun in the Summer Sun." Instead of a Guest of Honor, WPFW always has a Featured Artist.

Western Pennsylvania Furry Weekend

Name & Date	Location	Attendance	Parade
Western Pennsylvania Furry Weekend 2006 October 6–8, 2006	Comfort Inn Pittsburgh North, Pittsburgh, PA	71	7
Western Pennsylvania Furry Weekend 2007 October 5–7, 2007	Comfort Inn Pittsburgh North, Pittsburgh, PA	92	24
Western Pennsylvania Furry Weekend 2008 October 3–5, 2008	Comfort Inn, Pittsburgh North [and] Aspinwall Fireman's Memorial Park, Pittsburgh, PA	108	?
Western Pennsylvania Furry Weekend 2009 October 2–4, 2009	Comfort Inn, Pittsburgh North, Pittsburgh, PA	96	?
Western Pennsylvania Furry Weekend 2010 October 1–3, 2010	Comfort Inn, Pittsburgh North, Pittsburgh, PA	112	?
Western Pennsylvania Furry Weekend 2011 September 30–October 2, 2011	Comfort Inn, Pittsburgh North, Pittsburgh, PA	97	?
Western Pennsylvania Furry Weekend 2012 September 28–30, 2012	Comfort Inn, Pittsburgh North, Pittsburgh, PA	98	?
Western Pennsylvania Furry Weekend 2013 October 11–13, 2013	North Park Lodge, McCandless, PA	132	?
Western Pennsylvania Furry Weekend 2014 October 3–4, 2014	Boyce Park Four Seasons Activity Center, Plum, PA	133	?
Western Pennsylvania Furry Weekend 2015 October 9–10, 2015	North Park Lodge, McCandless, PA	?	?

Events

Western Pennsylvania Furry Weekend 2006: The charity auction raised $500, and by taking advantage of a pledge by an attendee to match the donations, and then of a pledge by a non-fan philanthropist to match donations, the total donation to Animal Friends was $2,000.
Guests of Honor: Shawntae Howard (featured artist)
Charity: Animal Friends ($2,000)
Chairmen or Organizers: Akira Shima (furry artist)

Western Pennsylvania Furry Weekend 2007: A Midnight Menagerie had eight acts.
Guests of Honor: Brendan Roo (featured artist)
Charity: Animal Friends ($657)
Chairmen or Organizers: Swift Fox

Western Pennsylvania Furry Weekend 2008: Fireman's Memorial Park had a shelter, horseshoe pits, basketball hoop, sliding board, swings, gym equipment, grills and picnic tables. The announced program was Friday evening socializing, Looney Labs Games, and fursuit photo shoot; Saturday, morning cartoons, hotel closed at noon and all events moved to park (lazer tag, group photo, drum circle, dinner, charity raffle), after 8:00 p.m. back at hotel, menagerie; Sunday noon, trip to Pittsburgh Zoo & PPG Aquarium (or Carnegie Museum of Natural History if bad weather), 6:00 p.m. dinner at Steak & Shake at Pittsburgh Mills Mall.

Guests of Honor: MehdniX (furry artist/fursuiter)
Charity: The Beaver County Humane Society ($1,200)
Chairmen or Organizers: Swift Fox

Western Pennsylvania Furry Weekend 2009: Events included games, a fursuit group photograph, Saturday morning cartoons, lazer tag, a Fursuit Menagerie, a Drum Circle at Fireman's Park, a charity raffle, a Saturday night dance, a Sunday outing to the Pittsburgh Zoo and PPG Aquarium, and a closing dinner at the Steak n Shake at the Pittsburgh Mills Mall.
Guests of Honor: Jon Starrazor (featured artist)
Charity: The Beaver County Humane Society ($1,200)
Chairmen or Organizers: Swift Fox

Western Pennsylvania Furry Weekend 2010:
Guests of Honor: Flanowa (featured artist)
Charity: The Beaver County Humane Society ($1,200)
Chairmen or Organizers: Swift Fox

Western Pennsylvania Furry Weekend 2011:
Guests of Honor: Kyote (featured artist)
Charity: ClarionPAWS ($1,700)
Chairmen or Organizers: Swift Fox

Western Pennsylvania Furry Weekend 2012: Swift Fox, the long-serving Director, resigned to let new leadership keep the WPFW vibrant.
Guests of Honor: Sunstreak Chakat (featured artist)
Charity: ClarionPAWS ($2,230)
Chairmen or Organizers: Swift Fox

Western Pennsylvania Furry Weekend 2013:
Guests of Honor: Akira Shima (featured artist)
Charity: Hide-e-Hole Ferret Rescue ($1,714)
Chairmen or Organizers: Blithe

Western Pennsylvania Furry Weekend 2014:
Guests of Honor: Sebastian Silverfox (featured artist)
Charity: Hide-e-Hole Ferret Rescue ($3,800+)
Chairmen or Organizers: Blithe

Western Pennsylvania Furry Weekend 2015:
Guests of Honor: PeeJay (Featured Artist)
Charity: Going Home Greyhounds, Inc. ($3,121)
Chairmen or Organizers: Blithe

What The Fur?

What The Fur? (capital T and ? optional but preferred) is a furry convention for Montréal and Eastern Canadian-area furs. It was started as yet another followup to the discontinued C-ACE by the two Montreal-area furry communities, MonFur and Francofur. It was intended as a full-scale furry convention with the usual Dealers' Den, Art Show, Gaming Room, Headless Lounge, Fursuit Parade, a Restaurant Guide to Montréal, etc. The convention was organized as Productions Anthromorphique, and was given active support by several other furry, s-f, and anime conventions, the Montréal s-f & furry community, and the staff of the 2009 s-f Worldcon in Montréal. The conbook is printed in both English and French.

What The Fur?

What The Fur? 2014 conbook. Art by Ookami Kemono. Used with permission.

Name & Date	Theme	Location	Attendance	Parade
What The Fur? 2010 June 4–6, 2010	Pirates vs. Ninjas	Hotel Espresso, Montreal, Quebec	232	21
What The Fur? 2011 June 3–5, 2011	Zombie Apocalypse: Night of the Furry Dead	Hotel Espresso, Montreal, Quebec	221	32
What The Fur? 2012 June 1–3, 2012	Creatures of the Night	Hotel Espresso, Montreal, Quebec	282	none
What The Fur? 2013 May 17–19, 2013	Fairy Tales	Delta Centre-Ville, Montreal, Quebec	297	41
What The Fur? 2014 May 23–25, 2014	A Steam Powered Celebration	Sheraton Montreal Airport Hotel, Dorval, Quebec	303	74
What The Fur? 2015 May 22–24, 2015	Time Travelin' Furries	Holiday Inn Hotel & Suites Pointe-Claire Montreal Airport Hotel, Pointe-Claire, Quebec	373	72

Events

What The Fur? 2010: There was an Iron Artist contest. Notable presentations included "Convention Horror Stories" by Belic Bear of FurFright, "Beyond Furry" by Blindsight of Furnal Equinox, "History of Furry Fandom" by Dronon (presented twice, in English and French), and "Publishing" by René Walling, the chairman of the 2009 Worldcon. The front and back of the T-shirt were by gNAW.
    Guests of Honor: Malcolm Earle (Max Blackrabbit), gNAW (furry artists)
    Charity: The EcoMuseum Zoo of the St.-Lawrence Valley Natural History Society (C$738.60)
    Chairmen or Organizers: Christopher Pilgrim (Feli)

What The Fur? 2011: WTF 2011 featured a convention-long game of Furries vs. Zombies. Players either tried to survive the weekend with their brains intact, or to convert as many people as they

could into zombies. At the closing ceremonies, the audience voted on the winners: the Zombies, by a large margin. The conbook cover was by Kalika, and the T-shirt by gNAW.
   Guests of Honor: Kalika Tybera, Demicoeur (furry artists)
   Charity: The EcoMuseum Zoo of the St.-Lawrence Valley Natural History Society (C$2,223)
   Chairmen or Organizers: Christopher Pilgrim (Feli)

What The Fur? 2012: Due to laws banning the wearing of masks during protest marches, WTF 2012 did not hold a Fursuit Parade. The conbook cover and T-shirt were by Kanthara. Feli cut off all his hair for the Canadian Cancer Society.
   Guests of Honor: Karine Charlebois (Kanthara)
   Charity: The EcoMuseum Zoo of the St.-Lawrence Valley Natural History Society (C$4,150.93)
   Chairmen or Organizers: Christopher Pilgrim (Feli)

What The Fur? 2013: The move to a larger hotel was expected to allow room for growth over several years. However, the Delta Centre-Ville closed on October 31, 2013, and was converted to student housing, forcing WTF to move after one year. The conbook cover and T-shirt were by HollyAnn.
   Guests of Honor: Lisa Cotton (HollyAnn, furry cartoonist)
   Charity: The EcoMuseum Zoo of the St.-Lawrence Valley Natural History Society (C$2,185.75)
   Chairmen or Organizers: Christopher Pilgrim (Feli)

What The Fur? 2014: Leading events were fursuit-related, such as the Fursuit Parade, Fursuit Games, and an International Fursuit Hockey League. Other events included an Iron Artist contest and a Chocolate Social. The conbook cover and T-shirt were by Ookami Kemono.
   Guests of Honor: Alex Cockburn (Ookami Kemono, furry artist)
   Charity: The EcoMuseum Zoo of the St.-Lawrence Valley Natural History Society (C$3,103.33)
   Chairmen or Organizers: Christopher Pilgrim (Feli)

What The Fur? 2015: WTF 2015 was originally announced for May 15–17. It moved to the Holiday Inn Point-Claire due to complaints about the 2014 hotel not meeting expectations. The Dealers' Room was filled by the previous January, and later applicants put on a waiting list. Fursuiting events led the games, dance competition, and hockey. A second dance was added on Friday evening. Other events included a life drawing session, an improv session, an Iron Artist competition, and a furry fandom history panel moderated by Dronon. The furry novel *Tinder Stricken* by Heidi C. Vlach was debuted. The conbook cover and T-shirt were by Cat-Monk Shiro.
   Guests of Honor: Cat-Monk Shiro
   Charity: The EcoMuseum Zoo of the St.-Lawrence Valley Natural History Society (C$3,000)
   Chairmen or Organizers: Christopher Pilgrim (Feli), Marc Ladouceur (Firebreath)

Wild Nights

Wild Nights is a furry outdoor camping event that split off from the Oklacon when its organizing body, the Oklahoma Association of Anthropomorphic Arts, dissolved. Wild Nights used the old OAAA charter and bylaws as a model, and organized Wild Nights to be a similar event and with the same charity, but at a different state park. The organizing body is the Missouri Exotic Species Art Association (MESA), a registered not-for-profit 501c7 tax-exempt organization. Since 2012 the convention's title is often modified to fit the theme of the year: "My Little Wild Nights: Furry Is Magic"; "Wild Nights of the Round Table"; "…in Sherwood Forest," etc. Wild Nights' long-running charity is Safari's Sanctuary, a private exotic wildlife rescue zoo (not open to the public) in Broken Arrow, OK. There has always been a T-shirt, usually by the Artist Guest-of-Honor.

Name & Date	Theme	Location	Attendance
Wild Nights 2009 April 23–27, 2009	none	Robbers Cave State Park, Wilburton, OK	49
Wild Nights 2010 April 22–26, 2010	none	Robbers Cave State Park, Wilburton, OK	99
Wild Nights 2011 April 21–25, 2011	Basic Training	Robbers Cave State Park, Wilburton, OK	126
Wild Nights 2012 April 26–30, 2012	My Little Wild Nights: Furry Is Magic	Robbers Cave State Park, Wilburton, OK	122
Wild Nights 2013 April 25–29, 2013	…of the Round Table	Robbers Cave State Park, Wilburton, OK	272
Wild Nights 2014 April 24–28, 2014	…in Sherwood Forest	Robbers Cave State Park, Wilburton, OK	302
Wild Nights 2015 April 23–28, 2015	Gears Through Time	Robbers Cave State Park, Wilburton, OK	231

Events

Wild Nights 2009: The original venue was Lake of the Ozarks State Park, MO, but this was denied by the Missouri Department of State Parks; so MESA moved the event to a similar state park in Oklahoma. Events included swimming, volleyball, basketball, and similar outdoor games, plus furry games such as Predator & Prey and a furry variety show. Attendees stayed in cabins that held 12 to 32 people in a single big room. The posters and badges of furry conventions were featured. There were eight acts in the variety show. There was no charity; an $800 surplus was put toward the next year's expenses.

Guests of Honor: Baka Sukonku (furry artist)
Chairmen or Organizers: MESA President: Joel Ricketts (Heros the Noisy Panther)

Wild Nights 2010:
[Did Wild Nights 2010 differ at all from 2009?]
Guests of Honor: Chris the Hybrid (furry artist, fursuiter), Tzup (fursuiter)
Charity: Safari's Sanctuary
Chairmen or Organizers: MESA President: Joel Ricketts (Heros the Noisy Panther)

Wild Nights 2011: USO Special Guests (Entertainment Guests) were Max DeGroot and Kwaz the Drumming Raccoon.
Guests of Honor: PacerFox, Eris Valgen (fursuit performers)
Charity: Safari's Sanctuary
Chairmen or Organizers: MESA President: Travis

Wild Nights 2012: The theme was originally "Furry Fallout." Rhubarb the Bear's musical play, "Fosgate: Ferret Loan Officer," was premiered. The event also showed SonicBlu's independent puppet films, and had a firearms marksmanship event, a variety show, and a campfire.
Guests of Honor: Brett Blumfield (SonicBlu Darkfold, puppeteer/filmmaker), Ned Wilkinson (Rhubarb the Bear, furry playwright/composer), Luthien Nightwolf (furry artist), Chad Laubach (WildWolf, fursuit maker)
Charity: Safari's Sanctuary
Chairmen or Organizers: MESA President: Travis

Wild Nights 2013: Events included a charity poker tournament. Jeff Goode's ten-person play "Fursona Non Grata" was performed to a standing ovation.

Guests of Honor: Artist G-o-H Andrea Radeck (Firefeathers), Musician G-o-H Buck Riley (Husky In Denial), Fursuiter G-o-H Buddy (a.k.a. JD Puppy)
Charity: Safari's Sanctuary ($2,742)
Chairmen or Organizers: MESA President: Joel Ricketts (Heros the Noisy Panther)

Wild Nights 2014: Margaret Carspecken drew the Wild Nights in Sherwood Forest logo.
Guests of Honor: Lucas Raymond (Potoroo, chairman of Camp Feral!, musician), OzFoxes (Robert & Margaret Carspecken, furry cartoonists), Bob Burns (Oki Doki Coyote, fursuit performer)
Charity: Safari's Sanctuary
Chairmen or Organizers: MESA President: Joel Ricketts (Heros the Noisy Panther)

Wild Nights 2015:
Guests of Honor: Artist G-o-H SpringDragon, Musician G-o-H Alexander James Adams
Charity: Safari's Sanctuary
Chairmen or Organizers: MESA President: Joel Ricketts (Heros the Noisy Panther)

WUFF

WUFF (Wild Ukrainian Furry Fun) began in May 2006 as a nameless furmeet gathering in Kiev (or Kyïv, for those who prefer the Ukrainian spelling—Kiev is Russian), Ukraine for a Spring picnic. May 9th is also a Victory Day holiday in Ukraine, Russia, and Belarus, celebrating the surrender of Nazi Germany in World War II. The 2006 and 2007 attendances were only 11 and 13. In 2008 it was upgraded into UkrMiniFurka, a furmeet/convention under a committee headed by Basil Lion, with a registration of 62. UkrMiniFurka for the first three or four years spread throughout Kiev and the neighboring forest and fields, with those from out of town staying as Kiev furs' houseguests or in a selected hostel. Gradually the hostel became more prominent with events scheduled there. The WUFF name was adopted in 2012. Today WUFF is a traditional hotel convention. WUFF does not have a theme, but it does have since 2011 an official animal and color each year, featured on the attendee badge and T-shirt. There are photographs and videos of fursuiters cavorting along the banks of the Dnieper River. The charity, the Kiev Society for Protection of Animals, receives volunteer help from the WUFF organizers throughout the year.

Name & Date	*Location*	*Attendance*
UkrMiniFurka 2008 May 9–11, 2008	None	62
UkrMiniFurka 2009 May 9–11, 2009	International Tatarka, Kiev (hostel)	67
UkrMiniFurka 2010 May 8–10, 2010	International Tatarka, Kiev (hostel)	95
UkrMiniFurka 2011 May 7–9, 2011	Lvivska Bramah, Kiev (hostel)	150
WUFF 2012 April 28–May 2, 2012	Prolisok, Kiev (youth hostel)	164
WUFF 2013 May 9–12, 2013	Hotel Sofiyevsky Posad, Kiev	219
WUFF 2014 May 7–11, 2014	Hotel Sofiyevsky Posad, Kiev	260
WUFF 2015 May 6–10, 2015	Hotel Gintama-Briz, Kiev	121

Events

UkrMiniFurka 2008: There was no hotel since all events were outdoors throughout Kiev.
Chairmen or Organizers: Basil Karpov (Basil Lion), Belo4ka, Jrik, Skar, Xopek

UkrMiniFurka 2009: Besides hanging out in Kiev, UkrMikiFurka 2009 included a visit to the Kiev zoo. A trip to Chernobyl was planned but not held due to not enough interest.
Chairmen or Organizers: Basil Karpov (Basil Lion), Belo4ka, Jrik, Skar, Xopek

UkrMiniFurka 2010: There was a Friday trip to Kamenetz-Podolsk, a Saturday morning visit to the Kiev zoo and an afternoon picnic in the woods, Sunday was free. A controversial open vote for a T-shirt was held. Many voters were not preregistered convention members. Everyone from Russia, whether a member or not, voted for a Russian artist. A second vote was held of preregistered WUFF members only, and Belo4ka (a Ukranian artist) won.
Chairmen or Organizers: Basil Karpov (Basil Lion), Belo4ka, Jrik

UkrMiniFurka 2011: UkrMiniFurka 2011 offered a choice between staying with friends or at the Bramah hostel. The vote for the official T-shirt was held among the organizers only before the convention; Belo4ka won. Registrants got a marsh-colored ("dark grey with a touch of green") T-shirt and a white badge featuring that year's animal, the puma. There was a trip to the Aeroclub Aeroprakt, 51 km. from Kiev, where attendees could fly in a sports plane.
Chairmen or Organizers: Basil Karpov (Basil Lion)

WUFF 2012: Events included the Saturday opening party in the hotel bar; a Sunday fursuit walk in the city center, opening of art exhibit, evening disco, quiz; a Monday dealers' room, table games, fur workshop, fursuit photo session, fursuit games, "pump it up" contest, and evening Lounge Party in the hotel barbar; and Tuesday BBQ in the forest, and the art exhibition close & auction. Besides this there were classes in drawing, photography, and board games in the hotel, or active games like Frisbee tossing, shooting, tightrope waking, and Twister in the woods. The T-shirt voted upon by the committee was by Belo4ka; attendees received a yellow badge and an orange T-shirt featuring a fox. There was the first exhibit of furry art in a Kiev art gallery, with sales donated to the convention's charity. The original planned hostel, Borysfen, was closed for repairs and WUFF 2012 had to reschedule to the Prolisok hostel. Many attendees complained, "This T-shirt art is total shit. Last year's was better."
Charity: Kiev Society for the Protection of Animals' Gostomel shelter for homeless animals
Chairmen or Organizers: Basil Karpov (Basil Lion), Belo4ka, Perihelion

WUFF 2013: The schedule was: the 9th hotel check in, WUFF opening, pump it up contest, an evening lounge party in the hotel bar; the 10th setup of the dealers den and artists' lounge, table and fursuit games, a fursuit photo-shoot, classes in creating furry games and fursuit making, a pump it up contest, and evening furry disco; the 11th a morning fursuit walk in the city center, and an afternoon forest BBQ; the 12th checkout. The T-shirt artist chosen was Belo4ka; attendees received a green badge and T-shirt featuring a panda. Many attendees complained, "This T-shirt art is total shit, while last year's was super cool!"
Charity: Kiev Society for the Protection of Animals' Gostomel shelter for homeless animals
Chairmen or Organizers: Basil Karpov (Basil Lion)

WUFF 2014: Events were similar, but there was no furwalk in the city center, and the BBQ was replaced by a picnic. WUFF 2014 was announced as about "Kiev-Maidan: Myths and Reality"; this is sometimes reported incorrectly as an official theme. Since the choice of the T-shirt artist was always dramatically criticized, the 2014 artist was not revealed (it was Belo4ka). Attendees received a purple badge and T-shirt featuring a raccoon. There was grumbling about "the super-secret T-shirt artist," but most attendees did not complain.

WUFF 2014 banner. Art by Belo4ka. Used with permission.

Charity: Kiev Society for the Protection of Animals' Gostomel shelter for homeless animals
Chairmen or Organizers: Basil Karpov (Basil Lion)

WUFF 2015: Events included fursuit and board games, an art competition and artists' lounge, a fursuit walk and photo shoot, dances including a disco dance, and a VIP party to which all attendees were invited. Outdoor events included a barbecue picnic on the bank of a lake in the nearby woods, a nightly campfire gathering, and the closing ceremony also at a picnic. All indoor events were carried on the hotel TV's Channel 1. Attendees received a red badge and T-shirt featuring a maned wolf. There were no complaints about the secret T-shirt artist (Belo4ka again). Part of the Art Show, Dealers' Den, and auction, either items or sales, plus post-convention surplus of funds were donated to the charity.

Charity: Kiev Society for the Protection of Animals' Gostomel shelter for homeless animals (12,000 hryvnia [about U.S.$520])

Chairmen or Organizers: Basil Karpov (Basil Lion)

Zampacon

Zampacon, "La Prima Convention Furry Italiana," means "Pawcon." Despite its small size, it has been enthusiastically supported by all Italian furs. The same art is used for the poster, conbook cover, and T-shirt each year. The badge artist is always Aledon Rex.

Name & Date	Theme	Location	Attendance
Zampacon '12 December 29, 2012–January 1, 2013	none	Due Torri youth hostel, near Bologna	31
Zampacon '13 September 4–8, 2013	At the Beach	Maria Gabriella Hotel, Rimini	41
Zampacon '14 September 3–7, 2014	Murrs Attacks!	Hotel Morri Oceania, Bellaria-Igea Marina	54
Zampacon '15 September 2–6, 2015	Fur Ro Dah!	Hotel Morri Oceania, Bellaria-Igea Marina	60

Events

Zampacon '12: The first Zampacon was limited to 34 registrants; the limit of the hostel. 4 cancelled at the last moment, and only one new fur registered. Games were held in the lobby in the morning, and panels in the evening. Movies were shown on two nights, and there was a New Year's celebration with a mini-disco, in the lobby, games on the upper floor, a midnight fireworks show, and a toast. The poster artist was Alpha0; there was no conbook or T-shirt.

Chairmen or Organizers: Ajani, Rov, Valion

Zampacon '13: Zampacon '13 moved to the Adriatic coast in Summer, and increased from four to five days. The larger hotel permitted the removal of the attendance limit. The convention was unofficially beach-themed, with furry beach activities. Zampacon '13 added a Dealers' Den, a 20-page conbook, and a T-shirt. The poster, conbook cover, and T-shirt artist was Aledon Rex.

Chairmen or Organizers: Ajani, Rov, Valion, Maxsteel

Zampacon '14: Zampacon '14 had a new hotel but was still on the Adriatic beaches; but beach activities were cancelled due to bad weather. The 54 attendees included some from Greece, Slovenia, and the U.S. The "Murrs Attacks!" theme was a reference to the *Mars Attacks!* movie, which was shown (in English, subtitled in Italian). Six attendees joined only for the fursuit activities, including an unofficial evening Fursuit Parade through the city streets. Convention upgrades included the adoption of two cartoon mascots, an anthro white Maremma sheepdog named Dante and a lynx named Beatrice, both dressed in Italian red-white-green, designed by Aledon Rex; a glow-in-the-dark waistband, a LAN tourney, a video game tournament, a larger conbook; more con-owned equipment; and the translation of key program items into English. There were volunteers for security, the dealers' den, and spotting. The poster, conbook cover, and T-shirt artist was Black Lion. As an April fool's joke, the hotel announced that the convention had added a guest of *honor:* a prominent Italian politician (who was revealed at the last minute as also a notorious porn star).

Chairmen or Organizers: Ajani, Rov, Valion, Aledon Rex

Zampacon '15: "Fur Ro Dah!" was a reference to the *Skyrim* fantasy RPG game. There was a pre-convention contest for writers to submit articles for the conbook. Beach games were again possible due to fair weather. Full English translations were provided of all website and forum text to enable English speakers to join more easily. The first fursuit street parade was held, with a city permit; it was mentioned positively in two newspapers. There was a fursuit photoshoot. Zampacon '15 featured a Zampacon Mystic Quest, a convention-long treasure hunt with all attendees assigned to one of six teams, that included exploring the whole city. The poster, conbook cover, and T-shirt artist was Alpha0, and there was a Zampacon color printed lanyard. As an April Fool's joke, it was announced that the theme was being changed to My Little Zampacon to accommodate a large number of German *MLP:FIM* fans who had just joined.

Chairmen or Organizers: Ajani, Rov, Valion, Aledon Rex, Scale

ZodiaCon

ZodiaCon is the Czech Republic's second furry convention. It is themed around the Zodiac, with each convention having an anthropomorphized animal mascot, originally representing that zodiac sign.

Name & Date	Theme	Location	Attendance
ZodiaCon 2011 May 20–22, 2011	The Dawn of Time	Tanvald, Czech Republic	60

Name & Date	Theme	Location	Attendance
ZodiaCon 2012 May 5–8, 2012	The Sky Is Falling	ŠARZ Vršov, Vršov near Pardubice, Czech Republic	67
ZodiaCon 2013 May 13–16, 2013	?	ŠARZ Vršov, Vršov near Pardubice, Czech Republic	74
ZodiaCon 2014 May 30–June 2, 2014	The Wild West	ŠARZ Vršov, Vršov near Pardubice, Czech Republic	95
ZodiaCon 2015 May 29–June 1, 2015	The Mayan Expedition	Vršovská Brána hotel, Horní Bradlo, Pardubice, Czech Republic	91

Events

ZodiaCon 2011: The attendees came from the Czech Republic, Slovakia, Poland, Germany, and Belgium. The mascot was Lambert the ram (for Aries). The first event, a Friday evening BBQ, has become traditional. Changer the Elder made both a poster and a T-shirt.
Guests of Honor: None
Charity: Český svaz ochránců přírody (Czech Union for Nature Conservation)
Chairmen or Organizers: Michal Valášek (Altair)

ZodiaCon 2012: The theme was of a post-catastrophe dystopian society. The mascot was Vartan the bull (for Taurus). Several thousand Kč were raised for charity. The T-shirt was by Changer the Elder.
Guests of Honor: AlectorFencer
Charity: Český svaz ochránců přírody (Czech Union for Nature Conservation)
Chairmen or Organizers: Michal Valášek (Altair)

ZodiaCon 2013: The mascot was Castor and Pollux, the zebra twins (for Gemini). Mikairu drew both a poster and the T-shirt.
Guests of Honor: None
Charity: Český svaz ochránců přírody (Czech Union for Nature Conservation)
Chairmen or Organizers: Michal Valášek (Altair)

ZodiaCon 2014: The mascot was Jack O'Hare, a rabbit "typical Wild West settler" (supposedly for Cancer. The 2011 logo shows all 12 animal mascots with several non-traditional characters including the anthro rabbit, the zebra twins, an eagle, a unicorn, and a shark). The T-shirt was by Mikairu.
Guests of Honor: Pan Hesekiel Shiroi (furry artist/puppeteer)
Charity: Český svaz ochránců přírody (Czech Union for Nature Conservation)
Chairmen or Organizers: Michal Valášek (Altair)

ZodiaCon 2015: The Mayan theme was emphasized in "South America, Indian temples, lots of gold, human sacrifices…" The 91 attendees were identified by their fursonas. The Vršovská Brána hotel ("Gateway to Vršov") was the same as the ŠARZ Vršov with a new name. The T-shirt was by Motomo Wahots and could be pre-ordered. The 2015 showed the animal mascot as a female cougar, but she was not named.
Guests of Honor: Keenora Fluffball (fursuit performer)
Charity: Český svaz ochránců přírody (Czech Union for Nature Conservation)
Chairmen or Organizers: Michal Valášek (Altair)

ZonieCon

The short-lived ZonieCon was organized by Scott Malcomson and a group of furry fans in Tucson, Arizona. It was named after its mascot, Arizona fan/cartoonist Michael-Scot McMurry's Zonie the

Coyote character. ZonieCon became known for its live gun target practices, its disorganization, and its bad luck, but despite this, it had a reputation of being informal fun. ZonieCon did not have a theme, charity or fursuits. There were no further furry conventions in Arizona until the annual Arizona Fur Con in Phoenix was started in 2013, although Malcolmson made a failed attempt to revive ZonieCon in 2011 with a Camaradie theme.

Name & Date	Location	Attendance
ZonieCon 1998 May 1–3, 1998	Francisco Grande Hotel and Golf Resort, Casa Grande, AZ	42
ZonieCon 1999 October 29–November 1, 1999	Best Western Executive Inn, Tucson, AZ	47
ZonieCon 2000 Not held		
ZonieCon 2001 October 19–21, 2001	Best Western Executive Inn, Tucson, AZ	57

Events

ZonieCon 1998: Machine-gun shoots were an advertised and highlighted event at each of the ZonieCons. Mitchell Beiro produced ZonieCon's flyers and publications, and a foamcore display. The first venue was the Francisco Grande Hotel and Golf Resort in Tucson's suburb of Casa Grande; the site of previous popular Coppercon s-f conventions. It turned out to be a "guerilla con." Attendees arrived to find six other conventions under way in the hotel, and none of the guaranteed facilities available. When Malcomson produced the signed contract with the hotel, the manager said, "So sue us!" The hotel did allow the fans to meet in the hotel, and grudgingly supplied some materials. The convention had planned model rocket flights on the hotel's open lawns. When the ZonieCon began, those lawns were full of tractors for a tractor company's tilling demonstrations. As soon as the tractors were gone, the rocket flights were held immediately. The ZonieCon took over the hotel's "Eagle's Nest" penthouse for its promised con suite. There were numerous no-shows. Two promised Society of Creative Anachronism groups failed to show up, leaving a few individual SCAers who did come feeling lonely. A half-dozen guests-of-honor declined or failed to reply at all, until Steve Addelsee accepted at the last minute. Despite the problems, or because of them, the attendees had a good time in a "us against the world" spirit. Events included a "meat meet" barbecue with free hamburgers and ribs, and a failed experiment to make root beer. The machine-gun shoot reportedly had some memorable conversations between two attendees and the Grand Matriarch of the Greater Arizona Women's Christian Organization (the Church Ladies). The most common exchange: "Hey, anybody got more 9 mm parabellum?" After the convention, Malcolmson did sue the hotel in small claims court. He lost.

Guests of Honor: Steve Addelsee (Furry artist)
Chairmen or Organizers: Scott Malcolmson

ZonieCon 1999: A scaled-back rocket shoot was held in a nearby park; there was a machine gun shoot at a local "wildcat range"; and "Art Spelunking" with lanterns and paint in an abandoned storm drain. A better Art Show was held with proper hanging materials. The convention was considered a success as a relaxed, sociable event.

Guests of Honor: Chuck Manley (rocket expert)
Chairmen or Organizers: Scott Malcolmson

ZonieCon 2000: There was no ZonieCon 2000. The Tucson convention was dependent on Scott Malcolmson's personal finances, and in 2000 he could not afford it.

ZonieCon 2001: The convention was dedicated to the memory of Michael-Scot McMurry, the creator of the convention's mascot, Zonie the Coyote, who had died of cancer in April. ZonieCon 2001 was billed as "The Con That Would Not Die," since it was returning after a one-year hiatus. It also suffered from a hotel that did not know that it was supposed to have a convention, due to the staffer who had signed the contract having left without telling anyone. Fortunately, that hotel did its best to honor the contract. The main problem was that the hotel had chosen that weekend of "no business" to remodel all the rooms, and the workmen had already started tearing them up. The Best Western manager got two nearby hotels to accept the conventioneers as "overflow" guests, and cleaned up one of its own function rooms for ZonieCon. Since the rooms were going to be painted anyway, the fans were allowed to graffiti all over them with markers. That was the last ZonieCon, though. Most of the attendees had been personal friends of the likeable and outgoing McMurry, and his lingering, painful death set a pall over the convention. Mostly, it was the result of Scott Malcolmson's moving from Tucson to Phoenix. He gave other Tucson fans his permission to continue the convention, but none cared to do so; especially since Malcolmson had personally lost $600 on the last ZonieCon.

Guests of Honor: Anthony M. Waters (s-f artist)
Chairmen or Organizers: Scott Malcolmson

Appendix: Furry Convention Attendance Milestones

6,000 attendees
Anthrocon 2015 1st

5,000 attendees
Anthrocon 2012 1st
Midwest FurFest 2015 2nd

4,000 attendees
Anthrocon 2010 1st
Midwest FurFest 2014 2nd

3,000 attendees
Anthrocon 2008 1st
Further Confusion 2012 2nd
Midwest FurFest 2012 3rd
Furry Weekend Atlanta 2015 4th

2,000 attendees
Anthrocon 2004 1st
Further Confusion 2007 2nd
Midwest FurFest 2009 3rd
Furry Weekend Atlanta 2013 4th
RainFurrest 2013 5th
EuroFurence 20 6th
Furry Fiesta 2015 7th
Biggest Little Fur Con 2015 8th

1,000 attendees
ConFurence 9 (1998) 1st
Anthrocon 2000 2nd
Further Confusion 2001 3rd
Midwest FurFest 2005 4th
Furry Weekend Atlanta 2009 5th
RainFurrest 2010 6th
FurFright 2010 7th
Furry Fiesta 2011 8th
Furry Connection North 2011 9th
EuroFurence 17 10th
CaliFur 9 11th
Rocky Mountain Fur Con 2013 12th
Biggest Little Fur Con 2014 13th
ConFuzzled 2014 14th
Megaplex XIII 15th
Furpocalypse 2014 16th
Furnal Equinox 2015 17th
Motor City Fur Con 2015 18th

Index

Real names are inverted; fursona pseudonyms are uninverted.

AAE, Inc. *see* Anthropomorphic Arts and Education, Inc.
Aalborg, Denmark 128
Aalto, Alflor 36, 116
Abando 7, 13–15, 42, 145
Abayomi (mascot) 51
Abenteuerzentrum Grunewald e.v. 28
Accipiter 78
Achseten holiday house 52, 54
ActFur on Air 95, 169
Adams, Alexander James 80, 81, 133, 187, 214
Adams, Richard 188
Adam's Mark Hotel 18, 20, 21, 22, 65
Adcox, Thom 84
Addelsee, Steve 219
Addison, Texas 114
Adelboden, Switzerland 52, 54
Adriatic Sea 217
Aelos (mascot) 41
Aeroclub Aeroprakt 215
Aerun Wolfsong 124
Aethan *see* French, Andrew
Aetobatus *see* Sawyer, Michael
The Age 169
Agent Elrond 16
Agheptonygm 94
A.I. 83
Airplane! 101
Airporter Garden Hotel 56, 59
Ajani 217
Akela Taka 50
Akeyla 52, 54, 165, 166
AkiFox 198, 199
Akins, Gary 19
Akira Shima 209, 210
Akonite 208
Aksakovo, Russia 202
ALAA *see* Anthropomorphic Literature and Arts Association (ALAA)
ALAA Hall of Fame 175, 176, 188
Alabama 192
Åland Islands 181
Alassa 51
Albany, New York 18, 66
Albany Anthrocon *see* Anthrocon
Al Bear 102
Albee, Amadhia 37, 136
Albee, Jessica Maia 120

Albee, Timothy 22, 79, 169, 189
Albers, Jon 162
Alberta 96
Albinotopaz 28
AlectorFencer 26, 67, 70, 75, 142, 165, 166, 218
Aledon Rex C2, 216, 217
Alex King 207
Alexander 103
Alexander, Heather 79, 132, 133
Alexandrova, Darya 207
Algonquin Provincial Park 38, 39
Algonquinos 44
Alice's Adventures in Wonderland 44
Alkali Bismuth 90, 91, 146
All Fur Fun 15–16, 70, 73, 186
AllFur Radio 23
Almedijar, Spain 145
The Aloft Hotel 135
Aloha 188
AlohaWolf *see* Johnson, Robert K., Jr.
Aloyen Youngblood *see* Wilbur, Roger
Alpha K-9 37
Alpha_Ki *see* Baumwolf, Karoline
Alpha0 217
Alps 52, 141, 142
Altair *see* Valášek, Michal
Alter-Ego 3
Altia 149
Amadhia 27
Amber Does Dallas 115
Amberley Suites Hotel 195
American Red Cross 161
AmoXcalli 4
Amsterdam, the Netherlands 115
Anaheim, California 56
Anakaine 103
Anatoliba 142, 166
Anbessa 164
Anderson, Karen 131, 132
Anderson, Poul 131
Andrews, Nancy 208
Ångström 14
Aniki Geelong 14
Animal Adoption Foundation (AAF) 177

Animal Aid PDX 106
Animal Farm 8, 175
Animal Friends 23, 209
Animal Haven 98
Animal Management in Rural and Remote Indigenous Communities (AMRRIC) 136
Animal Rescue Kansai (ARK) 37
Animal Rescue League's Wildlife Rehabilitation Center 24
Animal Rescue Team TAIWAN 148
Animal Welfare League of Queensland 96
Animals for Awareness 172, 173
The Animals' Island 180
Animalympics 37, 57
Animaniacs 63, 71
Animation Academy 35
Animation World Network 3
Anime Festival Asia (ALA) 125
"Anime Gets Furry!" 59
Anime Kemono 150
Anime Weekend Atlanta 120
ANIMEast 66
AnimeCat 194
Anklebones 41, 42
Ann Arbor, Michigan 112
Antarctic Press 63
Antheria 16
Anthrax 95, 104, 169
AnhroAsia 125
Anthrocon C1, 1, 5, 10, 11, 18–26, 62, 66, 82, 116, 118, 167, 174, 221
Anthrocon, Inc. 22, 23, 24, 25
Anthrofest 25–26
Anthro International Entertainment 16
Anthro New England (ANE) 16–18
Anthro New England, Inc. 16
AnthrOhio *see* Morphicon
Anthrolations 10
Anthropod 42
Anthropolis 16
Anthropomorphic Arts and Education, Inc. 130, 131, 132, 133, 134
Anthropomorphic Events of Ontario (AEO) 109
Anthropomorphic Literature and Arts Association (ALAA) 4, 11, 65

Index

Anthropomorphic Research Project *see* International Anthropomorphic Research Project (IARP)
Anyare 43
Aoino Broome 148
Aphinity 208
Apollo Husky 30
Apoxon 208
Arashi 141
Arbat, Moscow 200
Arc 182
Archie Comics 21
The Architect of Sleep 60
ArcticPete *see* Smith, Pete
ARFI (Art Russian Furry Initiative) 202
AR-15 *see* Colt AR-15 rifle
Arius 42, 43
Arizona 27, 218
Arizona Fur Con C1, 27–28, 119
Arizona Fur Convention LLC 27
Arlington Heights, Illinois 170
Armour, Iain 82, 84, 85, 96, 116, 158, 203, 204, 208
Armstrong, Gene 106, 186, 187, 188
Arnold 29
Aronen, Karri 60
The Arrow on Swanston Hotel 67, 167
Arrowroot 110
"The Art of Furry Fandom" 37
ARTE (Association Relative à la Télévision Européenne) 72
Asami, Yuko 148
Aschersleben, Germany 75
Ash *see* Risher, Eric
Ashanti *see* Verbeeten, Angelique
Ashtoreth *see* Haas, William
ASPCA of Louisiana 99
Astérix 81
Astolpho 188
Atalon the Deer *see* Kalkbrenner, Markus
Atamanov, Sergei 200, 215
Atlanta, Georgia 120, 121
Atlanta Pride Parade and Party 122
Atrium Hotel 33, 90
Atrium Marquis (mascot) 60
Atrium Marquis Hotel 56, 59
Atso Fox *see* Jones, Braden
Auchter, Karsten 68, 79, 114, 116, 133, 157, 164, 169
Auckland, New Zealand 92, 94
Aureth *see* Doolittle, Jim
Auri 104
AussieHusky 103, 104
Austin, Alicia 59
Austin, Texas 205
Australia 5, 10, 57, 67, 134, 166, 167, 190
Australia on Collins Restaurant 167
Australia Zoo Wildlife Warriors 96
Australian Fandom Conventions 4, 135
Australian Furry Association (AUSFA) 167
Avalon 142
Avantel Club Istra 200, 203
AvantGarden Gallery 37

"Avatar" 71
Avila, Ruben 60, 65
Avner, Dennis 187
awards 19, 20, 26, 60, 63
AzraFox 68
Azshara kletete 51
Azyl Pod Psim Aniołem 138

Babs Bunny 173, 177, 194
Back Alley McBeals 83
Bad Dog Books 42, 115
badge 10
The Badger Trust 68, 69
Bailey Bat 111
Baka Sukonku 213
Baker, Anna 85, 163
Baker, Mike 134
Bakus 141
Balaa 35
Balistreri, Ben 24
Baltimore, Maryland 91
Balto *see* Peña, Albert C.
Bambioid 57
bandana 196, 197, 198
B& From RivFur 192
Bandthro 116
Bane Ranaura 104
Bangkok, Thailand 7, 125
Barceló Hinckley Island Hotel 68
Barclay, Dave 133
Bard, Michael 110
Barks, Carl 188
Barnaby 118, 119
Barnes, Robert 190
Barnes & Noble 108
Baron of Blackwhite Castle 80
Barrett, John 41, 55, 83, 124, 178, 179
Barry R. Kirshner Wildlife Foundation 131, 132
Bartels, Stephan 78, 79
Bartlett, Chris 133, 134
Bartošova peč 48, 50
Bartrop, Richard 40
Baselbieter Chinderhus 141
Basil Lion *see* Karpov, Basil
Bates, Andrew 67
Battle Ground, Indiana 66
Baumwolf, Karoline 54, 79, 82, 165
Bavaria 137
Bay Area Bears/Good Bears of the World 132
Bay Area Furries 185
BayCon 9
Bayview Hotel Singapore 125
BC Siberian Husky Club 208
bcbreakaway 97
Beagle, Peter S. 24, 25, 61, 63, 81
Beast 201
Beastcub 37
Beatrice (mascot) C2, 217
Beaulieu, Trace 155
The Beaver County Humane Society 210
Becky A. 163
Bee Movie 167
Beedon, Jeff 146, 172, 173, 183
Beekse Bergen safari park 77
Beetlecat *see* Larsson, Deanna

Beetlejuice/Mac Dragon 100
Beiro, Mitchell 10, 59, 63, 71, 118, 219
Belic Bear 97, 98, 99, 100, 101, 102, 211
Bell, Clare 134
Bellaria-Igea Marina, Italy 216
Belo4ka 215, 216
Ben Raven 169
Berg Polarbear *see* Cardinale, Vincent
Bergey, Michael 73
BerliCon 28–30
The BerliCon Orga 29, 30
Berlin, Germany 10, 28, 75, 76, 77, 82, 206
Bern, Switzerland 52
Bernardyn Foundation for Polish lynx 138
Bernese Oberland, Switzerland 141
Beshon 69
Best Friends Animal Society 119
Best Friends—Haiti Fund 134
Best in Show: 15 Years of Outstanding Furry Fiction 4
Best Western Executive Inn (I) 70, 72
Best Western Executive Inn (II) 219
Best Western Executive Plaza 112
Best Western Hospitality Inn 32
Best Western Orlando East Inn & Suites 108
Best Western Sunrise Hotel 16
Best Western Victoria Park Suites Hotel 31
Betsy Beaver *see* Nichols, Betsy
BIABIA 52, 53
Biesmeyer, Deanna 28, 37, 89
Big Al's "Wild Arrows" shooting gallery 137
BigBlueFox *see* Auchter, Karsten
Biggest Little Fur Con 30–31, 119, 221
Bijoux DeFoxxe 105
Bilyk, Dennis 96, 97
Bingaman, Kory 116
Bingen, Germany 77
Bingo Dingo 191
Birdsell, James 70, 71, 72
Birmingham, England 68
Birmingham Hilton Metropole 68, 69
Birty 143
Bitter Lake 81, 181
Black Bison Saloon 137
Black Forest, Germany 145
Black Lion *see* Prokhorov, Dmitry
Black Teagan *see* Gavet, Teagan
Black Wolf 112, 201, 202, 203, 204
Blackfrost 162
Blackkrystal 204
Bladon, Lindsey 33
Blair, Paul 62
Blajn 138
Blake 201
Blanchard Park 107
Blanco, Angel Manuel 115
BLFC Staff 3
BLFCorp 30

Index

Blindsight 110, 111, 211
Bliss, David 63, 64
Blitz 94
Blitz Victor Foxtrot 48
Blitz Wolfang 157
Bloodhound Omega *see* Wrzosek, Maja
BlooFox *see* McKim, Ami
Bloom, Bard 178
Bloom, Rhys 178
Bloom, Victoria Borah 178
Bloomington, Minnesota 117
Blotch C5, 43, 67, 80, 81, 83, 116, 134, 167, 168, 169, 183, 196, 197
Blu the Dragon 136
Bluari 51
Blue Ash, Ohio 90
Blue Fox Fursuits 11
The Blue Hyena *see* Rudd, Alexis
Blue_Panther vi, 52, 54, 81, 165
BlueOtter 183, 184
Blumfield, Brett 213
Bluth, Toby 132
Blythe 210
Bob Drake's Cabinet of Curiosities 100
Bob Hope Airport 63
Bobcat *see* Schumacher, Sven
Bodstedt, Germany 75, 77
Bohemia 49, 79
Bohemia-Moravia 48, 49, 50, 51
Boise, Idaho 102
Boise Hotel and Conference Center 102
Boise Weekly 102
Bologna, Italy 216
Bolton, Colin 39
Bolton, Phil 71
Bonk 121
Booshie 204, 205
Boriss, Lis 114, 121
Bos'n C. Otter *see* Bartlett, Chris
Boston, Massachusetts 8, 152
Boston Furries Meetup Group 153
Boston Logan Hilton Hotel 152
Botanical Gardens 103
Bound By Fire 89
Bowman, Jeff 135
Box Hill Darkzone 167
Boyce Park Four Seasons Activity Center 209
Boyett, Steven R. 60
Boyle, Bob 24
Brady, Tom 172, 174
Branson, Missouri 89
Branton, Daniel 16
Branwyn *see* Desveaux, Dan
Braun, Dave 160
Bravo 146
Brazil 5, 10
Brementown Musicians 71
Brendan Roo 209
Breshears, Gene 173
Březová nad Svitavou, Czech Republic 48
Brighton 119
Brighton, England 9
Brill, Mark 187, 194
Brin, David 132

Brisbane, Queensland 94, 96, 190, 191
Brisbane River 190, 191
Bristow, Lindsey 175
Britannia Country House Hotel 68
BritFurs 68, 190
British Columbia 100, 207, 208
The British National Fox Welfare Society 80
Brno, Czech Republic 49
Brody Catsmouth 192, 193, 194, 195
Brok the Badger (mascot) 68, 69
Broken Arrow, Oklahoma 212
Brometheus Bear (mascot) 30, 31
Bronies of NSW 104
Brony 116
Brook, Jennifer 32
Brookfield, Wisconsin 90
Brookfield Outdoor Education Centre 93, 94
Brother Bear 108
Brown, Mark 169
Brown, Sherwyn 183
Brown Wolf 37
Brownlow-Pike, Warrick 82, 135
Bruton, Heather 21, 32, 71, 110, 116, 197
Bucker Fuskyote 185
Bucktown Tiger Live! 16, 89, 113, 146, 157, 158, 162, 178, 184, 195
Bucky Boy 182
Buddy *see* JDPuppy
Bueckert, Chelsey 208
Bugs Bunny 188
Bühl-Neusatzeck, Germany 144, 145
BumB sports and cultural hotel 205
Bumblebee *see* Bloom, Victoria Borah
Burgess, Phillip 131, 133, 134
Burnaby, British Columbia 207
Burns, Bob 89, 214
Burt, Matt 121
BushyCat *see* Frey, Rebecca Ann
Butler, Tracy 113
Butterscotch Vixen *see* Foxx, Susan
Byers, Tiffany 162

C-ACE 26, 31–32, 55, 56, 210
Cabungcai, John Razel M. C4, 186
Caesar, Julius 81
Café Retro 167
Cairyn *see* Klemp, Ronald W.
CajunFox Windrunner 55, 56
Cal-Furr 32–33
Calamity Coyote *see* McLaughlin, Loren
Calgary, Alberta 32
Calgary Furry Convention 33
California 16, 129, 185
California Wolf Center 37
CaliFur 16, 33–37, 116, 221
CaliFur Diego 38
CaliFur.11 150
CaliFur Train 35
Callahan, Bonnie 36
Caltroplay 55
CamashRed 138
Cambridge, Massachusetts 16
Camion, Jeffrey 188

Camp Algonquin 43
Camp Arowhon 38, 39, 40, 43
Camp Bloomington West 46
Camp Feral! C5, 7, 11, 13, 38–44, 109, 110, 145, 181, 182
Camp Rangi Woods 93
Campbell, Krista 27
Campfire Tails 44–45
CampFur 45
Camping, Harold 84
Canaan, Dan 15, 70, 71, 72, 73, 178, 179
Canada 96, 109, 207, 210
Canadian Anthro and Cartooning Expo 31
Canadian Cancer Society 212
Cancer Research U.K. 135
Canine Partners for Life 21
Canis Claxis *see* Wilson, David
Capital City KOA, Kansas 46
Capobianco, Michael 59
Cardinale, Vincent 135
Cardozo, S. "Aloha" 160
CARE (Center for Animal Research and Education) 115, 116
C.A.R.E. (Creating Animal Respect Education) 118, 154, 156, 157, 158
Caribou *see* Palmer, Sara "Caribou"
Carl Fox *see* Meyers, Karl F.
Carla Cougar (mascot) 66
Carnegie Library of Pittsburgh 26
Carnegie Museum of Natural History 209
Carnival 169
Carpenter, John Alden 8
Carroll, Lewis 70
Carspecken, Margaret 61, 78, 89, 172, 194, 214
Carspecken, Robert 89, 172, 194, 214
Cartoon Art Museum 131
Cartoon/Fantasy Organization (C/FO) 3
Cartoon Research 4
Carver, Jeffrey A. 20
Carykaiba 14
Casa Grande, Arizona 219
Casshan 14
Castaway Pet Rescue, Inc. 174
Castellón, Spain 145
Castor and Pollux the zebra twins (mascot) 218
Cat A Do Cat Co-op 27, 28
Cat House on the Kings 36, 134
Cat-Monk Shiro 212
The Cat Survival Trust 70
CATALES 99
Cataroo *see* Cawley, Rachel
Cats Don't Dance 113
Cavanaugh, Jack 58
Cawley, John 35, 57
Cawley, Rachel 35, 61, 62
CBS 11 Dallas 115
Ceilfox 204, 205
Cekuba 208
Centaur *see* Blair, Paul
Centennial Park 103, 104
Central Midwest Furmeet 46
Central Plains Fur Con 46–47

Index

Central Plains Fur Meet 47–48
Cerb 188
ČesFuR 48–51
Česká a Slovenská Federativni Republika 48
Ceška Paradisa 79
Český svaz ochránců přírody (Czech Union for nature Conservation) 218
C/FO see Cartoon/Fantasy Organization (C/FO)
CH-on 52, 54
Chairo see Strom, Lee
Chakat Goldfur see Doove, Bernard
Chama see Hagenfeldt, Thomas
Chambord, France 88
Chan, Justin 37
Chandler-Reaves, Brynne 59
Changa Lion 37
Changer the Elder 75, 81, 218
Chaos 71, 72, 73
Charlebois, Karine 84, 212
Charlotte's Web 188
Chaumes-en-Brie, France 88
Cheese fondue 52, 141, 142
Cheetah see Tegethoff, Sven
Cheetah Conservation Fund 203
Cheney, Kansas 47
Cheney Lake Campground 47
Chernobyl, Ukraine 138, 215
Cherry, Laura 133
Cherryh, C. J. 131, 175
Chibi-Marrow 82, 175
Chicago, Illinois 6, 170–176
Chicago Cubs 23
Chicago House anti-HIV and AIDS 172
Child's Play 127
Chile 7
Chilly see Rosengarten, Erika Leigh
Chimo Hotel 31
Chin, Jimmy 71, 81, 122
China 5, 10
"China Critter Festival" 52
China National Furry Party 51–53
Chip Unicorn see Edwards, Brent
Chippendale, Sydney, New South Wales 103
chlorine gas incident 175
Chris B. Critter 146, 178
Chris Pardus 41
Chris the Hybrid 213
Christmas 189
Chrzonsz, Matthias 165, 166
Chuck, a cat gold-miner 134
Chugo 92
Chun Yan Miu 189
Ciara 116
Cincinnati, Ohio 89
Ciran, France 88
Circles 41
Cirrel see Eggerding, Philip
Clarion Hotel 176
ClarionPAWS 210
Clark, Jared 37, 84, 92, 158, 185, 188
"Clash of Tails" 85
Clawcast 42
Clawshawt 140
Clean Room Contest 135, 175

CleanerWolf 29
Cleveland, Ohio 65, 66
Clinton Lake, Kansas 46
Clockwork Creature Studio 11, 91
The Clouded Leopard Project 188
CloudPouncer 122, 176
Club Stripes 42
Clyde (mascot) 139
Cnipur 27
Coal Silvermuzzle 208
Coates, Jacob 96
Cochran, Connor 24
Cockburn, Alex 101, 211, 212
Cocks, Louise 136
Codex 176
Cohn Jonner 185
Cola see Foster, Brian
CoLD SToRAGE 135
Cole, Foster 126
Cole, John 84, 157, 158
Colifox 69
Collins, Jerry 57
Cologne FurDance 5
Colonial Travel Lodge 108
Colorado 196
Colt AR-15 rifle 160
Columbus, Ohio 106, 176
Columbus-Worthington Holiday Inn 176, 177
"Come Find Me" 82
El Comercio 7
Comfort Inn Pittsburgh North 209
The Comic Book Legal Defense Fund 132, 133
ComicCon 119
Comic-Con International 9, 10, 56, 63, 73, 74
Comic Fiesta 125, 126
Comics Buyer's Guide 3
Comiket 148
Company Technical Document Center 3
"Con crud" 57
Con-Dor 61
Concepcion, Richard 172
Condition 55–56
Confoederatio Helvetica 52
ConFurence 1, 5, 9, 10, 11, 19, 24, 33, 56–65, 66, 73, 74, 75, 77, 81, 129, 221
ConFURence East 11, 61, 62, 65–67
The ConFurence Group 62, 73
ConFurgence 67, 135, 169, 170
ConFuzzled 54, 68–70, 221
ConFuzzled Focus 68
ConFuzzled UK 68
Conifur Northwest 15, 70–73
Connecticut Grand Hotel 98
Conservator's Center, Inc. 121, 122
Con*Tact Caffeine 208
Con-Version 33
Conway, Dr. Samuel C. 16, 19, 20, 21, 22, 23, 24, 25, 26, 27, 28, 40, 41, 42, 59, 67, 73, 79, 80, 81, 82, 90, 106, 113, 114, 121, 146, 154, 156, 157, 160, 167, 169, 172, 173, 174, 186, 189
Cooksey, David 132
Coon Spoon 163

Cooner see Nunnemacher, John
CopperCon 219
Cormack see Dadd, Cameron
Corsi 195
Cosmik 82, 109, 116
cosplay 3
Costa Mesa, California 5, 56
Costume-Con 111
"Cotillion" 60
Cotton, Lisa 212
Cougar Mountain Zoological Park 188, 189
Cougari 92
Coulter, Anita 134
Country Cat & City Kitty Cat/Kitten Rescue 114
Courtyard Ottawa Downtown Hotel 31
Coyote Marty 203
The Coyote Point Museum 130
"Coyote Yodel" 64
Cóyotl Awards 11
Crane, Walter 133
Crashheart Otter 158
Crash's Landing and Big Sid's Sanctuary 143
Cray Drygu 83
Crazy Corgi 91
Crimson Mist 194, 195
Crispin, A. C. 59
Critical Fail 121, 194
Critter Camp Exotic Pet Sanctuary 176
Critter Care Wildlife Society 187
CritterConDiego 10, 38, 63, 73–74
Critterlympics 132, 133
Croc 133, 188
Cromwell, Connecticut 98, 112
CrookedWolf 135
Crowne Plaza Addison 117
Crowne Plaza Cincinnati–Blue Ash 90
Crowne Plaza Cromwell 98, 112
Crowne Plaza Hotel 196
Crowne Plaza Philadelphia West 127
Crowne Plaza Hotel 114, 116
CrssaFox see St. Clair, Carissa 162
Crutcher, Spike 185
Crystal Lake 98
CTWolf 126
Cubby see Zubkov, Sergei
Cummings, Jim 26
The Cunning Little Vixen 79
Cupit, Christine 169, 191
Cupro Hastes 26
Curphy, Melitta 32, 175
Curtis, Carole 62, 118, 160, 177
Curtis, Ian 9
Curtis, Mike 62, 118, 160, 177
"Cute Furry Festival of the Divine Land" 52
Cutepuppy 184
Cybercat see Stone, Stephie
CynWolfe see Smith, Pete
Czech Republic 5, 10, 48, 49, 76, 79, 217
Czech Society for Ornithology 51
Czech Union for Nature Conservation 50

Index

"Czechnology" 79
Czerneda, Julie E. 32

Da-fox 100
Dadd, Cameron 135, 136
The Daily Eurofurence 80
Daily Howl 72, 73
The Daily Howl 98
Dale Fox 46, 47, 48
Dalgon 92
Dallas, Texas 114, 115
Dallas Morning News 115
Dallas Regional Anthropomorphic Meeting Association (D.R.A.M.A.) 114
Damon Husky 118, 119
Dan and Mab's Furry Adventures 36, 84
Dancing in the Moonlight 188
Danji 179
Danjiisthmus 28
Dante (mascot) C2, 217
Danyals, Rourke 153
Dapiko Dapaw 126
Darcus *see* Montjan, Klaus
Dark, Steve 160
Dark Cougar 112
Dark Natasha 64, 65, 67, 80, 111, 169, 196, 197
Darkmoor 183
Darky Gryphon 136
Darling Harbour 103, 104
DarthMeow 93, 94
Dasenbrock, Derrick 172
Daszh 142
Davecko 208
David L. Lawrence Convention Center 18
Davies, Beth 82, 97, 175, 176
Davies, Chuck 42
Davis, Dmitri 27
Davis, Matthew Wayne 15, 16, 20, 22, 24, 27, 28, 35, 42, 67, 73, 80, 81, 82, 83, 106, 112, 113, 120, 121, 133, 146, 154, 156, 157, 167, 169, 172, 173, 174, 183, 187, 189, 190, 194, 197
Dax Wildsong *see* Bowman, Jeff
Day of the Dead 90
Days Inn and Comfort Suites 99
DBruin *see* Beedon, Jeff
Deal Whitley scholarship fund 59, 60, 61, 62
DeCarlo, Dan 21
DeCarlo, Josie 21
DeCarvalho, Fernando 23, 25
Decatur, Alabama 195
de la Guardia, Mitch 31, 35
DeLorean 113
Delta Centre-Ville 211, 212
DeMello, Martin 63
Demicoeur 212
The Den 43
Denby, Robert 98
Denmark 128
Denver, Colorado 119, 196
Denver Adam's Mark Hotel 196
The Denver Zoo 197
DeoLoup 88

Deschutes National Forest 44
Despicable Me 191
Dessau, Germany 75
Destad, Bauske 161
Desveaux, Dan 41, 113
Detroit, Michigan 112, 179
Deuce 43
Devin 44
Devious Bruin *see* Beedon, Jeff
Dewalt, Candy 177
Dewalt, Ryan 177
Dickinson, Mike 110, 111
Didsbury, Greater Manchester, England 68
DietyOfDooky 103
DiFrancesco, Jon 208
Digi Dragon 119
Digital Game Museum 135
Dimonius 200, 201, 202, 203
Dingbat *see* Middendorf, Erin
Dinger, Katherine 133
Dingo Discovery Centre 169
Disney, Walt 188
Disney Comics 58
Disney Studios *see* Walt Disney Studios
Disney Television 37, 58, 59, 60
Disneyland 37, 57
DivineVixen *see* Gauffin, Martin
Division V 75
Dixon, Larry 25, 59
Dizmis 184
Djurens Ö 181
Djurskyddet Karlstad [Karlstad Animal Welfare] 123
Dnieper River 214
Doc Bolt 163
The Docks Hotel 104
DocMarcus 115
Dr. Demento 78
Dr. Seuss *see* Geisel, Theodore
Dr. Werner von Wolfenstein 187
Dr. Who 102
Doggy 54
Dogpatch Press 4
Dogz R. Barkin *see* Rowe, Santi
Le Domain du Ciran 88
Domanski, Steve 41
Donald Duck 8
"Don't Draw Them Bigger Than Her Head" 63
Don't Hug Cacti Studios 36, 180, 197
Dook 115
Doolittle, Jim 170, 172, 173
Doove, Bernard 167, 169
DoPE (Department of Pawpetry Entertainment) 78, 79, 80, 81, 82
Doran, Jeremy 134
Dorsai Irregulars 21, 22, 23, 113, 174
Dortmund, Germany 198
Dorval, Quebec 211
Dottar 94
DoubleTree by Hilton-San Jose Hotel 129, 130, 132, 185
DoubleTree by Hilton-Toronto Airport Hotel 109, 110
DoubleTree Hotel Denver 196, 197
Doubletree Plaza Hotel 26

Doubletree Suites 118
Douglas, Melissa 69
Dowden, Patrick 107, 108, 109
A Dozen Dead Furs 89
Draconis *see* McLaughlin, Loren
The Dragget Show 90
Dragi P 142
Dragon Mama 88, 89
Dragonboy 21
Dragon*Con 121
DragonDyne Publishing 188
Dragoneer 83, 84
Drake, Maxwell Anderson 37
Drake, Melissa 40
Drakon Vectarus 192
Dreamcatchers 80
Dreamous 31
DreamVision Creations 116
Drenthe, Netherlands 122
Dronon *see* Turrittin, Tom
Drury Plaza Hotel Broadview 47
Duane, Diane 22, 131
DucKon 6, 170, 172, 174
Dudman, Martin 77, 79
Dudziak, Marcus 29
Due Torri youth hostel 216
Duismann, Maik 79
Duke, Pat 160
Duncan, Jonathan Vair 112
Duncan da Husky *see* Brady, Tom
Duncan the Dog 100
Dungeons & Dragons 91
Dunn, Ben 6
Durango Dingo 184
Dustin 95
Dustin Friend *see* Destad, Bauske
Dustmeat *see* Giles, Megan
Duval, Shay 208
Dyatlenko, Vadim 200
Dye, Thomas K. 172, 173
Dzierzazna, Poland 137, 138

Earle, Malcolm 42, 72, 178, 211
EAST (episches Abfeiern Streunender Tiere) C2, 74, 75, 206
Easter 62
Eastern Suburbs Legion Club 104
Easy Virtue 169
Ebel, Matthew 16, 83, 84, 91, 92, 115, 121, 134, 157, 158
EbonyTigress *see* Brown, Sheryn
The EcoMuseum Zoo of the St.-Lawrence Valley Natural History Society 211, 212
Eddy, Jeff 117
Edge 44
Edi 139
Edmonton, Alberta 97
Edwards, Brent 19, 130
Eevachu 44, 55
Efteling amusement park 77
Eggerding, Philip 161, 162
Eging am See, Bavaria 137
Egypt Urnash *see* Trauth, Margaret
Eindhoven, the Netherlands 77
Ekevoo 13, 14
"ElevatorCon" 122
elevators 20, 21, 61, 122
Elizabeth, New Jersey 65

Index

Ellijay Wildlife Rehabilitation Sanctuary 121
Elliott, Eric 133
Elliott, Stephan 169
E.L.V.I.S. Convention Services 66
Elwetika 142
Embassy Suites 153, 193
Embassy Suites Phoenix-Scottsdale 27
EmptySet 185
End Tide 81
Endangered Animal Rescue Sanctuary (EARS) 100
Engel, Baron 131, 133
EngineFace 136
England 10, 68
Enigma 104
Entenwall Island, Germany 206
EosFoxx *see* Fischer, Marion
EPCOT Center 158
Epic Convention of Stray Animals (EAST) 74
Equine Angels Rescue 25
Equus 183
Eragon 167
MV *Erasmus* 189, 190
Erekson, Rock 197
Erika Leigh R 196
The Estrel Hotel 76, 82
Etheras 123, 124
Ettinger, Charles 162
Eureka Tower Sky Deck 167
EuroFurence C2, 9, 10, 11, 60, 61, 68, 69, 75–82, 87, 116, 133, 163, 165, 202, 204, 221
Eurofurence e.V. 78
EuroFurence Hymn 77
Euva 87
Evanier, Mark 23
Evans, Iestyn 82
Evil Nayo 43
Evil Simbaya 43
EvilKitty3 128
Evol Otter 161
Executive Plaza Airport Hotel 208
Executive Suites & Conference Centre 207
Exline, Darrel L. 62, 63, 64, 65, 71, 73, 74
Exotic Feline Breeding Compound 36, 63, 65, 132
Exotic Feline Rescue Center 146
"Eyes of the Night" 132
"Eyes of the Wolf" 57
EZwolf 51, 67, 82, 181

F3 Convention 88–89
FA Bucks 83
FA: United 82–84
FableFire 158
Facebook 92
Faert 202, 203
Fahrni, Dominik 52, 54, 142
Fahrstuhl 199
Fairmont San Jose 130, 134
Falcon's Grove 98
Falkenstein Jugendheim 74, 163
Fallout Coyote 97
Falstaff (mascot) 41
Fancher, Jane 131
"Fandoms United" 82
FANG 42
Fang 135
Fangcon 84–85
Fans and Freaks 160
Fantasia 63
Fantastic Furry Stories 10
Fantastic Journeys Publishing 102
Far from Fear e.V. 81
Farley (mascot) 40
Farore Nightclaw 135, 187
Fashion Square Mall 108
Fat Fluffs Rabbit Rescue and Rehome 70
FatCorgiOnyx 204
fatdrake 126
Fatkraken 190, 204
"The Fauna Project" 80
Fay, Timothy 60
Fayette Friends of Animals 24
FCN, Inc. *see* Furry Connection North, Inc.
FCX 133
FCY2K 131
Fear Liston 21
The Fearless Four 71
Feazle, Shaun 106
Federation Square 167
Feiten, Dave 132
Fel 120
Feli *see* Pilgrim, Christopher
Feline Conservation Center 65
Felines & Canines 175
Felix the Cat 8
Felorin *see* Shapiro, David
Felpur.Samael 162
The Fender Fursuit 83
Fendracus 142
FENEC Adventures 33
FENEK 137
Fennec, Juliana 15
Fennell, Amy 32
Fennell, Greg 27, 28
Feral! *see* Camp Feral!
FeralCom 39, 41, 42, 43
Ferme de Jean holiday camp 75
Fernando's Café 23, 25, 26
The Ferret Rescue Society 187
ferrets 71, 72, 73, 78, 79
Ferrets Unlimited Rescue Services (FURS) 177, 178, 179
Ferris *see* Davies, Chuck
Ferris, Jeff 61
Festival Internationale de l'Anthropomorphisme *see* Anthrofest
Festival of the Feral 181, 182
Fhloston Paradise 96
F.I.A. 79
Fido Award 169
Fife, Washington 70
Fificat 14
The Fifth Element 96
Final Fantasy 47
Fine Young Deviants 102
FinFur Animus 85–87
FinFur Summer Camp 85, 87
Firebreath *see* Ladouceur, Marc
Firefeathers *see* Radek, Andrea
Firehazard 178
Fireman's Memorial Park 209, 210
FirestormSix 27, 106, 110, 175, 179
Firr 91
Fischer, Marion 29, 30, 142, 165, 181
Fish, Leslie 62, 65
Fisher, Adam 113
Five Acres Animal Shelter 140
Fivel 18
Fizz 113
Fizz Otter 158
Fjordwolf 78
FL! Committee 125
Flain Falcon 42, 194
Flam 14
FlameDrake 95, 96, 191
Flanowa 210
Flare Starfire 101
"The Flat Cat Was Cute" 63
Flaydramon 103
Flayrah 4, 72
Fleki 203
Fletcher, Ken 35, 59, 117
Flinch 37
Flint Creek Wildlife Rehabilitation 173
Flint Otterhall *see* Cooksey, David
FlintHoof *see* Canaan, Dan
Floe 163
Floki *see* Bloom, Bard
Florida 107, 153
Florida Furs 108, 157
Fluke 83
Flye *see* Cocks, Louise
"Flying Purple Parking Meter" 58
Foglio, Phil 59
Foofaraw 3
Foofers *see* Burgess, Phillip
For a Few Dollars More 148
Forgotten Felines & Fidos 22
Forresters Hotel 104
"Fosgate: Ferret Loan Officer" 158, 213
Fossil the Undead Anthrosaur 36, 84, 179, 195
Foster, Alan Dean 59, 133, 188
Foster, Brian 55
Foster's Home for Imaginary Friends 24
Four Points by Sheraton 55, 195
4:2:5 156
Fox, Randy 19, 106, 109, 157, 158
Fox Amoore *see* Armour, Iain
Foxdale 104
Foxday 177, 178, 179
Foxfeather R. Zenkova 117, 174
Foxfire 34, 35
FoxSTAR *see* Matheson, Richard T.
Foxwell 124
Foxx, Susan 162
Foxy Fennec *see* Fennec, Juliana
Foxy Malone *see* Cupit, Christine
France 7, 10
Francis, Mike 68, 69
Francisco Grande Hotel and Golf Resort 219
Francofur 210
Frane, Kevin 43, 55
FranFurence 87–88

Index

Frankfurt, Germany 143
Freas, Frank Kelly 60
Freas, Laura 60
Frech, Michaela 30, 165, 166, 218
Freckleton, Grant 132
Fred Patten Special Collection on Science Fiction & Fantasy 4
Freedom Service Dogs 197, 198
Freese, Tanja C1, 25, 69, 78, 79, 80, 81, 82, 111, 114, 158, 165, 169, 188, 204
Freies Wort Suhl 81
Freizeitanlage Seeräuber 75
Fremer, Michael 37
French, Andrew 41
Freusburg Castle 75, 163, 164, 165
Frey, Rebecca Ann 40, 110
Friday the 13th 42
Friedrich, Zack vi
Friends of Feral 43
Friends of Lulu 133
Friends of the Sea Otter 131
Frisky's Wildlife & Primate Sanctuary 91, 92
Front Range Equine Rescue 197
Frost.Bite *see* Pike, Celina
Frostscar 55
Frozen Oasis 22, 23, 85, 100, 121, 123, 124, 133, 161, 162, 177, 178
Fry, Michael 134
Frýdštejn Castle 50
Frysco *see* Doran, Jeremy
FSB (Federal Security Service) 202
Fuckie C6, 141
Fukiage Station No. 5 151
Fulda, Germany 79
Fundacja Niechciane i Zapomniane 138
Funday PawPet Show 21, 157, 158, 173
Funny Animal Convention 154
Funny Animals and More: From Anime to Zoomorphics 4
"Funny Animals in World War II Propaganda" 4
Fur Affinity 46, 82, 83, 88
Fur Media 30
Fur Reality 89–90
Fur Squared 90–91
Fur the 'More 91–92
Fur What It's Worth 102
FurBest 92
FurbleFox *see* Francis, Mike
Furbo 27
Furboliche 5, 7
Furcadia 131
FurCon (I) 134
FurCon (II) 179
FurCon, e.V. 163
FurCoNZ 92–94
FurDU 94–96
Fur-Eh! 96–97
Fur-Eh! Organizing Committee 97
FurFright 1, 21, 97–102, 112, 211, 221
FurFright/Boston Bruins 102
FurFright, Inc. 98, 99, 100, 101
FurIdaho 102
FurJAM 94, 102–104
Furlandia 105–106

Furlaxation 106
Furlaxion, Inc. 106
Furloween 107–109, 117
furmeets
Furnal Equinox 102, 109–112, 211, 221
FurNation 40, 115, 182
Furp *see* Reed, Patrick
FurPlanet Productions vi, 11, 27, 114, 115, 188
Furpocalypse 102, 112, 221
"Furrier Transforms" 63
Furries from A to Z (Anthropomorphism to Zoomorphism) 2
Furrnion 6, 92
"Furry" 57
Furry Brasil 13
Furry Connection North C7, 112–114, 179, 221
Furry Connection North, Inc. 112, 113, 114
Furry CON(spiracy) 124
Furry Convention Leadership Roundtable vi
Furry Cruise 5
Furry Day 37
Furry Down Under 94
Furry Drama Show 85, 89
Furry End of the World Convention 123
Furry Fiesta C6, 114–117, 184, 205, 221
Furry Friends Foundation 173
Furry Hall of Fame 4, 67, 167, 169
Furry Migration 117
Furry Night Live 185
Furry Party 9
Furry Punk Rock Massacre 146
Furry Siesta 117
Furry Spring Break 117–118, 154
Furry Unlocked 118–119
Furry Weekend Atlanta C6, 120–122, 156, 157, 221
Furry Weekend Atlanta, Inc. 121
Furry Weekend Holland 122–123
"The Furry West Homestead Act of CF-2003" 64
Furry Western Australia Gathering 135
Furry Writers' Guild (FWG) 4, 11
Furry.ch—das schweizer Furryportal 52
FurryCon (I) 123
FurryCon (II) 123–124
FurryLah (FL!) 125
Furrymuck 19, 61, 62
FurryPhile 10
Furryratchet 75
Fursday 178, 179
fursona 9, 10
"Fursona Non Grata" 213
Fursonas 6
Furstivus 91, 126–127
Furstock 127
fursuit 1, 9, 10, 11, 24, 36, 57, 58, 170, 212
Fursuit Hockey League (FHL) 102
Fursuit Parade 10, 19, 21, 22, 26, 33, 34, 60, 79, 196

Furs Upon Malaysia (FURUM) 125–126
Furtastic 128
Furtasticon 10, 65
Further Confusion 11, 62, 68, 78, 129–135, 185, 221
Further Confusion ClubHouse in Critter Valley 133
Furtual Horizons; a Rainfurrest Anthology 188
FURUM *see* Furs Upon Malaysia (FURUM)
FurVention 135
FurVersion 10
Furville 203
FurWAG 135–136
FurWanted 136–137
Futerkon 137–138, 139, 140
Futrazakon 137, 138–139, 140
Futurecamp! 43
FuzzWolf vi
Fuzzy Productions, LLC 184
FWG *see* Furry Writers' Guild (FWG)

Gabapple *see* Douglas, Melissa
Gafford, Carl 58
Gafford, Crystal 127
Gagné, Michel 22
GalaxyOwls 85
Gale 125
Gallacci, Steve 4, 8, 10, 58, 80, 169, 189
Game of Thrones 87, 124
Garabedian, Laura 27, 47
Garcia, Dave 58
Garcia, Eric 64
Gargoyles 37, 59, 82, 84
Garman, Tess 67, 79, 82, 83, 116, 134, 173, 183, 196
Garra 142
Gateway FurMeet 139–140
Gauffin, Martin 77, 180
Gavet, Teagan 43, 67, 83, 116, 134, 183, 196
Gavin 112
Gawain *see* Seto, Gary Lee
The Gay Blades 83
Gdakanie (mascot) 140
Gdakon C6, 51, 137, 140–141
Gdakonek (mascot) 140
Gdansk, Poland 137, 140, 141
"Gdański konwent furry" 140
Geisel, Theodore 19
Geist (mascot) 41
Gembeck, Frank, Jr. 131
Gemeindehaus der Philipp Melanchthon Gemeinde 28
Gene Catlow *see* Temple, Albert
Genki *see* Pledger, Joey
"Gently Falling Rain" 59
GeorgiaFurs 122
Geraldton, Western Australia 136
Gerbasi, Dr. Kathy 25
Germany 5, 10, 75, 136, 137, 141, 143, 163, 164, 198, 206
Gertie Award 26
Geusz, Phil 15, 110, 160, 172, 187, 188

Index

Gez Tank Skunkrat 43
Ghostbusters 145
Giannoulas, Ted *see* San Diego Chicken
Gibson, Roz 35, 60, 63, 64
Gideon Artwolf 160
Gideon Hoss 42
Gilbert, David 173
Gilchrist, Guy 21, 22
Giles, Megan 37, 115
Ginger *see* Willard, Jessica
Gir Tygrin 113, 114
Gishkeshenh 43
Gizmo 45
Glacier Mr. Juggling Dragon 150
Glass Ferret 116
Gnadenhof Emmrich animal sanctuary 81
gNAW 211, 212
Gods with Fur: And Feathers, Scales. ... 4
Going Home Greyhounds, Inc. 210
Gold, Kyell 42, 43, 69, 82, 115, 116, 117, 122, 184, 187, 188, 197
Gold, Lee 60, 63
Gold Coast, Queensland 94, 96
Golden Leaves Con 54, 141–142
Golden Sydney Award 19, 60
Golden State Greyhound Adoption 133
Golden Tulip Hotel 80
Goldenwolf *see* Grandjean, Christy
Goldfur *see* Doove, Bernard
Goode, Jeff 184, 194, 213
Goodwin, Chris 32
Goorhuis, Henrieke C2, 70, 81, 142
Gordon, David 32
Göttingen, Germany 75, 78
Graafen Blackpaw 204, 205
Graf, Lia 58
Graf, Michael 52, 80, 142
Grainger, Colson 43, 69, 84
Grand Rapids, Michigan 142
Grand Sierra Resort, Nevada Foyer 30
Grandjean, Christy 132, 183, 196
Grandville 180, 181
Graphic Story Bookshop 3
Gravedigger 138, 139
Graveyard Greg 27, 187, 188
"The Great James Mountbatten-Windsor's Magnificent Zoological Extravaganza; or, The Mancunian Play" 68
Great Lakes Fur Con 142–143
Great Valley Nature Center 20
Greater California German Shepherd Rescue 134
Greater Philadelphia Search & Rescue 22
"Greenhouse World" 82
GreenReaper *see* Parry, Laurence
Greevixor 70, 180
Gre7g *see* Luterman, Greg
Greyfur 51
Greyhound Expressions 114
Greykitty C2
Griffin, Rick 70, 175, 196
Grimal 21, 43

Groat, Jim 10, 20, 58, 193
Growler 43
GrowlTiger 160
Growly 162
Grrrwolf *see* Spotswood, Brent
Grundwalheim Adventure Center 29
Gruppenhaus Bärgsunne 141
Gruppenhaus C'est la Vie 142
Guangzhou, China 52
Guide Dogs for the Blind 133, 134
Guinness Book of World Records 5, 22, 23
The Gunman at Sunset 148
Gunmouth *see* Burt, Matt
Gunn, Cassandra 190
Gunn, Marc 35
Gurney, James 24
Gusto 138
Gypsy Pirates 27, 28
Gyro Wolf 125
Gysenstein holiday house 52

H-Con 143–145
Haas, William 62
Hagen, Brian 133
Hagenfeldt, Thomas 77
Hahn, Moira 133
Halberd, Bunny 194
Hali 157
Haliburton Heights 38, 39, 40
Hall, Renee Carter 189
Hall of Firpine *see* Ebel, Matthew
Hallow Fox 24
Halloween 97, 98, 102, 108, 112, 119, 142, 147, 184
Hamburg, Germany 76
Hamill, Herbie 21, 80, 108, 109, 127, 154, 157, 158, 160
Hammet, Dashiell 152
Hampton Inn-Gateway Arch 139
Handicapped Wildlife Station 50
Hanover Marriott 83
Hanson, Christina 58, 131, 133
Hanson-Roberts, Mary 62, 172
Happy Hearts Feline Rescue 179, 180
Harlequin Inn 104
Harp, Brian 60
Harris, Joe 24
Hartford Courier 100
Harvst the Husky 184
Harz Mountains, Germany 74
Hasliberg, Switzerland 142
Haus Marchgraben 52
Hauschild, Dan 172, 173, 174, 175
Haven 117
HavenCon 117
HavocFox 193, 194
HAWS Waukesha 91
Hazard *see* McGaughy, Mekala
Head Madhatters 132
Headless Lounge 10
Heartdancer, Jaden 161
Heartlilly 205
Heath, Andy J. 82, 135
Heavy Horse *see* Loewen, Alan
Heeze, the Netherlands 75
Hefele, Christian 78

Heidelberg, Germany 143
Heinlein, Robert A. 3
Heitsch, Gerritt 75
"Hell Hath No Furries" 100
Hellfyre *see* Verezhensky, Sean 36
The Helm Bar 104
Helping Hands Humane Society 46
Helsinki, Finland 85, 87
Helvetic Confederation 52
Helvetica Bold *see* Burgess, Phillip
Henderson, Lauren 101, 122
Henrieke *see* Goorhuis, Henrieke
Henrik 14
Henry, Matt 118, 154
Henson Productions 131
Herbert, Alexander 93
Herbie Bearclaw *see* Hamill, Herbie
Heros the Noisy Panther *see* Ricketts, Joel
Hesse 143
Hibbary *see* Luetkemeyer, Hillary Renee
Hide-e-Hole Ferret Rescue 210
Higashi Shizuoka Station 150
Higgs, Michael 60
Higgs Raccoon vi
Highland Tiger: The Scottish Wildcat 204
Hiker 41, 43
Hikone, Japan 148
Hilda the Bambioid 57
Hill, Amber 47, 117, 174, 184
Hill, Robert 57
Hilton, Craig 169
Hilton Atlanta Hotel 120, 121
Hilton Bayfront Hotel 38
Hilton Burbank Airport & Convention Center 56, 63
Hilton Garden Inn 97, 193
Hilton Garden Inn Cincinnati/Sharonville 90
Hilton Indianapolis North 146
Hilton Leicester 69
Hilton Seattle Airport & Conference Center 186, 187
Himekawa, Akira 148
Hinckley, Leicestershire, England 68
Hittehund 181
Hixbi Fox 124
Hláska Hotel 48
H'Lven *see* Schulmayer, Andreas
Hofgard, Katie 15
Hogan, Lynn 84
Hogarth, M.C.A. 173
Holbrook, Bill 21, 121, 160, 193
Holcomb, Odis 161
Holcomb II 163
Holiday Inn 98
Holiday Inn Anaheim Resort 56, 58
Holiday Inn Atlanta Airport 120
Holiday Inn Atlanta Airport-North Hotel 120
Holiday Inn Bristol Plaza 33, 56, 58
Holiday Inn City Line 65
Holiday Inn Express 205
Holiday Inn Express & Suites Grand Rapids South 143
Holiday Inn Hotel & Suites Pointe-

Index

Claire Montreal Airport Hotel 211
Holiday Inn Independence 65
Holiday Inn Jetport 65
Holiday Inn Knoxville Downtown 84
Holiday Inn Knoxville West–Cedar Bluff Road 84
Holiday Inn on the Bay 73, 74
Holiday Inn Seattle—Sea-Tac Airport Hotel 186
Holiday Inn Select Hotel, Memphis International Airport 159
Holiday Inn Select Memphis East 158
"Hollow Hills" 61
HollyAnn *see* Cotton, Lisa
Holmgren, Jason 20
Hologram C2
Honrado, Jaime 186
Hood, Matthew 69, 70
Hope, British Columbia 45
"Hope by Her Smile" 58
Hopkins, David 73, 197
Hopper, Buck 28
Horizon Wings 99
Horne, Leon 132
HorrorFurence 14 80
H0rs3 112 [Note the zero rather than an o. Does this matter in the alphabetization?]
Horse's Ghost 183, 184
Horton Grand Hotel 38
Hossie 50
Hostel Bursztynek 140, 141
Hotel Amber 141
Hotel Dessau-Rosslau 75
Hotel Espresso 211
"The Hotel from Hell" 66
Hotel Gintama-Briz 214
Hotel Grand Chancellor 191
Hotel Luna 48, 49, 51
Hotel ML 83
Hotel Morri Oceania 216
Hotel Regency Cambridge 17
Hotel Skalský-Dvůr 49, 51
Hotel Sofiyevsky Posad 214
Hotel Vltava 48
Hounds for Heroes 204
The Hounds of Blackwhite Castle 80
House Avarryn 124
House Bark 124
House Bearathon 124
House Foxish 124
House Lyonstare 124
The House Rabbit Society 133, 134
House Taurgaryen 124
Housecon 9
Househead 102
Howard, Sara 36, 188
Howard, Shawntae 32, 179, 209
Howard Johnson Inn 158
Howard Johnson Inn and Convention Center 89
Hoyt *see* Dudziak, Marcus
Huffington Post 25
Hufnaar 138
Hughes Aircraft Company 3
La Hugoire 88

Huish, Linsey 31
Humane Animal Welfare Society (HAWS) 91
Humane Society of Huron Valley 113
Hundslund, Jutland, Denmark 128
The Hunger Games 43
Hunt Valley, Maryland 91
Hunt Valley Inn 91
Huntsville, Alabama 192, 193
Huntsville Airport 195
Hunua Ragebeetle 94
Hurricane Katrina 161
Huscoon 6
Husky in Denial *see* Riley, Buck
Husted, Ursula 161, 172
Hyatt Regency 33
Hyatt Regency Hotel 196
Hyatt Regency Minneapolis 117
Hyatt Regency O'Hare 170, 171, 174, 175
Hyatt Regency Woodfield 170, 173

Ianieri, Ivy 136
Ibercamp 145
ibis Styles Hotel 135, 136
Ice Age 3 96
Ice Cream Social 58
Ice TYP 90
ICEBANSHEE *see* Andrews, Nancy
Iceleron 169
I-CON 6
Idaho 102
Idess *see* Sherwood, 'Idess'
Idle Valley *see* Powell, Steven
Idylwild Fox *see* Crutcher, Spike
Ifus *see* Johnson, Stephanie
Iggi Eastwind 112
Ihaha 50, 51
Ijon Tichy: Raumpilot 165
Ikegawa, Lance 10, 80, 189
Ikkuma 185
"An Illustrated History of Furry Fandom, 1966–1996" 4
"I'm Going to ConFurence 5" 59
The Imaginarium of Doctor Parnassus 178
Immaterial *see* Knapp, Laura
Imperial Japanese Navy 82
Imperial March 115
Indianapolis, Indiana 146
Indianapolis Marriott East 146
Indy 179, 180
IndyFurCon (iFC) 146–147
The Infurnational Space Station 45
Infurnity C7, 147–148
InterCityHotel Magdeburg 81, 82
InterContinental Dallas 115, 116
International Anthropomorphic Convention and Exposition 57, 62
International Anthropomorphic Research Project (IARP) 25, 116
International Anthropomorphics Festival *see* Anthrofest
International Comics Festival 9
International Community of Banyakigezi 117
International Otter Survival Fund 69

International Tatarka 214
Internet 61, 76, 77, 78, 200
Intervales State Park 13
"Invasion" 62
Inverness, Scotland 203
Irvine, California 56
Irvine Hilton Hotel 56
Irvine Marriott 33
IsaacFox 142
Isacson, Henrik 77, 180
Isengrin 94
Isfacat 162, 195
Isra 14
Istanbul 115
Isuna *see* Nischan, Silke
Italy 5, 216
"It's Like Herding Cats, Only Moreso" 42
Ivybeth 43, 100
Ivy/Muttasaur 104
Iyu *see* Domanski, Steve

J Tigerclaw 16
J3T *see* Tong, Jodi
Jace 133
Jace Inugami 85
Jack O'Hare (mascot) 218
Jack-O-Lantern 98
Jacksonville, Florida 153, 156, 157
Jaekel, Andreas 78, 79
Jaggers Pawtucket 174
Jagu 201
Jakebe Sunraven 183
Jan *see* Chun Yan Miu
Janáček, Leoš 79
Janys 50
Japan 5, 10, 148–152, 205–206
Japan Guide Dog Association 148
Japan Meeting of Furries C3, 148
Japanese wedding party 35
Jar 203
Järvi, Santtu 87
Jase Husky 85
Jasper 25
Jaspian 162
Java Meerkat *see* Sensanbaugher, Margaret
Jaws 101
Jayrith 194
Jay Stoat *see* Coates, Jacob
JAZcabungcai *see* Cabungcai, John Razel M.
J.C. 148
JD Puppy 1, 100, 101, 116, 214
Jeanette, Tamara 6, 91, 98, 99, 101, 111
Jenner *see* Hilton, Craig
Jessie T. Wolf *see* Albee, Jessica Maia
Jet Dingo 192
Jethro *see* Kassis, Jethro
Jewel *see* Pinnegar, Michael
Jewlz 90
Jibba FoxCoon *see* Smith, Jason
Jill0r 114, 173
J.O. C7
Jobbins, Sheridan 169
Joecifur 194
Joey-Poey 178

Index

Joeyjoejoe 95, 96
Johis 69, 82
John Wayne Airport 57
Johnson, Robert K., Jr. 35
Johnson, Stephanie 137, 171, 176, 179
Jon Starrazor 210
Jonas 133
Jonas, Jeff 6
Jonas Pride 192
Jonathan Livingston Seagull 9
Jondi *see* DiFrancesco, Jon
Jones, Braden 105
Josepp 14
Josie and the Pussycats 21
Jrik 215
Jrrhack 13, 14
JTigerclaw 102
Jugendherberge Biggesee youth hostel 76
Jugendherberge Dessau-Rosslau 74
Jugendherberge Freusburg youth hostel 75, 78, 163, 164, 165
Jugendherberge Göttingen 75
Jugendherberge Hilders-Oberbernhards youth hostel 76
Juggendorf am Müggelsee youth camp 75, 77
Jugular Jaguar *see* McLaughlin, Loren
"Julie Bunny Must Die!" 158
Julien, Julie 207
Jumpy *see* Bartels, Stephan
Jurassic Park 96
Jürgen 142
Justin *see* Dyatlenko, Vadim
Jutland, Denmark 128

K-9 83
K-9 Stray Rescue League 179
Ka Hale o Ku'u Hoaloha Hula 133
Kabalo (mascot) 41
Kadath 102
Kagemushi *see* Conway, Dr. Samuel C.
Kahuki Lairu 196
Kaiser-Wilhelm-Koog, Germany 75, 76
Kaji 204
Kajito 54
Kalika Tybera 212
Kalkbrenner, Markus 144, 190
Kamadan 94
Kamenetz-Podolsk 215
Kami Cheetah 121
Kampgrounds of America 46
Kane Area Rehabilitation and Education for Wildlife 174
Kanouse Entertainment Group 123
Kanpai Japanese Sushi and Steak House 108
Kanthara *see* Charlebois, Karine
Kappy 139, 140
KaputOtter 190
KARE 60
Karlstad, Sweden 123
Karpov, Basil 201, 214, 215, 216
Kassis, Jethro 27, 28
Kat Aclysm 104

Katalina 102
Katmomma 84
Katowice, Poland 137
Katz, Alexander 193
Kawasaki City Industrial Promotion Hall 149, 205, 206
Kawazu 195
KayJay 166
Kazaleh, Mike 16, 63, 156, 157
Kaze, Ghost Warrior 79, 133
Kazusa Industrial Hall 149
KazzyCaboodles 191
KC Cabung-os 186
Keagos 119
Keefur 85, 124
Keenora Fluffball 218
Keepers of the Light 82
Keianza 112
Keihound 197
Keishana, Reimina 89, 122
Keller, Shawn 131
Kellic J. Tiger 117
Kellner, Christoph 142
Kellogg, Diana 83, 161, 162
Kelly, Carolyn 23
Kelly, Walt 23, 176
Kelsey, Lauren 135
Kemocon C7, 37, 148, 206
KemoCon Project 149
kemono 148, 151
Kemono Square 150
Kemper, Danielle 27, 28
Kempi's 116
Kendal 192
Kendra 94
Kenket *see* Garman, Tess
Kennedy, John 156
Kentucky 89
Keovi 36, 69, 181
Kerijiano 205
Kerry, Steve 57
Keto 81, 99, 100, 101
K'gra Leopard 97, 98, 99, 100, 101, 102
Khaki Dog *see* Vance, Alex
Khaosdog *see* Lemke, Saskia
KharCon 151
Kharkiv, Ukraine 151, 200
Kharkov *see* Kharkiv, Ukraine
Khiray of the River 132
Khranos 134, 179
Khyot *see* Luterman, Heather
Kiara Shiba 139, 140
Kiba Swiftpaw 191, 192
Kiba Wolf 26
Kidd, Paul 20, 66, 67, 134, 136, 167, 169
Kiev Society for the Protection of Animals 214
Kiev Society for the Protection of Animals' Gostomel shelter for homeless animals 215, 216
Kiev Zoo 215
Kigukemo 151–152
Kihu 44
Kijani 31
Kim 147
Kimba the White Lion 8
Kimberfox 121

Kimzie 184
Kinark Outdoor Centre 38, 39, 40, 41
King, Robert C. 1, 58, 170, 172, 195
King of Prussia, Pennsylvania 18, 20
KingTaibu *see* Kellner, Christoph
Kinky Turtle *see* Muchtler, Andrew
Kinyin 194
Kipper Otter 134, 174
Kirchen, Germany 75, 78
Kirrow 123
Kisaraku, Japan 149
Kisu 87
Kit Drago 91, 92
Kitsumi 35, 36, 105, 106
Kitt Foxx 177, 178
Kittee, Finland 87
kittiah 190
Kittitara 17
Kittrel *see* Gafford, Crystal
Kitty 87
Kitty-sama 94
Kiwanis Camp 93
Kiwi 92
Klemp, Ronald W. 78, 132, 164
Klik 119
Kline, Ed 130
Kling, Karen 177
Klinkler, Zas'nene 63
Klyk 202, 203
Knapp, Laura 27, 28Kneezle 204
Knight, E.E. 134
KnotCast 115, 184
Knott's Berry Farm 60
Knoxville Pride Parade 85
Knoxville, Tennessee 84
KO *see* Omel, Kevin
Kocur 75
Koda Bear 99
Kodi 188
Kodian 160
Koga Silverdragon 14
Köhler, Tobias 76
Koji C6, 116
Kokako Lodge 93, 94
Kokoushotelli Gustavelund 85
Kolja Wostock (mascot) 74
Kolmården Zoo 77
Koltas 142
Kompaniet, Pavel 51, 162, 201
Konu Eikuku Hentaru *see* Yoshikawa, Konu
Kopeikin, Paul 199, 200, 201
Köpenicker Kanusport Club 28, 29
Korrok 50
Korth 178
Koru 119
Kostrzyn nad odrą 127
Kot 138, 139
KotaHusky 18
Koul 202
Koush 14
Kouty, Czech Republic 48, 49
Kraden 169
Krado 125
Krahnos 41
Krakow, Poland 137
Kralle *see* Duismann, Maik
Krazy Kat 8

Index

Krazy Kat: A Jazz Pantomime 8
Kreecha, Zaen 167
Kreutzman, Kris 9
Kriske *see* Kurita, Yusuke
KROQ 36
Krueger, Chad 73, 157
Krueger, Sarah 15
Kryphos 109
Kuala Lumpur, Malaysia 125, 126
Kuddlepup *see* Cole, John
Kudlaty 139, 141
Kunako 141
Kunava 207
Kuragari 119
Kurganova, Russia 207
Kurita, Yusuke 148
Kuro-Kai *see* Rolentaes, Aisha
Kwaz the Drumming Raccoon 213
KWKAT 162
Kyïv, Ukraine 214
Kyle 169
Kyle, Richard 3
Kyote 210
Kyteria of Anevern 36
Kyubi 138, 139

The Labyrinth 122
Lackadaisy 113
Lackey, Mercedes 25, 59, 118
Lacy 122, 176
Ladouceur, Marc 212
Lady Foxglove *see* Hogan, Lynn
Lage, Daphne 19, 59
Laird, Peter 22
Lake, Santtu 87
Lake Afton Campground 47
Lake County Animal Education and Rescue 175
Lake Lucerne 52
Lake Nestea 40
Lake of the Ozarks State Park, Missouri 213
Laken SteelJaw 184
Lakota Wolf Preserve 83
Lambert the ram (mascot) 218
Lamper Fox 142, 143
Lamplighter Inn & Suites North 89
Lane, Jim 162
Lane, Julie 105
Lane, Kamber 55
Lanee, Bruce 58
Langenbruk, Switzerland 141
La Pine, Oregon 44
Large Hadron Collider 69
Larsson, Deanna 188
The Last Unicorn 200
LatinVixen 67, 113, 120, 196
Latte *see* Kelsey, Lauren
Laubach, Chad 109, 213
Lawrence, Kansas 46
LazerForce 103
Die Lebende Westernstadt 136
Ledeč nad Sázavou, Czech Republic 48
Ledger, Jared 114, 173, 197, 208
Lee, Razzy 208
Lem, Stanislaw 165
Lemke, Saskia 165, 166

Lemonade Coyote *see* McCormick, Timothy
Leniwiec 138
Leo Leopard 202, 203
Leo Lovely 194
LeoMearido 203
Leon 149
Lester, Paul 173
LeTigre 74, 75, 206
Lettres de Coquefredouille 4
Leu 74, 75
Lewis, T. 134
Lex Cypher *see* Herbert, Alexander
Libštát, Czech Republic 50
Licorice Monster 207
Liehm, Ray 104
Life Achievement Award 3
life-drawing class 131
Light, Michele 59, 60, 62, 66, 115, 196
Lightfoot Kyohti 183
Lightpaws 106
Likeshine 100, 112, 114
Lil Chu 119
Lily Night Road 198
Lima, Peru 7
Lindskold, Jane 133
Lingrimm 201
Linköping, Sweden 75, 76
Linköping University 76
Linnaeus 173
Lion Guardians 203
The Lion King 37, 177, 200
Lionel Scritchie's Dormitory 78
Lionitus 16
Lisek, Czech Republic 51
Little Blue Society 134
Little Shop of Horrors 177
Liverpool, England 135
Livingston, Scotland 204
Livingston(e), Monika 58, 63, 187
Lizardbeth *see* Boriss, Lis
Lizardlars 75
Llanowar 203
Loba Teimosa 14
Loch Ness 204
Łódź, Poland 137, 138
Łódź Animal shelter 138
Loewen, Alan 179
Loewi 79
Logn 18
Loial 188
Loisir Hotel 148
London, Ontario 55
London Boat Party 189
LondonFurs 189
Lone_Fox 88
Long, Lazarus 84
Look Left 84, 91
"Looking Back: 10 Years of Furry Parties" 60
Loopy 43
Loopy Wolf *see* Pidcock, Andrew
"Loot" 60
Loran Skunky *see* Thomas, Jason
Lorelei Rock, Germany 163
Loriana Vixen 161
The Lort Smith Animal Hospital 169

Los Angeles, California 56, 62
Los Angeles Public Library 3
Los Angeles Science Fantasy Society 3
Loscon 63
Lost Dogs Home 169
Louvelex *see* Henderson, Lauren
Love a Mutt Pet Rescue 188
Lu Ken 52
Lucian 112
Lucifur Fox 97
Lucky 180
Lucky Coyote 36, 115, 197
Lucky the Evil Dog 174
Luena, Ed 64
Luetkemeyer, Hillary Renee 122
Lumière Place Casino & Hotels 139
Lumio Draco 106
Luna Park 167
Lupie 95
Luschhoernchen 198
Luterman, Greg 85
Luterman, Heather 85, 173, 195
Lutherstadt Wittenberg, Germany 75
Luthien Nightwolf 48, 213
Luxen *see* Graf, Michael
Lvivska Bramah 214, 215
Lyctiger 94
Lyenuv 147
Lykourgos 184
Lyons, Brenda 92
Lyosha *see* Fennell, Amy
Lyrick 119

MA Vest-a-Dog 18
Ma, Lung 88
MacConaill, Niall 32
Mach Stormrunner *see* Dowden, Patrick
MacKinnon, Ted 32
MacNeal, Noel 158
MacQuillan, Cynthia 62
Macroceli 84, 95
Madman 169
MafunDi *see* Wiedemann, Jens-René
Magdeburg, Germany 76, 81
Magdeburg zoological gardens 81
Magic the Gathering 115, 120, 124
Magna, Leo 35
Magon, Jymn 58, 60, 63
Magus Lupus 54, 166
Mahrkale *see* Schaefer, M.
Maiden Voyage 136
Malahovka boarding house 199, 202
Malathar *see* Palivec, Kevin
Malaysia 5, 10, 126
Malcolmson, Scott 59, 218, 219, 220
The Maltese Falcon 152
Maltese Fur-Con 152–153
Maltese Fur-Con Committee 152
The Maltese Pigeon 153
Maly *see* Stout, Jana
Mammal Trust UK 190
The Man Show 64
Management 166
Manchester, England 68
Manchester Dogs Home 69

Index

Manchester International Youth Hostel 68
Mangusu 69
Manhattan Superbowl 104
Manila, Philippines 185
Manley, Chuck 219
Manly Harbour 103
"Mare de Deu de Gracia" hostel 92
Maremma sheepdog 217
Mari 162
Maria Gabriella Hotel 216
Marina Hotel 16
The Maritim Hotel 76, 81
Markaroo 118, 119
Markey, Dan 39
Marrickville Bowls Club 104
Marriott Denver Tech Center 196
Marriott Toronto Airport 111
Marriott's Fairfield Inn & Suites 83
Mars Attacks! 217
Marshall Space Flight Center 192
Martin, George R.R. 87, 124
Martin, Jim 24, 81
Martin, Steve 37, 57, 58, 157
Martin, Watts 19, 80
Martin Wolf 201
Marty *see* Martynov, Ivan
Martyn, Ian 64
Martynov, Ivan 200
Marvin Raptor 126
Mary Mouse *see* Minch, Mary C.
Maryland Furs 91
Mash 203
Maskwa 97
"Master of the Seventh Blade" 58
Mataeus DeVailo 198
Mather, Theresa 65
Matheson, Richard T. 78
Matrices *see* Howard, Sara
Matt Hollywood 95
Matt Lion *see* Hood, Matthew
Matty Blade 136
Mausie (mascot) 180, 181
Max BlackRabbit *see* Earle, Malcolm
Max Cat (mascot) 19
Max DeGroot *see* Smith, Craig E.
Max Goof *see* Smith, Craig E.
Maxsteel 217
Maxwell, Drew 61, 62
Mayhem 71, 72, 73
Mbili 50
McAdam, Marci 72, 111
McCandless, Pennsylvanis 209
McCarthy, Kyle 124
McCormick, Timothy 122
McCullar, Matt J. 172
McCullough, Strike 192
McGaughy, Mekala 89
McGrain, Daria 121
McGuire, Seanan 60
McKim, Ami 208
McKinley, Chris 41, 130
McLaughlin, Loren 85, 89, 118, 124, 183
McMurry, Michael-Scot 63, 218, 220
McPherson, Brian 160
Mearú Dreamsong 51
Medieval Madness 78
Medlar 208
Medosai 135
Meezer *see* Jeanette, Tamara
MegaPanther (mascot) 157
Megaplex 116, 153–158, 221
MehdniX 210
Mek "Stitch" 109
Mekki 199
Melbourne, Victoria 67, 92, 94, 166, 167
Melbourne Convention and Exhibition Centre 67
Melbourne in December Fur Meet 67, 166
Melbourne Zoo 167
Melendez, Noel 146, 173
Melman, Avi 59
MelSkunk *see* Drake, Melissa
Melville, Chuck 58, 73
Memburu 51
Memphis, Tennessee 84, 158
Memphis Flyer 161
Memphis International Airport 159
A Menagerie of Heroes 188
Meo 144
Mephit FurMeet 84, 158–163
Mephit MiniCon (MMC) 29, 163–166
Mephitis 203
Mercure Hotel 191
Mercure Inverness Hotel 203
Mercure Livingston Hotel 204
Merkindesr 46, 47, 48
Merlino, Mark 3, 9, 16, 56, 57, 58, 59, 60, 61, 62, 77, 78, 177, 183
Mermaid Lilith 27
Mermaid Lucia 27
Method 1 113
Metro Manila 185, 186
Mexikanisches Restaurant 137
Meyers, Karl F. 154, 156, 157
Mezösi, Thomas 77
Miami 43
Mickey Mouse 8
Mid-America Anthropomorphic and Arts Corporation 196
Mid-Atlantic Anthropomorphic Society 91
Middendorf, Erin 113, 116
Middletown, Connecticut 98
MiDFur 67, 92, 94, 102, 166–170
"Midnight Over Minerva" 71, 118
Midori 197
Mid-South and Tennessee Anthropomorphic Arts Association (MST3A) 160
Midwest FurFest 6, 135, 170–176, 221
Midwest Furry Fandom, Inc. 170, 174
Mighty Morphin Power Rangers 179
Mighty Tiny 63
Mikairu C8, 218
Miles, Kylen 63
Military Working Dogs 100
The Millennium Hotel 139
Millenium Maxwell House Hotel 84
Miller, Jannifer 175
Milwaukee, Wisconsin 90
Milwaukee Brewers 23
Minch, Mary C. 55, 113, 116, 158, 178
Minerva Mink 63, 71
Mines International Exhibition and Convention Center 126
Mines Wellness Hotel 126
Minicon 117
Minneapolis, Minnesota 60, 117
Minnesota Furs (MNFurs) 117
Minter, Jeff "Yak" 70
Minton, Tom 25
Mirabeau Park Hotel & Convention Center 15
Misha (mascot) 41
Misora 89
Miss Mab *see* Winters, Amber M.
Mississauga Humane Society 110, 111, 112
Missmonster Mel *see* Curphy, Melita
Missouri 88
Missouri Department of State Parks 213
Missouri Exotic Species Art Association 212
Missouri's Furries 88
MistyStriker 167, 191
Mitch DLG 115
Mitchell, Ellisa 59
Mitchroney, Ken 130
MitRa *see* Horne, Leon
Mitsu 99
Mitsuki-onega 92
Mitten, Cara 32
Mitti 36, 134, 135
MixedCandy Productions 90, 113
Miyagami, Kacey C7, 82, 105, 114
Miyazaki, Hayao 176
MMC Café 165
Mochi 36
Mogged, Brian 31
Mokusei Kaze 102
Molly (lioness) 200
Momotaro no Umiwashi 81
MonFur 210
Mongoose Ink 31
Mongrels 82, 135
Monkey Paw Entertainment 27
Monoyasha 116
Montjan, Klaus 137
Montréal, Quebec 26, 210, 211, 212
Montreal Canadians 102
Montréal Gazette 27
MoogiePower *see* Martyn, Ian
Moonridge Animal Park 100
Moonridge Zoo 35
Moorcat *see* Ravencraft, Sean
Moreau Awards 19, 20
MoreFurCon 66
Morph Parade 7
Morphic Tales 10
Morphicon 106, 176–179
The Morphicon Corporation 177
Morrissey, Phil 57, 118
Morschach, Switzerland 52
Morwood, Peter 131
Moscow, Russia 199, 200, 201, 202
Moser, Aura 194

Index

Moskviich (Moscovite) recreation center 199, 202
Mostyn, Pavia 178, 179
Mothra *see* Bloom, Rhys
Motomo Wahots 218
Motor City Furry Con 179–180, 221
Motor City Furry Con, LLC 179
Mounier C. S. 44, 45
Mt. Laurel, New Jersey 83
The Mountain Lion Foundation 134
Mouse *see* Sender, Terry
MP3 156
Muchtler, Andrew 194
Muddyfox 14
Municipal Cultural Center 137
The Muppet Show 63
Murono, Toby 174, 175, 176
Mursa 15
Muttasaur *see* Ianieri, Ivy
Mutts and Mutts Rescue League 114
My Little Pony: Equestria Girls 104
My Little Pony: Friendship Is Magic 27, 82, 217
Myenia C1, 27, 184
Myler, Jake 63
Mysh 50
Myst Xtreme 84
The Mysterious Affair of Giles 116
Mystery Science Theater 3000 172
Mystery Science Theater 3000: Prince of Space 101
MYSTIQE *see* Bueckert, Chelsey
Mythagoras 10

Nadezhda the sable (mascot) 207
Nagoya, Japan 151
Nagoya SME Promotion Center 151
Nakira 40
Nalina *see* Brook, Jennifer
Nambroth *see* Miller, Jennifer
Nan Fung International Convention & Exhibition Center 52
Nanook123 69
NARF Animal Rescue 134
Naros 77
Nashville, Tennessee 84, 160
Nastya 200
National Aviary 26
National Guard 172
National Hockey League 25
National Tiger Sanctuary 89
Native Animal Rescue 136
Natoli 199
Nature Conservation Agency 50
"Naturfreundehaus Ebberg" 198
Naughty Sexy Furry Writing: Enter at Your Own Risk 188
naut *see* Fahrni, Dominik
Nebra (Unstrut) youth hostel 74
NecroDrone 37
Neff, David 161
NekoDorei 106
Nekogami 83
Nekomon 100
Nelena 165
Nemeier, George F., Jr. 19, 40, 115, 160
Neo 198, 199
The Neo-Futurists 176

Neo-Geen 177
Neon Slushie 179
NeonBunny 185
Nera Akkari 50
Nerevar 139
The Netherlands 10, 122
Nevada Humane Society 31
Neverwhen 188
New Coyote 73
New England 97, 112
New Jersey 82
New Jersey SPCA 83
New Leash On Life 100
New Year's Furry Ball 126
New York 6
New York Yankees 23
New Zealand 10, 92
Newark, New Jersey 83
Newark Liberty International Airport 65, 83
Newark Liberty International Airport Marriott Hotel 83
NewEinstein 180, 181
Newtown Food Festival 103
Newtype USA 4
Nexion 202
Nexus Folf 18
Nexxus *see* Robertson, James
Niagara County Community College 23, 25
Nichols, Betsy 153
Nicodemus *see* Riggs, Adam
Nienna 180
NightWolf 88
Nihaler 162
NIIC the Singing Dog 85, 92
Nik Vulper 113
Nikita Hyena 191
Nikita Wolfpaw 191
Nikko 142
Nimbl *see* Remes, Antti
NimbleSquirrel 93, 94
Nimrais 165, 204
Nischan, Silke 29
"NitroCoon" 59
NitroShep 105
Niuxi 75
Niven, Larry 132
NJSPCA 84
Noben 197
Noble Park 167
Noble Wolf 27
Nootka *see* Vick, Diana
Nootka (mascot) 72
NordBayern Infonet 80
NordicFuzzCon 7, 180–181
Norman, Floyd 23, 24
Norman, Lisanne 21, 35, 62, 78
Normandy 88
North 187, 188
North Alabama Regional Furs 192
North Island, New Zealand 93
North Karelia Kittee 87
North Park Lodge 209
North Sea 76
Northbridge 136
NorthEast Anthropomorphic Association 82, 91
Northern Wolf 100

Northwest Wildlife Rehabilitation Center 188
Norton, Andre 3
NovaFox 29
Nové Město na Moravě 51
Novi, Michigan 113, 179
Novotny, Jeff 32
Nuka *see* Plante, Dr. Courtney
Nuneaton Warwickshire Wildlife Sanctuary 69
Nunnemacher, John 95, 131
Nuremberg, Bavaria, Germany 76
Nuremburg Castle 76
Nut-Case 179
Ny, Joseph 65, 66
Ny, Susan 65, 66, 67
Ny, Trish *see* Ny, Susan
Nynäshamn, Sweden 180
Nyxsiern 91

The Oakland Zoo 131
Oakley, Mark 32
Oakshadow, BanWynn 41, 42
Oberbernhards, Germany 76
Obi 14
The Occidental 104
Oceanworld 103
Ocelot 133
Oddy Redwing 113, 183
Odenwald Mümling, Germany 145
Ogden Group Camp 44
Ogwambi 81
Ognas 106
O'Hare International Airport 174
Ohio Alleycat Resource 90
Okami 37
O'Keefe, Dan 127
OkiDoki Coyote *see* Burns, Bob
Okill 123
Oklacon 47, 181–184, 212
Oklahoma 181, 182, 212
Oklahoma Association of Anthropomorphic Arts, Inc. (OAAA) 182, 183, 184, 212
O'Kun, Tempe 44
Old Doc Yak 8
Oldfreek 162, 193
Olive Branch, Mississippi 159, 162
OliverFox 29, 30
Olpe, North Rhine-Westphalia, Germany 76
Olufsborg Camp, Hundslund 128
Olven *see* Pasekova, Dagmar
"Omaha," the Cat Dancer 58, 117
Omega the Lioness 201
Omekin Lutz 208
Omel, Kevin 192, 193, 194, 195, 196
OMGSparky 143
Omni Albany Hotel 18
Omni William Penn Hotel 23, 24
Once Upon a Time in the West 148
One Tail at a Time 175
Onnanoko 208
Ontario 38, 55, 109
Ontario Furries 110
Ookami Kemono *see* Cockburn, Alex
Operation Desert Snow 80
Orange County, California 33, 56

Index

Orange County/John Wayne Airport 57, 59, 60
Orci 198, 199
Oregon 105
Oregon Trail 44
O'Riley, Rod 9, 37, 38, 56, 57, 58, 59, 60, 61, 62
Orlando Airport Marriott Lakeside 154
Orlando, Florida 107, 116, 117, 118, 153, 154, 156, 157
Orlando Elk's Lodge 107
Orleans *see* Novotny, Jeff
Orphen Sirius 203
Orwell, George 175
Ostsee Zeitung 77
Oswald the Lucky Rabbit 8
OTK 149
Ottawa, Ontario 26, 31
"Our Arbat" 199, 200
Outrigger Surfers Paradise 95
Over the Hedge 134
Overzen 118
Oz Kangaroo 95, 96, 184
OzFoxes *see* Carspecken, Margaret; Carspecken, Robert
OzFurry 166
Ozone Griffox 88
Ozzy Bat (mascot) 107

P. Pardus *see* Suzuki, Ken
Pablo 141
PacAnthro 185
PacerFox 213
Pacific Anthropomorphics League 185
Pacific Anthropomorphics Weekend (PAW) 185
Pacific Northwest 70
Paf! 41, 132
Painted Dog 112
Painted Dog Conservation, Inc. 136
Pakesh De *see* Dickinson, Mike
The Palace Hotel 104
Palivec, Kevin 132
Palladinthug 27
Palmer, Sara "Caribou" 20, 100
Pan Hesekiel Shiroi *see* Frech, Michaela
Pancakes on the Rocks 103
PandaGuy *see* Albers, Jon
Pandez Panda 90, 147
Pandoracon 89, 90
PANJA! 149
Paperback Grove 104
Pardubice, Czech Republic 218
Parenting Children of a Different Species (PCDS) 193, 194, 195, 196
Parry, Laurence 173
Pasekova, Dagmar 49, 50, 51, 79, 80
Pasterz 138
Patches (I) 42
Patches (II) 178
Patchouli 41, 42
Path 116
Pathfinder RPG 115
Patrick the Dog 75
Patrix 52, 54, 166

Patten, Fred 35, 58, 61, 63, 169, 188
Patto 43
Patton, Fiona 32
Paulfox 104
Paulsen, Rob 23
Paulus, Sarah 166
Pavlov, Czech Republic 50, 51
Paw of the King Soron 124
"Paw on Globe" 63
PAWcon 185
Pawel Lemurr 75
PawFur 30
Pawnee (mascot) 42, 43, 44
Pawpet Live Experiences, Inc. (PLEx) 154
Pawpet Megaplex *see* Megaplex
"Pawpet Show—The Story" 82
Pawpet Theater 172
PawPrints Fanzine 10
Paws for a Cause 113
Paws with a Cause (PAWS) 143
Paxton, Ian 9
Payne, Michael H. 58, 59, 60, 64, 130
Pays de L'ours 100
PeacePaw Yote 139
Pearl Possum 59
PeeJay 210
Peek 78
Pegasus *see* Paulus, Sarah
Pehl, Mary Jo 172
Peña, Albert C. 184, 188
Penh Gwyn *see* Hagen, Brian
Pennsylvania 20, 21, 22, 23, 24, 25, 26, 126, 127, 209, 210
Pepper Coyote *see* Clark, Jared
Perian, Strype and Cooper 55
Perihelion 215
Pernštejn Castle 51
Perro *see* Murono, Toby
Perth, Western Australia 135
Peru 7
Peso 50
Pet Connecton 46
Petboy 51
Peteranderl, Philipp 79
The Petershof near Erbach/Erbuch, Germany 144
Pets Are Wonderful Support (PAWS) 132
Pfluftel 52, 54
The Phantom of the Pawpet Show 79
Phelan 29
Philadelphia Inquirer 21
Philcon 65
Philadelphia, Pennsylvania 10, 18, 20, 22, 65, 82, 126, 127
Philippine Anthro Festival C4, 185–186
Philippines 10
Phoenix, Arizona 27, 119
PhoenixTV 207
Phoenix Wolf 198
Pidcock, Andrew 32
Pidgeon, Jeff 134
Pike, Celina 27
Pilgrim, Christopher 32, 211, 212
Pinnegar, Michael 177, 178, 179
Pirates of the Caribbean 137

Pittsburgh *see* Anthrocon
Pittsburgh, Pennsylvania 6, 18, 22, 23, 24, 25, 26, 82, 208, 209
Pittsburgh Mills Mall 209, 210
Pittsburgh Parrot Rescue 24
Pittsburgh Pirates 23
Pittsburgh Post-Gazette 24, 26
Pittsburgh Zoo & PPG Aquarium 209, 210
Pixar Animation Studios 131
Plante, Dr. Courtney 24, 25
Pledger, Joey 21, 41, 83, 133, 183
Plonq *see* Braun, Dave
Plum, Pennsylvania 209
Plunkett, Steve 19, 20, 172, 178
PMoss *see* Mostyn, Pavia
Poe, Edgar Allan 91
Poetigress *see* Hall, Renee Carter
Pogo Possum 8, 23, 35
Pointe-Claire, Quebec 211
Pointe Hilton Squaw Peak Resort 27
Poke 78, 79
Poland 5, 10, 127, 139, 140, 141
Polfurs 127, 138
Poliou 92
Pompeii 81
poppawolf 147
Portland, Oregon 105
Portland PAW Team 105
"PotatoCon" 102
Potoroo *see* Raymond, Lucas
Pounce the Panther (mascot) 157
Pounds, Roy D., II 36, 64, 65, 71
Pournelle, Jerry 133
Poutine Social 97
Powell, Steven 47, 48
Power Morphicon 179
Prague, Czech Republic 48, 50
Praha-Jinonice 50
Prales detem 51
Prell, Karen 131
The Press 83
PRguitarman *see* Torres, Chris
The Pride of Chanur 175
The Prince of Knaves 116
Princess Rei *see* Keishana, Reimina
Productions Anthropomorphique 210
Prokhorov, Dmitry 200, 201, 203, 217
Prolisok 214
Pronovost, Amy 32
Przystanek Woodstock 127
Pullman City 181
Pulver, David L. 19
Punkva Caves 49
The Puppits 50
PuppyDog 92
Purple Nurple Live! 20, 60, 130
Put a Tiger at Your Table 161
PWN_3 102
Pyrmont Bridge Hotel 104

Quality Hotel Winn Haninge 180
Quicksilver 98
Quinn, Mike 131
Quintaglio trilogy 61
Quoth the Raven (mascot) 91
Qzurr 49, 51, 81, 203

Index

Rabbit Meadows Sanctuary & Adoption Center 188
Rabbit Tracks 132
Rabbit Valley Books/Comics 11, 31, 41, 119
Rabbitt, Andrew 31, 41
Rabbitt, Sean 31, 41
Raczoon 194
Radek, Andrea 214
Radio Comix 10, 160
Radio Russia 200
Radisson (mascot) 60
Radisson Hotel 176
Radisson Plaza Hotel 60
Radisson Riverside Rochester 123
Radisson Suite Hotel Huntsville 192, 193
Radisson WorldGate Resort Orlando Hotel 154
Radix 109
Rafferty *see* Holmgren, Jason
Rage 66
Rags 108
Raid Zero 185
Raika 51
Rails and Tails 162
RAIn, Inc. 105, 186
Rainbow Animal Assisted Therapy 174
RainFurrest 6, 14, 35, 70, 105, 186–189, 221
RainFurrest Anthropomorphics International (RAIn) 186
RainFurrest charity anthology 188
Raksha 140, 141
Ramada Edmonton Hotel & Conference Centre 96
Ramada Jarvis Hotel 203
Ramada Minneapolis Airport Hotel 117
Ramada Newark Airport International Hotel 83
Ramada Plaza Grand Rapids 143
Ramada Plaza Inn and Conference Center 106
Ramada Resort and Convention Center 118, 153
Randon 87
Rankin, Susan 154, 194
Rapid T. Rabbit *see* Concepcion, Richard
Rapid T. Rabbit and Friends 172
Rapido 189, 190
Raptor Protection of Slovakia 51
Raschkar *see* Vogt, Heribert
Rasputch 88
Rattie Ratz 133
Raubtier- und Exotenasyl e.v 81
raven 91
"The Raven" 91
Ravencraft, Sean 15
Ray 74, 75
Rayan Wolffe 162
RayFkm 145
Raymond, Lucas 14, 41, 42, 43, 44, 55, 85, 214
Razzek *see* Byers, Tiffany
RBW 166, 189–190
Reaves, Michael 59

Rebel Empire Workshops 136
"Recreational Trubnik" 207
Red Lion Costa Mesa 56, 57, 58, 59
RedCoatCat *see* Jeanette, Tamara
RedHyena 189
Redondo Beach, California 16
Redstone Arsenal 192
Reed, Patrick 134
Regália 50
Regap of Connecticut 100
Rei Meerkat 143
Rei Vagan 96
Reins of Life 21
Reiza 90
Remes, Antti 77, 78
Rendezvous Studio Hotel 135
Reno, Nevada 30, 119
Reno Area Anthropomorphic Arts and Recreations (RAAAR) 30
Reptile and Amphibian Rescue Network (RARN) 35
Revaivwra 198
Revar 62
Reven, Thea 188, 208
Revit 106
Rex Wolf 189
Reynolds, Brian 156
Reyes Wolf 13, 14
Rhari *see* Duval, Shay
Rhubarb the Bear *see* Wilkinson, Ned
Richard Nightpaw 204
Richex 204
Richmond, British Columbia 208
Ricketts, Joel 183, 213, 214
Ridpath Hotel 15
Rieko 46
Riffuchs *see* Wilke, Kai-Uwe
Rigel 133
Riggs, Adam 187
Rikoshi Kisaragi *see* Frane, Kevin
Riley, Buck 85, 158, 195, 214
Rimini, Italy 216
Ringberg Resort Hotel 76, 80
Ringo 123
Ringtail Café Productions LLC 90, 184
Rio Tanuki 176
Risher, Eric 178
Ritka 138
River Spree 29
River Thames 189
Rivercoon *see* Bliss, David
RivFur 94, 102, 190–192
Riyeko 46
Rizzorat 69
RKTDWG *see* Erekson, Rock
Roarey Raccoon 69
Robbers Cave State Park 213
Robertson, James 40, 115, 182
Robey, John "The Gneech" 69, 91, 161
Robin Hood 8, 175
Robinson, Benjamin Eren 39, 40
Robinson, Dr. Jane 61
Rochester, New York 123
Rocket City FurMeet 192–196
Rocket City FurMeet, Inc. 192
Rocket Dog Rescue 135

The Rocks 103
The Rocky Horror Picture Show 115, 156, 157
Rocky Horror Picture Show Pool Party 100, 101
Rocky Mountain Fur Con 119, 196–198, 221
Rocky Mountain Raptor Program 196
Rog Minotaur 161
Rogers, Mark E. 21, 22
Roihu 87
Rok Kaiser 113
Roki (mascot) 118
RokiRed 119
Rolentaes, Aisha 205
Roman Nose State Park 181, 182, 184
Rome (theme) 81
Roochi 119
Roolipeliyhdistys FinFur Ry 87
Rory 156
Rosales, Joe 160
Rose (pub at The Rose Hotel) 103, 104
Rose Quoll 191
Rosemont, Illinois 170, 171
Rosengarten, Erika Leigh 156, 173
Ross, David 24
Ross, Tiffany 115
Roth, Christopher 160, 161, 162, 163, 193
Rourkie *see* Danyals, Rourke
Rov 217
Rowe, Santi 79
Rowley, Christopher 63
Rowrbrazzle 4, 8, 37, 59
Roxas 146
Roxicat *see* Barrett, John
Royal-Pain-In-The-Ass 198
RSPCA 167, 190, 192
Rubah Fox 169
Rudd, Alexis 70, 174
Ruger (mascot) 42
Ruggels, Scott 32
Rugunda, Ruhakana 117
Ruhr Valley, Germany 198
Ruhrcon 198–199
Rukis 27, 47, 111, 122, 197
Rund, Lance 132
Runton, Andy 25
Rupert Bear 8
"Rus" boarding house 199, 202
RusCon 199
RusFURence vi, 51, 199–203, 207
The Rush Limbaugh Show 133
Rüsselsheim, Germany 163
Russia 5, 10, 199, 207
Rust Rat 162
RustyFox 50
Ryan Blackpaw 139
Ryd, Linköping, Sweden 76
Rydges Hotel 167
Rydges on Swanson Hotel 167
Rydsskolan college dormitory 75, 76
Ryoga 149

SA Furs 166
Saber 198, 199

Index

Sabretoothed Ermine *see* Davies, Beth
Sabrina Bear 194, 195
Sabrina, the Teen-Age Witch 21
SachenFurs 141
Sachsen-Anhalt, Germany 74
Safar, Jonah E. 20
Safari's Interactive Animal Sanctuary 89, 183, 184, 212, 213, 214
Safe Haven Rescue Zoo 31
Safe Haven Wildlife Refuge 173
St. Clair, Carissa 162
St. Louis, Missouri 139
St. Paul, Minnesota 117
St. Valentine's Day *see* Valentine Day
saint-yves 207
saitenyo 181
Sakai, Stan 16, 22, 81, 169
Sal 90
Salem, Spain 145
Salthaven Wildlife Rehabilitation and Education Centre 55
Salt Lake City, Utah 118, 119
Salt Lake City Radisson Hotel 118
Salt Lake City Sheraton *see* Sheraton Salt Lake City Hotel
Samarindus 77
Sam Spade 152
Sample, Ken 57, 58, 62
Sample, Lisa 177
Samurai Cat 22
San Diego, California 9, 56, 61, 62, 73
San Diego Chicken (mascot) 26
San Diego Comic-Con *see* Comic-Con International
San Diego Convention Center 73
San Diego Union-Tribune 175
San Francisco, California 129, 185
San Francisco International Airport 131
San Jose, California 9, 129, 185
San Jose Convention Center, Marriott and Hilton Hotels 130
San Jose Garden Airport Hotel 185
San Mateo, California 129, 132
San Mateo Marriott 129, 131
Sanborn, Will A. 173
Sanchez, Edgardo 43
Sanctuary Under Dog Angel Foundation *see* Azyl Pod Psim Aniołem
Sanguine Games 116
Sankt Goarshausen, Germany 163, 164
Santa Ana, California 37, 61
Santa Clara, California 129
Santa Fox 194
São Paulo, Brazil 5, 13
Sapphire 83
Sarduyon 25, 67, 82
Sari NeoChaos 197
The Sarvey Wildlife Center 187
ŠARZ Vršov 218
Saturios 198
Satyrday 177, 178, 179
Sauron 203
Savannah Horrocks 135
Save-a-Vet 176

Save Our Tazzie Devils 67
Save the European Lynx 139
Savino, Chris 134
Sawredge Inn 97
Sawyer, Michael 132
Sawyer, Robert J. 61
Saxony-Anhalt, Germany 75
Scani 112
Scape Goat 195
Scarborough, Elizabeth Ann 188
Schaefer, M. 176
Scharbach/Odenwald, Germany 143
Scharff, Steven 173, 185, 198
Schaumberg, Illinois 170
Scheriff 50
Schneider, Ron 158
Schreiber, Sandy 111
Schulmayer, Andreas 163, 164, 165
Schumacher, Sven 144
Schwartz, Anya 32
Schwartz, Eric W. 19, 60, 177
Schwerte, North Rhine-Westphalia, Germany 198
Schytte, Peter 129
science-fiction fandom 6
"Science, Pseudoscience and Outright Crap" 114
Sci-Fi Channel 58, 66
ScotiaCon 203–205
ScotiaCon UK Ltd. 203
Scotland 10, 203, 204, 205
Scottish Owl Centre 205
Scottsdale Resort at McCormick 27
Scrapper 166, 167
Scribblefox *see* Ledger, Jared
Scruff E. Coyote 64
SeaTac, Washington 70
SeaTac Clarion Hotel 70
Sea-Tac Radisson Airport 70, 73
Seattle, Washington 14, 70, 71, 105, 186, 187
Seattle Airport Marriott Hotel 186
Seattle Tacoma Hotel and Convention Center 70
Seattle-Tacoma International Airport 70
SeaWorld Orlando 156
Sebastian Silverfox 210
Second Chance Cat Rescue 192
Second Life 133
The Secret of NIMH 176
Sedge Hare 98
Seeheim, Germany 163, 164
Sema JayHawk 90
Sender, Terry 156
Seng, Jennifer 32, 83, 173, 174
Sensanbaugher, Margaret 89
Seraph 110
Serena 166
Serengeti 81
Sesame Street 24
Sethaa 29, 166
Seto, Gary Lee 62
Setsu-P 193, 194, 195
Severus Blackpaw 30
SewerRat *see* Hefele, Christian
Seylyn 208
The Seymour Marine Discovery Center 132

Shade 137
Shadow (I) 14
Shadow (II) 104
Shadow Snow 87
Shadow Wolf *see* Hofgard, Katie
Shakleford, Rusty 37, 122, 198
Shanda Fantasy Arts 62, 177
Shandower 73
Shapero, Kay 57, 61
Shapiro, David 131
Sharley 50, 51
Sharon Sakai medical expenses 67
Sharon Woods Park 176, 177
Sharonville, Ohio 90
Sharpe, Rebecca 27, 143
Sharpe19 *see* Sharpe, Rebecca
Shaterri *see* Stadnicki, Steven
Shaw!, Scott 22
Shep Otterpaw 109
Sheraton Arlington Park 170
Sheraton Bradley Hotel 98, 99
Sheraton Detroit Novi Hotel 113, 179
Sheraton Gateway Atlanta Airport Hotel 120, 121
Sheraton Indianapolis Hotel at Keystone Crossing 146
Sheraton Milwaukee Brookfield Hotel 90
Sheraton Montreal Airport Hotel 211
Sheraton Portland Airport Hotel 105
Sheraton Premiere Hotel 91
Sheraton Salt Lake City Hotel 118
Sheraton Studio City Resort 153
Sheraton Tacoma Convention Center 70, 72
Sheraton Toronto Airport Hotel and Conference Centre 110
Sheraton World Resort 153, 156
Sherwood 37
Sherwood, M. "Idess" 197
Shex 166
Shiner Bock Beer 205
ShinigamiGirl 82, 97, 198
Shinji 178, 179
Shirokuma 195
ShiroTora 109
Shitty Grape Lollipops 83
Shiva 116
Shizuoka, Japan 150
Shizuoka Convention & Arts Center 150
Shizuoka Kemono Square 150
Shorty (I) 74, 75
Shorty (II) 94
Shy Matsi 82, 83
Sia, Benjamin 186
Siberian Husky Rescue 67
Sidian *see* Huish, Linsey
Sierra de Mariola "parque natural" 145
Sierra Racs 97
Sigil 56, 179
Sikamor Rooney 83
Silber *see* Peteranderl, Philipp
Sidian 198
Silent Ravyn 97, 134

Index

Silfur *see* Markey, Dan
Silver, Jonas 132
Silver Huskywolf *see* Bladon, Lindsey; Bristow, Lindsey
Silver Wolf 112
Silverbolt 14
SilverDeni 82
SilverFox 96, 203
Silverfox Publications 19
Silverfox5213 C6, 7, 122, 126
Silverfoxwolf 204, 205
Simba *see* Robinson, Benjamin Eren
SimBa *see* Dimonius
Simplewolf 201
Simpson, David C. 172, 178
Singapore 5, 7, 10, 125
Sithy 123
Sitio Maio 13
Sito, Tom 37
16th Street Mall 196
Sixth Column 3
Skaifox 69
Skar *see* Atamanov, Sergei
Sketch Dalmatian *see* Blanco, Angel Manuel
Sketchkat 190
SkippyFox 126
Skroy 146
Skulldog 84, 101, 179
Skunk, Dan 110
Skunkday 177, 178, 179
Skunkfuckers Party 9
Skunki 77
Skyrim 217
Slamdance Film Festival 6
Slappy the Tiger (mascot) 128
slashersivi 162
Sled Dog Welfare 190
Sli 104
Slovakia 49
Sluneční zátoka campground 48
SlvWolf *see* Järvi, Santtu; Lake, Santtu
SM Megatrade Conference Center 185
SmackJackal *see* Wally, Sean
Smirnoff 204
Smith, Craig E. 178, 213
Smith, Jason 16, 113, 169
Smith, Mary Mae 163
Smith, Pete 67, 167, 169
Smith, Terrie 10, 19, 58, 59, 66, 77
Smith, Tom 22
Snap 179
Snout *see* Isacson, Henrik
Snowshadow 86, 87
SnowWolf 41
Society and Animals 2
Society of Creative Anachronism 219
Södertälje Katthem 180
Sofawolf Press 11, 23, 82, 117, 134, 169
Softpaw Magazine 80, 133
Soki 105
Solaxe 138
SolidAsp 83, 91
Solion 194
Sologne, France 88

SomaCat 124
Something Awful 205
somewolf *see* Chrzonsz, Matthias
Sonderjen 175
Songs of the Old Ages 79
SonicBlu Darkfold *see* Blumfield, Brett
Sophia Ferret (mascot) 19
Sophia's Pizza Restaurant 167
Sorin Kat 197, 198
Soron 123
Soulscape *see* Reven, Thea
South Bank Parklands 191
South Bank Piazza 191
The Southern Fandom Confederation Bulletin 193
South Fur Lands 10, 166, 167
Southside Animal Shelter 146
Southwest Airlines 64
Sovipaw Air Force 187
Sowers, Darcy 174
Sowers, Matt 174
Space Center 24
Space Jam 66
Spacehyena *see* Mitten, Cara
Spain 6, 92, 145
Sparf 91
Sparky 94
Sparky Nekomi 198
Special Awards Committee 65
Special Interest Group 57, 66
Spectra Vixen 162
Spelunker Sal 31
Spirit Creations 69
Spiritraptor 204
Spirituality Leader Yotewah Californicus 193
Spitfire Jackal 153
Spokane, Washington 14, 73
Spokane Convention Center 186
Sport and Recreation Center Wawrzkowizna 137
Sportareál Samopše sports center 76
Spots and Stripes (SAS) 123
Spotswood, Brent 73
Spring Dragon 214
Springfield, Missouri 89
Spring Lake Park, Minnesota 117
Spunky *see* Seng, Jennifer
STA Ferret Rescue 70
Stadnicki, Steven 62
Staeger, Rod 21
Stairwell Appreciation Duty 174
Stake & Shake 209, 210
Stalking Cat *see* Avner, Dennis
Stangel, Heiko 144, 145
Stanislaus Wildlife Care Center 133
The Star Diaries 165
Star Trek 145
Star Wars 115
Starfinder 133
StarShadow 169
Starwind 183
State Board of Equalization 61
State Capital Theatre 104
State University of New York 25
Statosky, Eltee 194
"Stay As You Are" 82
Steamfox *see* Pounds, Roy D. II

Steel the Wolf 46
Steele 207
Stephanie de la Loba Negra 184
StephenQuoll 169
Sternberg, Omaha 58, 64
Stevens, Zsa'nene 35, 36, 37
StickDevil 194
Stiftung Fledermaus 82
Stigmata *see* Duncan, Jonathan Vair
Stockholm, Sweden 7, 180
Stoller, Peter 19
Stone, Stephie 99, 100
Stone Castle Hotel & Convention Center 89
Stories of Camp Rainfurrest 188
Stout, Jana 208
The Stranger 72
Strawberry Neko 97
Stray Rescue of St. Louis 139
Streamline Pictures 3
Středočeský kraj, Czech Republic 76
Strider Orion 121
Strom, Lee 78, 132
Stromberg (RP), Germany 144
Strype 84, 97
Stu Cat 95, 96
Stuart, Shannon 35, 63
"Stumbles the Hill Husky" 184
Sub-level 03 34, 35, 115, 121, 133, 161, 162, 183, 184, 194
Sue Deer *see* Rankin, Susan
Suhl, Germany 76
Sumida Industrial Center 149
Sumie-dh 50
Summer Jackel 178
Sunny the Bear (mascot) 128
Sunroute Hikone 148
Sunstreak Chakat 210
Suntec City 125
"¡Supermen South!" 3
Support Our Shelters 22
Surfers Paradise, Queensland 95
Susman, Tim 169
Suzuki, Ken 39, 40, 41, 42, 184
Svey 47
Swann, S. Andrew 20, 60, 66
Sweden 7, 10, 75, 123, 180
Swift Fox 209, 210
Swiss Alps 52
Swissfurs.ch 52
Switzerland vi, 5, 10, 52, 54, 141, 163
Swycaffer, Jefferson 35
Syber 197, 205
SyberFox 106
Sydney, New South Wales 94, 102, 103
Sydney Fisher (mascot) 57, 60
Sydney Park 104
SylCon 5
Sylys Sable *see* Merlino, Mark

Taala Ruhun 94
Tabalon *see* Jaekel, Andreas
Tabbie *see* Zsapka, Josef
TabbieFox 50, 68, 69
Tacoma, Washington 70
Taffka Unicorn vi, 202, 203
Tailchaser's Song 9
Tails of a Clockwork World 188

Index

Taipei 147
Taiwan 10
The Tak 90
Takaza J. Wolf *see* Hauschild, Dan
Talbot, Brian 181
Tales of the Tai-Pan Universe 70
TaleSpin 58, 60
Talisman 115
TallyHawk 194
Talzhemir 131
Tamu 50, 51
TaniDaReal *see* Freese, Tanja
"Tank Vixens" 79
Tanuki Gohuki 14
Tanvald, Czech Republic 217
Taronga Zoo 103
Taurin Fox 99, 100
Tavi Munk 162, 163
Taya 106
"Tears Like Rain" 60
Teddy Ruxspin 118
Teer, Tanith 57
Tegethoff, Sven 61, 68, 69, 77, 78, 79, 80, 81, 82, 131, 190
Tegler Forest 29
Telephone *see* Biesmeyer, Deanna
Temperance 124, 188
Temple, Albert 61
Temrin 207, 208
Tenax Raccoon 118, 119
Tennessee 84
TeR 199
Terril *see* Schytte, Peter
Tes-Tui-H'ar *see* Heitsch, Gerritt
Těsnohlídek, Rudolf 79
Tevionbee 192
Texas 114, 117, 205
Texas Furry Con 205
Texas Furry Fiesta (TFF) 114, 117
Tezuka, Osamu 188
Thai Tails 125
Thailand 10
Thallanor Rasmuson *see* Bilyk, Dennis
Thames River 189
Thanksgiving 170, 175
Thatcher, Richard 177
Thazumi 83
Thearmjing 74
TheKarelia 137
Therapy Dogs, Inc. 20
Therapy Pets 130, 133, 134
The Thing 131
13th St. Cats 134
Thomas, Jason 133, 134, 160
Thornwolf 175
ThrashWolf 203
Through Fox's Eyes 178
Thumper 208
Tiamat 14
Tibo *see* Birdsell, James
Tiger Eyes *see* Stevens, Zsa'nene
Tiger Fox 121
Tiger Haven 85, 160, 161, 162, 163
Tiger Paw 120, 121, 122
Tiger Touch University Retreat 132
Tigerden Internet Services 115, 160
Tigerwolf *see* Nemeier, George F. Jr.
Tigon 208

Tigurstar 102
TILT Longtail 101, 121, 180
Timduru 88, 190
Time Warner Community Service Grant 23
Timezone 95, 96
Timon b 103, 104
Timothy Rabbit 173
Tincrash *see* Melendez, Noel
Tinder Stricken 212
Tingriel 202
Tinintri 194
Tiny Toon Adventures 60
Tirrel 155, 158
Titana 165, 166
Titash 138
Tobias Amaranth 94
toboe-chan92 106
Tockar, Lee 26
Tojo the Thief 105
Tokinosumika Hotel 150
Tokyo, Japan 149, 205, 206
Tong, Jodi 161
Too Much Light Makes the Baby Go Blind 174, 176
Toonseum: Pittsburgh Museum of Cartoon Art 25, 26
Tooth Less 185, 186
Topeka, Kansas 46
TopFox *see* Cawley, John
Tora NightProwler 146
toranor 75
Torkelson, Peter 130, 131, 133
Toronto, Ontario 39, 40, 41, 109, 110
Toronto Role-playing and Anthropomorphic Animal Costuming Society (TRAACS) 39
Torres, Chris 135
Touch My Badger *see* Tremblay, Mitti
Toulouse 136
Town and Country Resort and Convention Center 56, 62
Town Cats of Morgan Hill 134
Toxic Audio 154, 156
Toyohashi, Japan 148
Toyohashi Zoo & Botanical Park 148
Tracer Moonshadow 89
Training and Recreation Centre Dzierzązna 137
Tran, Kimlinh 26
Transformers 191
TransFur 148, 205–206
Transportation Security Administration 160, 195
Trapa *see* Winters, Tank
Trauth, Margaret 134, 188
Travelodge 108
Travelodge Orlando Downtown Centroplex 108
Travis 213
Trax 180, 181
Trekwolf 102
Tremblay, Mitti 36
Trick *see* Kemper, Danielle
Tricky Shoes 83
TriggerFox 192
Triss Winterdusk *see* Feazle, Shaun

Tristan 198
Trix Rabbit 24
Trixie Wolf 177
TrojanCentaur 93
Tropicon 74, 206
True Blue 198
tryst_fel_cath *see* Barnes, Robert
Tsaiwolf 204
Tucson, Arizona 218, 219, 220
Tugs 119
Tui 14
"Tumbles the Stairdragon" 121
Turistická ubytovna Pohoda 48
Turku, Finland 60
Turner- und Jugendheim Loreley e.v. youth hostel 163
Turnov, Czech Republic 48
Turrittin, Tom 6, 211, 212
Tuusula, Finland 85
TV Dave *see* Neff, David
Tweehek (Groups Accommodation) 122
25th anniversary of furry conventions 135
Twice 166, 198
Twitch Da Woof 146
Twitter 92
2 Sense 113
2, the Ranting Gryphon *see* Davis, Matthew Wayne
Tyco 31
Tyger 165
TygerCowboy *see* Roth, Christopher
Tygger *see* Graf, Lia
Tygřík 50
Tyler 56
Tyson's Corner, Virginia 91
Tyvdalhøj 128
Tyzin 143
Tzologist 85
Tzup 213

UCLA 3
Uderzo, Albert 81
Uffington Horse 133
Uganda 117
Ugly Little Monster 184
UK Fur CON 9
UK Wolf Conservation Trust 190
Ukiwa the cheetah *see* Kopeikin, Paul
Ukraine 5, 10, 151, 200, 201, 202, 214, 215, 216
UkrMiniFurka 214
Ultraviolet *see* Gunn, Cassandra
unci_narynin *see* Köhler, Tobias
Uncle Kage *see* Conway, Dr. Samuel C.
Uncle Kage's Story Hour 21, 22, 24, 113, 131, 154, 156, 157, 158, 173
Uncle Oakie *see* Oakshadow, BanWynn
Un-Con 118
Underdog 24
Unicorn 77, 78
United Publications 77, 79
U.S. Space and Rocket Center 192
The United States War Dogs Association, Inc. 100, 101, 102, 112, 153

Index

Universal City Florida 154
University of California, Riverside 4
University of New South Wales 104
University of Waterloo [Ontario] 24
University Place Hotel & Convention Center 105
The Unlucky Thirteen 80
Unthrocon *see* Furry Unlocked
The Unwanted and Forgotten Foundation *see* Fundacja Niechciane i Zapomniane
UralFurence 207
Ursa Major Awards 11, 15, 22, 32, 36, 37, 63, 64, 65, 83, 175, 178, 179, 194
Urson 109
USB flash drive 83
USO Special Guests 213
Utah 118, 119
Utahraptor 118
Utsikten Meetings 180
Utsuke, Maito 148

Valášek, Michal 50
Valencia 145
Valentine's Day 120, 121
Valgen, Eris 213
Valhund 18
Valion 217
Valley Forge Hilton 18, 20
Valley of the Kings Sanctuary & Retreat 172
Van Camp, Susan 57, 67
Vance, Alex 115, 203
VancouFur 207–208
Vancouver, British Columbia 207, 208
Vancouver Orphan Kitten Rescue Association (VOKRA) 208
Vanderlugt 90
Vandrav *see* Baker, Mike
Vantid *see* Hill, Amber
Variety 6
Vartan the bull (mascot) 218
Ventana's 174
Verbeeten, Angelique 81
Verec 41
Verezhensky, Sean 36
Vermy Fox 106
Vernon, Ursula 82, 134, 173, 174
Veteran Military Dog Handlers 100
"Veteran of the Psychotic Wars" 58
Viacom 105
Viacommix 105
Vibe Hotel Gold Coast 95
Vick, Diana 71
Vick, Edd 73
Victoria Hotel 167
Victory Day 214
VidWulf Silentstrider Spiritweaver *see* Chan, Justin
Viking 199
Vilareal, Castellón, Spain 92
Vincent VanLeopard 194
Ving card room keys 60
Vital Ground 98, 99
VitaniDaReal *see* Freese, Tanja
Vixgeck, Alex 145
Vlach, Heidi C. 212

Vlk00 50, 51
Vogt, Heribert 78
Vogt, Lionel 194
von Fur, Dixie 56
Vootie 8
Vorpal Bunny 205
Vršov, Czech Republic 218
Vršovská Brána hotel 218
Vurt 96

Wacom 169
Wagensveld, Richard 79
Wagner, Martin 58
Waitangi Day 92, 94
The Waldzoo Offenbach 80
Wales 68
Walker, D. 101
Wallaby 102
Wallace (mascot) 203, 204
Waller, Reed 58, 59, 117
Walling, René 211
Wally, Sean 134
Walt Disney Studios 7, 8, 23, 35, 175, 200
Walter, Dominik 78, 70
Waltham, Massachusetts 153
Walton, Jo 32
Wamndog 183
Wan, Adam 157
Warlick, Clint 34
Warner Bros. 60, 63, 66, 71
Warsaw, Poland 137
Wasatch Regional Anthropomorphic Arts and Entertainment (WRAAE) 118, 119
Washington 15, 70, 186
Washington State Ferret Rescue and Shelter 72, 73
Watani *see* Wagensveld, Richard
Watching Anime, Reading Manga: 25 Years of Essays and Reviews 4
Waterbury, Connecticut 98
Waterford Lakes Town Center 109
Watermark Hotel 95
Waters, Anthony M. 220
Watership Down 8, 188
WaterWorks 103
Watonga, Oklahoma 182
Wawrzkowizna, Poland 137, 138, 139
Wayne Suburban 21
Wayne, Taral 58
WBAI 99.5 66
WDVE 102.5 23
Wear, Brian 34, 35
Weasely 95
Weeko (mascot) 42
Wein, Len 58
Weisman, Greg 37, 84
Wellington, New Zealand 93
We're Back: A Dinosaur Story 113
Weremagnus *see* Kadatz, Amanda
WerePuppy *see* Brill, Mark
Wessner, Terry 39, 41, 42
West, Gemily 124
West Kissimmee, Florida 153
Westercon 9
Western Pennsylvania Furry Weekend 166, 208–210

Western Pennsylvania Humane Society 26
Western Pennsylvania National Wild Animal Orphanage 22
Westin Chicago North Shore 170
Westin Hotel 18, 22, 23, 24
Westin Peachtree Plaza 120, 122
Westin Santa Clara 129
What The Fur? 102, 110, 210–212
Wheel OF Blame 193
Wheeling, Illinois 170
Whelan, Laschita 162
Whippany, New Jersey 83
Whisker Rescue 117
Whiskers 20
Whispering Woods Hotel & Conference Center 159, 162
White, E.B. 188
White Raccoon 14
White Wolf *see* Kellogg, Diana
White Wolf Game Studios 66, 67
WhiteFire *see* Torkelson, Peter
Whitley, Deal 58, 59
WhiteyFawks *see* Scharff, Steven
Who Framed Roger Rabbit 63
WhoozFur, Inc. 146
Whose Lion Is It, Anyway? 90, 113, 114, 146, 173
Wichita, Kansas 46, 47
Wicked Sarah *see* Krueger, Sarah
Wicker 27, 67
Wiedemann, Jens-René 29, 142
Wiehltal Bridge 79
WikiFur vi, 173
Wilbur, Roger 19, 20
Wilburton, Oklahoma 213
The Wild Animal Park, Suhl 81
Wild Nights 212–214
Wild West 136, 137
Wild Wild West 139
Wildcare 133
The Wildfowl and Wetlands Trust 190
Wildlife Companions 133, 185
Wildlife Heritage Foundation 69
Wildlife in Need 173
Wildlife Rescue & Rehabilitation Center 134
Wildtierhilfe Fiel e.v. 82
WildWolf *see* Laubach, Chad
Wilfredian League of Gugnuncs 8
Wilke, Kai-Uwe 29, 30
Wilkinson, Ned 82, 115, 116, 158, 213
Will King 207
Willard, Jessica 41, 172
Williams, Amber M. 36, 55, 84
Wills, Tod 100, 101
Wilson, David 161
Wilykat *see* Bolton, Colin
Winckler, Erin 160
The Wind in the Willows 35
Windfalcon *see* Lyons, Brenda
Windmelodie 166
Windpaw Coyote 182, 183
Windsor Locks, Connecticut 98
WindyCon 174
WinFox 202
Winnie Woodpecker 63

Index

Winnipeg, Manitoba 6
"Winter Charge" 57
Winters, Tank 35, 36, 186, 187, 208
The Wizard of Oz 47
WLF the dragon 207
Wolever Wuff 208
Wolf Behavior Seminar 66
Wolf Park 66, 67, 172
Wolf Pup Wielder 163
Wolf Sanctuary 196
Wolf Studios/Haunted Verdun Manor 172
Wolfaya 48
Wolfaya *see* Baker, Anna
Wolfbird 56
Wolff 184
Wolffire *see* Stangel, Heiko
Wolfgem's medical expenses 124
Wolfgem *see* West, Gemily
"Wolfie Shorts" 64
Wolfpup TK 31
Wolf's Den 110, 111
Wolfy-Nail *see* Kompaniet, Pavel
Wood, Tim 176
Woodfield Mall 172
Woody *see* Wood, Tim
Wookiee 40, 95
World Horse Welfare 204
World Science Fiction Convention 3, 4, 8, 9
World Tree 178
World Wildlife Fund (WWF) 37, 139
Worldcon *see* World Science Fiction Convention
Worley, Kate 58
The Wormwood 41, 42

Worthington, Ohio 176, 177
Wotan 41
Wow! Wow! Wubbzy! 24
Wroclaw, Poland 137
Wrzosek, Maja 79, 165
WToboe 13, 14
WUFF 214–216
Wyman, Vicky 19, 20, 58, 66
Wyndham Franklin Plaza Hotel 18
Wyndham Jacksonville Riverwalk 154

The X-Files 145
Xan *see* Walter, Dominik
Xander the Blue 90, 91
Xen Wirder 207
Xenotropis 112
XianJaguar 195
Xkůň 49, 50, 51
xodingo 67
Xopek 215
Xyrus Chase 186

YamiBliss *see* Camion, Jeffrey
Yanazaki 14
Yappy Fox; Yappy SlyFox *see* Fox, Randy
Yarf!: The Journal of Applied Anthropomorphics 4, 10, 19, 34, 57
Yateley, England 9
Year of the Rat 81
Yekatinburg, Russia 207
YellowBronco 139
Yiff: The Card Game 73
Yonoa 176
Yorkdale Mall 43
Yoshikawa, Konu C2, 74, 75, 206

Young Frankenstein 102
YouTube 43, 61
Ysengrin Werewolf 172
Yuki 111

Zahzu 48
Zakkun 42
Zaloom, Paul 157
Zampacon C2, 216–217
Zaslove, Mark 58
Zato Bull 119
Zeltlagerplatz e.v. campground/hostel 28
ZEN 110, 190
Zhai Shi 52
Zhivago D *see* Shakleford, Rusty
Zigzag 72
Zillercon 5
Zilvan C7
Zilven 137, 147
Zlenice, Czech Republic 48, 50
Zodiac 217
ZodiaCon C8, 217–218
Zolna, Ed 59
Zonie the Coyote (mascot) 218, 220
ZonieCon 218–220
Zoological Garden (Brno) 49
Zoomorphica 10
Zootopia 7
El Zorrito (mascot) 92
"Zorro the fox" 57
Zsa Zsa Gabortion 83
Zsapka, Josef 68
Zubkov, Sergei 200
Zuo Yiyi 52
Zvenigorodskiy boarding house 199, 200, 201, 202, 203